Unity 4 Fundamentals

Unity 4 Fundamentals

Get Started at Making Games with Unity

Alan Thorn

Focal Press
Taylor & Francis Group
NEW YORK AND LONDON

First published 2014 by Focal Press
70 Blanchard Road, Suite 402, Burlington, MA 01803

And in the UK by Focal Press
2 Park Square, Milton Park, Abingdon, Oxon OX14 4RN

Focal Press is an imprint of the Taylor & Francis Group, an informa business

Notices

Knowledge and best practice in this field are constantly changing. As new research and experience broaden our understanding, changes in research methods, professional practices, or medical treatment may become necessary.

Practitioners and researchers must always rely on their own experience and knowledge in evaluating and using any information, methods, compounds, or experiments described herein. In using such information or methods they should be mindful of their own safety and the safety of others, including parties for whom they have a professional responsibility.

Product or corporate names may be trademarks or registered trademarks, and are used only for identification and explanation without intent to infringe.

Library of Congress Cataloging-in-Publication Data
Thorn, Alan.
Unity 4 fundamentals: making games with Unity / Alan Thorn.—First edition.
pages cm.
1. Computer games—Programming. 2. Video games—Design.
3. Unity (Electronic resource) I. Title.
QA76.76.C672T498 2013
794.8'1526—dc23
2013023842

ISBN: 978-0-415-82383-8 (pbk)
ISBN: 978-0-203-54960-5 (ebk)

Typeset in Myriad Pro
By Apex CoVantage, LLC

Printed in Canada

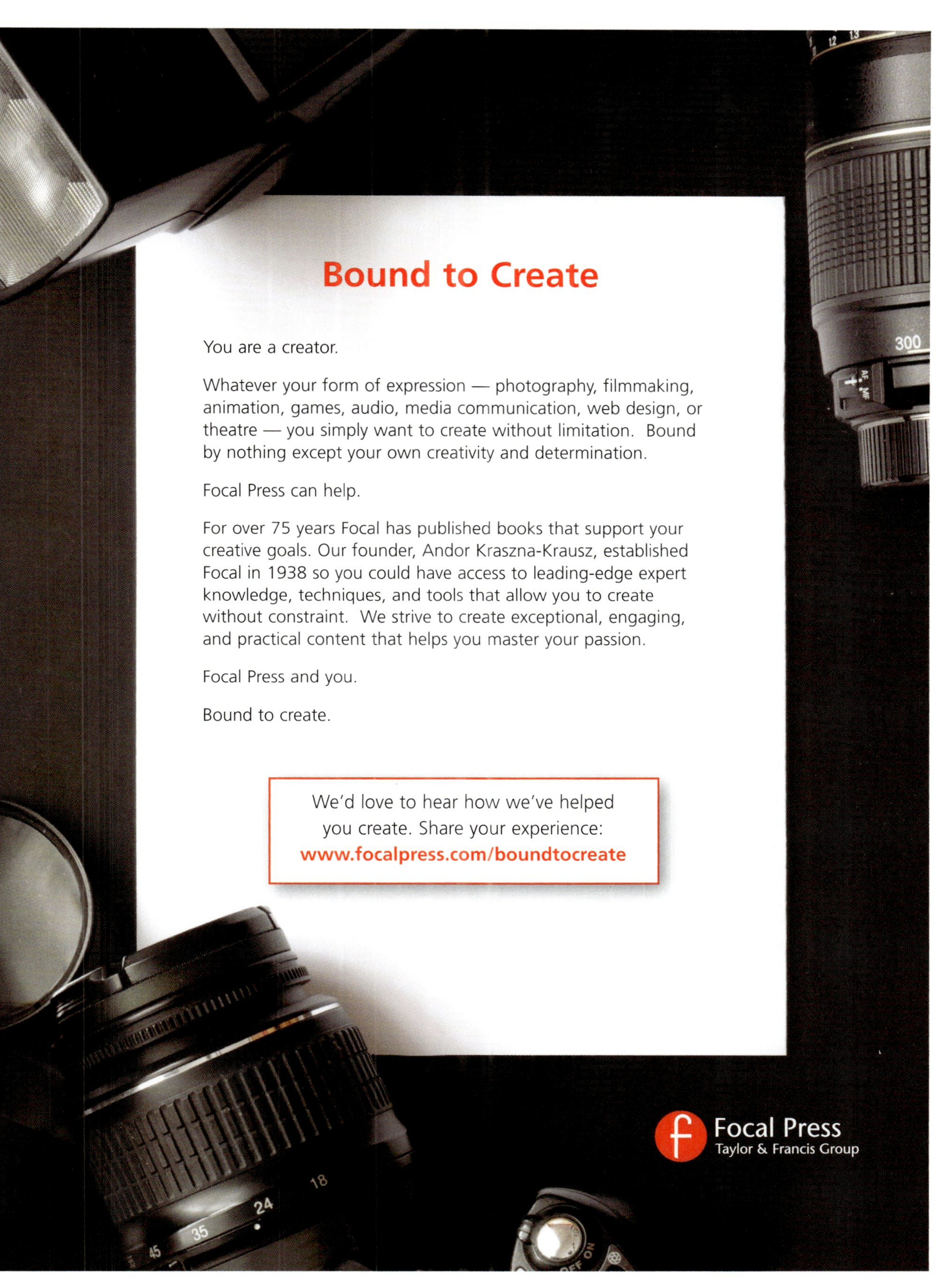

Bound to Create
You are a creator.
Whatever your form of expression — photography, filmmaking, animation, games, audio, media communication, web design, or theatre — you simply want to create without limitation. Bound by nothing except your own creativity and determination.
Focal Press can help.
For over 75 years Focal has published books that support your creative goals. Our founder, Andor Kraszna-Krausz, established Focal in 1938 so you could have access to leading-edge expert knowledge, techniques, and tools that allow you to create without constraint. We strive to create exceptional, engaging, and practical content that helps you master your passion.
Focal Press and you.
Bound to create.
We'd love to hear how we've helped you create. Share your experience:
www.focalpress.com/boundtocreate
Focal Press
Taylor & Francis Group

Contents

Acknowledgements

This book would not have been possible without the valuable help and skills of many people. There are too many to list here individually, but I feel specific mention should go to Sean Connelly for arranging the book in the first place and for his ideas and suggestions along the way, and to Caitlin Murphy for editing and coordinating my work. I'd also like to give thanks to the technical reviewers, for spotting my slip-ups and mistakes, and to the rest of the Focal Press team who contributed in some way but whom I never got to know. And finally, I'd like to thank you, the reader, for taking the time and effort to explore the Unity engine through this book. I hope you find it helpful.

Alan Thorn, London, 2013

About the Author

Alan Thorn is a game developer, author, and freelance programmer with over 12 years of industry experience. He is the founder of the London-based game studio, Wax Lyrical Games, and the creator of the award-winning adventure game Baron Wittard: Nemesis of Ragnarok. He has worked freelance on over 500 projects worldwide including games, simulators, kiosks and augmented reality software for game studios, museums and theme parks. He has spoken on game development at universities throughout the UK and is the author of nine books on game development, including Teach Yourself Games Programming, Game Engine Design and Implementation, and UDK Game Development. He is also a contributor at 3DMotive.com, a video training service for computer game professionals. More information on Alan Thorn and his start-up Wax Lyrical Games can be found at: http://ww.alanthorn.net and http://www.waxlyricalgames.com

Introduction

The contemporary video games industry is experienced by most gamers and developers as a busy and bustling place, a hub of creative and technical activity where little or nothing remains the same for long. Here, the only constant and assured factor among the confusion is a constant state of change: changes in hardware, gamers, development studios, ideas, platforms and fads and fashions. Two recent changes, however, stand apart from most of the others, due mainly to their unprecedented nature. The first is a new and rapid surge in the number of game development start-ups; that is, newly created companies founded often by recent graduates or by breakaway industry veterans all hoping to release blockbuster games. It seems that now, more than ever before, more people are able to realise their dreams of creating video games that can reach sizeable and profitable markets. The second change is akin to a 'paradigmatic shift' in the kinds of technologies and hardware on which games are now made available to the public. Games can now be found on a greater selection of devices than ever before: from traditional home PCs and consoles to mobile phones, tablet computers, cable TV packages – even embedded in web pages. Both of these changes are taking place against the background of an industry generally moving towards the 'democratisation of game development'. This is a popular trend aiming to make the activity of game development as accessible to as many people as possible, in as many markets as possible. This is not without some risk, of course: the consequence of democratising game development is that more people can become game developers, targeting many platforms. More developers mean more games, and more games mean more *choice* for the consumer. But the game-loving consumer, though faced with ever-increasing choice, still has the limitations of a finite wallet and finite resources. A consumer must therefore make purchasing decisions *between* games, choosing to acquire one game rather than another because they cannot afford them all. The developers, then, create their products in a climate of competition, each struggling against the others to gain the attention and enjoyment of the gamers. To succeed in this furious and perhaps unfortunate competition, developers are forever striving to find ways to make their work simpler so they can concentrate less on technicalities, regulations and platform-specifics and more on the content and gameplay of their games. One of the tools that many developers are choosing to use for creating games, and perhaps the fastest growing tool today, is the Unity engine. This engine forms the subject matter of this book.

What is this Book About?

This book can be seen as an introductory course on the 'Unity 4 Engine', a term I shall abbreviate from hereon as simply 'Unity' or 'Unity 4'. It assumes that you, the reader, know little or nothing about Unity, and it explains the engine so as to equip you with the skills and knowledge necessary to use Unity independently for making interactive software – specifically games. Over the course of its chapters this book discusses Unity in three discrete stages: it begins by defining clearly both what Unity is and what it is not, and considers the reasons why developers might want to use the engine as well as reasons why they might not. Then it proceeds to examine the core, the critical or most basic set of features underpinning almost all work in Unity. These are foundational matters every Unity developer needs to know to work successfully with the engine. Then finally it moves on to the wide and powerful range of ancillary features and techniques resting on the foundation, which, once learnt, lead in the direction of intermediate competency. Together these three stages describe and explore the fundamentals of Unity, the most common and widely used features for making video games. However, while it's true to say this book is first and foremost about Unity, it would not be true to say that Unity is the *only* subject it covers. This is because much of what is said about Unity and game development applies to creating games more generally, whether using Unity or not. This means that much of what is learned here is transferable. Concepts such as assets, meshes, transformations, lightmapping, animation, rigging, and coordinate systems are but a few of the concepts used in Unity *and* beyond.

Who is this Book For?

Every book is written with a 'target audience' in mind; that is, in the *mind of the author*. The target audience is an imaginary caricature embodying all the assumptions I, the author, must inevitably make about you, the reader. Making assumptions is a dangerous prospect and certainly not something I enjoy, primarily because assumptions can so often be mistaken or prejudicial. However, this case demands that I do make some assumptions about the reader's current knowledge, experience and skills, mainly to ensure the book is written in clear and accessible language and contains subject matter that matches reader expectations. To make my assumptions about the target audience clear I shall state them in the form of character profiles: specifically, three people for whom this book was written, and two people for whom this book was not written. That being said, however, none of the profiles given below should be taken as complete gospel. It is no part of my purpose to discourage anyone eager to learn, willing to adapt and keen to tackle new challenges, regardless of their background. Game development is infinitely knowable stuff, and nobody who has ever lived was born a game developer; everybody had to begin somewhere. So feel free to continue with this book even if the character profiles differ radically from yours: you will not be discouraged if you are determined enough.

This book is probably for you if you match any of the following three profiles:

- Andrea is a student pursuing a course in Art and Design, focussing on video game art. She plays and enjoys many games and hopes one day to work in the industry as an artist in a large development studio. She understands that having knowledge of a game engine, such as Unity, can give her many career advantages. She understands how to create art but is keen to know more generally about how games come together.
- Kevin is a hobbyist game developer hoping to leave his current job as a sales assistant and move into the world of indie games, where he can run his own company and sell his own ideas. He has experience of C++, C# and Javascript and has made a few simple games in his spare time, but has no experience of Unity. He sees Unity as an opportunity to realise his dream of making games, either on his own or with some friends.
- Mohammed does not really enjoy *playing* video games at all. He sees video games as a creative art form and is keen to express himself in that form *as a developer* because he likes technical challenges. He has some basic understanding of what a programming language is and is enrolled on a game development course starting a few months from now. He has heard about Unity and its power for creating games and is keen to find out more.

This book is probably not for you if you match any of the following two profiles:

- Betty is currently deciding what to study at university. She has never really enjoyed playing games and has no experience of making them. She is indecisive about her future and about the career she wishes to pursue. She sees game development as an easy option and a shortcut to making lots of money. She's heard that a lot of developers use Unity and is prepared to read a little about it, but doesn't wish to learn any programming.
- Thomas has been making games with Unity since its first release and is very familiar with the tools. He's not seeking an introductory guide to the software but is only looking for a book that discusses the features and additions *new* to version 4. He *only* wants a 'What's new' guide written for the experienced developer.

Why is this Book Necessary?

There might be some readers who are sceptical about the value or importance of such a book as this, even after reading everything in the introduction so far. Their view might be that this book is simply not necessary. They might hold this view for a number of different reasons, and this section aims to address at least most of these concerns in a question-and-answer format. First, some might argue that this book cannot possibly say much that is new about Unity, since there is already a wide range of books on the subject claiming to target the newcomer. In response to this, it needs to be said that, at the time of writing, almost all of these books focus on *earlier* versions of Unity, such as Unity 3 and Unity 2. This book in contrast focusses specifically on the latest version of the software, 4, about which comparatively little has been said so far. That being said, however, some might wonder why this book does not simply focus *only* on the new features of the software, leaving the hang-over or constant features from earlier versions unexplained and relying on information provided in earlier books. It's true that this approach could have been taken, but it has not been taken here – and for an important reason: this book is supposed to act as an *all-in-one* guide or course targeted at complete newcomers to the engine; a book that can be read profitably from begin to end. It's structured and arranged so that readers will not need to look elsewhere in order to understand and learn the fundamentals of the engine.

In addition to this concern, another common objection might arise. It runs something like this: this book must be unnecessary because every feature, concept or principle it discusses *can already be learned elsewhere* for free, simply by researching online through video tutorials, programmer blogs and community forums. However, this line of reasoning cannot to be taken as a legitimate criticism of the book, just as an encyclopaedia is not to be criticised for containing information that can be learned elsewhere by those who spend enough time researching it. It's true that everything in this book can probably be learned elsewhere and for free by individuals willing to invest hours, days, even weeks or months on research. The aim of this book is *not* to impart or reveal magical or obscure wisdom that is impossible to discover otherwise. Rather, it is to select the relevant details from the overwhelming mass of information available on the Unity engine and to present those details to the newcomer in clear language, in a logical order and as a comprehensive fundamentals course. I share my knowledge, skills and experience with you as a convenience, to save you the time and effort of researching and learning the hard way.

The final objection some might raise about the book's relevance is subtler and more person-relative. It's the idea that this book does not say all there is to say on the subject of Unity: that it either does not cover everything there is to know, or it does not contain a detailed explanation of how to make *this* or *that specific* game, or how to create *this* or *that* specific behaviour. In response, it is important to emphasise that this book indeed does *not* cover everything there is to know about the Unity engine. That is because *no* book could hope to achieve such a feat, just as no person can hope to make a circle square. Even taking into account the mass of information available online, there is still much left unsaid because people continually find new ways of adapting and using the software. In short, this book is called *comprehensive*, but the term is to be understood in a relative and not an absolute sense. This book is *comprehensive for* a fundamentals course, for a course aimed at showing newcomers the most critical and important features of Unity that offers them a solid foundation for further learning. It is not, however, comprehensive period; it is not a solution for learning all there is to know and for making every game imaginable.

How Should this Book be Read?

The chapters and sub-sections of this book have been written and arranged so as to be amenable to two main kinds of reader: the reference reader and the tutorial reader. The reference reader largely prefers to learn on their own, only resorting to the book when absolutely essential. They flick through chapters and paragraphs to find the relevant section, skim-reading and checking headings and diagrams. The tutorial reader by contrast sees the book as both guide and companion and reads it from start to finish, chapter by chapter, as it is presented. Though both kinds of reader can benefit from this book, it is mainly the tutorial reader who will gain the most. This is because the chapters are written and ordered the way I would present them if I were teaching the Unity engine in a classroom environment. The advantage of the book over the classroom is that the book can be read and re-read to confirm and brush-up on information. My personal recommendation to you from the outset is to read this title first as a tutorial reader and then later as a reference reader. This will increase your chances of getting the most the book has to offer.

Is this Book out of Date Already?

Every book that is written has a 'lifetime'. This is the length of time after a book's release that its contents are relevant for and of value to its readership. Any reader who picks up a 'living' book can expect to find worthwhile information within. Some books have almost an infinite lifetime because their contents are in some sense timeless, such as novels or books about the basics of arithmetic. Other books, however, such as computing books, have distinctly finite lifetimes because they document a subject that is continually evolving and which is always threatening to invalidate whatever came before. So the question arises as to the lifetime of this (computing) book. How far does the static text on these pages relate to the changing, moving games industry? In particular, the reader has a vested interest in knowing not only that the information here is valid at the present moment but also that it stands a more than reasonable chance of remaining valid for the foreseeable future. At first sight it might seem that this book is already threatened with obsolescence because updates to Unity are so frequently released. However, reasoning this way is akin to saying that no book can meaningfully be written about Microsoft Windows because Microsoft releases updates and patches on a regular basis. This concern ignores the fact that the lifetime of a book is determined not simply by the frequency of change but also by its extent. Once this is taken into account, the prognosis for the lifetime of this book begins to look much better because, despite changes and additions to the software, the fundamentals of the Unity engine and its associated workflows have remained relatively consistent. It is likely that between my writing this book and your reading it, further Unity changes and updates will have been released. This will mean that the software you are using is already different from the version I am using, even though both our versions fall within the version 4 release cycles. However, this frequency and extent of change, in the form of updates, repairs and improvements, need not concern us unduly because it is unlikely to be of a kind to invalidate the instructions and guidance I give here. It is unlikely to have dramatic implications for how the software is *used* from the perspective of developers. Thus, the Unity-specific details discussed here can reasonably be expected to hold for all updates and revisions within the version 4 release cycles, and perhaps even beyond to version 5. The game development concepts and theories also discussed in the book will have a still longer life expectancy – possibly taking you through the entirety of your career.

Conventions and Companion Files

The term 'conventions' in this section is used to refer to the linguistic and stylistic elements that occur repeatedly throughout the book, such as icons and underlining, which serve to attract your attention. They are used to raise your awareness and make a statement about the significance of specific sentences or paragraphs of text. Specifically, keywords or important terms – such as 'mesh' or 'asset' – will be highlighted in bold at their first use, then afterwards appear in standard formatting. Side boxes and note boxes will also accompany the main paragraphs of text to further detail ideas or to diverge onto related subjects of importance. These side boxes can be ignored unless otherwise stated, but my recommendation is to read everything. Further italics are used to stress specific words or phrases, to emphasise their significance.

This book also features a complement of associated companion files and online resources, some of which have an impact on the formatting and conventions used. Specifically, a bold exclamation icon will be inserted along with a text box whenever a section of text relates to the companion files. The text box will provide instructions on how to access the associated files. This book features a range of companion files and resources. These include: game assets, project files, video tutorials, and PowerPoint presentations for classroom learning. More will be discussed on the specifics of these as and when required. To access the project files for this title, please visit: http://www.alanthorn.net.

CHAPTER 1

Getting Started with Unity

By the end of this chapter you should:

1. Understand what Unity is and is intended to achieve
2. Understand the range of features and tools Unity offers
3. Have a firm grasp of the interface basics
4. Be able to install and configure Unity
5. Be able to create a project and a basic scene

The chances are high that you already have some idea about what Unity is and what it can do, even if that idea is not comprehensive or easily expressed in words. The phrases 'game engine' or 'game-making software' often spring to mind when thinking of Unity in a general sense. However, it's important for us as developers to be clearer and more precise than this about what Unity is and is not, what it's intended to do and what it's not intended to do. In short, it's necessary to begin the process of learning Unity with a clear understanding of what it is. This approach might initially seem trivial or pointless, particularly to those who have already studied Unity or are simply eager to get started. However, it's an approach we must take if we are to understand Unity in depth and avoid possible confusions and errors in our thinking further along the line. The reason is this: learning Unity, or any game development tool, can be likened to the challenge faced by a traveller who must navigate a large and maze-like city that is strange to him (or her), a city of plazas and winding streets. To travel to any destination within that city the traveller must use one of two methods: trial and error, or following a map. The former method involves much guessing, wandering, taking of wrong turns and hitting dead ends before the destination is finally reached by accident. The latter method involves reading the map, determining the shortest route, and then travelling that route from start to finish without having to fear any dead ends at all. The map method, being preferable for its greater efficiency, is only possible, however, when the layout and details of the city are *sufficiently understood*. Consequently, the first half of this chapter is mainly concerned with building a 'mental map' of Unity; an understanding of the software that allows us to see what Unity is by understanding the parts or components from which it is made. After reaching that point we can install and configure Unity on our computers, and then finally use Unity to create our first functional project.

1.1 What is Unity?

The title 'Unity' is an umbrella term referring to a suite of technologies and tools whose collective purpose is to help developers create interactive software products, most notably games (see Figure 1.1) but also augmented reality applications and simulators. Unity, in short, is game-making software. But further clarification is required here, to avoid the mistaken view that knowledge of Unity is, on its own, *everything* you need to create games. This is a mistaken view because games are made from many different components from across many disciplines, ranging from programming and scripting to graphics and music. The remit of Unity is only a selection of those components. Unity is not, strictly speaking, an asset creation application such as 3DS Max or Maya or Photoshop or FL Studio. Developers do not typically use Unity to *create* the graphics, music, sounds, ideas, concepts, voices, animations, movies and other **assets** that feature in the game. These assets are

Figure 1.1 Bounders and Cads, a causal/strategy game by Wax Lyrical Games. It is one of many games created using the Unity engine

typically created beforehand by artists, musicians and other developers using tools and techniques outside of Unity. The role of Unity by contrast is to take those pre-created assets as individual files, add extra information to them and make them work together in a synthesis that is a *completed* game product, just as a car manufacturing plant will assemble a car from an assortment of ready-made parts or pieces. Unity is in that narrower sense a game-making tool. It is software used largely by designers and programmers for bringing to life a final game on the basis of pre-created assets. For this reason this book will not discuss techniques for creating models and graphics in 3D software or creating music and sound. Rather, it assumes such assets have already been created and then explores how Unity can be of help.

Unity as a tool consists mainly of three separate components or parts. These are: 1) the engine; 2) the editor; and 3) the publishing or output modules. These three parts together are the essence of Unity and the source of its power as game-making software. These components are now considered sequentially in more detail.

1.1.1 The Engine

Unity is commonly designated a 'game engine', but this description really only highlights one of its three components. The engine is the most fundamental, or core, part of the Unity package and all games created with it, just as the heart and brain are among the most fundamental parts of the body. The Unity **engine** is a piece of software that is not immediately obvious to the user or developer but is always working 'under the hood'. Without any explicit mention being made of it, it will be built or embedded into *every* game made with Unity. There it acts as the logical core or unseen infrastructure on which the game rests. The engine can be likened to a vanilla template that is dressed and customised to produce different games, just as a car engine is attached to different frames to produce different models of car. The engine is, of course, different from each of the other two components of Unity (the editor and distribution modules), as we shall see. It is also different from game assets. The assets of a game refer to its content; to the graphics and sounds and animations and models that exist *in the game world*. The engine in contrast is responsible for making the world exist and operate in the first place. It acts as the 'laws of the game universe' and gives us an empty world to dress and populate with our assets and imagination.

1.1.2 The Editor

The Unity editor (See Figure 1.2) is the most tangible part of the software. It is where most developers will spend their time when working with Unity; the gamer on the other hand will not know of the editor at all when they play a game – unless, of course, they happen to be Unity developers as well! But even then they would know about it only because they'd used the editor to make their own games, not because the editor is included in any completed games. The editor is only used by developers during the development phase of the game. It encompasses all the interface, windows, tools and menus that form a part of Unity. When a developer launches Unity from their desktop and begins using the tools to create a game, they are using the Unity editor to do so. The editor features access to different tools, windows and modules that either ship

Figure 1.2 Unity scene-editing tools allow developers to design and build game worlds

with Unity or which can be extended through add-ons. Further, the kinds of options that are made available by the editor vary with editions of Unity, from the free version to the professional version – as we shall see throughout this book. The most notable parts of the editor include: 1) the scene tab or 'world editor' where game levels and environments are constructed using a drag and drop interface (see B of Figure 1.7); 2) the Windows menu, used for opening different editors and tools (see A of Figure 1.7); and 3) the MonoDevelop editor for creating and compiling programming in the form of scripted statements in the JavaScript, C# or Boo languages (See Figure 1.6).

1.1.3 The Distribution Modules

Unity is noted for its cross-platform philosophy, which can be described, albeit simplistically, as 'Build once, deploy everywhere'. In short, Unity aims to be a development tool allowing developers to make games targeted for many platforms and systems, all from only one project or code set. Unity 4 supports: Windows, Mac, Linux, Web, Android, iOS, Flash, Xbox 360, Wii, and PS3. Support for the first four desktop platforms is provided 'out of the box' with the standard Unity package, in both the free and professional versions. Support for the remaining platforms must be purchased through extras or add-ons, and some of those (such as the game console modules) are made available only to 'approved developers'. Regardless of the specifics, however, the distribution modules are the components or pieces of Unity that make compilation and deployment of a game possible with the engine. The distribution modules effectively have the power to combine the engine with game data, made using the editor, so that the game becomes an independent, stand-alone entity.

Stand-alone means it can be distributed successfully and run by the end user without their needing to have the Unity software themselves.

1.2 Why Use Unity? And Why Not?

Unity is fast becoming the 'default choice' of engine for many game studios, especially the so-called 'indie developers' – that is, small teams on tight budgets creating games without the support of a large publisher. There are various technical, logistical and economic reasons for this. Some of these are stated below.

- **Unity can make game development cheaper and easier**. The cost of game development in terms of time can be considerable. This is especially so for smaller teams which, in the absence of a pre-made engine, must develop the technologies and tools for powering their games before they can even start. If they use Unity, developers don't need to create their own engines, editors or distribution modules. These important components are provided 'pre-made' with Unity, which means that developers can focus less on the underlying technicalities of their games and more on the content and game worlds themselves.
- **Unity supports industry-standard file formats.** Unity accepts game assets (meshes, graphics, sounds, etc.) from a variety of industry-standard file formats such as FBX, 3DS, MA, MB, WAV, PNG, PSD and others. There will be more on this subject in Chapter 2. But in short: Unity accepts assets from an extensive range of well-established and common formats. This makes it convenient for artists and developers familiar with established tools to get their assets quickly and easily into their games.
- **Unity saves developers time.** Unity has a RAD (Rapid Application Development) flavour. By being an 'out of the box' engine, it empowers developers to create cross-platform games immediately without having to concern themselves unduly with hardware specifics. Further, Unity is used and therefore *tested* on a daily basis by a large community of users – estimated in 2012 to number around a million. This group consists of both full and part-time developers, and most of them notify the community of potential bugs or errors with the software so Unity developers can correct and patch the problems. This lends a certain weight or 'tried-and-tested' flavour to the software that might not exist for a custom-made engine or with less well-known tools.

Despite the growing popularity of Unity, there are nonetheless times when a developer may for good reason avoid using Unity. In almost all these cases, the reason will be that Unity is not the most appropriate tool for the purpose. It is important to consider here at least three situations where Unity might not be appropriate, if only to paint a more complete picture of when it *is* suited to your needs.

- Situation 1: Unity might be avoided when creating 2D games – that is, games played orthographically in two-dimensions, for example retro side-scrolling shooters or classic platform games. This is because Unity's toolset is tailored *primarily* for 3D games. Unity's tools can be and often are used creatively to make 2D games, sometimes very successfully. But there are engines available dedicated to 2D. These include: GameMaker: Studio, Stenycl, Torque 2D and Construct 2.

- Situation 2: Unity might be avoided even in cases of 3D game development. This usually happens when a developer prefers the workflow or design of a different engine or when they value some other feature Unity does not currently offer, such as Source Code access or built-in GUI editors or the ability to embed Adobe Flash without having to purchase further add-ons. Alternative 3D engines include: UDK, CryEngine, Shiva, DX Studio, OGRE 3D and Panda 3D.
- Situation 3: Third and finally, a developer might avoid Unity (or *any* pre-made engine!), preferring to make their own tool from scratch. This often happens when a game is 'avant-garde' or of such an unconventional nature that it could not be created easily by any tool except one made for purpose. Determining whether your game falls into this category requires experience, as well as time spent creating prototypes in different tools to see which offers the smoothest workflow and produces the best-quality results.

1.3 Unity Versions and Features

Unity is available in two main versions: the free version (as in 'free of charge', not 'open source free software') and the 'pro' or professional version, which is available for a fee. Both of these versions can be downloaded from the Unity homepage at http://www.unity3d.com. The professional version differs significantly from the free version: it not only has a darker graphite interface but also offers full access to the complete range of development tools in the editor. However, both versions can be and have been used to create commercial games. Although this book will not make assumptions as to which version you might have, it will nonetheless consider an extensive range of features, some of which are only available in the professional version. The following sections highlight in overview some of the main features of Unity this book will be detailing, all of them accessible through the editor.

1.3.1 The Scene-editing Tools

The scene-editing tools, as shown in Figure 1.2, are considered more deeply later in the chapter when we pursue our first project. They are mentioned here only briefly for the purpose of introduction. The scene editor refers to a collection of fundamental tools that occupy the largest part of the Unity interface. They are what developers will spend most of their time using when they build games. These tools include the *Scene View*, the *Navigation controls* and the transformation tools of *Translate*, *Rotate* and *Scale*. Together these features allow developers to see their levels in a live preview, assemble and edit them, and generally build them in a WYSIWIG way (*What You See Is What You Get*).

1.3.2 Terrain Tools

Games featuring outdoor scenes, or at least scenes where the outdoors can be seen, even if it's only from a window, will likely make use of the terrain tools. These are a

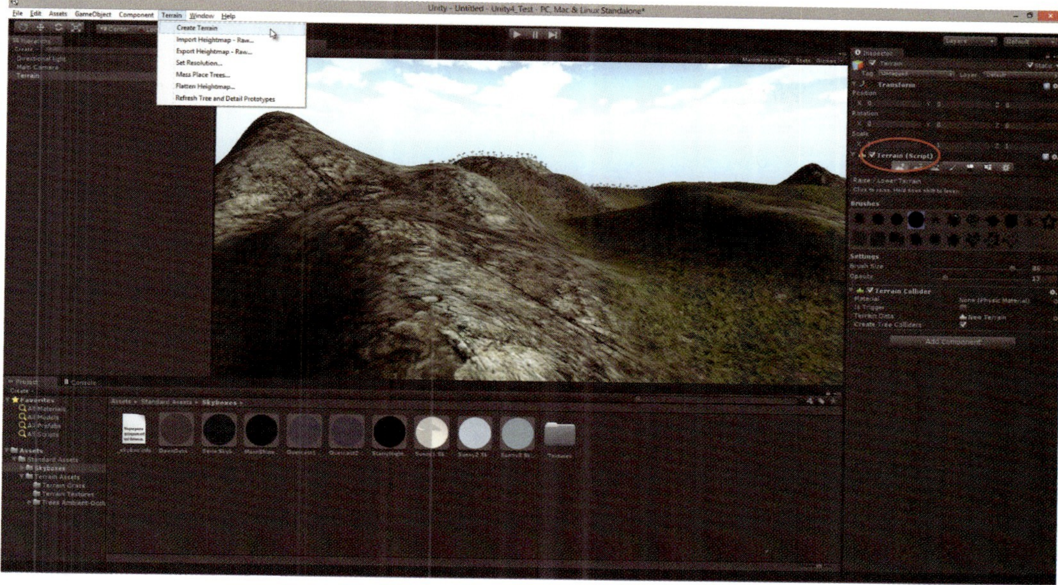

Figure 1.3 Terrain tools are used to sculpt, shape, paint and embellish landscape meshes

range of sculpting and painting tools whose collective purpose is to generate natural-looking 'landscapes' and geographical elements – hills, mountains, crevices, rivers, plains, fields and so on. Developers use the terrain tools to create terrain by way of four main steps. First, a flat and highly tessellated plane is generated into the scene or level. Next, a range of sculpting and shaping tools are used to push and pull elements of the plane into shape like a lump of clay to form a final landscape. The sculpted landscape is then painted with terrain textures, such as grass and dirt, to make it look more believable. Finally, the terrain is decorated or set-dressed with props and elements in the form of trees, bushes, grass, rocks and debris. The terrain tools are considered further in Chapter 4.

1.3.3 The Beast Lightmapper

Chapter 5 details the process of lighting and lightmapping scenes in Unity. Here it is enough to say that the role of the Beast lightmapper is to bake or separate all the complex effects of lighting in the scene into a set of textures *prior* to the game being executed or compiled. These textures are then stored and shipped with the game to be blended onto the objects in the scene *when the game is running*, to make the scene appear illuminated, without incurring any of the performance penalties associated with real-time lighting calculations. As we'll see, the Beast lightmapper offers our games substantial benefits for creating realistic-looking scenes and levels.

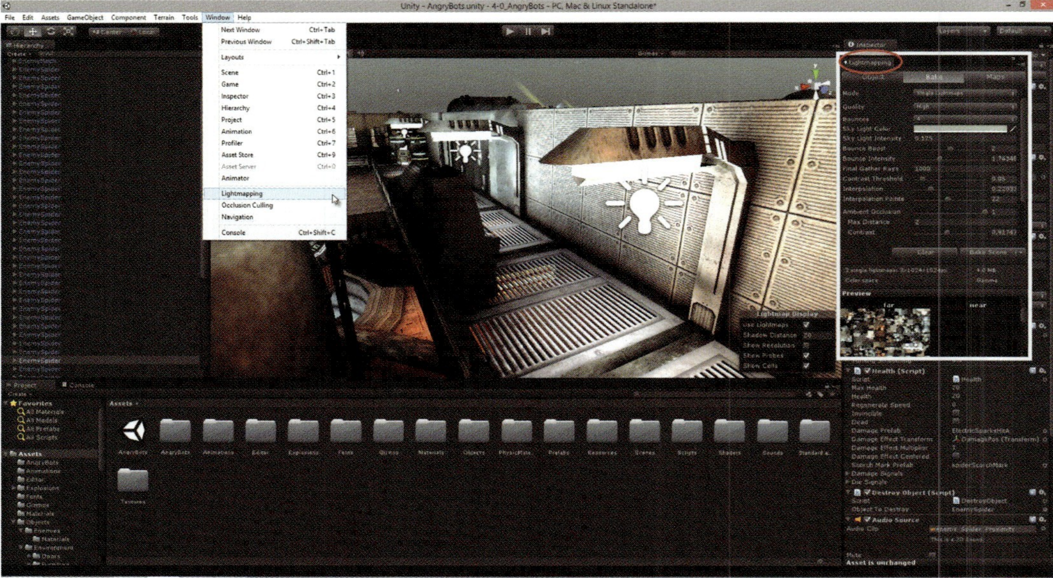

Figure 1.4 The Beast lightmapper is used to create realistic lighting for 3D scenes

1.3.4 Shuriken Particles

Most 3D games made with Unity feature at least one particle system, and many feature far more. The particle system is a special structure or entity used to create a range of animated special effects, almost all of which rely on swarm-like patterns or behaviours that emerge when many small pieces or things come together. For example, the particle system is especially suited for creating effects such as rain, smoke, fog, fairy dust, magical particles, armies of ants, swarms of bees and flocks of birds. The Shuriken particle editor is the feature developers will call upon in Unity to make particle system animations for their games. Shuriken is examined further in Chapter 6.

1.3.5 Animation and Mecanim

In addition to animations created through particle systems, Unity supports two other kinds of animation systems: general *key-frame-based animation* and *character-rigging animation*. These forms of animation are accessible through the two editors: the animation editor (which is a legacy feature) and the Mecanim editor, which is a feature new to Unity 4. The animation editor and Mecanim can be used together for editing key-frame animations; they make it possible for rigid objects as well as non-organic entities such as cars, doors, planes and robots to change over time. Developers can make sliding doors open, trains travel along train tracks, propellers spin and elevators rise. In addition, Mecanim makes it possible to animate rigged character models from within the Unity editor: to make them walk, run, attack and jump, for instance. The new animation tools are detailed in Chapter 11.

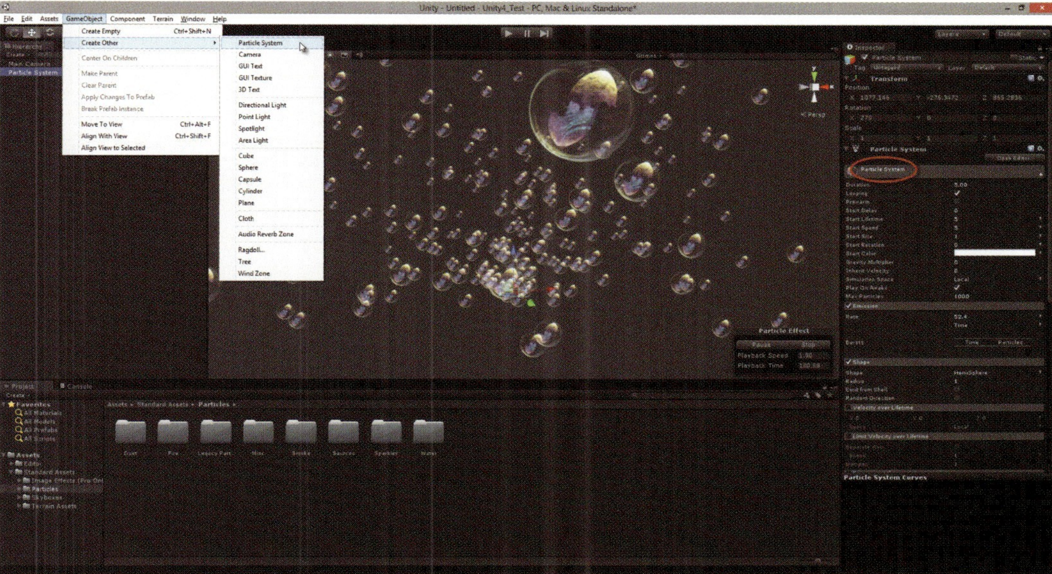

Figure 1.5 Lots of bubbles! Shuriken is used to generate special effects: for creating snow, rain, magic, dust and more

1.3.6 Pathfinding and Physics

In most games, NPCs (Non-Player Characters) – characters controlled by the computer – tend not to stand motionless and aimless in the level. Rather, they appear to identify targets and places to visit, and they travel 'intelligently', navigating around obstacles and using the most sensible route. These 'intelligent properties' are the result of features supported by Unity in the form of 1) pathfinding, for calculating and travelling routes, and 2) physics for collision-detection, among other features. These features are discussed in some detail in Chapter 10 as well as in other chapters.

1.3.7 Scripting and MonoDevelop

Nearly all games are governed by an underlying logic or set of rules, a fundamental set of mechanics or instructions telling the game how to behave or work. A game, for example, needs to be told *how* to respond to user input when it is received, *when* the game is lost or won, *how* enemies behave and *where* events should or should not happen. The total set of 'hows, whens, wheres, and whys' found in a game are defined in Unity by programming in the form of scripting, using any one of the three languages Unity supports – JavaScript (or *UnityScript*), C# and Boo. Source code in these languages can be written using a third-party code editor provided with Unity, named MonoDevelop – although developers do have the option to use an alternative editor, such as Microsoft Visual Studio, if preferred.

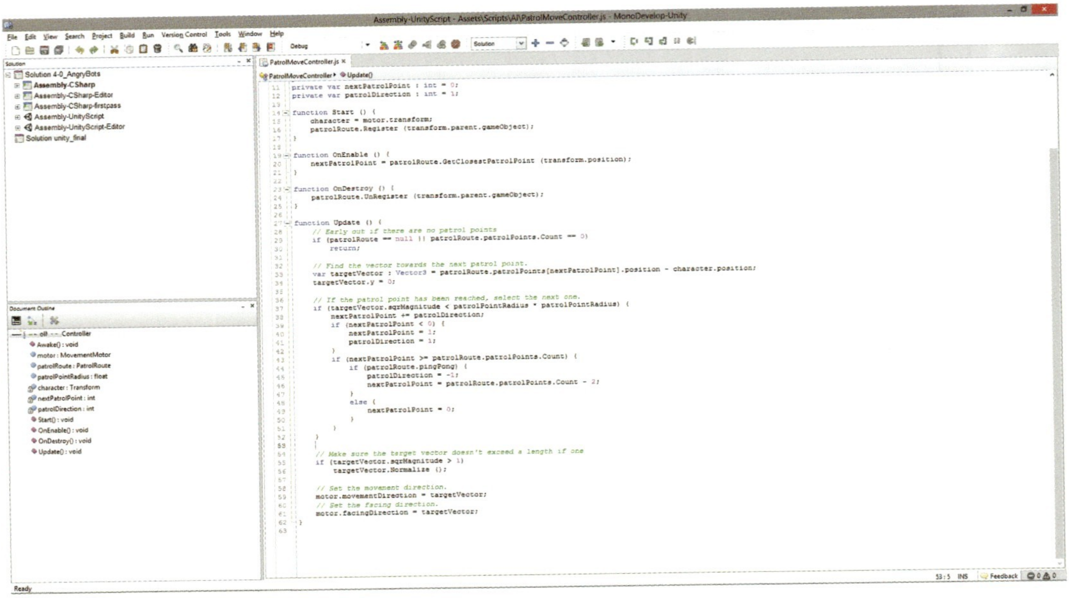

Figure 1.6 MonoDevelop is an IDE (Integrated Development Environment) for writing code in any of the three languages supported by Unity: C#, Javascript or Boo

1.4 Unity – The First Guided Tour

Previous sections of this chapter introduced Unity by stating what it is and is not and generally describing the features it offers for game development. This section moves on and takes a 'dive in the deep end'. We're going to pursue a practical project, one that will be simple but nonetheless functional as a basic 'game'. It will act as an introductory springboard to using Unity. The project will feature one room with a piece of modern sculpture at its centre and the room will be explored in first-person perspective using the standard WASD keys on the keyboard. That is, the room will be explored with a free-roaming camera showing the world from the eye view of the main game character. In creating this project, a range of Unity features and concepts will be introduced and consolidated, many of which will be examined in depth in later chapters.

This section and the remainder of the chapter will require you, the reader, not just to *read* and *think* but also *do*. Specifically, you'll need to be seated at your desktop or notebook and follow me step by step from beginning to end as we progress through the tutorial, repeating in Unity on your system the instructions you'll read below. Consequently, the remaining sections will have fewer descriptive statements like 'This is X' or 'X is about Y' and more instructional statements like 'Press button X' or 'Open Window Y'.

Some might doubt the usefulness of this 'diving in' approach to learning Unity, complaining that it puts the cart before the horse, requiring the use of features and tools that haven't even been introduced. I maintain, however, that this 'diving in' approach is both useful and effective for at least three reasons: first, descriptions without concrete examples can seem dull and clinical and, perhaps more importantly, are detached from real-world workflows. For example, this book *could* have begun with a discussion of the Unity GUI and each and every one of its menu items, one by one (*Edit* > *Copy* and *GameObject* > *Create Other* > *Particle System*, etc.). But even then it would not be clear how exactly these options and features fit together or are supposed to be used in real-world projects. Better then is the method of witnessing someone creating a project and then using that example to appreciate how the features are relevant and have importance. Some descriptions and explanations will *accompany* the steps of the tutorial for the purpose of introducing subjects and features. But these descriptions will generally be brief, partly because an example speaks a thousand words and partly because many of these features will be examined in more depth later on. The second reason to begin with a practical example is that Unity is large and extensive. It is an application in which it can be difficult for newcomers to orientate themselves and see where to begin or how to get started. By focussing on a hands-on project it becomes easier to understand the key features of the software, to rank, organize and relate them conceptually – features such as level editing, asset importing, cameras and meshes. The third and final reason is simply this: I want to show you how easy it is to get started using Unity!

1.4.1 Installing Unity

The first step in using Unity for those completely new to the software is to install it on your computer if you have not already done so – and this applies whether you're using Windows or a Mac. Unity – both the free and professional version – can be downloaded from the Unity Technologies home page at: http://unity3d.com/. The installation process is simple: just download and run the installer. This is a process that needs to be performed only once unless you unfortunately experience data corruption or virus activity and require a re-install or are updating to a newer version of the software.

1.4.2 Running Unity for the First Time

On running Unity for the first time you'll likely be presented with the 'Welcome to Unity' tips window after the editor opens. There'll be a sample project (a *game*) open in the editor with a scene (a *level*) visible in the Scene View, and the interface will be in its default arrangement, as shown in Figure 1.7. This figure also labels the main GUI components, such as the File menu and toolbar, the Scene View, the Game View, the Object Inspector, the Project panel, and the Hierarchy panel. To get started, perform the following steps in order.

Figure 1.7 The Unity editor in its default arrangement. Demonstrates the default GUI layout for Unity. GUI components are: A) the File menu and toolbar: Here live the most common and general application commands, as well as access to most other editors available in the software; B) the Scene View tab displays a large rectangular view showing the contents of the currently open scene in the project; C) the Game tab is used to offer a final real-time preview of how the scene will appear *to the gamer*; D) the Object Inspector shows all significant and editable properties associated with the object currently selected in the Scene View; E) the Project panel lists all assets associated with the project – graphics, sounds, animations, scripts, etc.; F) the Hierarchy panel lists all objects in the currently open scene.

See Video: *Chapter01_Vid01_UnityConfigure* for a video tutorial on how to configure and set up the Unity interface if your interface arrangement and appearance differ from Figure 1.7.

1. Close the 'Welcome to Unity' window that appears at application-start, assuming it does appear, but leave its 'Show at Startup' checkbox ticked so it appears again should you need to use it. This window is filled with helpful resources for newcomers and experienced alike, providing links and references to community forums, documentation and also the Unity Answers website (http://answers.unity3d.com). There, the community provides a concentrated support network for each other in the form of question and answer (Q&A) solutions. The welcome window can be ignored, however, for this tutorial.
2. Carefully examine the interface in its default layout, the layout used throughout this book: the Scene and Game views together as tabs, the Object Inspector aligned to the right of the window,

the Project panel to the bottom of the window, and the Hierarchy panel to the left. Notice the **Scene View,** which is listed in a tab, besides the **Game View**. These are marked by labels B and C in Figure 1.7. The Scene tab will be active by default and will show the contents of the **scene** or level under construction, which on the first run of Unity will be a sample level that ships with the Unity software. If, however, you have already opened and explored Unity, the Scene View might be blank or empty, or show a different scene. In this case, be sure to check out the video *Chapter01_Vid01_UnityConfigure*.

1.5 Working with Unity – Getting Started

Games and applications developed with Unity differ greatly from one another in both their style and content. Unity has been used to develop platform games, RPGs, sports games, first-person shooter games, adventure games and others. Despite radical differences between these game types, almost all will have been made from start to finish using a common pattern or workflow that we might call the *Unity workflow*. This workflow comprises six main steps. These are the six steps to successfully making a game. They come out of how Unity has been designed and constructed, how Unity *conceives* the game development process. So, whenever a developer sets out to make a new game, they make it *first* by understanding and *then* by *following* this six-stage workflow. The workflow takes the following form and applies to almost all game projects in Unity.

Six Steps of Unity Development

1. Start by creating a new project to contain and hold together all the files for the game.
2. Import assets into the project (graphics and sounds, etc.) that are to feature in the game.
3. Add scenes (levels) to the project to contain all game objects in a unified coordinate space or environment.
4. Build the scenes by populating them with game objects. That is, use the Unity editor like a level editor to transform the assets into game objects, and use a range of other editing tools for positioning and arranging those objects spatially in the scene.
5. Next, configure and customise the behaviour of game objects and scenes with scripting, via any of three supported languages: C#, JavaScript or Boo.
6. Finally, build the project through the distribution modules into an executable and stand-alone form that can be distributed to end users.

These six steps together encompass the complete game development workflow. Many of them will be followed right now as we create our project.

1.5.1 Stage 1 – Create a New Project

The first of the six stages involves creating a new project. It marks the beginning of the development process, just as creating a new document in a word processor marks the beginning of a new document. Unity is a 'project-based' application in the same way that asset-creation software like Maya, 3DS Max and Blender are project-based applications. The role of a project is mainly *compositional*: allowing users to import a set of files into the project, to arrange and *manage* those files, to bring them together and *relate* them in specific ways, and then to save the result as a final composition or project which still depends on all the imported files, until finally the project is built into a stand-alone form fit for distribution. In 3D software, users create projects for creating rendered artwork, or movies, or animations. In Unity, developers create projects to make games. For this reason 1 Project = 1 Game (generally speaking). To create a new game we must create a new project, and to save our work we must save the project. The project acts as the container or home for all our work on a *specific* game: the scenes, assets, scripts, data, sound and animations belonging to the same game will all be part of the same project – the project will be their *owner*. The following steps detail how to create a new project for our first game.

1. Open Unity and, starting from the editor interface, click the menu option *File > New Project* (**not** *File > New Scene*). Doing this will show the Unity Project Wizard for specifying the main properties of the project to be created.
2. From the Project Creation dialog, enter a folder location on the local hard drive where the project should be saved and ensure no check boxes are ticked in the *Import Packages* list (none are selected by default). Import packages are discussed in brief later in this chapter and in more detail in Chapter 3. Finally, click the *Create* button to generate a new project.
3. That's it! Creating a new project really is that simple. However, there is more to say about the creation process and the project generally. To be specific, navigate to the folder on your hard drive where the project was created. To get there quickly from the Unity editor, hover the mouse cursor anywhere within the *project panel* at the bottom of the interface (in the default layout). Once there, right-click the mouse to show a context menu, and from the menu choose the option *Show in Explorer*. This opens the project folder in a browser where its contents and files can be seen.
4. The Unity Project folder typically contains four sub-folders: *Assets*, *Library*, *Project Settings* and *Temp*. The latter three folders contain project *meta-data* (data about the data of the project). This is data Unity uses 'under the hood' to maintain and work successfully with projects. They are folders we hardly ever need to explore. The first folder, *Assets,* by contrast *is* relevant to us as Unity users. It will be used to house all of the asset files for the project, including images, sounds, movies and more. In short, each file imported into the project as an asset will in some way be contained inside the Asset folder, either directly in the Asset folder itself or indirectly in one of its sub-folders. The Asset folder contents correspond *directly* to the files and items that appear within the Project panel of the Unity interface. The Project panel can be thought of as a browser window into the Assets folder. Newly created projects feature an empty Project panel, and this reflects an empty Asset folder. This means that a new project begins with no assets, as expected.

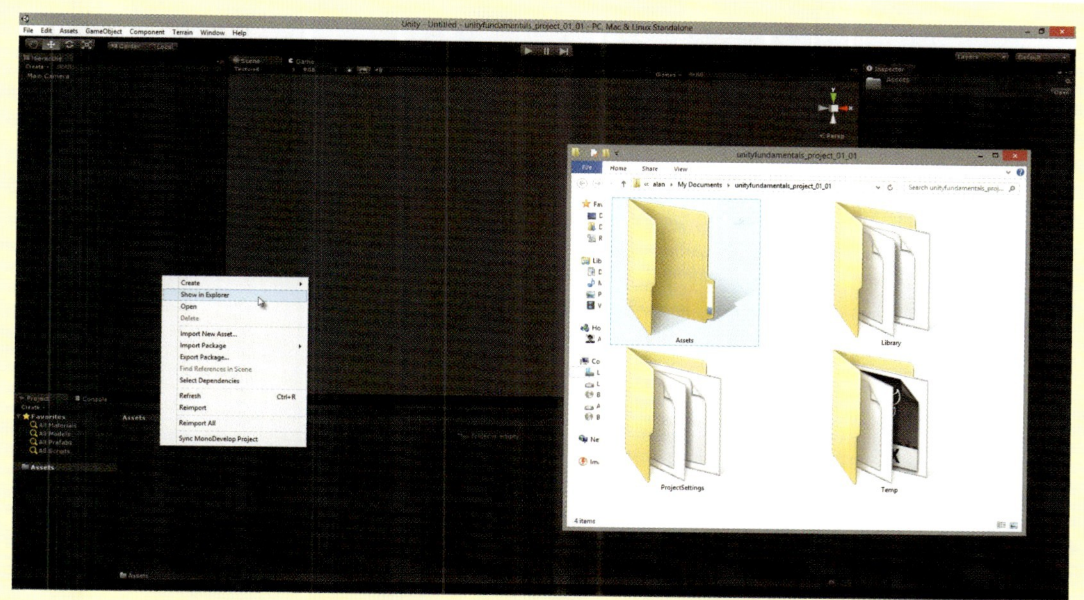

Figure 1.8 Select *Show in Explorer* from the Project panel to view the project folder on the local hard drive

IMPORTANT: One Unity project corresponds to one folder on the hard drive. This contains a further four sub-folders, as we have seen: *Assets*, *Library*, *Project Settings* and *Temp*. These four folders all contain *project critical* data. This data should not be edited or changed or moved manually outside of the Unity interface. Editing the contents of these folders at the explorer level without notifying the Unity software *could* result in a broken or damaged project. That is, a project that Unity no longer recognises or understands correctly because the synchronisation between the software and the folder has been corrupted. In a case such as this, and where no backup copy is available, the developer must either attempt to repair the project through trial and error or begin the project again. So be careful!

1.5.2 Stage 2 – Import Assets

Assets refer to *all* the independent files imported into the project for use at some point in the game. These files are typically created by artists and other developers using applications outside the Unity software and *before* the game itself is created. A project can have none, one or a potentially limitless number of assets. They include image files such as PNGs and Photoshop images used as textures, and 3D Models (.max or .Ma files) used in the game as meshes. Assets also include audio files such as sound and music (WAVs and OGGs), as well movie files in the OGG Theora format and source code in the form of script files in any of the Unity-supported languages. Note that importing an asset into a project does *not* mean the asset will automatically or certainly feature in the game, but only that Unity is configured and made aware of the asset so that it *can* be used, if and when required; the asset is put into a readied state. Once the asset is imported into a Unity project it becomes a part or dependency of that project unless it is explicitly removed. The project to be created in this chapter will contain a range of assets; specifically: meshes for the walls, floor and ceiling of the room, a mesh for the central sculpture, and a texture graphic to be applied to the sculpture. The following steps indicate how to import the mesh and texture graphic – the remaining resources will be imported in later steps.

1. Right-click inside the *Project panel* of the Unity interface to show the Project Context menu. From the menu choose *Import New Asset*. This same option can also be accessed by clicking *Assets > Import New Asset* from the application main menu. This displays a file selection dialog where assets files in any valid format can be selected for import. Import the sculpture mesh asset (sculpture.ma; MA format – Maya Ascii) from the Chapter 1 companion files. Repeat this process for the *sculpture_texture.png* texture asset.
2. The Project panel in the Unity editor now contains a total of two asset files, although an additional materials folder might have been generated by Unity automatically after importing the mesh file. To explore these assets in more detail, open the Project folder in a browser window by right-clicking any vacant space inside the Project panel and selecting the *Show in Explorer* option. Notice the Asset folder now contains both the imported assets that appear in the Project panel.

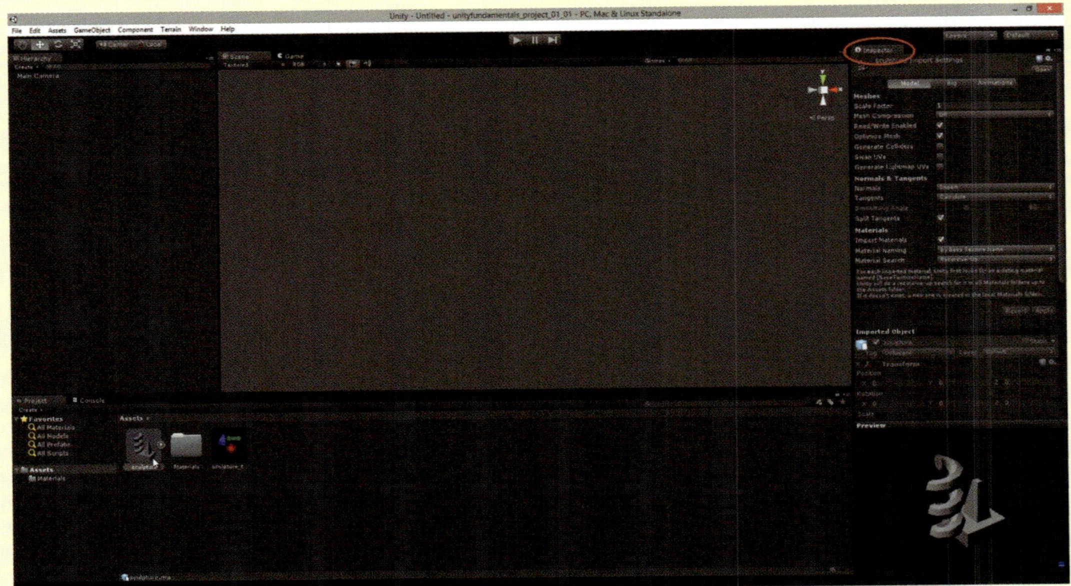

Figure 1.9 Select an object in the Project panel to see its properties in the Object Inspector

Note here that importing an asset into Unity leaves the *original* file, selected from the *File | Open Dialog*, intact. Unity makes a *copy* of that file in the Asset folder and continues to reference only that copy. Changing or updating the original file will therefore have no appreciable effect on the asset imported into Unity; though changes and edits made to the copy in the Asset folder *will* have an effect.

3. Select each of the assets in the Project panel and notice how the contents of the Object Inspector panel (at the right-hand side of the interface) changes according to the selection. The Object Inspector is *context-sensitive* in that it shows the critical properties for the selected item in the editor. It does this regardless of whether the selected item is in the Project panel, the Hierarchy panel, the Scene View, or anywhere else. For now the settings will be left as they are, but we'll return to the Object Inspector at a later stage of this chapter.

1.5.3 Stage 3 – Create Scene

One Unity project can contain none, one or more scenes. One scene is equivalent to one level. Specifically, the scene refers to a single, three-dimensional coordinate space in which game objects can exist. Unity treats a scene as an asset – a special kind of asset. In essence, the scene is a container for all things that will exist in a game level. Thus, a game that features ten levels will typically have ten scenes, with each scene corresponding to one level and containing all the things that exist in that level – enemies, scenery props, lighting, effects and so on. Game worlds or levels are therefore built or assembled through scenes and the scene is thus a critical asset for a game. A game project that contains no scenes is therefore neither a playable nor a functional project. Our sample project in this chapter will contain only one room that acts as a single level; it will consequently have only one scene. *By default* all new projects will contain a new scene, and this scene will be visible in the Scene viewport. Consider the following steps to examine scenes further.

1. Every new project is created by default with a new scene; however, this scene is not automatically saved and added as a bona fide member of the project. To see this, take a look at the project panel, which appears empty apart from the assets already imported and which does not list any scene as an asset of the project. To add the auto-generated scene as a member of the project, simply click the *File > Save Scene* option from the application menu or press the *Ctrl + S* keyboard shortcut. Name the scene *MainScene* and confirm the operation. The scene is now officially added to the project and appears in the Project panel alongside the other assets.

NOTE: If the project *did not* begin with a scene in the viewport, however, or if you removed the scene, then a new scene can be created and added to the project using the *File > New Scene* command from the application main menu. The scene must still be saved after performing the New Scene operation.

1.5.4 Stage 4 – Build Scene; Getting Started

The first three stages of the six-stage process involve creating a project, importing assets and creating as many scenes as required – in this case only one. The fourth stage is perhaps one of the most enjoyable and engaging stages because it's where the game begins to 'come together'. Our project so far has some assets and a scene, but the scene contains practically nothing of interest – it's an empty coordinate space, a world with nothing in it. It's now time to change that and act as the level designer; time to begin creating the game world and make things exist. The following steps demonstrate how to do this.

1. The Unity editor features two main viewports: the *Scene* viewport and the *Game* viewport (see Figure 1.7). The Scene viewport shows us the game scene from a director's eye view; it presents the scene in the way a game developer requires for making a game world. The Game viewport shows us the same scene but presents it as though we were the gamer – it show us what the level would look like if we played it in-game. More of this will become clear as we use the tools. For now, ensure the Scene viewport is selected, *not* the Game viewport. The Scene viewport will allow us to build and edit the level. Also ensure your Scene toolbar looks like mine, as shown in Figure 1.7.
2. Let's begin scene creation by creating a floor for the room; the surface on which the player will walk. Typically, the floor will be created on the basis of a mesh that will have been imported into the project as an asset, just as we imported the sculpture asset. But here (since our scene will be 'simple') we'll simply use some of the pre-made primitive objects that Unity can generate for us. The floor will be created from a *plane* primitive. To create this, select *GameObject > Create Other > Plane* from the application main menu. Figure 1.10 illustrates what the scene should look like once the plane object has been added. Look at the next section for information on viewport navigation.

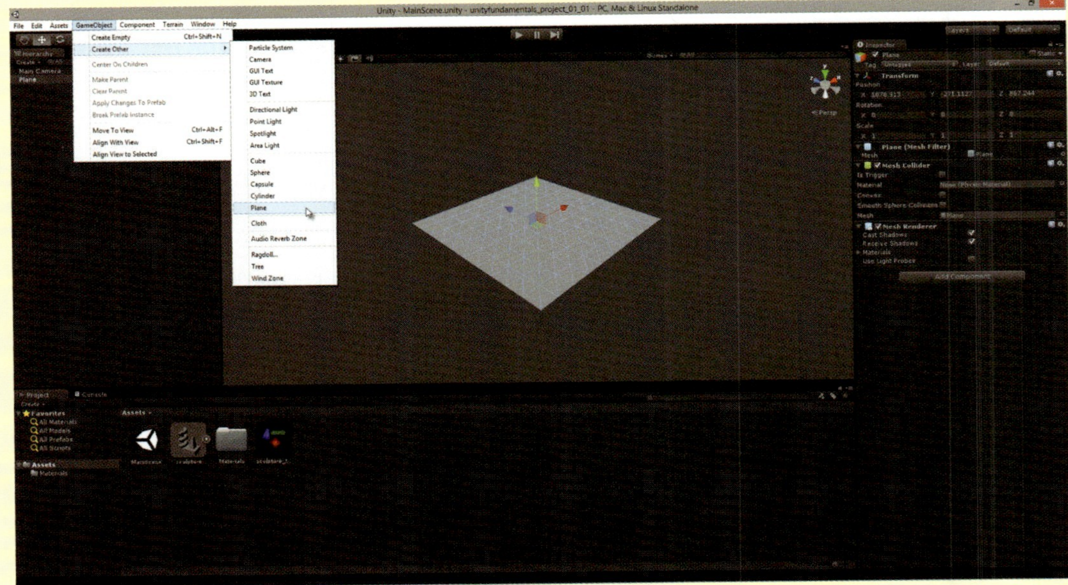

Figure 1.10 Scene with a floor plane added

1.5.4 Stage 4 – Viewport Navigation

One of the critical and most essential skills of any successful level designer in Unity is that of navigating viewports – that is, being able to move the camera around in the viewport using keyboard and mouse controls to see the scene from different angles and perspectives. This section provides a comprehensive tutorial on the most important navigation techniques. Users familiar with Maya, however, are in for a real treat. This is because most of the navigation controls and level-editing keyboard shortcuts in Unity are borrowed from or based on those in Maya. More information on the viewport navigation modes can be seen in the companion video tutorials for Chapter 1 where different navigation techniques are demonstrated.

See Video: *Chapter01_Vid02_ViewportNavigation* for a video tutorial on how to navigate scene viewports.

- **Pan Mode**. Panning is the process of moving the viewport camera up, down, left or right, but does not involve turning or rotation. Pan mode is enabled in one of two ways: either by pressing the *Pan tool* button in the Editor Toolbar, as shown in Figure 1.7, or by holding down the middle mouse button. Pan mode will be active as long as that button is held down. With pan mode active, simply move the mouse; moving it right to pan right, and left to pan left, etc. Pan mode is especially useful for taking in an overall glance or inspection of the level.
- **Zoom/Dollying**. Zoom mode is a misnomer because true zooming involves holding the camera position *constant* and making distant objects *appear* nearer by changing the camera focal length. The Unity zoom mode is closer to 'dollying', in which the viewport camera actually moves forwards and backwards, coming closer to or moving further from objects in the scene. To dolly in this way, simply scroll the mouse wheel: up to move forwards and down to move backwards. This method of navigation – like all methods – can be combined with others.
- **Rotation**. The viewport camera can be rotated to view the scene from any angle. Rotation occurs by *holding down* the right mouse button and moving the mouse to control the viewing angle. Try combining the methods of panning, zooming and rotation to navigate the scene viewport.
- **Framing**. There are often times during scene construction when it's useful to move the viewport camera quickly to focus on a particular object in the scene. That is, to have the camera move automatically such that a specific object is at the centre of our view. This process is called framing. To frame an object, active any of the transform buttons on the toolbar *except for* Pan (you cannot select objects while the Pan tool is active). Then select an object in the viewport by left-clicking the mouse on the object. Then press the *F* key on the keyboard to centre the view on the selected object.
- **Orbiting**. Orbiting is the process of rotating the viewport camera around the *framed* object, just as the Earth rotates around the sun. Orbiting treats the framed object as though it were the pivot point of the camera, or its centre of rotation. A framed object is the object in the scene that was last framed with a framing operation using the keyboard shortcut *F*. To orbit around the framed object, hold down both

the *Alt* key on the keyboard and the *left-button* on the mouse, and then move the mouse to control the angle of rotation around the object.

- **First-person Controls**. One of the fastest and most convenient methods for navigating the viewport, 'first-person' navigation enables you to experience the level from close-up. This method allows developers to navigate the viewport using a free-floating first-person camera, seeing the world through the eyes of someone who is in it and has the ability to fly or float in every direction. To use this method, hold down the right-mouse button to enable rotation mode, and then use the WASD keys on the keyboard to control the forward, backwards and sideways movement of the camera.
- **Hovering**. The last method of navigation is hovering: this is accessible through the directional arrow keys on the keyboard. It works by holding the camera height constant and allowing the camera position to change on the X and Z axes (forwards, backwards, and left and right). The camera speed increases the longer the keys are held down. This technique is useful for navigating across large and expansive levels.

1.5.5 Stage 4 – Continuing Scene Construction

This section will see us complete the creation of our scene by adding the remaining elements; these include the walls, the sculpture at the room centre and a light to illuminate the scene. Follow the steps below.

1. Frame the floor plane in the viewport by selecting it with the mouse and then press the *F* key on the keyboard. Try rotating around the plane using orbiting – holding the *Alt* key and *left-mouse* button while moving the mouse. Notice that, with the plane selected in the viewport, its properties are shown in the Object Inspector panel. Its properties are grouped into various sections or groups named **components**, separated from each other by divider lines. Consider Figure 1.11. Move to the Transform component in the inspector and type the position of the object in World Space into the X, Y and Z edit boxes, setting the position of the object to the World origin at X:0, Y:0, Z:0. In doing this, the object might vanish from the viewport if the viewport does not have a clear view of the origin. In this case, simply press the *F* key again on the keyboard to centre the camera on the plane object. Make sure the plane is selected before pressing *F*!
2. Add a wall to the scene by generating a box primitive from the main menu with *GameObject > Create Other > Cube*. This creates a cube in the scene that intersects with the floor plane and, at present, looks nothing like a wall. The object will be adjusted or transformed: specifically, it will need to be made longer and thinner and it will also need to be moved. To do this, we can use the Transform controls. These are all accessible from the toolbar at the top of the editor (see Figure 1.7) but can also be accessed with keyboard shortcuts matching those in Maya: *Q* (Pan), *W* (Move or Translate), *E* (Rotate) and *R* (Scale).
3. Select the cube object in the viewport and change its size using the Scale tool. To do this, select the Scale tool with the *R* key. With the Scale tool selected, the Gizmo icon centred on the cube in the viewport changes to offer us control over the object scaling. In short, by clicking and dragging with the mouse over the centre grey cube (on the gizmo) we change the cube's size or scale in all three dimensions. By clicking and dragging over any of the other coloured cubes, we stretch or shrink the cube in a *single* dimension – along only one axis. Scale down the cube in the X axis (red) to create the thickness of the wall. Keep an eye on the object inspector as the scale changes. Notice the values

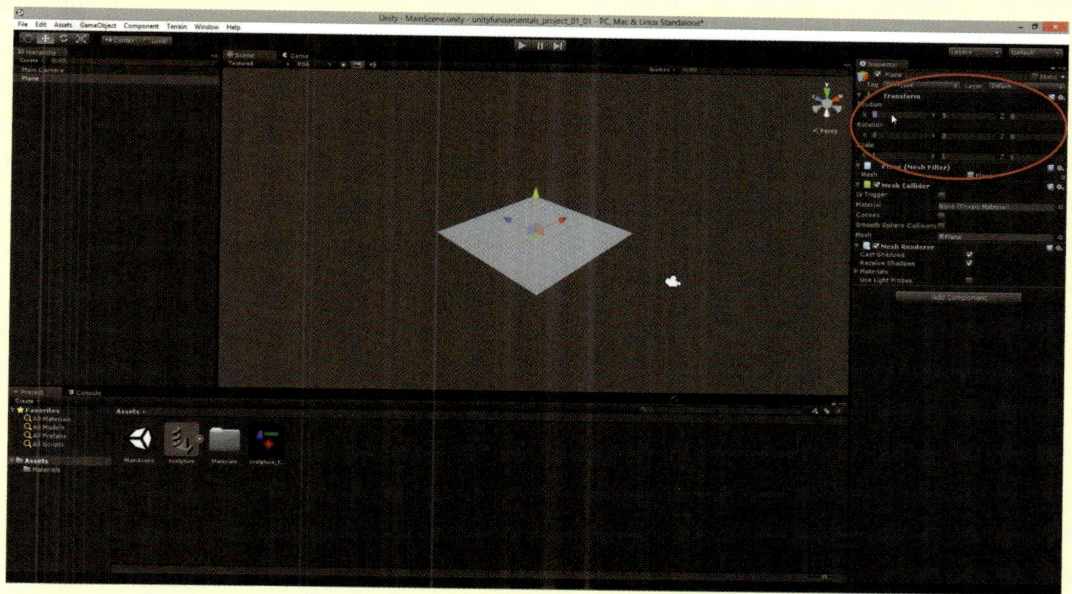

Figure 1.11 Editing the properties of the selected object using Components in the Object Inspector

in the scale type-in fields update to reflect the changes. Then upscale the object in both the Z and Y axes (blue and green) to create a width and height of wall to match the floor plane. Remember to use viewport navigation to check on the scaling operation from different angles. See Figure 1.12.

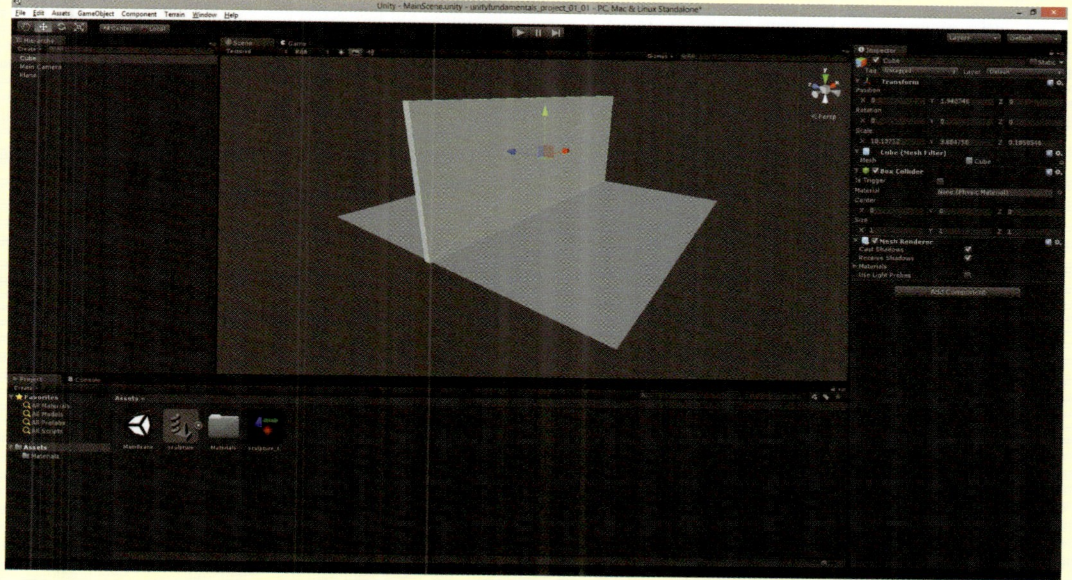

Figure 1.12 Use the Scale gizmo handles to edit the scale of the selected object

4. The wall has now been scaled appropriately but is still not positioned correctly in relation to the floor. To move the wall to a new position, select the Translate tool using the keyboard shortcut *W*, or by pressing the Translate button on the toolbar (see Figure 1.7). Like the scaling tool, the Translate tool draws a gizmo at the centre of the object in the Scene viewport (but not the Game viewport!). Clicking and dragging over any of the arrows will move/translate the object along that axis (red = left and right, blue = forwards and backwards, and green = up and down). Use the Translate tool to position the wall at the edge of the floor plane, making sure the bottom of the wall touches or intersects with the floor. Return to the Scale tool and tweak the size of the wall, if required.
5. You can make the bottom near corner of the wall *align exactly* with the nearest corner of the floor. This can be achieved using **vertex snapping**. Vertex snapping is useful for aligning the vertices (points/corners) of different objects, ensuring the objects meet or touch exactly and cleanly at the edges rather than penetrating slightly through each other, as the wall might pass through the floor if not aligned exactly. To do this, select the wall object and ensure the Translate tool is active. Then hold down the *V* key on the keyboard. While pressed, the cursor can be hovered over the vertices (or corners) of the wall object and the gizmo will snap or lock itself onto the nearest vertex. Again, this is visible only in the Scene viewport, not in the Game viewport. Find the near edge of the wall and then *click and drag* this to the corner of the floor plane to align the wall to the floor exactly. See the Chapter 1 companion video on building this project for a demonstration of vertex snapping – the video is listed at the end of this section.
6. Let us make the Scene viewport full-screen to get a clearer and more detailed view of our work. To do this we will use the 'space-bar full-screen' toggle. Hover the mouse cursor over the *Scene viewport*, *not* over a different panel. Then press the space-bar on the keyboard to enable full-screen mode. Pressing space bar again will return the viewport back to its original size.
7. One wall has now been created and sized successfully in relation to the floor, but the room will need three more walls to enclose each side of the floor. These can be created by repeating the above

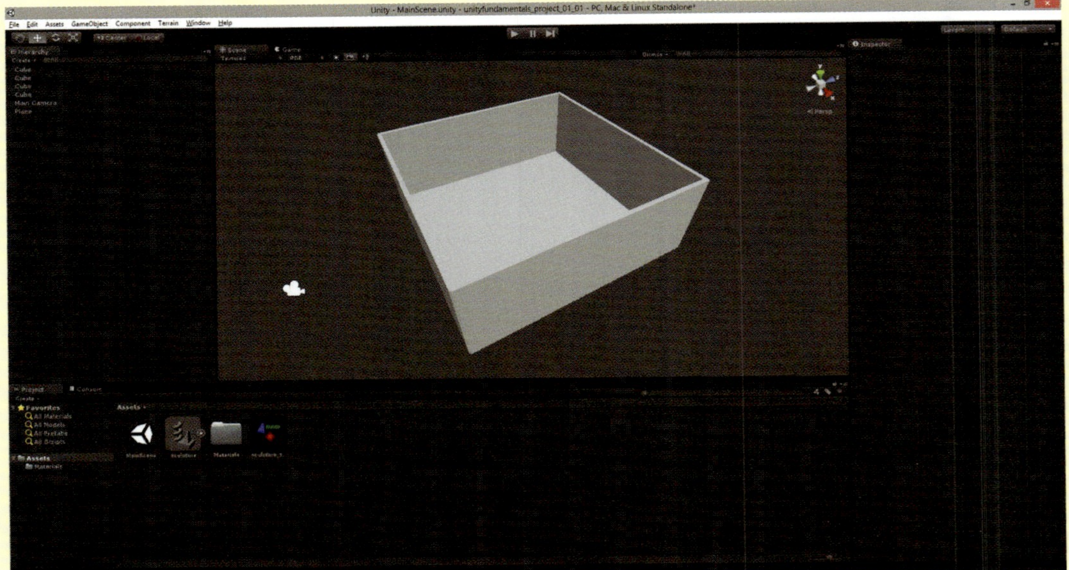

Figure 1.13 The level is coming together, with four walls and a floor

steps for each of the other walls, or a faster method is to use **object duplication**. This involves creating duplicates of our original wall – which has already been sized and scaled – and then simply 'transforming' the duplicates into their appropriate places. To do this, select the existing wall object and press *Ctrl* + *D* on the keyboard to duplicate the selected object (again, using the same keyboard shortcut as featured in Maya). An alternative method is to select *Edit* > *Duplicate* from the application main menu. Once duplicated, use the transformation tools and vertex snapping to move the duplicates into place for each side of the floor.

8. Two of the walls, however, will need to be rotated into place using the Rotate transformation tool, accessible with the keyboard shortcut *E*. Using the gizmo surrounding the selected object, rotate the wall around the Y axis (*Yaw*) by clicking and dragging along the green rotation handles. The rotation tool supports two modes of rotation: continuous and discrete. These modes influence how freely the object can rotate. Continuous rotation allows objects to be rotated around an axis by *any* quantity in degrees, including decimal values, while discrete rotation *snaps* the rotation to specified increments, such as increments of 10 or 15 degrees. Continuous rotation is the default behaviour of the tool, but discrete rotation can be used while holding down the *Ctrl* key on the keyboard and rotating the object. Use discrete rotation to rotate the walls 90 degrees to match the other two sides of the room. Check the rotation values in the object inspector as the object rotates to see discrete rotation in action and to check the object is correctly rotated.
9. Now that all four walls are in place we will insert the sculpture mesh asset into the centre of the room. To do this, simply *drag and drop* the sculpture mesh asset *from* the Project panel *into* the Scene viewport. The sculpture is added to the level but still needs to be transformed into place at the room's centre using the Translate tool. You might also want to scale the object. Notice how objects are added to the list inside the Hierarchy panel at the bottom left-hand side of the editor interface (see Figure 1.13). This panel, considered in more detail in Chapter 3, lists each and every object in the active scene that is shown in the viewport, including the floor and wall objects added earlier. It is important to emphasise that when we inserted the sculpture into the room by dragging and dropping the mesh asset from the Project panel, we did not move the asset from one panel to another in a 'cut and paste' fashion. The sculpture asset still appears in the Project panel even though the sculpture is now in the level as a game object. Rather, we created an *instance* or *instantiation* of the asset in the level, and the instantiation is listed in the Hierarchy panel. Unity calls each instance of an asset in the scene a **game object**; each unique thing in the scene is a game object. Notice that the sculpture asset can be dragged and dropped into the level multiple times to create many instances or copies of the object in the scene.
10. It is now time to add some texture to the surface of the sculpture. To do this, drag and drop the texture asset from the Project panel over the sculpture game object in the Scene viewport. The sculpture will now be 'shaded' with the appropriate texture. If the object does not appear shaded with a texture after the drag-and-drop operation, be sure the *Scene Shading* mode is set to **Textured** from the drop-down list in the Scene view toolbar, as shown in Figure 1.7.
11. Our first 'simple' level is almost completed, with two main exceptions: first, there is no light in the scene to properly illuminate any of the objects; and second, there is no way of playing or testing the scene in first-person mode. The scene is obviously being illuminated since the objects are visible to us in the viewport – Unity applies default lighting to the scene, as we shall see in later chapters. However, the lighting could be improved. These two issues of lighting and play-testing will now be addressed. Inserting a light into the scene is simple: click *GameObject* > *Create Other* > *Point Light* from the application main menu, or alternatively click the *Create* button in the Hierarchy panel and select *Point Light* from the context menu. Use the transformation tool to position the light and use

Figure 1.14 Adding and configuring a light in the scene

the scale to increase the range of the light. The brightness of the light can be increased by raising the **Intensity** property found in the Object Inspector when the light is selected.

12. Play-testing the game is even simpler than adding a light to the scene: simply press the large 'Play' button on the application toolbar. Pressing this button has the effect of *running the game*, allowing us to play and preview our work as a gamer. Be sure to press the *Play* button with either the Game (not Scene) tab active, or with the Scene tab active but showing in standard size not full-screen mode (this can be toggled with the space bar). Pressing the *Play* button a second time will exit *Play* mode and return us back to *Design* mode. You will see that in Play mode we are, at present, unable to do much in our game. A view of our scene is shown in the Game tab, but the camera does not respond to our input and cannot be used to explore the scene. We want to make this a first-person game, one in which the gamer, using standard WASD controls, can walk forwards, backwards and sideways, and also use the mouse to control the rotation of the player's head. Unity provides some pre-made scripts and behaviours to get up and running quickly with these sorts of controls. To access them, select *Assets > Import Package > Character Controller*. From the dialog that appears accept the default settings and click the *Import* Button to load the full range of pre-made assets into the project relating to first-person controls, and these assets will appear directly in the Project panel in the folder *Standard Assets*.
13. Open the folder *Standard Assets* in the Project panel, then open the folder *Character Controllers* and drag and drop the *First Person Controller* asset into the scene, positioning it somewhere in the room and above the floor to indicate the player start location – that is, the position in the scene where the player will begin when the game starts. Ensure the first-person controller does not intersect any scene geometry such as the floor, walls, or the sculpture, or else it will not behave as intended. Position the controller so that the camera icon attached to it is around eye level – the camera indicates the position of the player's eyes. Before pressing the *Play* button, move over to the Hierarchy panel and delete the Main Camera object from the scene – select the object in the Project

panel and press the delete key on the keyboard. This is because our scene now has a new main camera attached to the first-person controller and keeping both of the cameras will cause a conflict between the two. So the original camera should be deleted from the scene. Once deleted, press the *Play* button from the toolbar. Congratulations! You have now completed your first Unity project. Take a tour around the level and enjoy your hard work. During the tour you are likely to notice a few 'issues'; later chapters will detail a whole range of features that will help you resolve them. For example: the camera will sometimes allow you to see through the walls when you walk very close to them; or you will be able to walk through the sculpture in the centre of the room even though you can't walk through the walls or floor.

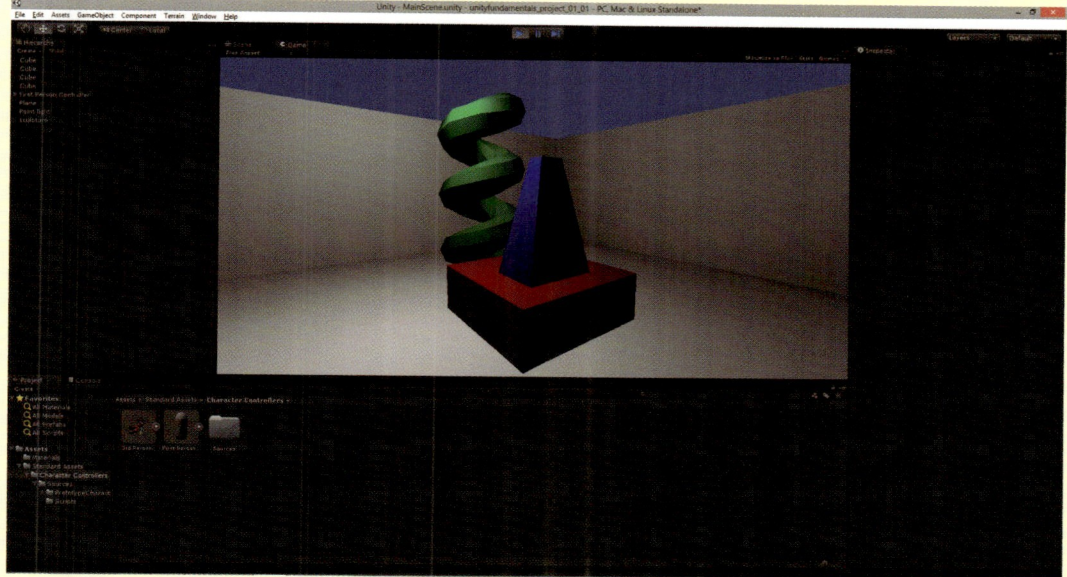

Figure 1.15 The completed project explored in first-person mode

See Video: *Chapter01_Vid03_BuildingTheProject* for a video tutorial on how to construct the project described in this chapter.

1.6 Conclusion

This chapter introduced the fundamentals of Unity – what Unity is and is not and the kinds of uses to which Unity can be put. Its conclusion was that Unity is primarily a game development or game composition tool: it takes game assets as an input, allows them to be assembled together in a unified game world, and finally outputs the result in the form of a stand-alone, executable game. In completing this chapter we've seen how a basic but workable project can be constructed in Unity from the ground up. Starting with a new project, we imported and configured assets; brought them into a scene; constructed a scene using the transformation tools (Translate, Scale and Rotate); then finalised the level by adding lighting and a first-person camera controller. The result is a scene that can be explored in first-person mode, and in constructing it we have put to use some of the most versatile and critical tools that Unity has to offer, tools that will come into play time and time again. The remaining chapters of this book begin where this chapter ends. They take the subjects we have looked at here as starting points for examining particular issues in more depth. The next chapter considers assets and asset workflows.

CHAPTER 2

Assets and Asset Management

By the end of this chapter you should:

1. Understand the different types of assets
2. Learn optimal methods for importing assets
3. Be able to use the Unity Project panel
4. Understand the benefits of asset management
5. Know how to search the Unity Asset Store

Section 1.5 of Chapter 1 outlined the six-stage workflow for Unity. Step 2 of that workflow focussed on assets. For this reason it is appropriate to consider assets early in this book. If you followed through the project of Chapter 1, you'll have already used assets in abundance. Now it's time to extend our knowledge of them. The Oxford English Dictionary defines 'Asset' as a 'useful or valuable thing or person'. For video games, assets are not only 'useful things' but indispensable things. Assets refer to *all* the independent files and data on which a game rests or depends – typically data originally created in software outside of Unity. The files imported into a Unity project for use in the game constitute the assets for that project. Consequently, assets include the graphics, animations, sounds, music, movies and all other data featured in the game. This data is typically imported into Unity by way of various files and file formats, such as PNG files for images and OGG files for movies and music. For this reason, the extent of support Unity provides for such files and file formats determines the range of assets that can be successfully imported, and thereby the kinds of applications and software you can use to create assets for your games. It's important, therefore, whenever you begin any new game in Unity, to be sure of two main points regarding asset creation: first, that you're using asset creation software (like Photoshop, Maya, 3DS Max or Blender) which can export or save assets in a format Unity recognises and understands; and, second, that your asset creation software provides the tools and features necessary to optimise and configure your assets for the best performance possible when imported into Unity. The issues associated with both compatible file formats and asset optimisation techniques are considered throughout this chapter.

NOTE: Assets do not refer to the specific copies or instances of assets in a scene, each of which has its own position and size: for example, a door object, a table object, or an enemy object. These are more technically termed **game objects**, not assets, because they live *in the scene*. They have a position and size in the scene. Assets never have a position or size in the scene because they don't live in scenes. Assets refer to the more abstract meshes, textures and data that live *in the project* – they are the template or raw materials from which specific game objects are made.

2.1 Assets – Graphics, Audio, Animation and Other Data

Assets, as we've seen, come in various forms regardless of file formats. They can be, for example, graphics, sounds, animations or movies. They provide the raw materials from which games and game objects are made and are thus critical to every game. The project in Chapter 1, for example, involved our constructing a room with a modern art sculpture at its centre; a room we could explore in first-person perspective. In creating this project it was necessary to make use not of only many assets but also many *different types of* asset: We created a *scene* asset to act as a world or space in which game objects could live and exist; we created plane and box *primitive* assets to act as the walls and floor of the room; we imported a *texture* and *mesh* asset for the sculpture at the room centre; we imported a first-person camera *package* with scripted source code to make the camera behave in first-person mode; and finally, we generated a *light* asset to illuminate the environment and enhance its believability. In that sample project alone many different assets were used. The following sub-sections consider each of these asset types in more detail and also provide information on the software used to create them, as well as important guidelines for importing them into Unity optimally.

2.1.1 Textures

Texture refers to *any* imported, standard pixel-based 2D image, *regardless* of its use in the project. Textures include all images made in software, such as Adobe Photoshop, Adobe PhotoShop Elements, GIMP and Corel PaintShop Pro. The supported file formats for textures include: PSD, TIFF, JPEG, PNG, GIF, BMP, TGA, IFF, and PICT. Thus, if your texture creation software supports saving and exporting to any of these formats then it can be used to create textures for import into Unity. A texture serves one of two main purposes in Unity: first, it can be *mapped* like a skin onto the surfaces of 3D mesh objects to make those objects *appear* more realistic or *look* more stylised. Second, it can be projected directly into screen space to create Graphical User Interface (GUI) elements for a game – such as its menus, buttons, edit boxes, fonts and other interface

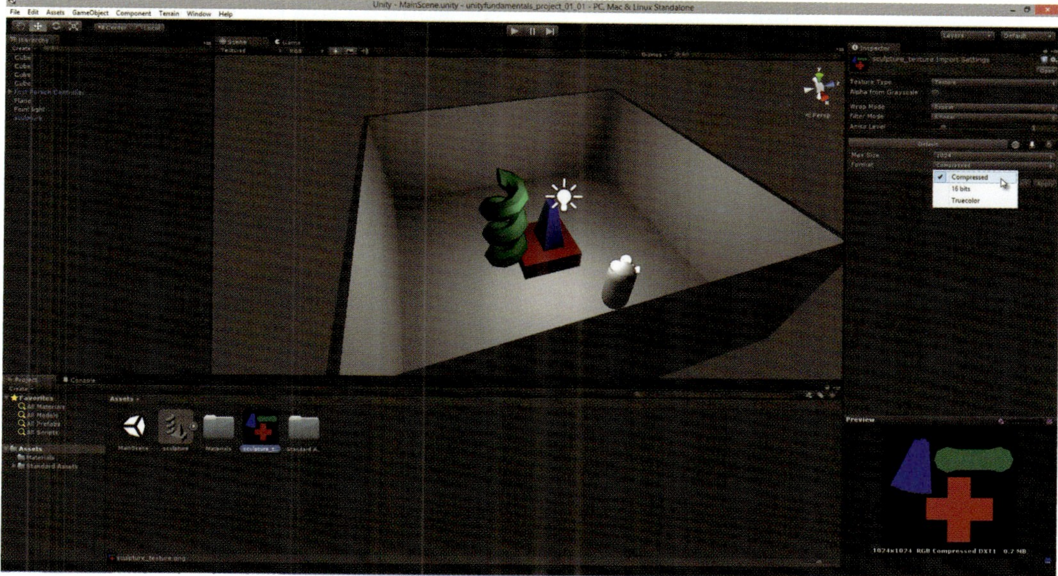

Figure 2.1 Configuring texture properties from the Object Inspector

widgets. Most Unity projects make use of many textures – sometimes thousands! Some of these textures will be used for mapping onto 3D objects and some for GUI elements.

NOTE: Open up the Unity project from Chapter 1 and select the sculpture texture file in the Project panel to examine its associated properties in the Object Inspector. See Figure 2.1. Note that changes applied to the texture asset in the Project panel will be propagated to *all* appearances of the texture on objects throughout the scene. Some of these properties are considered in more detail later in this section.

Texture Import Guidelines

Officially, Unity supports a wide range of image file formats for textures and allows textures to be of practically any pixel dimensions, but this does not mean that every format and any size file will perform equally well when imported into Unity. Indeed, the reverse is true. Consequently, there is a more restricted set of guidelines or workflows or 'best practices' that I recommend you follow and make habitual when creating *all* textures, to ensure they're optimised and configured for best performance when imported into Unity. These guidelines follow in the form of two general rules.

Texture Rule # 1 – Import in the Highest Quality Format and The Largest Size Available

Make it a habit to import the highest quality texture at its largest size into Unity wherever possible, unless there's some compelling reason not to. This often translates to mean: import in the Photoshop PSD format and at a size of 4096x4096 for square textures. Importing in the highest quality format means importing in the format that allows the artist to retain the greatest amount of image data from the original. PSD and Layered TIFF files generally satisfy this requirement because they both use lossless compression (data is not lost during a save operation) and retain all the layered pixel information (they do not flatten the layers in the image when saved). Importing at the largest size means importing the texture at the maximum pixel dimensions allowed by Unity, which is 4096 pixels in each dimension. These two mini-rules taken together might seem like a policy of madness. Surely no real-time game engine could possibly sustain all textures in those formats and at that size, given current hardware? However, the issue becomes clearer as soon as we see that Unity internally generates its *own* optimised textures on the basis of the imported versions. Thus, using 'premium assets' offers two main benefits: first, Unity generates a game-suitable texture from the highest quality version; and second, the developer still has access to the original layered artwork even after it has been imported into Unity.

To see this at work, consider the texture asset included with the project in Chapter 1. Select this asset in the Project panel of the Unity interface and adjust the *Max Size* value in the Object Inspector to edit the pixel dimensions of the texture. Change the size to a lower resolution and then click the *Apply* button to observe how the texture in the viewport reduces in quality because of its reduction in size. Now change the size back to its original setting and observe how the quality is 'restored' to the texture in the viewport. Unity has not **upsized** the shrunken texture back to its original settings. Rather it has referenced the original high-quality texture to generate a new version based on the settings specified in the Object Inspector. In this way, developers can import high resolution textures and have Unity maintain an internal version which can be downscaled or upscaled to the intended resolution without a loss in quality and without even having to leave the Unity editor.

Texture Rule # 2 – Use Power-2 pixel dimensions for all Standard Textures. Use any evenly numbered pixel dimensions for GUI textures

If your texture file is *not* intended for use as a GUI component (such as a button or window or text box) then ensure its width and height in pixels are of a 'power-2' size. That is, ensure their size is any of the following numbers: 32, 64, 128, 256, 512, 1024, 2048 or 4096. These sizes are said to be power-2 because $2^5 = 32$, $2^6 = 64$, $2^7 = 128$, and $2^8 = 256$, etc. Note that having the dimensions of a texture at a power-2 size does *not* mean the texture must be square, such as 256x256 – though square sizes are valid and often preferable. But equally valid are non-square power-2 sizes such as 256x1024, 512x64, or 1024x2048, etc. Using these sizes ensures your textures will be compatible and will perform well with the greatest range of graphics hardware available. The exception to power-2 sizes include textures for GUIs. These textures are configured to perform well at any size that is an even number (such as 200x150 or 348x222), but they cannot be applied to 3D meshes or other objects in the scene.

NOTE: The use of a texture, whether GUI or not, must be explicitly stated to Unity after import. This is achieved through the *Texture Type* field in the *Texture Settings* of the Object Inspector. It is visible whenever a texture asset is selected in the Project Panel. Consider Figure 2.1. The Texture Type field can be a range of values: the *Texture* value is the default and refers to standard textures applied to 3D meshes. The value *GUI* is for textures used in GUIs. Other values can be chosen for specialised textures; some of which are explored later in this book. Be sure to click the *Apply* button on the Object Inspector after changing any settings to texture assets to ensure the changes are applied.

See Video: *Chapter02_Vid01_UnityTextures* for a video tutorial on best-practice workflows for importing textures, including textures with transparent regions.

2.1.2 Meshes

The term 'mesh' is the name Unity gives to any asset, animated or not, that represents 3D geometry – that represents a model or 3D object. Buildings, enemies, doors, walls, weapons, characters, trees, ammo crates, spaceships – almost every visible game entity in a 3D game is a separate mesh. Meshes contain several distinct channels or pieces

Figure 2.2 Mesh geometry in Maya 2013, with UV information at the side

of information: **Geometry**, **UV Mapping**, **Rigging** and **Animation**. The Geometry channel contains all the data defining the geometric structure or constitution of the mesh – all the components that build the mesh. These consist of vertices, edges and polygons: together these components form the tangible form of meshes that we see when they appear in a scene. The UV Mapping information represents mathematical instructions specifying how textures are to be wrapped or projected onto the surface of the model, as defined in the Geometry channel. And the Animation and Rigging channels store all **key frames** that together define how the mesh changes or animates over time (if it animates at all – buildings and static objects, for instance, do not animate). The exact details of how meshes are created and structured are beyond the scope of this book, although the subjects of UV Mapping and Animation will be revisited in later chapters. Meshes can be created in content-creation software such as Maya, Blender and 3DS Max. Unity supports the following file formats for meshes: ma, mb, 3ds, max, jas, c4d, dae, fbx, blend, and obj. The rest of this section focusses on meshes and on the guidelines for structuring them for a clean and optimised import into Unity. As such, it will mainly address content creators already familiar with the modelling process.

Mesh Rule # 1 – Minimise Polygons and Vertices

Excess is wastage. The resolution or detail of a mesh is determined by its polygon count – the total number of polygons in the mesh. More polygons mean more geometric detail, but the detail theoretically comes at a performance cost – it costs more in computing power for Unity to render the mesh. That cost rises exponentially with the level of detail. Generally speaking, if mesh A has fewer polygons than mesh B but both meshes appear identical to each other and animate equally well, then mesh A is to be preferred for its simplicity, because that simplicity means it will perform better when running in Unity. In short, model your meshes to be as simple as possible in terms of polygons but without compromising on the quality you require for your game. Like many things, this is easier said than done. Optimising mesh geometry is a process that frequently requires tweaking and 'trial and error'. It will likely involve the following workflow: import model into Unity, see how it performs during gameplay, identify problems, tweak model in creation software, import again, see how it performs, and so on . . .

Mesh Rule # 2 – Minimise UV Seams and Reduce Materials

The UV Mapping coordinates of a mesh are mathematical instructions, but if they could be pictured they would essentially be what the mesh would be like if it were unfolded from its 3D form and flattened out on a sheet of paper or on a plane (see Figure 2.2). On that basis a 2D texture can be wrapped or projected onto the 3D surface of the mesh – the UV Mapping coordinates act exactly like a map. However, this unravelling or flattening out of the mesh in 2D inevitably means there will be places on the mesh where it must be cut or ripped apart. These lines of breakage are known as **seams** because they represent the borders where the texture ends or wraps around itself. With each of these seams in Unity there'll be a duplication of all the vertices along the seam. This 'doubling up' of vertices at the seams will indirectly increase the vertex count of the mesh. Consequently, the number of UV seams in the mesh should be minimised wherever practically possible – see the documentation for your modelling software on how to do this. Further, extra performance can be gained by ensuring that a mesh uses only one material rather than multiple materials.

Mesh Rule # 3 – Batch Local Meshes

If a group of meshes always appear closely together in your game (such as a pile of books or a set of tables and chairs), then these can be optimised for import into Unity by first being combined into a single mesh. Due to the way Unity renders meshes, this gives performance improvements over each mesh being imported separately.

NOTE: Select a mesh in the Project panel of the Unity editor (for example, the sculpture from the project in the previous chapter) and examine the properties listed in the Object Inspector. Examine them carefully and play around with them. There will be more on these properties later in the book.

2.1.3 Audio and other Data

The guidelines for importing the highest quality assets into Unity, which applied to texture assets, apply equally to audio and video assets. For audio assets, Unity officially supports the following formats: WAV, OGG, MP3, AIFF, MOD, IT, S3M, and XM. For movies, Unity officially supports: AVI, MOV, MPG, MPEG, MP4VIDEO, ASF and OGG Theora. However, despite the list of *officially* supported formats, some formats are preferable to others for quality reasons. For audio, uncompressed WAV files are recommended, since audio files might be transcoded internally by Unity to other lossy formats such as MP3, depending on the platform for which the game is being made. In the case of video, uncompressed AVIs or OGG Theora files are recommended.

NOTE: Files of practically any format can be imported into a Unity project and be accessible from the Project Panel: including Word Documents, PDF files, Excel Spreadsheets, XML Files and text documents. These sorts of files or assets will not, understandably, become part of the *content of the game* due to their nature, but can be used for the benefit of developers will who be using and working with the Unity project. It's a useful way of attaching design documents, specification sheets, schedules and work plans to a project. To add them, simply drag and drop the files from Windows explorer into the project panel of the Unity interface.

2.2 Asset Management – Working with the Project Panel

Practically all previous sections of this chapter discussed the 'best' or 'optimal' way to *create* assets for Unity – whether mesh or texture assets. As such they related to a time before the asset was imported into Unity, a time when the asset was being made. However, once the assets are created, they can be imported through the Unity Project panel. The Project panel is one of the most fundamental and critical features of Unity: it acts as file or asset manager and works in many respects like *Windows Explorer* in Windows or the *Finder* on the Mac. In Unity 4 it also sports a range of useful enhancements. The Project panel is a structured and hierarchical list of *all* assets currently available to the active project, that is, all assets that can be inserted or added into a scene, or used in the game being made. It is *not* however a list of all the objects and instances in the scene currently open in the scene tab, nor is it a list of all the assets currently on your hard drive. It is the *Hierarchy panel* that lists all objects in the active scene, and it is possible, even likely, that your hard drive contains far more potential assets than the Project panel does. The Project panel lists only the assets that have *either* been imported into the project from a file on the hard drive *or* which are

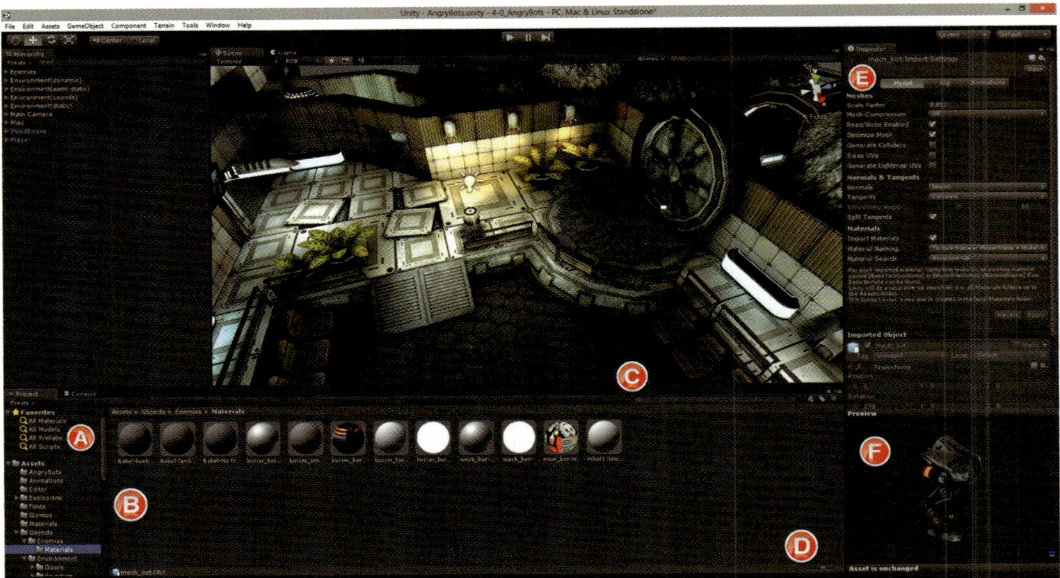

Figure 2.3 The Project panel and its associated features. **A**: Folder hierarchy listing the folder structure and Favorites for assets – click a folder or Favorite to view its contents in the folder view. Click the *Create* button here to create new folders and assets. **B**: Folder view lists all folders and assets contained in the folder selected in the Folder hierarchy. Folder structure can also be seen written in a line at the top of the folder view. Drag and drop assets here to add them to the project. **C**: Search panel used for searching assets – enter a search term and results are shown in the folder view. **D**: Scale Slider. Can be used to increase or decrease the size of thumbnails in the folder view. **E**: Object Inspector will show properties of the selected asset. **F**: Preview window of Object Inspector shows larger preview of visual assets: meshes and textures

available online for free or purchase from the Unity Asset Store. Further, importing an asset into the Project panel does not mean that it *will* feature in your game, only that it *can* now feature in the game if you choose – only assets from the Project panel can be added to scenes and levels.

NOTE: Try following through the next sections with a copy of the Unity Angry Bots sample project open. This project is provided with Unity 4, and is also available for free from the Unity Asset Store. To access this sample project, click *File > Open Project*. Then navigate to *Documents > Unity Project > Angry Bots*.

2.2.1 Importing Assets into the Project

Every new project in Unity begins with a Project panel that is empty or clean of assets. There are three methods for importing assets from a file: one is to use the application main menu by selecting *Assets > Import New Asset*. A second method is to right-click with the mouse in any empty region of the folder view of the Project panel and select *Import New Asset* from the context menu. Neither of these methods is much used in comparison with the third method: drag and drop your asset files from Windows Explorer or the Finder directly into the folder view of the Project panel. Developers typically prefer this last method because it supports the import of *multiple files* simultaneously, whereas methods 1 and 2 require individual files to be imported one at a time in sequence. On import, Unity will make *copies* of the files, leaving the originals unchanged and unreferenced, and storing the copies inside the Assets folder of the Project folder – from then on, Unity makes reference only to the copies. The Project panel is essentially a specialised view of the Assets folder of the project on the hard drive, and the folder can be opened and accessed directly in Windows Explorer or Finder by right-clicking in the Project panel and selecting *Show in Explorer* from the context menu. However, as discussed in Chapter 1, making changes and edits to this folder and its files at the OS level is not recommended. Instead, file operations (such as moving and deleting files and folders) should occur through the Project panel only, to avoid the risk of 'breaking the project' and its meta-data.

NOTE: Mesh assets can be added into a scene by dragging them from the Project panel folder view (see item B in Figure 2.3) directly into the scene via the Scene tab. Textures can be dragged and dropped onto meshes in the Scene View to apply them as a material. Double-clicking any scene asset from the Project panel will open the selected scene in the Scene View. Double-clicking other assets will open them in their default editor application. See Chapter 1 for introductory information on scenes. Chapter 3 considers the scene in greater depth.

2.2.2 Navigating the Project Panel and Examining Asset Properties with the Object Inspector

Nearly every type of asset, whether it's a mesh, a texture or an audio clip, has a range of type-specific properties. These properties control how all instances of the asset behave or appear in Unity. Texture assets feature size information and quality settings. Mesh assets feature topological properties (such as UVs, normals, tangents), as well as Rigging and Animation properties controlling how the mesh moves or animates – if it moves/animates at all. The properties of assets can be viewed and changed through the Object Inspector panel: simply single-click any asset in the Project panel to select it, and then see its properties appear in the Object Inspector at the right-hand side of the interface. Note that, for most assets, an image preview is shown both as a thumbnail in the Project panel folder view and in a larger form in the Object Inspector. See Figure 2.3. The properties for specific asset types will be discussed in more detail in later chapters of this book.

Navigating the Project panel is like using Windows Explorer or Finder. Double-click a folder to 'dig into' that folder and see its contents, or single-click on a folder inside the folder hierarchy found on the left side of the Project panel. See Figure 2.3 for more details on how to work with the Project panel.

2.2.3 Asset Management with Folders, Labels and Favorites

There's one working practice that stands out in Unity game development because of the extent to which it has laid waste to so many promising projects. It's the view that once assets are imported into a project, there is nothing left to do with them apart from putting them into the game. This view is dangerous because it underestimates the benefits to be had from investing just a little extra time at the start of a project in organising assets into folders and hierarchies. In short: this attitude underestimates the value of asset management. Asset management is born quickly from the realisation that a game relies on hundreds or maybe even thousands of imported assets, which can easily become jumbled together meaninglessly in folders unless strictly organised by specific criteria. Indeed, a disregard of asset organisation can lead to such a confusing mess that even the person who initially imported the assets can no longer make any sense of them – only a few hours after importing them. There's a sense in which asset organisation reflects the state of a developer's mind: muddled assets reflect muddled thinking, and that is a recipe for disaster. Thankfully, Unity 4 offers a range of intuitive and powerful asset management tools that can help developers 'tame' their assets into a workable state. These features are **Folders**, **Favorites** and **Labels**, described in more detail below. The construction of a new mini-project project in Chapter 3 will put most of these concepts into practice.

Folders

Folders in the Unity Project panel (as seen in item A of Figure 2.3) are used for grouping together a collection of related assets. There are no clear right or wrong answers as to the naming convention that should be used for folders or exactly how assets should be grouped among folders. These decisions will be project-specific. That being said, it is common to find textures grouped into a 'Textures' folder, and meshes into a 'Meshes' folder, and so on. Open the Unity Sample AngryBots project to see a 'real-world' example of asset organisation in the Project panel. Folders created in the Project panel function exactly as they do in Windows Explorer or Finder. In fact, creating a folder in the Project panel will create an identically named folder inside the Asset folder of the Project folder – the Project panel mirrors the folder structure found in the Project folder. To create a folder from the Unity interface, two main methods are available. First, use the application main menu to select *Assets > Create > Folder*; or right-click inside the folder view of the Project panel and choose *Create > Folder*. An alternative is to click the *Create* button at the top of the Project panel folder hierarchy. See item A in Figure 2.3. The newly created folder will be located inside the folder that was selected in the Project panel at the time of creation. Once created, assets can be transferred between folders through the familiar drag-and-drop technique.

Favorites

'Favorites 'are a feature new to Unity 4. They are virtual folders or shortcuts either to specific *folders* within the folder hierarchy or to *searches*, which are considered in the next section. In short: making a folder a Favorite means creating a *shortcut* to that folder, and the shortcut will be listed in the Favorites section of the Project panel. Thus, clicking on a Favorite will open up the associated folder or search in the main folder view, as though you had double-clicked on the folder directly. To create a Favorite, find a folder in the Project panel and drag and drop it onto the Favorite node at the top of the Project panel hierarchy. Note: you can only Favorite folders and searches, not individual assets. The 'favorited' folder will then be generated in the hierarchy and will remain clickable unless deleted (the selected Favorite can be deleted with the *Delete* key on the keyboard). The chief benefit of Favorites is that they enable developers to quickly access frequently used folders without having to find them manually by digging through a hierarchy of potentially numerous folders and subfolders. In this sense Favorites act as a shortcut. Notice from Figure 2.3 that Unity provides a number of defaults or pre-made Favorites, which can be used to filter through all assets of a project to find those of a specific type: *All Materials*, *All Scripts*, *and All Models*, etc. Note that deleting a Favorite will not delete its associated folder.

Labels

The concept of a 'label' in Unity is equivalent to the 'tag' or 'keyword' concepts used throughout the web and social media. Using labels, developers can 'stick' or 'attach' descriptive and meaningful words to their assets for categorising and sorting them. For example, the labels 'enemy' and 'boss' might be attached, or 'stuck', to an enemy mesh asset used as an evil boss character encountered at the end of a shooter game. Labelling assets is an important part of asset organisation because it allows developers to stick common sense and *searchable* descriptors onto assets that do not contain those descriptors explicitly in their filenames. In the next section we'll see how the assets of the project can be searched by labels. To create a label and attach it to an asset, try the following:

Figure 2.4 Add, edit and remove asset labels using the controls on the Preview panel of the Object Inspector

1. Select an asset in the Project panel, one that is to receive one or more labels. Then click the blue ellipsis button at the bottom right-hand corner of the preview window in the Object Inspector. See Figure 2.4.
2. Clicking this button will display a list of selectable tags, including *Audio*, *Terrain*, *Prop*, etc. (at least, in the AngryBots Project). Clicking the tags in the list toggles the applicability of the tag to the selected object; clicking once attaches the tag and clicking again removes the tag. In this way multiple tags are attached to a single object.
3. In addition, entirely new labels can be created by simply entering them into the text field and pressing the *Enter* or *Return* key on the keyboard. The list of labels on the selected object is shown below the Preview window of the Object Inspector, as shown in Figure 2.4.

2.2.4 Searching for Assets

Searching is about Unity automatically finding your desired asset or assets from among all the assets in the Project panel, based on search criteria. It's a feature that is especially important for both projects with many assets and development teams with many members. Unity 4 has significantly enhanced the speed and effectiveness of asset searches in the Project panel so you can more easily find the assets you need. The search feature behaves in real time, meaning that searches are performed as search terms are entered. Simply enter some text into the search field and the search updates, showing the results in the folder view of the Project panel. The search features can be found at the top right-hand corner of the project panel, as listed in item C of Figure 2.3. It consists of the search field, and some filter buttons to restrict the search results.

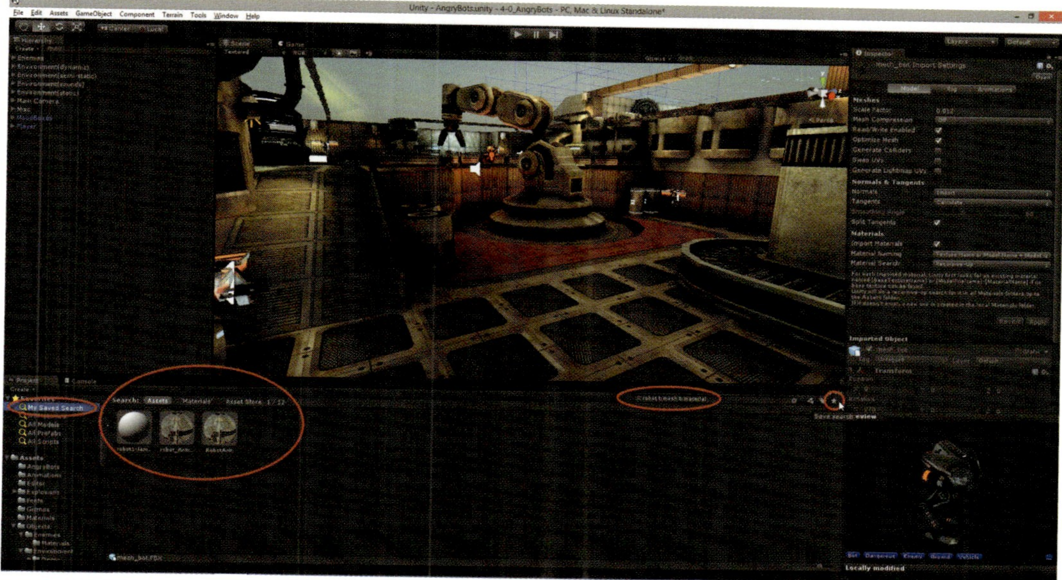

Figure 2.5 Searching for assets in the project

There are two main parts to a Unity search: the search keywords and the search filters. The search keywords are entered into the search field as a string to specify as exactly as possible the asset to be found. The more words that are included among the keywords, the more narrowed and precise the search becomes; thus, a search for 'weapon rifle' is narrower than 'weapon' since it singles out 'rifle' in addition to 'weapon'. Keywords may include the filename of the asset, or a word or name that appears within in the filename, or any labels attached to the asset, or the folder name containing the asset. The search filters further narrow or specify the search results and can be accessed using the buttons listed on the right-hand side of the search field. Specifically, search results can be filtered by either asset type (*Texture*, *Mesh*, *Scene*, *Script* and so on) or asset label. Simply click a filter button and pick a category to narrow the search.

NOTE: Filters can also be included in the search text using a set of switches or commands. These are useful for abbreviating the search process, saving us from having to use the mouse to select filters with the filter buttons. For example, the search: *Grenade t:mesh t:material l:friendly* will work as follows: it will search for every asset in the Project panel where the word 'Grenade' figures. Then those results will be restricted or reduced by a set of filters. Specifically, the restricted results will show only assets of the *mesh* and *material* type (since the command *t* specifies type) which also have a matching label of *friendly* (since the command *l* specifies label).

NOTE: The search results are presented in the folder view of the Project panel, typically arranged in three tabs, as shown in Figure 2.5. The leftmost tab 'Assets' applies the search across *all* assets in the project. The second tab takes its name from the selected folder in the Project panel, if any, and applies the search only to assets within the selected folder and its subfolders. The final tab applies the search across assets listed at the Unity Asset Store, as discussed later in this chapter.

One of the great advantages of Favorites is the ability it gives you to save searches – that is, the ability to store the keywords and filters of a search as a Favorite so that, by clicking that Favorite, the search can be repeated at any time on all the assets in the Project panel. To add a search as a Favorite, simply perform a search using keywords and filters as usual, and then click the Save Search button, as shown in Figure 2.5.

2.2.5 Browsing the Asset Store from Unity

The Unity Asset store is an online store or repository maintained by Unity Technologies. It offers third-party pre-made game assets and Unity add-ons, both for sale and for free, to all Unity users. The Asset Store requires an internet connection and a Unity Community Account, and can be accessed directly from the editor by clicking *Window > Asset Store* from the application main menu (or *Ctrl + 9* on the keyboard). However, in Unity 4 the Asset Store has also been tightly integrated into the Project panel. This means that assets and products at the store can be searched, browsed, previewed and imported directly from the Project panel as though they were standard assets on the hard drive already available to the project. To see this in action, perform the following steps.

1. Enter the term *weapon* in the search field of the Project panel. This produces, like all searches, a tabbed result in the folder view of the Project panel. Search results listed under the Asset Store tab in the folder view will show a list of all products in the store that match the search.
2. Assets listed in the Asset Store search results can be filtered further by *Paid* and *Free* categories; see Figure 2.6. These categories can be expanded and collapsed to show or hide their contents.
3. Selecting an asset in the Asset Store search results will show its appropriate purchase and download options in the Object Inspector, as well as display information regarding product version and author.

Figure 2.6 Searching for assets at the Unity Asset Store

2.3 Conclusion

This chapter focussed primarily on the raw materials of all Unity projects, namely assets. These refer to all the images, graphics, textures, meshes, audio, music, animation and other data imported into a Unity project for use in a game. Assets are typically created in third-party content-creation software such as Maya, Max and Blender, and, when completed, are imported into Unity from files saved in industry-standard file formats. Section 2.1 considered general guidelines and recommendations for optimising assets – such as mesh assets and texture assets – for import. Section 2.2 then considered how to import and manage those assets from the Unity editor using the Project panel, specifically using the features of folder creation, Favorites, labels and searching.

CHAPTER 3

Scenes, Assets and Game Objects

By the end of this chapter you should:

1. Understand the difference between assets and game objects
2. Appreciate the anatomy of game objects
3. Understand scenes as coordinate spaces
4. Be able to configure assets for a scene
5. Understand scene hierarchies and transformations

This chapter is mainly about how to make levels. In Unity, a level is called a 'scene', and one scene equals one level. The process of building a scene, as discussed here, corresponds to steps 3 and 4 of the six-stage Unity development workflow listed in Chapter 1. This chapter demonstrates scene construction and its associated features *by example*. It will require you to be seated at the computer with Unity 4 ready and follow me every step of the way to create a solar system scene, complete with starry background, orbiting planets and an animated camera. The completed project will not look particularly spectacular, nor will it make use of AAA quality assets; nor is it likely to become the basis for the next gaming blockbuster. It has been specifically designed to use a range of concepts which are all critical to working effectively with Unity scenes, regardless of their complexity. These concepts include the hierarchy panel, game objects (or GameObjects), components, parenting, cascading transformations, prefabs, asset packages and pivot points, amongst others. Along the way I'll be pausing to discuss and explain these concepts in depth. Understanding them will greatly increase your power as a level designer and Unity game developer. For this reason, I recommend reading over this chapter as many times as it takes for you to feel comfortable and 'at one' using the tools it discusses.

3.1 Creating the Solar System Project

Let's get started now with our project! Creating a new game in Unity means creating a new project – this is Step 1 of the Unity workflow. It was demonstrated in Chapter 1 but will be repeated here for completeness. To create the solar system project, open the Unity editor and select *File > New Project* from the menu, giving the project a suitable name (such as *project_solarsystem*) in the Project Wizard dialog. Click the *Create* button: and finally a new and empty project awaits us. Notice that, as with the project in Chapter 1, the Project panel is empty *even though* there is an auto-generated scene in the Scene tab. We should now make this scene officially an asset of the project: to do this, simply save the scene by clicking *File > Save Scene (Ctrl + Shift + S)* from the application menu, giving the scene a suitable name (such as: *scene_solarsystem*). This step of *adding a scene* is actually a part of Step 3 in the workflow, but we can safely perform it here.

TIP: This section demonstrates a habit or working practice that will be repeated throughout the chapter and which I recommend you apply to your projects. Specifically, the habit of prefixing asset names with descriptors or tags: for example, the project was not called simply '*solarsystem*' but '**project**_*solarsystem*', and the scene was not called simply '*solarsystem*', but '**scene**_*solarsystem*'. Including the asset type in the name of the asset itself as a prefix can help you: first, to see what kind the asset is simply by its name; and second, to arrange similar kinds of assets together alphabetically, since all like assets with the same prefix will share the same first letter in their name. Other prefixes for assets include: *texture_*, *audio_*, *music_*, *material_*, *video_*, *mesh_*, *script_*, *text_*.

3.2 Importing Assets

Step 2 of the Unity Workflow requires us to import assets into the project (see Chapter 2 for more information on assets). The project we'll create here is a solar system setting in which a collection of planets will orbit one another. This project will rely on only three external asset files that we'll import, despite the fact that our scene will contain many more than three objects. These three assets are included in the Chapter 3 folder of the companion files associated with this book. The first asset is a starry background texture (*texture_star_background.png*) that'll be used to create a specialised material called a **Skybox**. The Skybox allows us to surround the scene with stars. The second asset is a sphere mesh (*mesh_planet.ma*), to be used as the basis for all the planets in the level; and the third asset is a planet texture (*texture_planet_surface.png*), which will be applied to the planet mesh to shade its

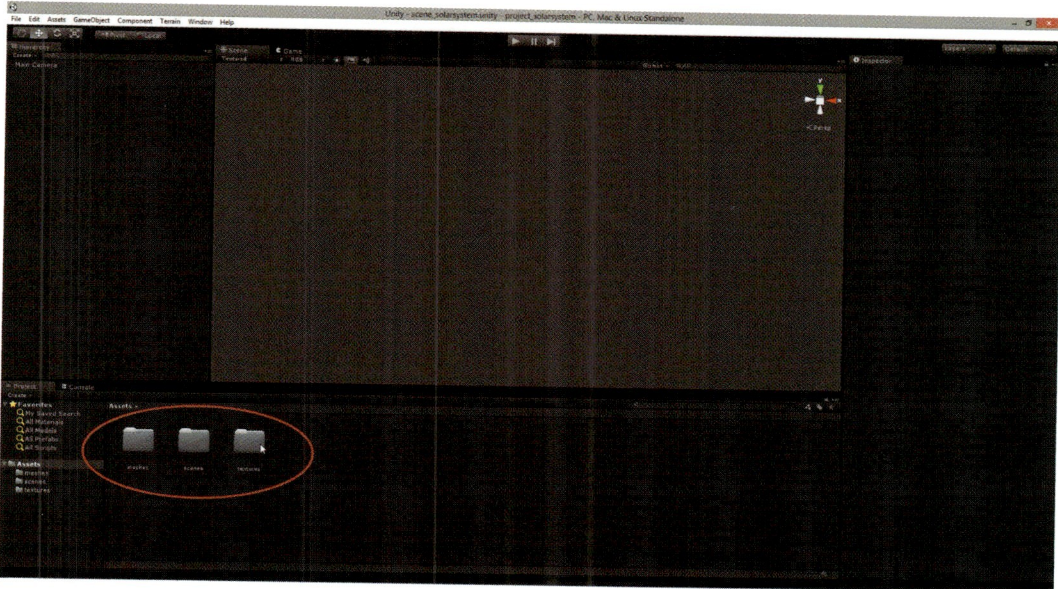

Figure 3.1 Assets imported into the solar system project

surface. To import these assets, simply drag and drop all three files together from Windows Explorer or Finder into the Unity Project panel – assets of different kinds can be imported in one operation. Be sure to organise these assets. Note from the Project panel in Figure 3.1 that I've arranged textures together in a *Textures* folder, the mesh inside a *Meshes* folder, and the scene in a *Scene* folder. Remember that as you import the mesh asset, Unity might automatically generate a Material folder and a material – these can be deleted.

3.3 Creating a Skybox Asset

Our project so far contains a total of four assets – the three imported files and the one scene that has been saved. The three imported assets, however, are not added to the scene in any way, even though they are a part of the project. Clicking the *Play* button from the toolbar will only display an empty scene in the Game tab, as seen from the *MainCamera* object that was created by default in the scene when it was first made. This camera can be seen listed in the hierarchy panel. Our first objective in this project is to give the scene a starry background to make it look as though it were in outer space. However, since this is a three-dimensional and not a two-dimensional project, the kind of background we need is not just a flat image or texture wallpapered to the back of the screen, but a background that truly wraps around or surrounds the scene so that it will be seen no matter the angle of the camera. For this reason, our flat two-dimensional texture of stars will not be enough on its own to act as the background for the scene. We'll need to create a *new* asset manually that will use or *make reference to* our existing star background asset. We'll need to create a **Skybox** asset – a special kind of **material**. This asset will surround our scene with a polygonal box, and each face of the box will be textured with our starry background texture, making it appear to surround the scene. To create a SkyBox that can be applied as the background of a scene, consider the following steps:

NOTE: A 'material' is an asset type that tells Unity how to blend or combine one or more texture assets together to display appropriately in a 3D world: whether on the surface of a mesh or as a SkyBox around the level. Textures cannot be applied directly onto models or objects in the scene. Textures can *only* make their way into scenes through materials. Even in Chapter 1, when dragging and dropping a texture asset onto a sculpture model, we did not apply the texture to the model. Unity *automatically* generated and configured a material on the basis of the texture, and applied the material, not the texture, to the sculpture model. This can be confirmed by examining the Project panel after the drop operation – a new material will have been created there.

1. Create a new material in the Project panel. To do this, right-click the mouse on any vacant space in the folder view and, from the context menu, click *Create > Material*. Name this new material: *material_solarsystem_skybox*.
2. From the outset, I recommend applying the principles of *asset management*: organise this material asset in a new *Materials* folder in the Project panel. Then select the asset and examine its properties in the Object Inspector panel. Notice, in the drop-down list at the top of the Object Inspector, Unity will have set a default **shader** for this material as *Diffuse*. Shaders define the kind of material created, and *Diffuse* represents the most common or basic kind of material: one allowing a standard texture to be applied to a 3D object with little or no change to the texture appearance. In many cases, the Diffuse shader is appropriate. For example, it'll be used for our planet object. But it's not suitable for skyboxes. Change this setting by clicking in the drop-down list and selecting *RenderFX > Skybox* from the menu. Clicking this option sets the material's shader to *Skybox*.

   The Skybox shader features a lot of options. These consist mainly of six texture swatches, one for each of the six faces of the cube: front, up, down, left, right, and back. Drag and drop the same starry texture from the project
3. panel into each of the slots, one at a time. Or, click the *Select* button on each texture swatch of the Skybox material and select the starry texture from the *Select Texture* Dialog. The starry texture is tileable in both the U and V direction and can be applied to each face of the cube to surround the level seamlessly with stars. See Figure 3.2.

Figure 3.2 Configured Skybox material with a starry texture applied to each of the six texture directions of the cube

NOTE: If you accidentally change your folder or asset selection in the main view of the Project panel while dragging and dropping the starry texture into the Skybox material swatches, you'll change what appears in the Object Inspector because the Inspector always changes to show properties for the selected item. This means that you'll no longer see the Skybox material properties for dragging and dropping once the selection changes. You can work around this 'issue' in one of two ways: you can select folders in the Project panel *folder hierarchy* section instead of the main folder view (and this does not affect the contents of the Object Inspector), or you can click the **Padlock** icon at the top-right corner of the Object Inspector with the Skybox material active, to 'lock' the Inspector to that material. Locking the Inspector to an asset or object means that its properties will *always* be shown regardless of subsequent selections. The lock feature is toggle-able, meaning it can be enabled and disabled through repeated alternative clicks of the padlock icon.

4. To set the Skybox material as the background for the scene, click *Edit > Render Settings* from the application menu, to show the default settings for a scene. For the setting *Skybox Material*, either drag and drop the Skybox material into this slot, or click the slot and select the Skybox material from the *Select Material* dialog. The Skybox material will be then applied as the background for the scene. See Figure 3.3. If the Skybox background is not visible in the Scene tab, then ensure the *Toggle Skybox* button is enabled from the Scene tab toolbar.

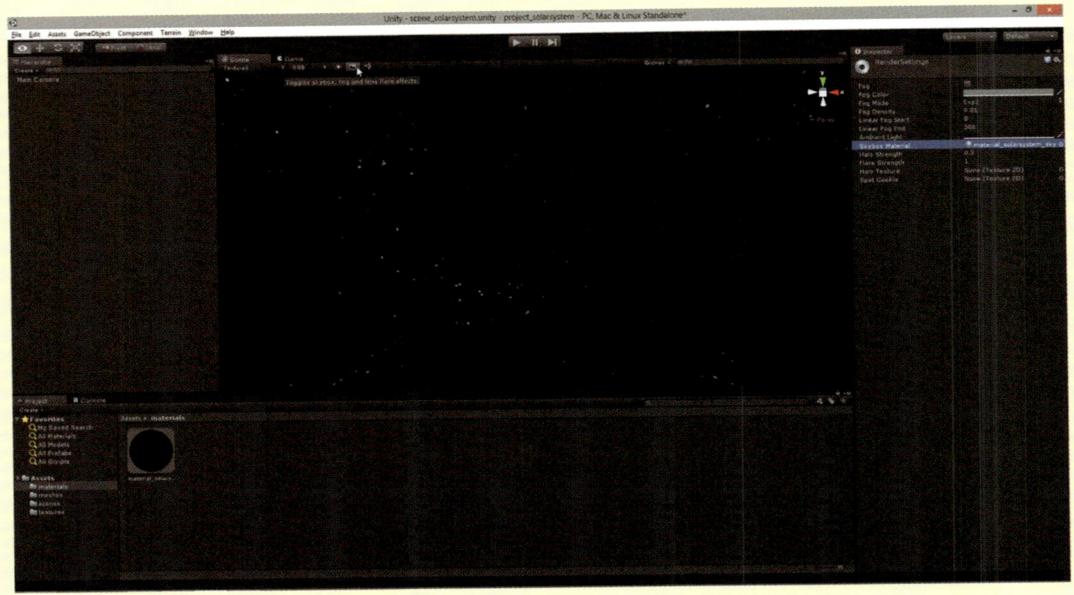

Figure 3.3 Render Settings dialog accessed via *Edit > Render Settings*. This can be used to assign a Skybox background to a scene that can be viewed in both the Scene and Game viewports

3.4 Putting Planets in the Scene

The scene so far features a Skybox background to create the illusion of endless space in all directions. This effect works on the basis of two main assets: a Skybox material asset that we created manually in Unity and a starry background texture asset that we imported. It's now time to populate the scene with planets to comprise a solar system: that is, a group of planets in orbit around a central star or sun. All these planets and the central star will be created from the same planet mesh asset. Each planet in the scene and, in fact, every object in the scene (including the camera) is known as a **GameObject**. All GameObjects have a distinguishing set of features. Specifically, they exist as part of the scene and they have a position, orientation and scale. To know whether an entity in a Unity project is a game object you simply need to ask: 'Is this thing listed in the scene's hierarchy panel?' (see item F of Figure 1.7 in Chapter 1). If the answer is in the affirmative, then it *is* a GameObject. The following steps demonstrate how to create a solar system in the scene with each planet a separate GameObject.

1. Select the *mesh_planet* asset in the *Project panel* and drag and drop it into the scene via the *Scene tab*. This will add an *instance* of the asset into the scene as a *GameObject*. The newly added GameObject should be selected automatically and will now be listed in the Scene hierarchy panel as a member of the scene. The game object might be bright purple in colour to indicate that it currently has no assigned material. Notice that in the Object Inspector the object will have transformation properties: position, rotation and scale. See 1.5.5 of Chapter 1 for more information on using the Transformation tools to move and arrange objects in the scene. The first planet in the scene will be the sun. For this

reason, rename this GameObject *obj_sun*. You can rename this object either by typing the name into the *Name* text field at the top of the Object Inspector when the object is selected, or by double-clicking the name of the object in the *hierarchy panel*. Set the position of the sun to the exact world centre at (0, 0, 0) and set its scale to (2, 2, 2).

UNITY UNITS: In Unity, position values in the scene are measured in the generic *Unity Unit*. Thus, an X value of 5, means 5 Unity Units from the origin. Unity Units are generic because they mean whatever you want them to mean: they don't have an official correspondence with any standardised measure, such as millimetres or inches. However, Unity Units are understood by the Physics system to correspond directly to metres. Consequently, most developers take the view that 1uu (Unity Unit) = 1 metre. Most artists and content creators therefore synchronise their modelling software and tools to use this system of units.

2. The added mesh will act as the sun, even though it looks like a textureless blob at present. A material will be added later. First, however, there will need to be orbiting planets to form a solar system. Add some extra planets using the duplicate method shown in Chapter 1: select the sun object in the scene and press the *Ctrl+D* shortcut, or select *Edit > Duplicate* from the application menu. Alternatively, you drag and drop more planet meshes into the scene. Transform the duplicates to new positions around the sun, giving each its own scale and own name (such as: *obj_planet_01*. . .) to add realism. Remember, you can also select the object by clicking its name in the hierarchy panel. See Figure 3.4.

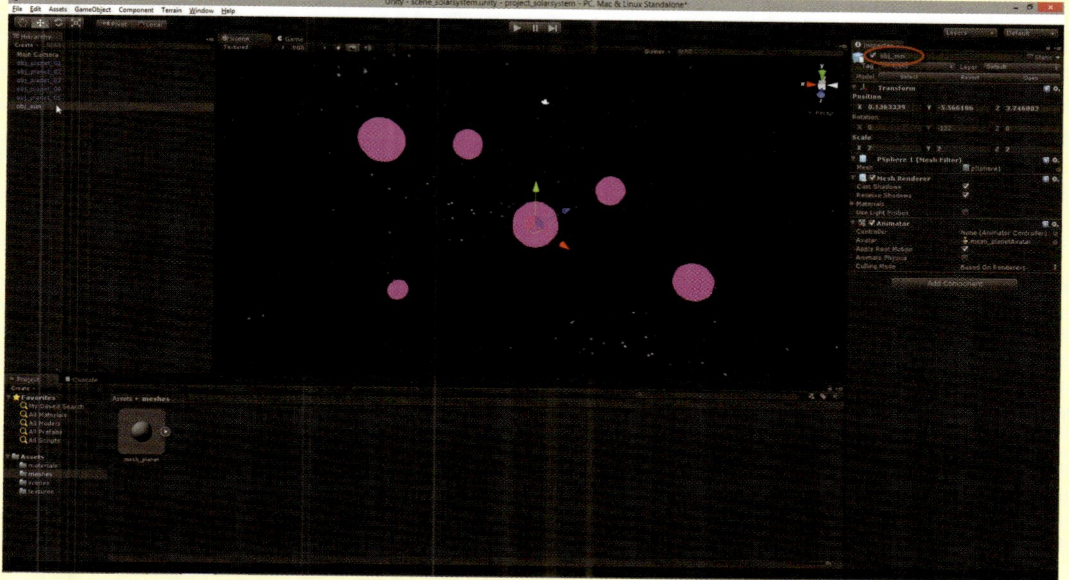

Figure 3.4 A selection of planets orbiting a sun object. Object names can be specified in the Object Inspector

3.5 Assigning Materials to the Planets

Our scene now sports a new and easily made solar system, which is essentially a collection of spherical mesh GameObjects, each with its own name, scale, position and orientation. However, none of these celestial bodies (whether sun or planet) looks like the genuine article because they have no material applied. The objects don't look like planets – their surfaces don't appear rough, coloured or rock-like. They are either bold purple to indicate they have no material applied, or a dull shade of grey (if you didn't delete the auto-generated material when the mesh was imported). The following steps focus on the procedure required to create new material assets on the basis of imported planet texture – one material for each planet to customise its look – and to assign those assets to the planet and sun meshes in the scene.

1. Let's start by creating a new material asset for one of the planets in the solar system. To do this, right-click in vacant space inside the Project panel folder view, and from the context menu select *Create > Material*. Or else, select *Assets > Create > Material* from the application main menu. Assign the material the name *material_planet_01*, and file this material under the Materials folder. You have a Material folder, right? Or, better still, create the material *while* the material folder is active in the Project panel – to ensure the newly created material will be generated in that folder.
2. Unity will have assigned this material the default **Diffuse** shader, as it did with our Skybox material earlier, and this time we should accept the default, leaving it unchanged. Click the texture swatch in the properties of the new material in the Object Inspector, to display the *Select Texture* dialog. From

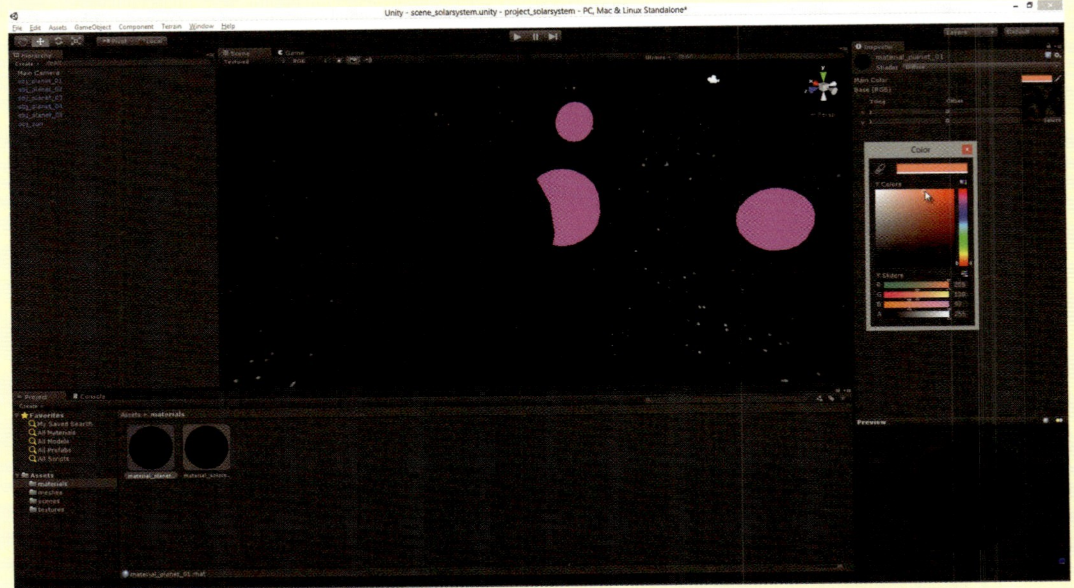

Figure 3.5 Creating a material for a planet using the *texture_planet_surface* texture. The Main Color swatch in the Diffuse material properties can be used to 'colorize' textures

this dialog, select the *texture_planet_surface* texture. The alternative method is to drag and drop that texture into the texture swatch. Click and drag the ball in the Preview Panel of the Object Inspector to rotate the view and observe the texture when applied to a sphere. This gives us some sort of preview of how the material will look in the scene.

3. The texture is in 'greyscale' (shades of grey) and doesn't look especially realistic – unless we want our game to look 'black and white'. However, this texture can be *colorized* by using the *Main Color* swatch. Click this swatch and select a brownish-red hue from the colour picker to simulate the look of planet Mars. Then drag and drop the material from the Project panel to any of the planet objects in the scene, and the selected planet will have the material applied instantly. Notice that dragging and dropping a material onto a planet didn't create a new GameObject in the scene as dragging and dropping a mesh did. Instead, Unity *modified* the material properties of the selected object. Select the planet object in the scene and observe its properties in the Object Inspector, in the *MeshRenderer* group or **component**. Expand the *Materials* field and note that *material_planet_01* has been assigned to *Element 0* of the materials array – the default material slot. GameObjects can have more than one material applied, but only one material per object is recommended in the interests of performance.
4. Now let's create materials for each of the other planets. We could do this by repeating steps 1–3 for each planet. But we can also use the technique of duplication. Just as we used duplication to create new planet objects in the scene, we can duplicate new materials and modify the MainColor setting for each duplicate. Select the *material_planet_01* in the Project panel and press *Ctrl+D* on the keyboard, or select *Edit > Duplicate* from the application menu to generate a duplicate material. In this case, the duplicated material should automatically be renamed to *material_planet_02*. If it is not, then rename it here. Select a different colour for this material and assign it to a different planet in the scene. Repeat this process for all remaining planets, leaving only the sun without a material. It's important to emphasise here that creating multiple materials *does not* duplicate the texture involved. We do have multiple materials that customise the look of each planet, but each of these materials reference the same texture asset. In this way we can vary the appearance of many game objects without increasing our texture memory usage. Unity likes to recycle!

NOTE: Don't forget to save your project and scene regularly. *File > Save Scene*, and *File > Save Project*.

5. The material for the sun object will use a different shader to Diffuse, which is applicable to most real-world objects. The sun in contrast should be bright, since it's a *light source*. It cannot receive shadows and cannot be in darkness because it's a photon emitter. Create a new material in the *Materials* folder and name it *material_sun*. For the shader select *Self-Illumin > Diffuse*. Materials in the Self-Illumin group are *self-illuminated* materials – always bold and bright and never affected by the lighting in a scene. Leave the texture swatch as completely white, and select a gold or yellow colour for the *MainColor* swatch. Then assign the material to the sun object in the scene. This completes the material assignments for our planets, but there's still other work to do. See Figure 3.6.

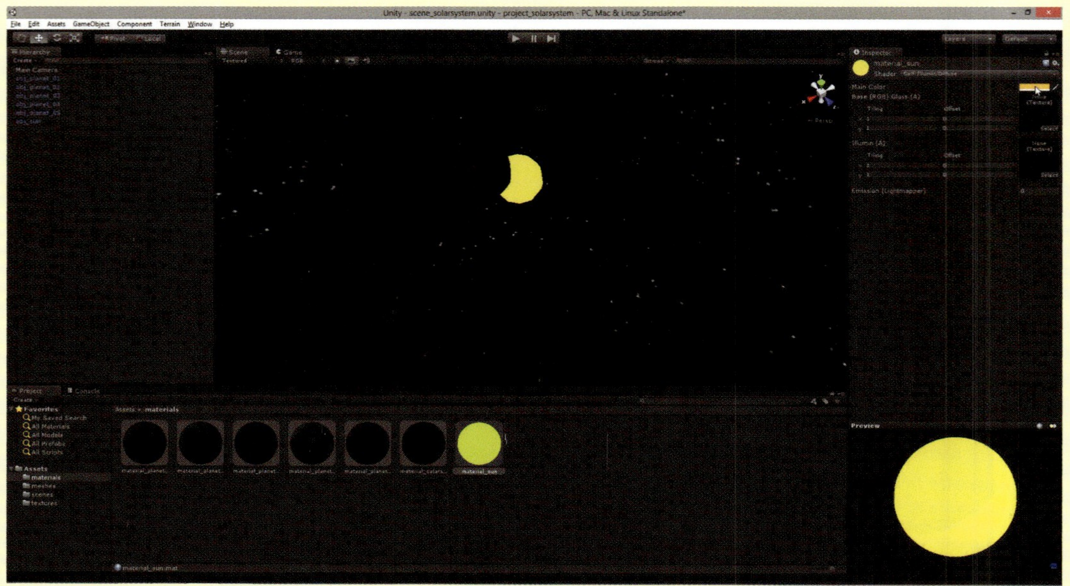

Figure 3.6 Creating Diffuse shader materials for planets and a Self-Illumin shader material for the sun. Notice the list of materials in the Project panel

3.6 Adding Light to the Scene

Now we've created some materials for the planets and a material for the sun. The scene is looking better, although the planets appear too dark considering their closeness to the sun. This issue will now be fixed by adding lights to the scene. Consider the following steps.

1. Start by creating a **Point Light** in the scene at the position of the sun. The Point Light casts light radially in all directions from an infinitesimally small point at its centre. To create a point light, click *GameObject > Create Other > Point Light* from the application main menu. This will add a 'light' game object to the scene, which will appear in the hierarchy panel along with all other GameObjects. Select the light and position it at the centre of the sun, which should be at position (0, 0, 0). Notice that *prior* to adding a light to the scene, Unity applied a general default lighting. Once a light is added, however, the default illumination is overridden, *even if* all lights are subsequently removed from the scene.
2. The range of the newly added Point Light might be too small or narrow to illuminate the surrounding planet objects. To receive illumination the planets must be inside the imaginary sphere that is drawn around the Point Light(represented by the gizmo object, which appears in the Scene tab when the light is selected). If the planets are too dark, increase the range of the point light by one of the following methods: 1) type in a new value for the Range field of the light in the Object Inspector; 2) click and drag over the Range title beside the text field, to *scrub* through the range values like a slider; or C) click and drag in the Scene view any of the gizmo handles on the sphere surrounding the light,

to increase its range. Increase the intensity (brightness) of the light to a value of 5 or thereabouts using the Intensity slider in the Object Inspector. In addition, click the light's Color slider to tint the light a shade of yellow or gold to emphasise its 'sunny disposition'.

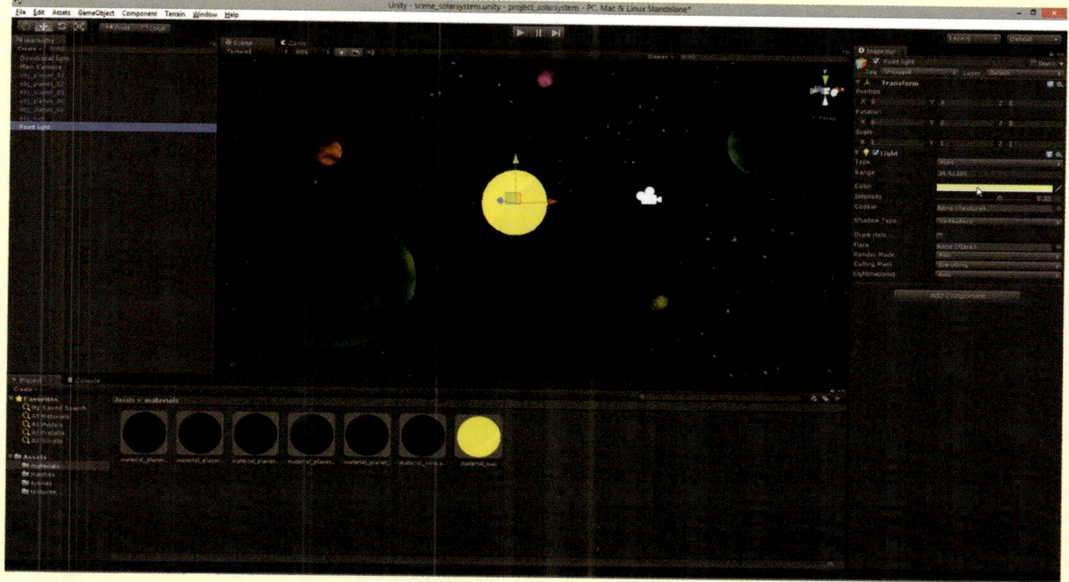

Figure 3.7 Using a 'point light' to simulate the sun and a 'directional light' to simulate bounced illumination on the backs of the planets

3. Consider adding a **Directional Light** of low intensity, positioned in the scene at a remote location away from the planets to simulate bounced light – that is, to simulate light that has *bounced around* and partially illuminated sides of the planets not directly in the way of the sun. To do this, click *GameObject > Create Other > Directional Light* from the application menu, and transform the light into place. Consider Figure 3.7. Bounced light is discussed further in Chapter 5.

Now we've come this far, try a very simple but important exercise, one that we'll explore in more detail later in the chapter. Select every object in the scene, one at a time and in sequence, clicking on the topmost object in the hierarchy panel and moving down one by one. On selecting each object, examine its properties and components in the Object Inspector and compare them to the components found on the object selected before. Notice that the *only* type of component that objects in the scene have in common is the **Transform** component, which appears at the top of the Object Inspector and contains values for an object's position, orientation and scale. All objects have components of other types, but these types vary on a per object basis: all mesh objects have the same type of components; all light objects have the same type; all cameras, and so on. As we'll see in a later section, components are the *building blocks* or constituent ingredients of GameObjects – the GameObject is the sum of its components.

3.7 Animating the Planets

Clicking the *Play* button on the toolbar will preview our solar system scene in the Game tab from the perspective of the *MainCamera* object. The scene, however, suffers from two main problems: first, the camera view is unlikely to be ideal – perhaps not all planets are visible to the camera and a different viewing angle could add some extra drama and atmosphere. Second, the planets are motionless when they should at least be spinning on their own axes. These problems will now be addressed in turn through the following steps.

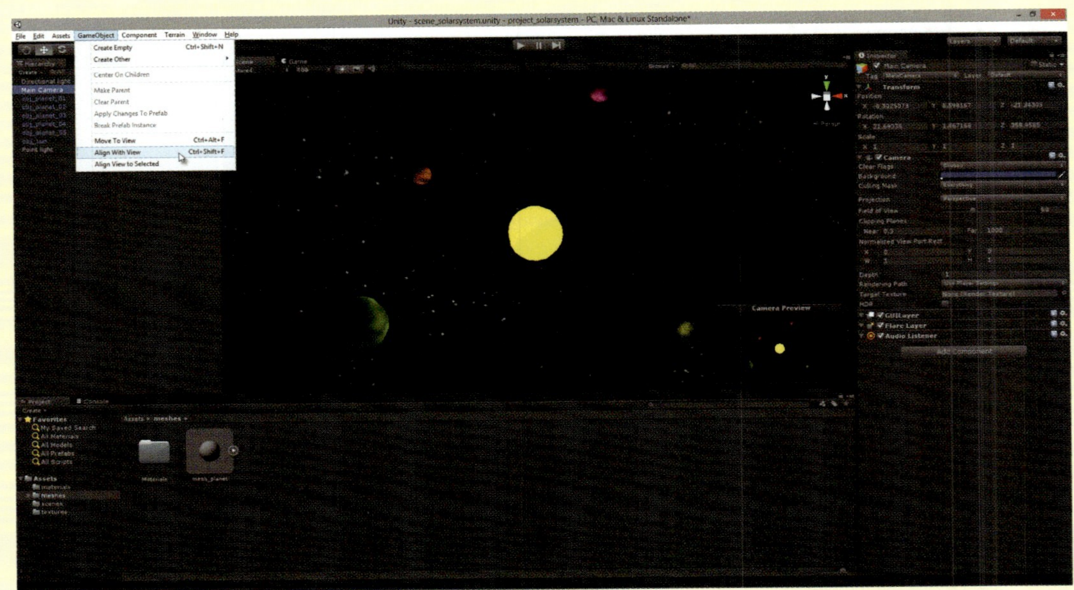

Figure 3.8 Positioning the camera in the scene on the basis of the Scene viewport

1. The position of the game camera can be changed easily by simply moving or transforming the camera (*MainCamera*) just like any other game object: the camera has its own position and orientation in the scene. With the camera selected in the viewport, notice the camera preview window that appears in the bottom right-hand corner and displays the scene as seen from the camera. This is useful for ensuring the camera is positioned to show the view we intend. However, it's also possible to set the position and orientation of the camera (or any object) based on the position and orientation of the scene viewport itself – that is, the implicit scene camera we use for exploring the scene in the Scene tab. To position the camera according to the viewport, select the *MainCamera* in the scene, either by selecting it in the Scene viewport or by selecting it from the hierarchy list. Then click *GameObject > Align with View* from the application menu, or press the keyboard shortcut *Ctrl + Shift + F*. Now press *Play* from the toolbar and experience the scene from the new perspective.
2. Using the camera aligning and positioning techniques in the previous step, the scene can be now be previewed from practically any position or angle. The planets in the scene, however, are still

motionless. The planet mesh was created in the modelling software Maya, with animation data built-in or 'baked' into it. Specifically, the mesh contains a rotation animation – an animation that rotates the planet over time for one complete 360° revolution about its own axis. This animation does not, however, play by default in Unity, hence the reason the planets appear motionless right now. But the animation can be *enabled* by editing the import settings for the mesh. To do this, start by selecting the mesh asset in the Project panel – **not** any of the individual instances or game objects in the scene, which are listed in the hierarchy panel.

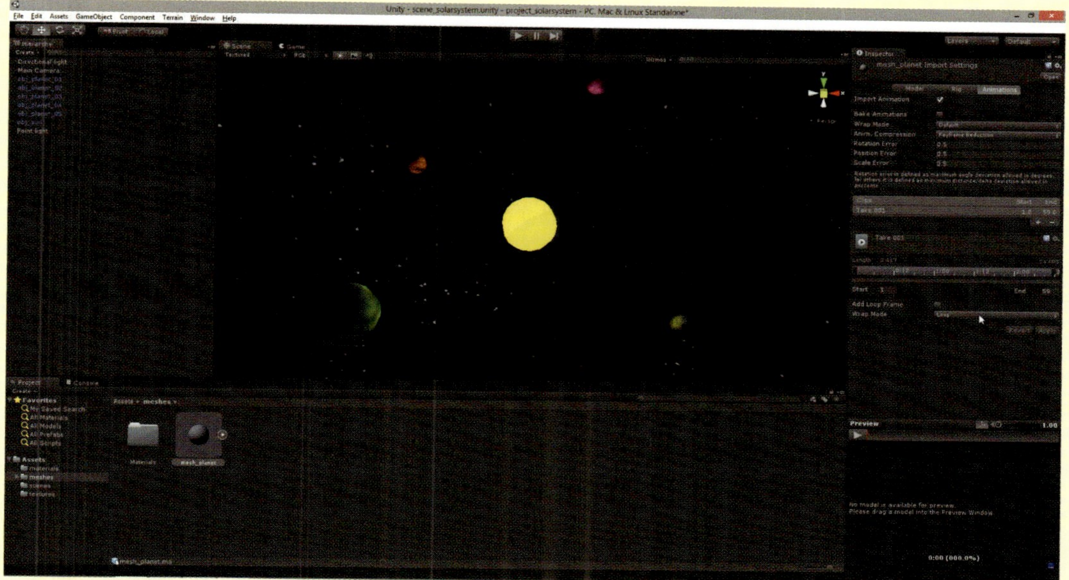

Figure 3.9 Configuring animation properties for a mesh object

3. With the planet mesh asset selected in the Project panel, examine its properties in the Object Inspector. From there, select the *Rig* tab to access and edit the structure or configuration of the object for animation, and select *Legacy* from the *Animation Type* drop-down to configure this object for a 'simple' key-frame animation. Click the *Apply* button to accept the changes and move to the *Animation* tab. Ensure the *Import Animation* checkbox is ticked, and notice the animation is listed under the 'Clips' panel as 'Take 001'. Click this 'animation clip' to expand the panel and see more animation-specific options. It'll show a *timeline* marking the total length or extent of the animation from first to last frame. The timeline features two sliders or markers with a shaded region between; together these highlight the section of the animation that is used for this mesh. Select all of the animation by ensuring the entire timeline is selected, clicking and dragging the end slider to the end of the timeline and the starting slider to the beginning of the animation. Since the animation is for a perpetually rotating planet it will also need to be played on a loop – that is, played over and over again endlessly. To do this, ensure *Loop* is selected from the *Wrap Mode* drop-down list – and do not forget to click the *Apply* button to accept all changes on this panel. See Figure 3.9. Note the three-stage work-flow pattern that emerges for configuring assets: 1) select asset in the Project panel; 2) edit asset properties in the Inspector; 3) click *Apply* to confirm the changes.

4. The animation changes applied to the planet mesh asset are now *propagated* to all instances of the mesh in the scene, and no further changes need to be applied for the meshes to animate. Click the *Play* button on the toolbar and all planet meshes will rotate or spin on their local axis at their default animation speed.

3.8 Using Hierarchies to Rotate Planets around the Sun

Each planet in our solar system in the scene now spins around its central axis as a result of enabling the animation baked into the mesh asset. However, the planets do not behave or move realistically *in relation* to one another. Specifically, the planets should rotate around or orbit the central star of the system, in addition to spinning on their own axis. The sun should act as their pivot or centre of rotation as they move throughout the universe. This problem is but a specific instance of a more general problem that game developers frequently face as soon as they begin to develop games where objects must move or behave *in relation* to other objects. Other include: 'How can I make the camera follow an object?'; 'How can I move objects together as though they were connected or part of the same entity?'; 'How can I move a car or a bus or a plane and have the people inside move along with it? The planets of our system, for example, do not exist in isolation: their position, movement and rotation are *dependent* on the central star. Thus, there is a connection or dependence between game objects, and this relationship should place restrictions and limitations on how the objects may move. Developers solve this important problem in many different and creative ways, and Unity offers at least one 'out of the box' solution in the form of the *Scene hierarchy,* as seen directly from the *hierarchy panel*. Through the following steps, this section will demonstrate the awesome power and potential of scene hierarchies and **cascading transformations**. By skilfully and inventively arranging the object hierarchy in a scene, it's possible to create implicit relationships and connections between objects that'll impact how they move and affect the believability of a scene, all without writing a single line of code.

1. Consider the relationship between objects in the solar system scene: *all* the planets must revolve *around* the sun, and the sun revolves in position around its own axis. In this relationship, a **hierarchy** can be identified: the sun is the **parent**, and the planets are the **children**. The planets are the **children** of the sun: not literally in that the planets were *born* from the sun, but metaphorically in that they depend on the sun to act as the pivot for their rotation. As the sun rotates around its axis, the planets rotate synchronously around the sun and maintain the same relative distance from the sun. The hierarchy panel can be used to encode this 'parent and child' relationship between game objects. To do this, select all planet objects via their entries in the hierarchy panel, and then drag and drop them over the sun entry. In response, the planet objects will be **parented** to the sun object: they will be its children. Visually in the hierarchy panel, this means all planet nodes will collapse under the sun node, and the sun node can be expanded (by clicking the Arrow icon) to reveal all the planet objects that are now its children.

2. To see this parent-child relationship at work in the scene, select the sun object and use the translate tool (*W* key) to move the sun to a different position. In doing so, the planet objects will *automatically* move and follow the sun *while still* retaining the same relative distance from each other. This is an example of a 'cascading transformation', because a transformation applied to the parent object will cascade downwards, like water in a waterfall, to all child objects beneath. In contrast, now select one of the planet objects and use the translate tool to move it to a different position in the scene. Here, notice the movement of the planet does *not* cascade upwards to the parent, or sideways to the **siblings** (the other planets which are its brothers and sisters). Thus, a child transforms independently of its parent, but the parent transforms affect all children.

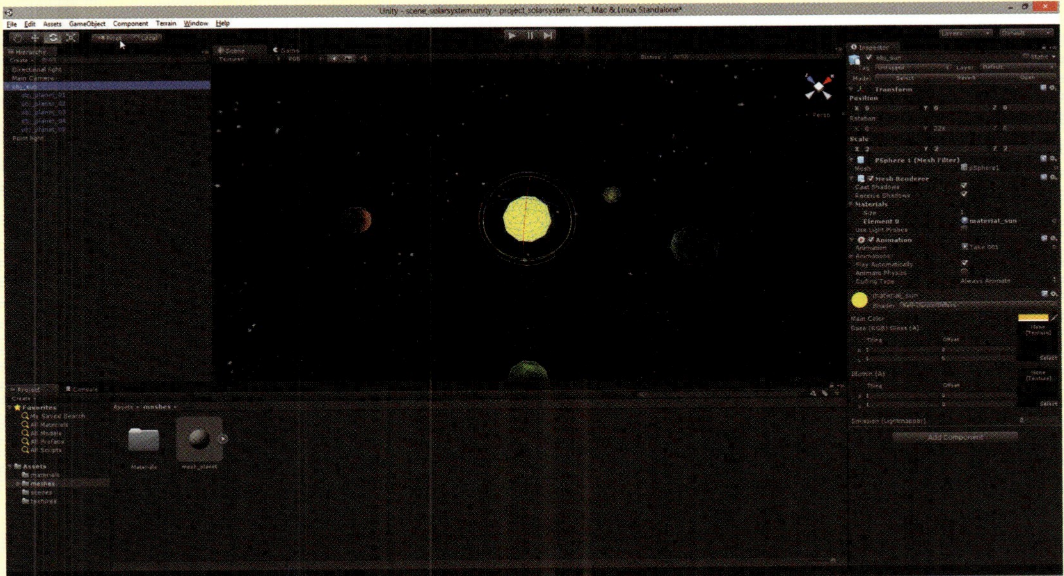

Figure 3.10 Rotation transformations cascading to child objects

3. This parent-child relationship and the concept of cascading transformations hold the key to orbiting the planets around the sun. To see how, *undo* all transformations applied to the sun and planets to reset the planets and sun back to their original positions. Be sure not to undo the hierarchical relationship – keep that. Then select the rotate tool (*R* key) and make sure that *Pivot* is set for the *Tool Handle*, from the toolbar. See Figure 3.10. The *Pivot* mode ensures rotation will occur from the pivot of the parent object – the centre of the sun. The *Center* option will instead base the rotation not on the sun's pivot but on the centre of the *selection* or *group*, which is an averaged centre generated from the sun and all of its child planets. With Rotate mode active and Pivot mode set, rotate the sun object in the scene and observe how all planets follow, rotating around the sun as it turns. Thus, the sun rotation is locked or linked to the planet rotation. Click the *Play* button on the toolbar to see this rotation in action: as the sun rotates on the basis of its baked animation, all planet objects will rotate in synch around the sun, to create the effect of a complete and interconnected solar system. And all of this was created simply through one 'drag'n'drop' operation: dragging the planets beneath the sun to create a parent-child relationship.

TIP: Experiment with parent-and-child relationships using the MainCamera. For example, first parent the camera to the sun object. That is, make the camera a child of the sun. Press *Play* and see the result: the camera rotates around the sun as it turns. Then parent the camera to one of the planet objects to create a nested parent-child relationship: the planets are the children of the sun and the camera is a child of one of the planets. The result is that the camera rotates around a planet instead of the sun.

3.9 Creating a Moon Object for a Planet

This section focusses on creating a moon object that will orbit a planet in the solar system. Creating this is something that we could actually achieve right away, just by duplicating a planet object, scaling it down, and then parenting it to any of the other planets. But this section will use an entirely different method, not because it is the most suitable or convenient – generally speaking, it is not – but rather for the sake of demonstrating and exploring the GameObject anatomy in more depth. Specifically, this section will look at how to create a moon GameObject entirely from scratch: beginning from an empty GameObject, and then by building that object component by component using the component-based paradigm, also known as component-based design (**CBD**). The aim is to show you the anatomy of a GameObject as being the sum of many parts, with each of those parts called a 'component'.

1. Let's create a moon. Start by selecting *GameObject > Create Empty* from the application menu, or press the keyboard shortcut *Ctrl + Shift + N*. This will create a new, empty GameObject in the scene, which is also added to the hierarchy. When deselected, this object will be entirely invisible in the Scene and Game viewports. The only evidence of its existence is its listing in the hierarchy panel. Selecting this object will show its properties in the Object Inspector, and there it can be seen to have one component named **Transform**. This component is common to all GameObjects, and contains the fundamental properties for any Game Object: position, scale, and orientation. Notice that, when selected, the empty Game Object can be transformed, rotated and scaled in the scene, as though it were a tangible object such as a mesh, even though changing these settings has little appreciable effect – at least, at the moment! Ensure the scale on X, Y and Z is set to 1. Rename the object in the hierarchy panel *obj_moon*.
2. The task here then is to transform this bare and simple GameObject into a tangible moon that can be seen in the viewport and which will orbit a planet just as they orbit the sun. To guide us in the construction of the moon object, consider the component composition of a planet. Select a planet in the scene and examine its list of components in the Object Inspector, namely: *Transform*, *MeshFilter*, *MeshRenderer* and *Animation*. These kinds of game object, with these specific components, were created automatically for us when we dragged and dropped the mesh into the scene from the Project

Figure 3.11 GameObjects are created from components

panel. For our moon to act like any of these planets, it must therefore have the *same* components with the *same* kind of settings. This is because a GameObject is the *sum of its components*. Thus, two objects with the same components at the same settings with behave identically to each other, even though Unity will still recognise them as two separate GameObjects in the Scene hierarchy. We could, of course, drag and drop the planet mesh into the scene to have Unity generate such an object for us as it did before, but we will build it manually this time. So select the *obj_moon* object and click the Add Component button in the Object Inspector to add a new component. From the list that appears, select *Mesh* > *Mesh Filter*. See Figure 3.11.

3. The *obj_moon* GameObject now has its first component, a mesh filter. The MeshFilter component allows a GameObject to act as a mesh or *reference* a mesh asset, such as the planet asset. It does not in itself allow the object to **render** or show that mesh in the scene – the **MeshRenderer** component will do that. Rather, it's a way of assigning to the object a reference to the mesh asset. To reference the planet mesh, click the Mesh Browser button on the Inspector from the *Mesh* field of the *MeshFilter* component, and select the planet mesh – which might be listed as *pShere1*. To add a mesh renderer component and show the mesh in the scene, click the *Add Component* button again from the Object Inspector and select *Mesh* > *MeshRenderer*. An alternative method is to select *Component* > *Mesh* > *MeshRenderer* from the application menu. The mesh will now be visible in the viewport, albeit untextured. If it's not immediately visible, however, ensure the object is not being obscured by another mesh in the scene – use the F key on the keyboard to frame the object at the centre of the view if necessary.
4. Create a new material for the moon by duplicating a material from one of the planet materials created earlier in this chapter. The moon material can be assigned to the moon object either through 'dragging and dropping' from the project panel to the scene view, or by way of the *MeshRenderer* component in the Object Inspector, using *Slot 0* of the Materials field. The moon GameObject now lacks one component in comparison to the other planet objects, namely the *Animation component*, which allows the mesh to animate on the basis of the baked animation. To add this, click the *Add*

Component button, and select *Miscellaneous > Animation* (*not Miscellaneous > Animator*). Once added, click the Animation slot on the Object Inspector and select the 'Take 001' animation clip from the browser to assign the animation to the mesh object. And in these four steps we have created a moon object from scratch, component by component. To complete the moon object and its relationship to other bodies, position it close to its parent planet and use the parenting feature of the hierarchy panel to add the moon as a child of the planet. Finally, take the level for a test run. The result: a rotating sun, planets that rotate around that sun, and a moon that rotates around one of the planets.

3.10 The Second Solar System

There are estimated to be in the universe around six sextillion planets across a total of ten thousand galaxies – depending, of course, on the 'latest' definitions of 'planet' and 'galaxy'. Our scene so far contains only a handful of planets in one galaxy, but I think we should go ahead and add more in the form of a brand new solar system. One way to add this solar system would be by copying and pasting: that is, by selecting all objects in the current system, duplicating them, and then moving the duplicates to a different part of the scene. This method is neither right nor wrong per se. However, this section will demonstrate a different method as a way of introducing yet another feature of Unity: the **Prefab**. The Prefab allows us to select many different but related objects in the scene and then to package them together into a single asset. This asset can then be added or instanced many times in a scene so that, for each instance, all the objects included in the package are treated together as though they were part of one mesh or one entity. The following steps demonstrate how prefabs work for creating a second, duplicate solar system that works just like the original.

1. Select the sun object in the scene, which will in turn select all child objects and thus the planets. To create a Prefab from these selected objects, drag and drop them from the Scene or hierarchy panel into the folder view of the Project panel. Unity will automatically generate a Prefab from the objects, and then add the Prefab as an asset to the Project panel, generating an appropriate thumbnail representation of the asset. Consider Figure 3.12.
2. The duplicate solar system can be now be created by dragging and dropping the Prefab asset from the Project panel back into the scene, just like a regular mesh asset. In fact, the Prefab can be instanced many times, creating many solar systems.
3. One useful set of features worth noting here, and which have been enhanced for Unity 4, are the *Dependency Inspection* features. Every game object in the scene is composed from one or more components, and these in turn can reference or *depend on* a selection of assets throughout the project. Take a look back over the previous sections and you'll see that the MeshFilter component, for example, depends on a mesh asset; the Material component on a material and texture asset; and other components, such as the **AudioSource** component, rely on audio assets, as we'll see later in this book. The sum total of references that a game object makes to assets is known as the object's **dependencies**. This is because the object can become broken or dysfunctional if its referenced assets are removed or changed after the fact – such as when a mesh asset is deleted from the project when there are dependent game objects in the scene. To help us keep track of the intricate relationships and webs of dependencies between objects and assets, Unity offers two main dependency

Figure 3.12 Creating prefabs from GameObjects

inspection features. These can be found under the *Assets* heading in the application main menu. These features are especially useful for identifying connections between objects to determine whether it's 'safe' to remove or change a specific asset – that is, whether an asset can be removed or changed without breaking existing game objects.

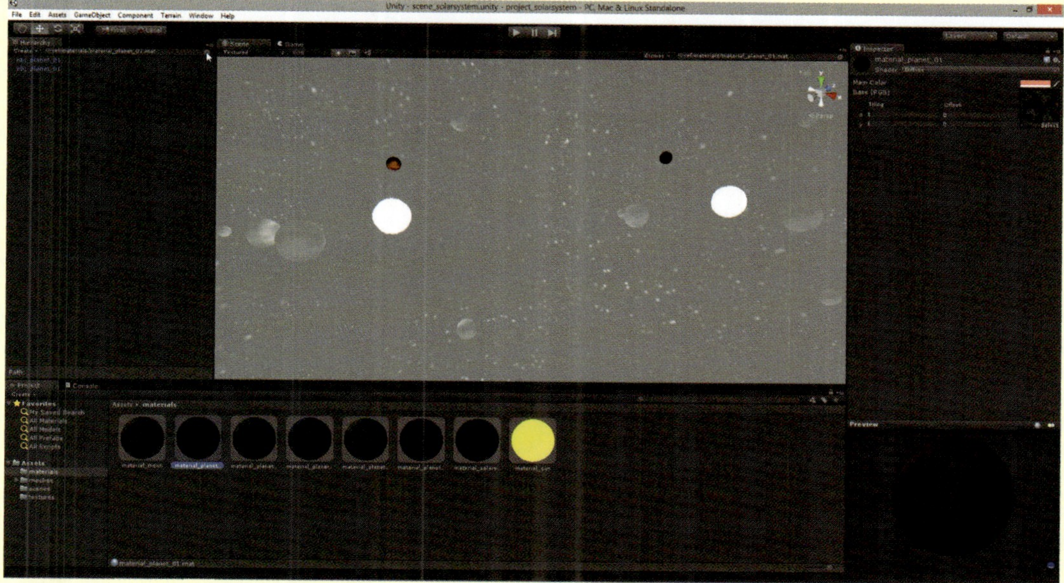

Figure 3.13 Searching for dependencies in the scene

4. To find all the dependencies of a selected game object in the scene, select a game object in the Scene tab – let's say one of the planet objects of our solar system – and then click *Assets > Select Dependencies* from the application menu. The Object Inspector is then filled with a *Narrow Selection* list, listing all the types of assets on which the object depends. In the case of a planet, this should be: *Materials, Textures, GameObjects* and *Meshes*. Click each of these groups in turn from the Object Inspector to see a more complete list of the associated assets in the Project panel view. Based on our project so far, a planet game object will depend on: a Prefab asset since the planet was added to a Prefab; a mesh asset since the planet MeshFilter component references a planet mesh, and a *selection* of materials, not just one – this is because the planet is part of a Prefab asset along with a range of other planets, and together these depend on many materials because each planet has its own material.
5. It's also possible to inspect dependencies in reverse order: that is, to select an asset and see which game objects depend on it. To do this, select an asset in the Project panel and then choose *Assets > Find References in Scene* from the application main menu. Doing this will filter the hierarchy panel with only a list of matching game objects in the scene; the scene tab will be coloured to highlight all matching objects. To exit this view, just click the Close button from the search box on the hierarchy panel. See Figure 3.13.

3.11 Showing and Hiding Solar Systems with Layers

We could go ahead at this stage and add many duplicates of our solar system Prefab throughout the scene in order to populate our universe with lots of planets. We could also go further and add asteroid fields between solar systems! If we did this, however, the scene would soon become filled with objects, which would present us with two main problems. First, the Scene view might become so cluttered with objects that it would be difficult to select the ones we wanted and easy to accidentally select and transform others. Second, we might want to show only *some* of the solar systems to the player, leaving others hidden until a later time – and it would be tedious to have to select each and every planet to show and hide. We can solve both of these problems – and all similar kinds of problem – using the feature of **layers**. With layers we can show and hide groups of objects: we can select a group of objects in the scene, mark them all as belonging to the same layer, and then either show or hide the layer to control the visibility of all objects on the layer. The term 'layer' is not so appropriate a term as 'group', in my view. This is because layers do not really specify the draw order of objects in the scene, nor do they specify how objects are layered on top of one another, as their name implies. Layers just specify *groups* of objects that can be shown or hidden together. Let us add some layers to our solar system scene through the following steps and see how layers can benefit our workflow.

1. Our scene will now feature many solar systems because I've duplicated the Prefab many times. Select two of the solar system prefabs by clicking on them from the Scene tab. At present, it's very easy when selecting objects to accidentally select and transform the wrong solar system, simply because

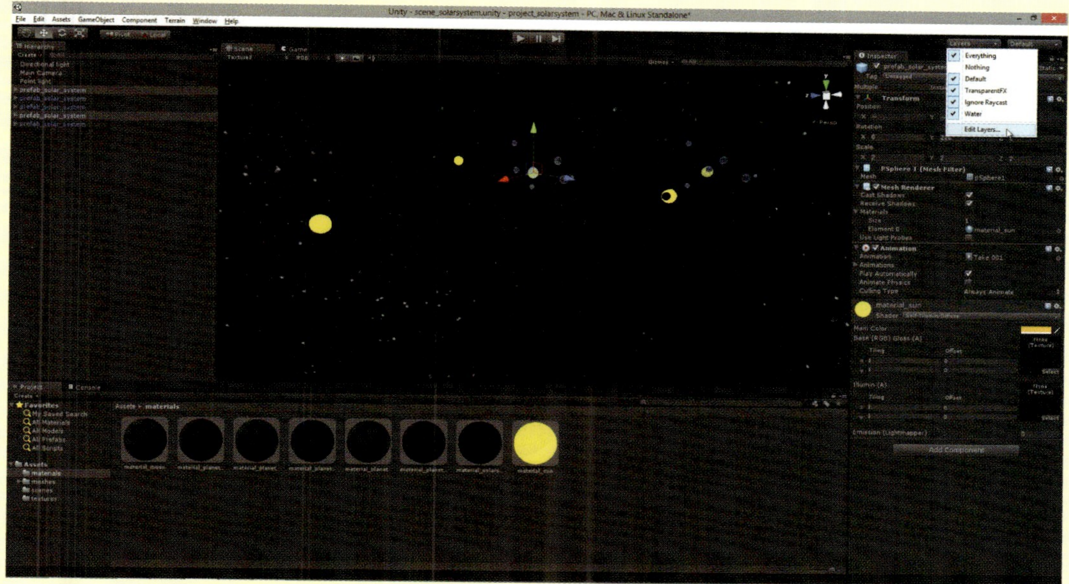

Figure 3.14 Creating a new, customised layer

there are so many of them. To avoid making this kind of mistake, it would be useful to hide a number of solar systems in the Scene view to make our workflow easier but without hiding the same objects when the game is run. We could toggle the visibility of the selected objects directly using the *Active* check box in the Object Inspector – this appears at the top-left corner of the Object Inspector, besides the Object Name. However, disabling this property will hide the objects during the game as well, and it also requires us to select every object to show or hide every time we want to show or hide them. Instead, we can use layers, because the visibility of layers can be different for both the run-time and design-time states of the game. Click the *Layers* drop-down menu from the application toolbar, selecting the option *Edit Layers* from the menu to create a new and custom layer. See Figure 3.14 for further details.

2. The *Layers and Tag Manager* is now shown in the Object Inspector, listing all of the existing layers, and showing a range of available slots for creating new layers. Available slots are labelled 'User Layer' and suffixed with a number. Select the topmost available slot, and click its right-hand column to begin entering a new name for the layer – in this case: *Solar System Layer*. This creates a new layer with the matching name. To confirm the layer has been created successfully, select the *Layers* drop-down menu again from the application toolbar and the newly named layer should be listed.
3. The new layer has been created but currently no objects from the scene are assigned to it. So ensure both solar systems are selected in the scene and click the *Layer* (singular) drop-down menu at the top of the Object Inspector not the *Layers* drop-down menu on the application toolbar. The former is for assigning objects to an existing layer and the latter is for creating the layers themselves. Assign the selected objects to the *Solar System Layer*; see Figure 3.15. On clicking this, a message dialog might appear asking whether the change in layer assignment should be applied to only the selected game objects or to both the selected game objects and all their children in the scene hierarchy. Be sure to apply changes to the children too by clicking the button 'Yes, change children'.
4. The two solar system objects are now added to a layer and we have global control over their visibility, even though they remain visible by default. To hide the layer and its objects: click the *Layers*

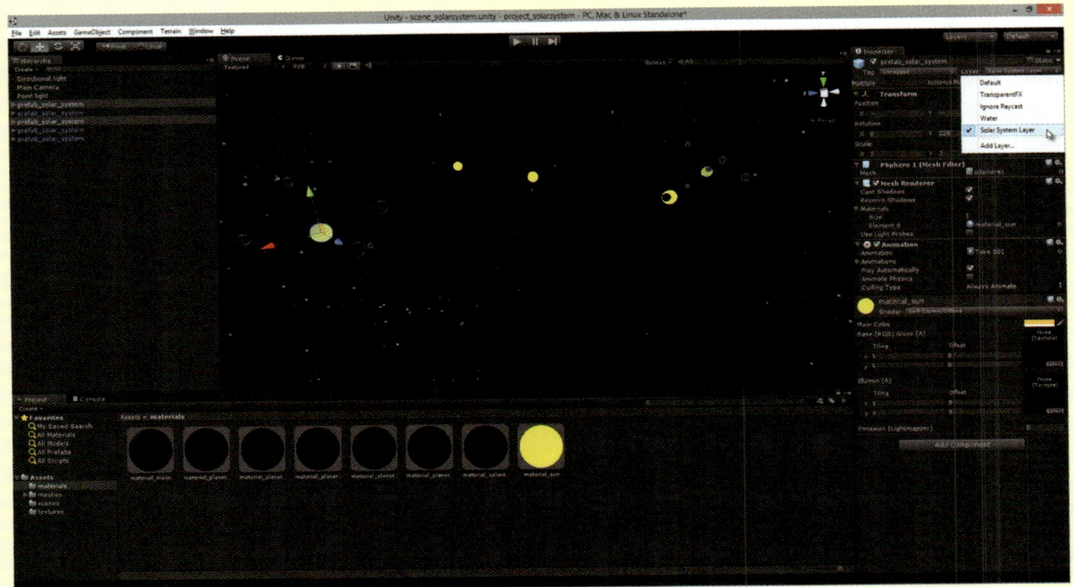

Figure 3.15 Assigning objects to layers

drop-down menu from the application toolbar, and uncheck the *Solar System Layer* from the menu. In response, all the layer's associated objects are hidden in the scene view – though they will still display during the game. This solves our problem of keeping objects visible in-game while avoiding accidental selection and transformation in the editor, because hidden objects cannot be selected using the mouse from the scene viewport. Note that the objects can still be selected from the hierarchy panel, just as they could before.

5. Show the solar system again in the scene view by re-enabling the visibility of the *Solar System Layer* from the *Layers* drop-down menu on the toolbar. For the sake of argument let us assume that we want to keep the solar system visible in the design view but hide it from the camera *during the game* – perhaps the solar system is concealed from human vision due to the incredible cloaking properties of the system's local gases! To do that, select from the Scene hierarchy the *Main Camera* object, which represents the view from which the scene is **rendered** (or shown) during the game. From the Object Inspector, select the *Culling Mask* and then disable or uncheck all layers that are to be hidden from this camera – namely the *Solar System Layer*. Now run the game and observe, or fail to observe, the hidden solar system.

3.12 Using Root Nodes

One technique regarding scene hierarchies that I frequently use in my own game projects for extra control and consistency – but which is by no means an official requirement or standard – is to parent *all* the objects in the scene beneath a single **root node** or Game Object. That is, to create a single, empty game object as the ultimate ancestor or parent for all other objects in the scene. Doing this has several distinct advantages: first, it means all objects in the scene can be transformed together as one by simply transforming the root node. Rotate the root node and the scene rotates; translate the root node and the scene translates. Second, it offers (as we'll see later) a number of scripting advantages: specifically it will allows us to call a function on the root node by name and to have that call cascade downwards through the object hierarchy, calling the same function on each and every child object – which can be useful if we need to execute a scene-wide behaviour on all objects. The following steps demonstrate how to work with root nodes.

1. Create a Root Node object. To do this, select *GameObject > Create Empty* from the application menu and name this object *Root*. Be sure to 'zero out' the transformations of the node. That is, from the Transformation component in the Object Inspector, be sure to set the translation and rotation values of the object to 0 on the X, Y and Z axes and the scale values to 1 on the X, Y and Z axes, if they are not already set to these values by default.

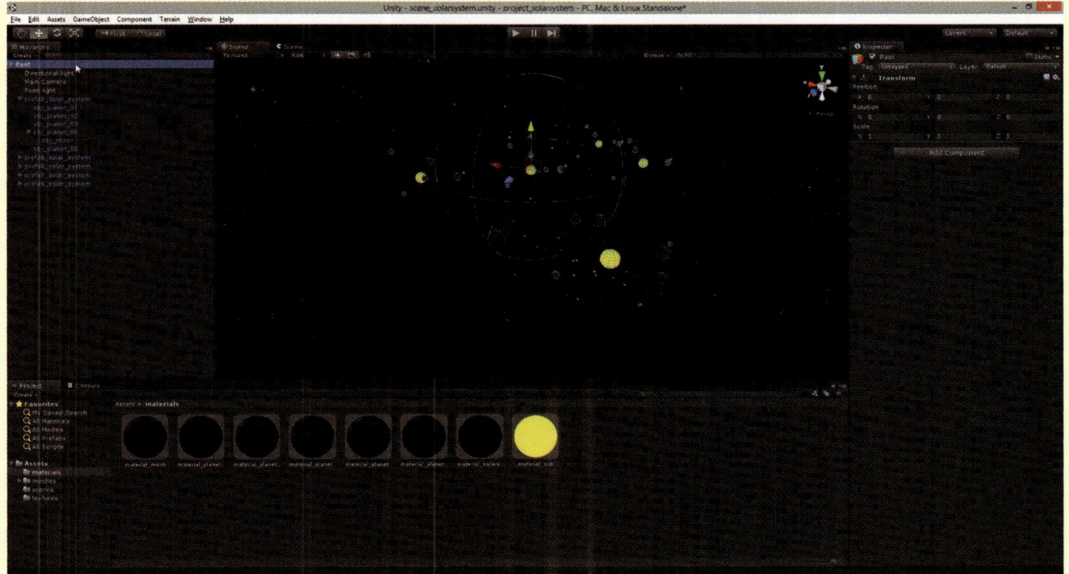

Figure 3.16 Creating a scene with a root node

2. Then select all other objects in the scene, and drag and drop them beneath the newly created root node to make them children or descendants of that node. In doing this, the root node has been created. See Figure 3.16. Test the root node: translate it, rotate, and scale it, and see how the entire scene inherits its transformation and properties. Further, uncheck the active check box on the Object Inspector and see the entire scene hide to match the root node's visibility status.

See Video: *Chapter03_Vid01_UnityStarProject* for a video tutorial on how to build the project in this video.

3.13 Expanding the Scene

The project in this chapter could be improved and expanded in many different directions. It could, for example, become the foundation of a 4X space simulation game or an educational game for physics, astronomy or even astrology classes. The expansion of this project will be left largely as an exercise for you, the reader, as you explore Unity on your own initiative. But I will make one further addition here that will help introduce some of Unity's scripting features, which will be covered in more detail later in the book. Specifically, I will you show how to customise the functionality of the game camera so that, during the game, it can focus or centre its view on a specified planet and allow us to circle the camera around the planet, much in the same way that framing and orbiting works with the camera in the Scene View tab. Consider the following steps on how to do this.

1. The camera behaviour, like the behaviour of most Unity objects, can be customised or changed by script. Unity provides us with the Monodevelop software to write scripted statements as an asset, and then to attach the script asset to a GameObject to control how it works during the game. In this sample, the camera behaviour will be customised using a pre-made script that Unity provides through an 'asset package'. To import the package (and thus to import the script) click *Assets > Import Package > Scripts* from the application menu. The import dialog appears in response. Accept its default settings and click the *Import* button to import all script files – these are added to the project as assets and can be viewed from the Project panel.

NOTE: On import, some yellow-coloured warnings might appear in the **console window**, depending on your system and version of Unity. The console window is for displaying debug statements. This window can be shown by pressing *Ctrl + Shift + C* or by clicking the *Console* tab besides the Project panel. To clear and hide the warnings, press the *Clear* button on the top-left side of the toolbar on the Console Window.

2. The scripts are added to the project, by default, in the folder *Standard Assets > Camera Scripts*. This folder contains three unique JavaScript files. Double-clicking a file will open it inside the MonoDevelop editor where the source code can be seen – although we will not need to edit the code for this exercise. Select the file MouseOrbit from the Project panel and drag and drop onto the Camera object in the scene. Select the Camera object, and see from the Object Inspector that the script has been attached as a Script component.
3. The properties and fields of the Script component correspond directly to public member variables defined in the script – changing these values will change the values of the associated variable. The *MouseOrbit* script has a property *Target*, which specifies the object in the scene for the game camera to *Look At*, or the object to *Frame* when the game is running. Leave this value at its default setting of *None* for the moment, and click the *Play* button on the toolbar to play-test the game in the Game tab.

Nothing appears to have changed yet; that is because the camera currently has no target and the script does require a target in order to work correctly. We *could* assign the script a target by exiting game mode, returning to the scene view and dragging and dropping any game object (such as a planet) into the *Target* field to frame it when the game is run again. But we can also change the value *while the game is running* and have the camera object update in real time to reflect the change. To see this at work, leave the game running and then just drag and drop a planet object from the hierarchy panel into the *Target* field of the camera in the Object Inspector. The camera will update immediately to reflect the change and will centre on the targeted object. With an object now targeted, it is possible to use the standard mouse controls to orbit the object – click and hold the left-mouse button while dragging to orbit around the target.

3.14 Conclusion

This chapter considered some of the most fundamental and critical features in Unity. They are critical in that almost every Unity project will make use of them, and for this reason alone almost every Unity developer will need to know about them. Practically every project from the simplest to the most complex will require a scene, assets and game objects and a developer capable of managing them effectively. It's worth recapping here to consolidate our knowledge and see how it fits with the Unity game development workflow. The project refers to a game, which is a collection of assets and game objects. Assets refer to all the abstract entities on which the game relies: graphics, sound, text, script, materials, textures, movies and so on. Unity GameObjects are the specific entities that live within the coordinate space of game world, and which rely on assets to get their work done. Specifically, the Game Object is a conglomeration of components the sum total of which defines the behaviour for the game object. Different objects are different *because* they differ in their component constitution, and two identical objects will share the same component constitution. Regardless of their internal structure, however, all game objects live inside a scene and are arranged in a Scene hierarchy, which expresses how objects are spatially related to each other. Objects, whose position and movement depend on another object, are said to be child objects of a parent; and transformations applied to the parent will cascade downwards to all children. In the next chapter we'll move forwards and consider what Unity has to offer us in terms of building and painting 'terrain'.

CHAPTER 4

Terrain and Audio

By the end of this chapter you should:

1. Understand what 'terrain' is
2. Be able to generate and sculpt terrain for your games
3. Know how to paint and decorate terrain
4. Be able to explore terrain in first-person mode
5. Know how to create and use 3D Audio

In this chapter we'll examine 'terrain' in Unity, an issue falling squarely within steps 3 and 4 of the six-step Unity workflow. These steps describe the process of 'level building' or 'scene creation' using the Unity editor tools. Like the previous chapter, this chapter will focus on a practical project: we'll use the Terrain tools to create a scene featuring a mountainous landscape environment that we'll explore in first-person mode, complete with a Skybox, textures and some basic foliage. Further, we'll also call upon the Unity audio tools to add realistic 3D sound effects to the scene. Before getting started, however, it's important to consider what terrain is and how it works in overview. It was mentioned in Chapter 2 that Unity is definitely not a content-creation tool in the sense that Maya, Max, Blender or Photoshop are content-creation tools: Unity is not used for modelling meshes or images. Rather, it's used for importing existing assets into a real-time 3D environment for inclusion into video games. Terrain, however, is an exception to this general rule. This is because it's an instance when Unity *does* act as a content-creation tool – a tool for creating a specific kind of mesh, namely, a Terrain mesh. The Terrain mesh is a single, procedurally generated mesh for creating natural landscapes or for a scene: mountains, hills, plains, fields, volcanic regions, and so on. Such terrain could, of course, be created in a modelling application by artists and then imported into Unity like any other regular mesh, but Unity offers a suite of built-in tools as a convenient way of creating them, and these tools are the 'Terrain tools'. So, if you need to create a quick and customisable landscape to act as a base layer for your scene, then the Terrain tools might be the solution. The following sections of this chapter explore how Terrain tools work in practice.

4.1 Creating a Terrain Object

Let's get started with the terrain project. This project will begin from an empty Unity project, featuring one empty scene. The first step in creating terrain for a scene is to generate the Terrain mesh – the mesh asset (vertices, edges and polygons) that will act as the terrain. This Terrain mesh will begin its life as a highly tessellated plane – that is, a flat surface whose topology consists of densely packed and regularly spaced vertices. It'll be our job as the project progresses to use the Terrain tools to sculpt and mould that initial terrain into its final shape, just as a sculptor shapes a composition from an initially formless lump of clay. Consider the following steps.

1. Select *Terrain* > *Create Terrain* from the application main menu. (STOP PRESS. In Unity 4.2 or above, Terrains are created by selecting *Game Object* > *Create Other* > *Terraine*.) Clicking this will generate a new Terrain mesh in the scene. In practice, two things happen here 'under the hood': first, a terrain *Asset* is generated in the Project panel; and second, a terrain *Mesh* is added to the scene as a game object on the basis of the asset. The newly created game object will have both a **Terrain component** and a **Terrain collider component**. The former will allow us to sculpt and texture the terrain and the latter to detect collisions with the terrain so that the player character and enemies will walk on top of the terrain as opposed to falling through and descending into oblivion.

NOTE: Almost all of the options considered so far in this chapter will be related to the Terrain group on the application menu.

2. The terrain is generated in the scene as a plane and its default size is 2000x2000 world units, which equates to a gargantuan surface area of 4,000,000 m^2! To reduce the size of the terrain, select *Terrain* > *Set Resolution* from the application menu. This important dialog allows us to set and edit a selection of fundamental properties for the terrain, not only its size. Almost all of these properties should be set *before* the terrain is sculpted and textured, because they ultimately influence the underlying structure and constitution of the Terrain mesh. Reduce the terrain *Width* and *Length* to 500 world units, and leave the terrain *Height* at 600 units. Note that editing the *Terrain Height* setting has no immediate and appreciable effect on the mesh in the viewport. Rather, this setting specifies a potential height or a maximum height: the tallest peak or height at which any mountain or outcrop of the terrain could reach when sculpted, if we so chose. See Figure 4.1.
3. The Height Map Resolution setting of the Resolution dialog specifies the pixel dimensions of a special internal, square texture, known as the *Height Map*. This texture has a direct and managerial connection to the Terrain mesh. Specifically, the greyscale values of texels (texture pixels) of the 'Height Map' map onto and control the elevation of vertices in the Terrain mesh. Black pixels refer to

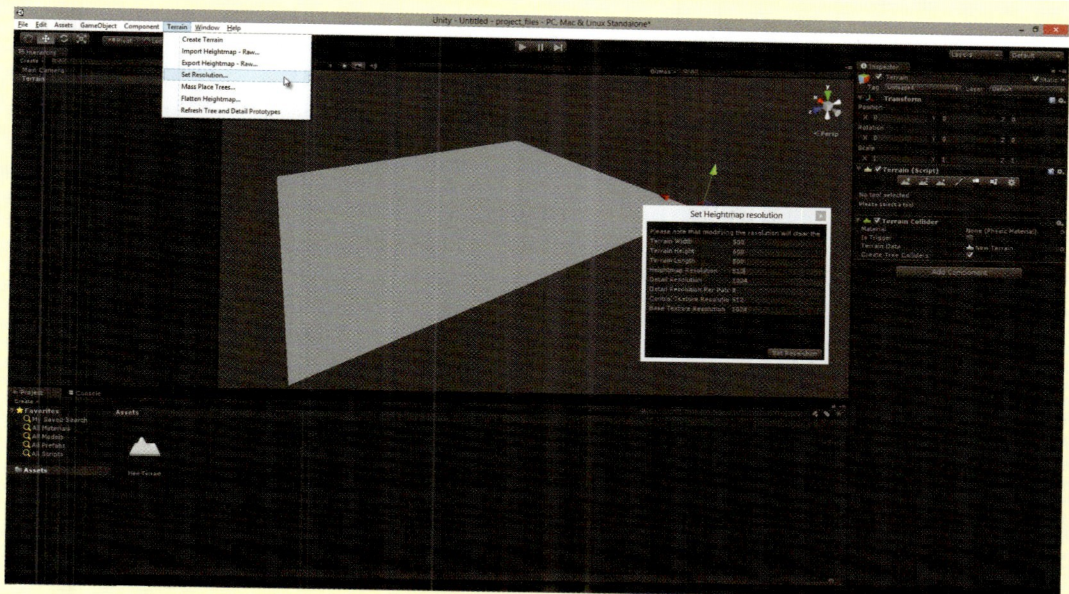

Figure 4.1 Configuring terrain properties through the Set Resolution dialog

depressions or sunken areas in the terrain (such as canyons), white pixels to extrusions or elevations (such as mountains), and shades in between to intermediate levels of elevation. The sculpting tools act as brushes and allow us to push and pull the terrain into shape. They actually work 'under the hood' by painting colour values directly onto the height map to indirectly deform or shape the Terrain mesh accordingly. The *Detail Resolution* and *Control Texture Resolution* settings work in a similar way but relate to other aspects of the terrain, as we'll see later. Leave all these settings at their defaults for this project: in short, the higher the values, the more detail and control you have over the Terrain mesh. This control and detail comes at a performance cost, however. Consequently, these values should be set as low as possible for your needs.

NOTE: The height map method of generating terrain means a tessellated, *three-dimensional* plane is deformed or displaced on the basis of pixel values in a *two-dimensional* texture file. This method hints at a possible limitation for terrain: you cannot use the Terrain tools to create alcoves, caves, holes, tunnels or crevice-like regions in which an interior space is carved out inside the terrain. This is because a two-dimensional texture lacks the necessary dimensions of information to store this detail. The height map only encodes levels of elevation for the terrain surface. Thus, insofar as the Unity Terrain tools offer sculpting features, they can only be used to raise and lower regions of a plane mesh.

4.2 Sculpting Terrain

The project so far has a flat plane mesh for a terrain, which looks more like an artificial super-smooth floor than a natural landscape with rugged and irregular details. Let us now mould or sculpt the terrain into shape, with valleys, hills, mountains and canyons. To do this, we'll use the terrain-sculpting tools, all of which are accessible from the Terrain component of the Terrain mesh in the scene. Though these tools seem like brushes which paint or operate interactively on the terrain mesh in the viewport, as we saw in the previous section they really paint pixel values into an internal height map texture. Consider the following steps.

1. Let's create the highest mountain in the terrain. To do this, select the Terrain mesh object in the scene viewport and click the *Raise/Lower* terrain tool in the Object Inspector to activate it (the leftmost button in the *Terrain Component*). When this tool is active, try hovering your mouse over the Terrain mesh to see a soft-edged blue circle appear beneath the cursor where it intersects the terrain. The blue circle is a visual indicator of brush size and strength. Click and hold the left mouse button while hovering over the terrain, and drag the mouse to start painting soft extrusions onto the Terrain mesh. Continue to paint and repaint over your work. See how, with each brush stroke, the terrain elevates according to the brush settings. Use the *Brush Size* slider in the Object Inspector to increase the diameter of the brush and use the *Opacity* slider to control the strength of the brush: higher values produce stronger brushes. This setting is termed *Opacity* rather than *Strength* because it controls the transparency or opacity of the colour values painted into the height map. Change both the *Brush Size* and *Opacity* settings to create a mountain. Don't worry about making mistakes: the terrain can always be reset to its default state, as we'll see in the next step. Continue to paint a mountain as high

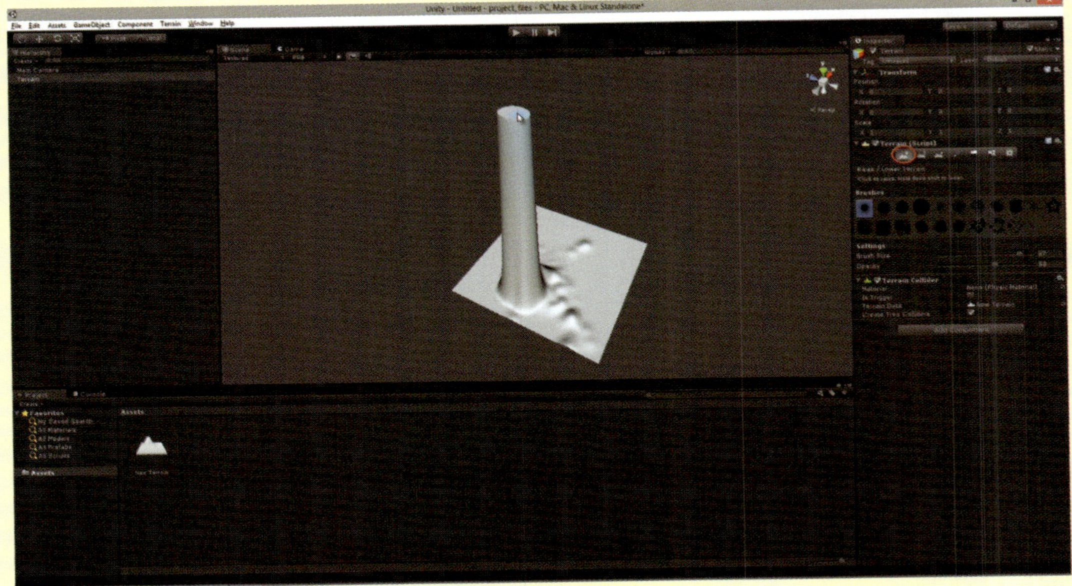

Figure 4.2 Creating a mountain for a Terrain mesh. Its height is capped by Terrain height

as possible to capture the absurd, and notice the mountain height is capped at the Terrain *Height* of 600 units; at this point, the mountain top flattens into a plateau. See Figure 4.2.

2. The mountain created in Figure 4.2 is too high and needs to be lowered. We *can* lower it manually using the *Raise/Lower* tool from the Object Inspector by holding down the *Shift* key on the keyboard while clicking on the terrain with the selected brush. Note: we can select brushes of different shapes and sizes from the Brushes palette (again, see Figure 4.2). This lower method works exactly as the opposite or reverse of the raise tool. However, despite the fact that we can lower the terrain manually, let's completely reset the terrain back to its starting settings and begin afresh, erasing our past brush mistakes and messes. To do that, click *Terrain > Flatten Heightmap* {. . .} from the application menu and use the dialog to flood-fill all pixels in the height map with a single colour – in this case the default height of 0. Click the *Flatten* button and the terrain is reset to its starting state.
3. This time use the *Raise/Lower* tool to really create the mountainous landscape we're aiming for. Use 'raise' to extrude our mountainous areas and use the lower tool to refine the height of the mountains and carve dips, recesses and canyons. Use a selection of brushes to 'rough up' the look of the mountains to add some natural-looking irregularities and cavities. If the terrain is looking too rough or jagged as a result of rougher brushes, then select the *Smooth Height* tool (third button on the Terrain component) and begin painting 'smoothness' into the rough areas, using it just like the *Raise/Lower* tool. See Figure 4.3 for more details.

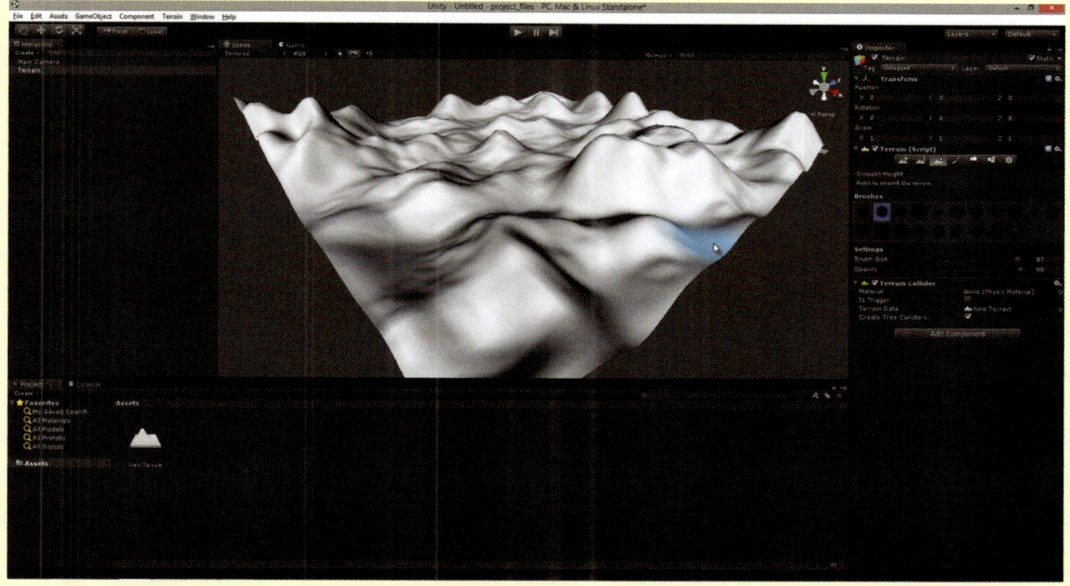

Figure 4.3 Toning down ultra-rough landscapes using the Smooth Height tool

4.3 Texturing the Terrain

The first three buttons or modes on the Terrain component relate to terrain sculpting – the process of shaping the terrain through elevation and depression. All of them work using the regular brush workflow, meaning they require you to select a brush, change its settings and then paint onto the terrain or height map. The first of these three tools is the *Raise/Lower* tool, for raising and lowering the height of the terrain. The second is the *Paint Height* tool: using this tool you can select a sample height by *Shift-clicking* a point on the terrain and then painting elsewhere to raise that region to the sampled height – it can be useful for creating cliff edges and other regions that share a similar height. The third and final tool is the Smooth Height tool for averaging between the vertices of the mesh to smooth out some of jaggedness and irregularities that can result from using rougher brushes with the Raise/Lower tool. Using the first and last of these tools we have successfully sculpted a Terrain mesh, but it still looks synthetic because it lacks texture: its surface is shaded with the default grey material and does not resemble a 'real-life' landscape. We shall now construct a texture for terrain using the Terrain painting tools and a selection of texture assets.

1. To get started painting the terrain with realistic-looking textures such as grass, rock and dirt, we must import suitable textures into the project. You can import and use any textures you want for terrains, but for the project in this chapter I'll make use of a selection of terrain textures that come pre-packaged with Unity in a Terrain Asset package. To import this package and its associated textures, click *Assets > Import Package > Terrain Assets* from the application main menu. Then click the *Import* button from the Import dialog that opens, to add the texture assets to the project. Once imported, some appropriate terrain textures can be found in the Project panel under *Standard Assets > Terrain Assets > Terrain Textures* – specifically, the Texture files *Cliff, GoodDirt, Grass* and *Grass&Rock*. Our aim now will be to use the Terrain tools to paint and blend combinations of these textures onto the terrain surface to form a complete and composite texture.
2. To start painting, select the Terrain mesh in the viewport and click the *Paint Texture* button from the Terrain component in the Object Inspector (the middle button). Once activated, click the *Edit*

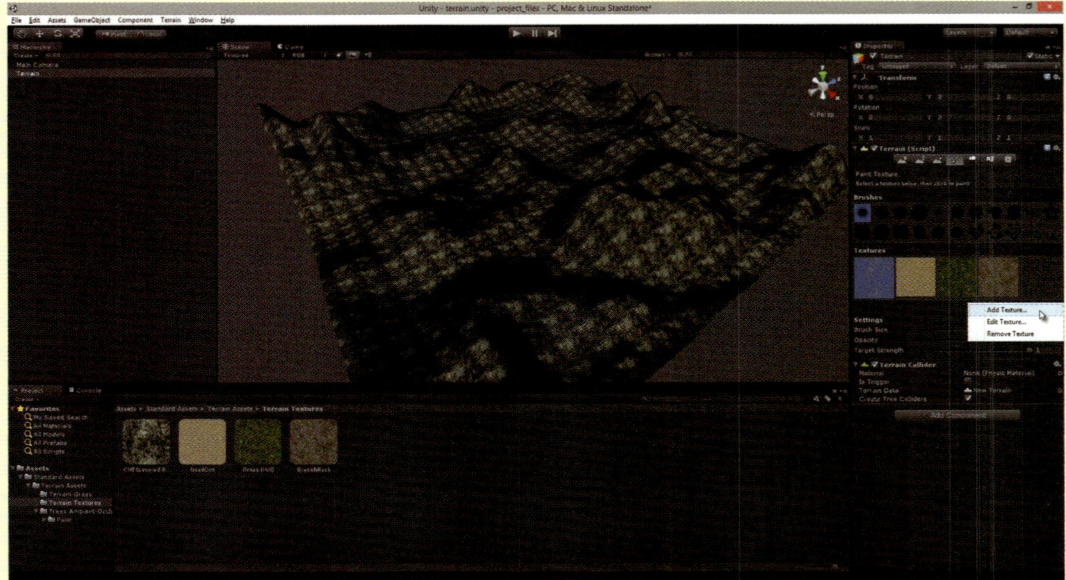

Figure 4.4 Using the Paint Texture tool to create a palette of texture brushes for painting onto the terrain surface

Texture {. . .} button and select *Add Texture* from the drop-down menu, and then select the first of our four terrain textures (*Cliff*) for the texture swatch, leaving the *Normal Map* slot empty and the *Tiling* values set to their defaults at 15. On clicking the *Add* button, the selected texture is added as the first or base texture in a palette of textures that can be chosen like brushes and painted on the terrain surface. The terrain in the viewport will also be textured with the newly added texture. Before painting, however, repeat the texture-adding process for the remaining three textures to complete the palette of four textures: see Figure 4.4.

NOTE: Adding subsequent textures to the palette of textures in the Paint Texture editor will not change or update the appearance of the Terrain mesh in the viewport, even though it did update after adding the first *Cliff* texture. The first texture in the palette is treated by Unity as the *default* or **base** texture for the terrain, the bottommost layer on top of which all other textures will be painted or layered.

3. The terrain now has a base texture applied and it's tiled across the terrain according to the texture's tiling settings. Is the tiling appropriate, however, for the terrain? In the case of a large expansive object like a terrain it's not always easy to tell when the terrain is viewed from a distance in the viewport. To get a clearer idea of how the texture tiling will look *to the gamer*, it will be necessary to move the viewport camera nearer to the terrain surface and see the effects of texture tiling from ground level. Seen from here it can reasonably be argued that the tiling is in need of adjustment: the tiles are too small, repeated too many times across the terrain surface, and it's noticeable even at ground level. To reduce the tiling, select the base texture in the texture palette of the Object Inspector, if it's not selected already, and click the *Edit Texture* {. . .} button, then click *Edit Texture* from the drop-down menu that appears. The tiling settings are specified in the *X* and *Y* edit boxes of the *Edit Texture dialog*; they represent the horizontal and vertical tiling respectively across the terrain surface. The default setting is *15* in both directions, and this does **not** mean that the texture is tiled 15 times in each direction. The value of 15 specifies the *total size* of *one* tile in world units on the terrain surface. Reducing the tiling across the terrain therefore means *increasing* rather than *decreasing* the tiling values, because you are decreasing the size of each tile. Thus, change the tiling settings from *15* to *70* for both X and Y and accept the changes. The result looks better, as can be seen in Figure 4.5.
4. The tiling settings for the base texture are now looking better for the terrain, and these tiling settings should be applied to all the other textures in the palette. Once applied, textures can be painted onto the terrain using the following method: select a texture from the palette by clicking its thumbnail, configure brush settings (size and shape), and then paint onto the terrain in the viewport to apply the texture onto the base layer. To get started, let's add some grassy plains to the lower levels of elevation. Select the grass texture from the palette, increase the *Brush Size* to around 87, set the *Opacity* to 100 and the *Target Strength* to 1. Then click and hold the mouse button while painting onto the terrain surface in the viewport. This will paint a grass layer on top of the base texture. The *Opacity* setting specifies the transparency of a *single brush stroke* but allows multiple overlapping strokes to bolden or strengthen the colour of the texture. Thus, make a mark and the texture is drawn according to its opacity; make another mark on top of the previous one and the colour of the

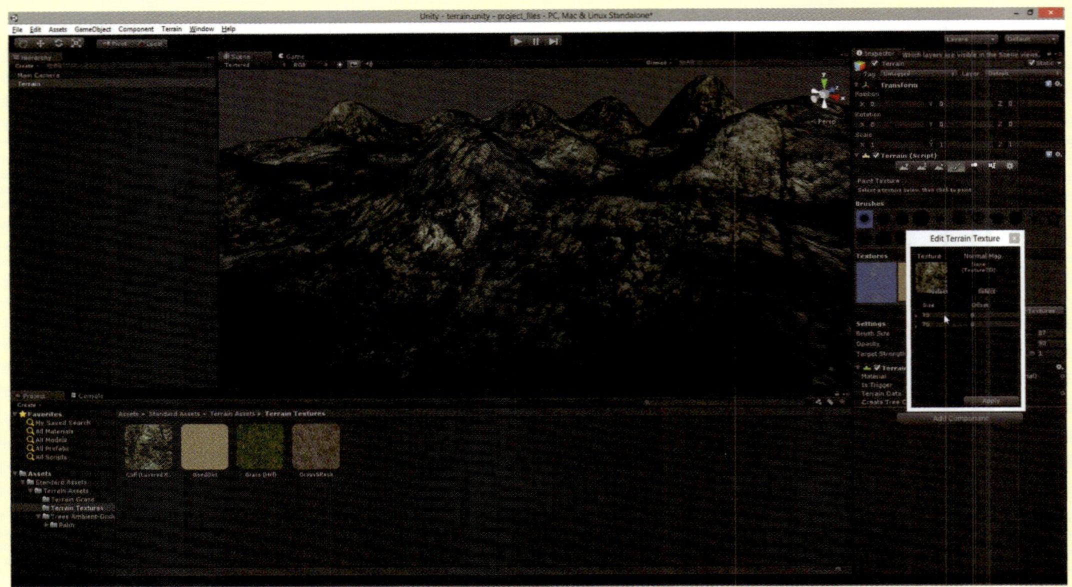

Figure 4.5 Increase the size of texture tiles for the base layer and improve the look of the Terrain mesh

texture is strengthened. The *Target Strength* setting in contrast specifies a maximum opacity for *all* brush strokes with that brush and texture, and it is a limit above which the opacity cannot reach; no amount of overlapping strokes can bolden the texture opacity beyond the *Target Strength*. The Target Strength is thus an *Opacity capping* value. Go ahead and use this technique to paint in the grassy plains.

See Video: *Chapter04_Vid01_TerrainProject* for a video tutorial on how to build the project in this chapter.

5. Repeat the process for painting the grass texture for the other textures in the palette to bring variation to the terrain, adding sand and dirt regions. Be certain to vary the opacity levels of the brush for each texture at the areas where two different terrain types meet in order to blend seamlessly between one texture and another. Failing to blend the textures will result in harsh-edged transition zones that'll make the terrain look artificial, because such zones are hardly ever found in 'real life'. Continue painting in textured regions in order to completely texture the surface of the terrain.
6. To add some polish to the terrain and the scene more generally, let's now add a Directional Light to simulate the sun, and a Skybox material to act as the background to the scene. The Directional Light can be added, as we've seen from Chapter 3, by selecting *Game Object > Create Other > Directional Light* from the application main menu. Selecting this option will allow us to position the light source in the scene and to configure its Brightness or Intensity properties using the Object Inspector. I set the intensity for my light at *0.8* and assigned it a desaturated (pale) golden colour – but feel

free to deviate from these values for your own project should you prefer different settings. To add the Skybox material, we *could,* of course, use our own custom-made Skybox material made from imported textures. Or, we can – as I will here – use a pre-made Skybox material that ships with the Unity engine. To import this into the project, we must import the *Skybox Asset package*. To do this, select *Assets > Import Package > SkyBoxes* from the application menu, and then click the Import button to accept the defaults and import the Skyboxes. This package features a range of Skybox materials for day and night scenes, and these will all be arranged by default in the Project panel into the folder *Standard Assets > SkyBoxes*.

7. Find an appropriate Skybox for the scene from the imported package by browsing the Skybox materials using the Project panel and the Object Inspector. You should by now be reasonably comfortable and familiar browsing assets using the Project panel. For this project, I have selected the Skybox *Sunny2*. To make this the background for the scene, select *Edit > Render Settings* from the application menu and choose a Skybox material for the *SkyBox Material* field in the Object Inspector. Again, this process and these settings were covered in some detail in the previous chapter, so they will not be covered in depth here. Take a look at Figure 4.6 below to see the scene composed so far.

Figure 4.6 The scene so far: sculptured terrain with textures, a directional light source to simulate sunlight and a Skybox background for the clouds

4.4 Decorating the Terrain

The previous sections have seen us create a detailed landscape for a level in a comparatively short time – short, that is, in comparison to the time it'd take us to develop our own terrain system from scratch. The landscape created so far, as well as the workflow used to create it, together offer an insight into the awesome potential of Unity as a game engine as well as, more generally, a time-saving tool.

The problem with our terrain at this stage is not its shape, form or texturing but rather its sparseness, its lack of set-dressing or props. The terrain is desolate: it has none of the hallmarks of a real-life terrain – no trees or grass or vegetation, no flourishing verdant life of any kind. It's time for us now to fix that issue by adding trees and grass; and we'll also add a first-person controller to the project so we can explore the terrain as a game character would be able to do. Consider the following steps.

1. Let's add some trees to the level. The terrain package imported earlier in this chapter already contains a palm tree mesh that we can add to the terrain. This can be found in the Project panel under the folder *Standard Assets > Trees Ambient-Occlusion > Palm*. One way to add the palm tree would simply be dragging and dropping the tree mesh from the Project panel into the viewport and positioning it onto the terrain surface, just as we would with any other 'regular' mesh file. However, this approach would soon become problematic for at least two reasons. First, terrains typically feature many trees, and duplicating a tree mesh for each tree on the terrain would quickly become tedious work. Second, the terrain elevates and has contours, and we want each tree on the terrain to be positioned so that it matches the flow and elevation of the terrain: again, we *could* manually position each tree using the Transformation tools, but this too would be tedious work. The Terrain tools therefore offer a solution to this problem: they allow us to use the brush workflow again to paint the meshes onto the surface of the terrain. This means we can paint multiple meshes in one brush stroke and have all of those meshes conform to the elevation. To access these tools, select the Terrain mesh in the viewport, and press the *Place Trees* button from the Object Inspector – it appears on the right-hand side of the *Paint Texture* button; see Figure 4.7 for more details.

Figure 4.7 Preparing to paint trees onto the terrain

Figure 4.8 Painting trees onto the terrain

2. Painting trees onto the terrain works much like painting textures. We must first add a set of tree brushes to the tree palette. Once added, we select them from the palette and use the brush tool to paint them onto the terrain. To add the palm tree as a brush to the palette, click the *Edit Trees* button from the Object Inspector and then choose the *Add Tree* option from the context menu. The *Add Tree* dialog appears in response. Click inside the Tree field and select the Palm Tree mesh from the GameObject browser to select the palm as the mesh to be added. Then click the Add button and the selected palm tree object is added as a brush to the tree palette.
3. Now let's paint the palm onto the terrain. Select the palm brush from the palette and the associated brush settings for the brush appear beneath in the Object Inspector. The *Brush Size* option controls the radius of the brush used to paint the tree meshes, and the *Tree Density* setting controls how tightly packed together each tree mesh will be when painted onto the terrain using the brush. Notice also the three subsequent options for variation: *color variation*, *height variation* and *width variation*. These settings can be tweaked to define a margin or range of possible values for a tree so that, when the trees are painted, each tree painted by the brush will be given a unique and random height, width and colour selected from within that range. This is to add variation and deviance to the appearance of the trees, reducing the 'sameness' look that is often entailed by duplicated meshes. A value of 0 for any of the variation options will ensure that all trees share the same value for that setting – it specifies no variation. For this project I have set the brush size to 40, the tree density to 50, the colour variation to 0.8, the height variation to 25, and the width variation to 0 to ensure all trees have the same width. Once set, paint the trees onto the terrain as though the brush tool were painting textures – click to stamp the trees onto the terrain. Notice how the meshes are automatically positioned to rest on the terrain surface according to its levels of elevation and also the variation in detail among the trees as specified by the variation settings. Continue adding trees to the level. Consider Figure 4.8.

NOTE: At this stage, why not add a first-person controller to the scene to explore the terrain close up and in first-person mode? The instructions for doing this can be found in Chapter 1, where a first-person controller was added to our scene for exploring a room from first-person perspective. Testing the scene with the first-person controller is the point at which the true vastness of the Terrain mesh becomes apparent. Be careful therefore in future terrain projects to scale your terrain appropriately for your needs. If your game will be a first-person game, then I recommend adding a first-person controller *before* creating the terrain to act as a point of reference for sizing the Terrain mesh.

4. The next step involves adding grass to the terrain, continuing with the brush-and-painting technique that we have now grown used to for adding details to the terrain. Details such as blades of grass, leaves, bushes, shrubs, flowers and other terrain minutiae are typically added as **billboard** objects rather than as standard meshes for performance reasons. The billboard is a special rectangular mesh (a **quad**) that is textured with an image (such as a blade of grass) and then configured so as to a rotate to directly face the camera wherever the camera is looking. Billboards are therefore a computationally inexpensive way to present numerous tiny but important details to the user, and they enhance the realism of the scene when used properly. To add grass to the scene as billboards, select the Terrain mesh in the viewport and click the *Paint Details* button from the Object Inspector – the penultimate button in the Terrain component. Then click the *Edit Details* button and select *Add Grass Texture* from the context menu. See Figure 4.9.

Figure 4.9 Adding grass to the terrain as billboards

5. The *Add Grass Texture* dialog displays and allows us to select a grass texture from the project assets. This texture will be applied to the billboard objects that we will paint onto the terrain using the standard brush workflow that we employed before. This time we will not be painting a *mesh* of our choosing – such as a tree mesh – but billboard or quad objects textured with a grass texture. Click in the *Detail Texture* field and select a grass texture from among the assets included in the Terrain Package; specifically *Grass2* (located inside *Standard Assets > Terrain Assets > Terrain Grass*). See that the dialog also contains settings for adding variation to the appearance of the texture as applied to each billboard mesh. The *Min* and *Max* settings for width and height control the range of possible values, out of which one will be randomly selected for the width and height of each painted quad or billboard. Further, the *Healthy Color* and *Dry Color* settings specify colours that are multiplied with the grass texture on a per billboard basis to *colorize* each billboard differently, again adding variation across billboards. Accept the default settings of this dialog and click the *Add* button to add the grass texture as a billboard brush to the *Details* palette in the Object Inspector.
6. Select the Grass Texture brush from the palette and begin painting grass into the viewport. On doing so, you may see one of two results: you may see grass being painted onto the terrain (if the viewport camera is close to the terrain surface), or you may see no immediate effect at all (if the viewport camera is zoomed out and away from the terrain). You should find that the visibility of the painted grass changes from visible to non-visible depending on the distance between terrain and camera. This feature is active as a performance enhancer to prevent the camera rendering unnecessary distant detail, such as grass and flowers. The distance itself can be controlled by the *Detail Distance* setting on the final tab or mode of the Terrain component in the Object Inspector, *Terrain Settings*. By default the Detail Distance slider is set to 80 world units, meaning that as the camera moves more than 80 units away from the terrain, the grass becomes hidden in the viewport (note – this does not mean that the grass will be invisible to the player during the game!). The visibility of the grass to the player also depends on the player's distance from the grass. Ensure the grass can be seen in the viewport, either by moving the camera closer to the terrain surface or increasing the *Detail Distance* slider in the *Terrain Settings*. Then continue the painting process.

Figure 4.10 Completed terrain with grass billboards

7. The density of the grass within the radius of the brush is controlled by the brush Opacity settings: increase Opacity to densely pack the grass billboards together and decrease Opacity to thin-out or reduce the density. Settle on a density that works for your scene; here, I have chosen 0.15. Continue adding grass to produce a scene resembling Figure 4.10. Take the scene for a test run using the first-person controller, and see how the grass is automatically configured to sway and bend with the wind.

4.5 Terrain and Audio

The completed terrain is now looking much better than before and is ripe for exploration in first-person mode. Congratulations! Taking this project as a base, a wide range of games could be created, from RPGs to simulators. However, the scene is silent; that is, literally silent in that no sounds can be heard. Let's use this opportunity to take a brief but instructive look at how Unity deals with sounds and then give the scene some atmosphere. In the world of Unity Audio there are two main elements to consider: *audio 'sources'* and *audio 'listeners'*. AudioListeners are components attached to things or entities that can *hear* sounds or music; any thing or person in the game with the ability to hear should have an **AudioListener component**. The AudioSource, in contrast, is a component attached to things or entities in the game that will *make* sounds: guns, bullets, fireworks, jukeboxes, people, cars – almost everything. If an object needs to be heard at all, then it must have an **AudioSource component**. Provided this basic rule is adhered to when attaching components to objects, Unity will happily take care of practically everything else to do with audio playback in your game. The following steps demonstrate the Unity audio framework in action, although audio will be considered again in more detail in later chapters.

1. Before we can play or hear any sound, the terrain project will need to have audio assets imported – it needs to have some audio to play. Unity accepts audio assets in a range of formats, including .WAV, .MP3 and .OGG, as well as other tracker formats such as .MOD and .IT. However, for most purposes and for best quality, uncompressed and lossless WAV formats are recommended for importing audio, regardless of whether the audio is a five-second effect or a five-minute musical score. For this project we can use some sound effects available to us for free from the Unity Asset Store. To access these sounds, search the Project panel for sounds and switch the search filter to Free Assets from the Asset Store, as seen in Figure 4.11. Select the *Sci-fi_AmbienceLoop1* track in the folder view of the Project panel – this asset is part of a larger package ('Free SFX Package' by Bleep Blop Audio). With the track selected in the Project panel, click the *Import* button on the Object Inspector to download the assets from the Asset Store and import them into the current project. Downloading the asset does require a free Unity Asset Store account.
2. Once downloaded, select the newly imported *Sci-fi_AmbienceLoop1* track asset in the folder view of the Project panel and preview it by clicking the *Play* button in the Object Inspector preview pane (bottom-right hand side of the Unity window). The intention here is to add this track to the scene as an ambient music loop to set a menacing and foreboding atmosphere and create a landscape of mystery, intrigue and suspense. As mentioned, for this sound to be played and heard the

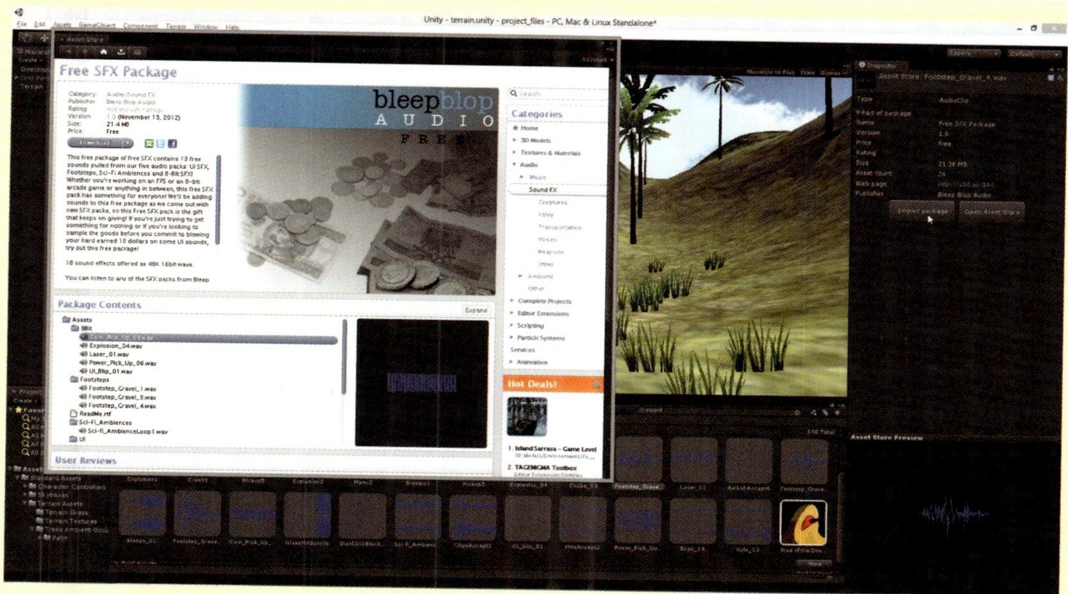

Figure 4.11 Importing audio assets from the Unity Asset Store

scene requires both an *AudioSource* to play the music and an *AudioListener* to hear the music. The AudioListener should already have been added to the scene automatically: it will have been attached either to the default camera as a component or to the first-person controller camera that was imported into the scene. To confirm this, select the camera object of the first-person controller in the viewport or Scene hierarchy, and then scan the active components in the Object Inspector to find the AudioListener component. If none exists, then an AudioListener component can be added manually to the camera by selecting *Component > Audio > Audio Listener* from the application main menu, with the camera selected. In a first-person game such as this one, the camera should generally have the AudioListener component, since it represents the position of the player.

3. The camera has an AudioListener component but still nothing can be heard since the scene contains no AudioSource to emit the music. Before adding this, select the *Sci-fi_AmbienceLoop1* track in the folder view of the Project panel, ensure the 3D Sound check box is un-checked (not ticked) in the Object Inspector, then click *Apply*. This ensures the ambient loop track will be treated as music and not as 3D sound – that is, as something that should play and be heard by the player wherever they are in the level, as opposed to a sound whose volume diminishes the further the player moves away from it. The music *does not* have a position in 3D space and hence it is not a 3D sound – it is an emotional commentary that exists above and beyond the space of the scene. With the 3D sound setting disabled, the sound can be added to the level as an Audio Source. To do this, create a new game object anywhere in the level by clicking *GameObject > Create Empty* from the application main menu. Name this object 'Music Track'.
4. Select the newly created game object and add to it an AudioSource component. To do that, select *Component > Audio > Audio Source*. Examine the AudioSource component in the Object Inspector and complete the field Audio Clip: that is, click on the field and select the *Sci-fi_AmbienceLoop1* audio asset from the browser. The Audio component is now correctly configured for playback. Now, simply hit the *Play* button in the toolbar to test the game, then complete with eerie music. See Figure 4.12.

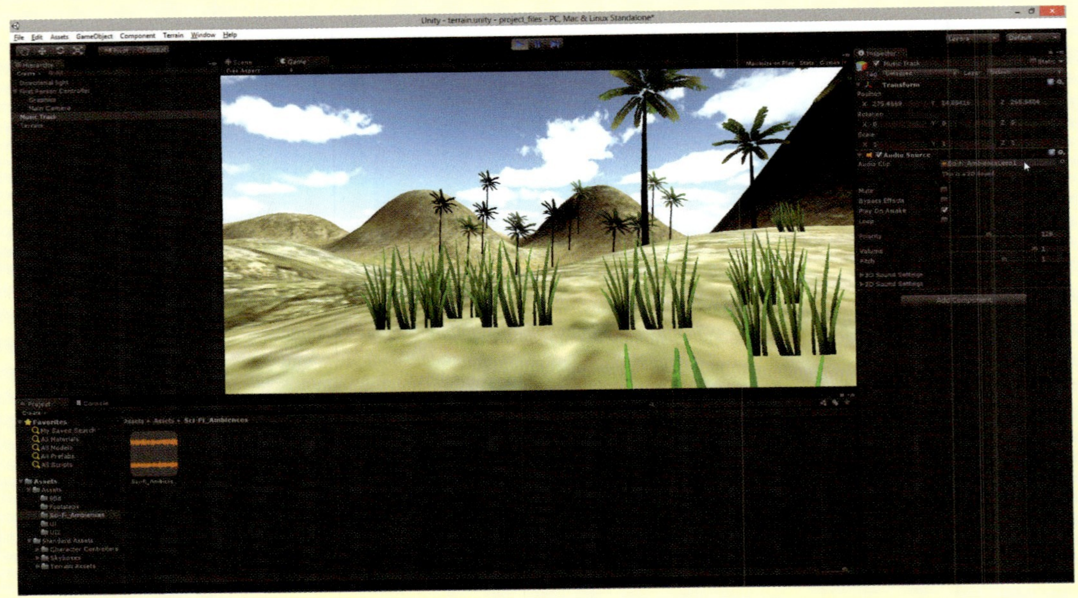

Figure 4.12 GameObject with AudioSource component attached

4.6 Conclusion

The focus of this chapter was primarily on terrain and secondarily on audio. The Unity Terrain tools offer an intuitive and easy to use suite of sculpting, texturing and decorating brushes for carving out landscapes for your scenes. However, these tools are not without limitations, particularly in relation to height maps, as Unity terrains cannot have interior spaces – such as caves and cavities – carved into them. To achieve these effects, a developer must either resort to a creative workaround or use an alternative method for creating terrains, such as modelling them manually in a 3D modelling package. Nevertheless, the terrain system is, as we have seen, powerful in that it offers sculpting and texturing features, as well as a means for painting meshes onto the surface of the terrain, matching its contours. Furthermore, this chapter demonstrated just how quickly a developer can be playing music and sound effects with the Unity audio system simply by using audio source and listener components. The next chapter enters the exciting and important world of lighting and lightmapping. There is perhaps no rendering task more computationally expensive than that of lighting and the calculation of lighting effects and this aspect of a game is thus critical to its performance.

CHAPTER 5

Lighting and Lightmapping

By the end of this chapter you should:

1. Understand how to work with lights in Unity scenes.
2. Understand what a lightmap is and how lightmapping works.
3. Be able to use the Beast Lightmapper.
4. Know how to build scenes using the Modular Building Method.
5. Understand the limitations of lightmapping.

Let's now take a summary tour of Unity's lighting features – at least, most of its key features. If there's one simple rule that applies to lighting in games, it is this: keep things as simple as possible. If your level looks correct under different lighting setups, then choose the one that involves the fewest number of lights and the fewest complications. If your objects do not need to cast shadows, then disable the shadow-casting feature. If your objects do not need to be affected by lights, then give them a special 'self-illumination' material to exclude them from lighting calculations. As we'll see, lighting and lighting calculations are computationally expensive. They're perhaps the single greatest performance overhead that can be placed on a real-time 3D video game. The concepts of 'optimisation' and 'performance improvement' should therefore be at the forefront of your mind when working with lighting (although ideally they'll be in your mind when working on almost any aspect of game development).

In this chapter we'll explore many of the lighting features Unity has to offer, including the different light types, real-time lighting, ambient lighting and lightmapping. We'll consider these features, as we've considered others in previous chapters, by pursuing a project. This project will have a flavour distinctly reminiscent of the sci-fi horror movie 'Event Horizon'. Specifically, we'll travel to an abandoned space station. We'll build this location using the **Modular Building Method** and, once it's constructed, we'll call upon a range of Unity's lighting features to convey a menacing atmosphere. Then finally, we'll add a first-person controller to explore the environment.

5.1 Build the Space Station using the Modular Building Method

To get going with the 'spooky space station' project, create an new empty project in Unity, making sure to save the project as well as the auto-generated scene – the latter will act as our main scene. This marks our starting point. From here, go ahead and import the associated project files for this chapter as assets of the project – these are assets I have specifically made for this chapter. The asset files to import include four architectural meshes and one texture that'll be applied to the meshes. The Mesh file names are: *mesh_corner.ma*, *mesh_intersection.ma*, *mesh_straight_through.ma*, and *mesh_straight_end.ma*. The Texture file name is: *texture_sci_fi_texture.tif*. Be sure to organise the assets of your project in the project panel using folders: Mesh assets inside the *meshes* folder, Texture assets inside the *textures* folder, and so on. Having reached this stage, we're ready to start building the scene environment. We'll do this using a popular and commonly used technique in game development called the *Modular Building Method*. Consider the following steps.

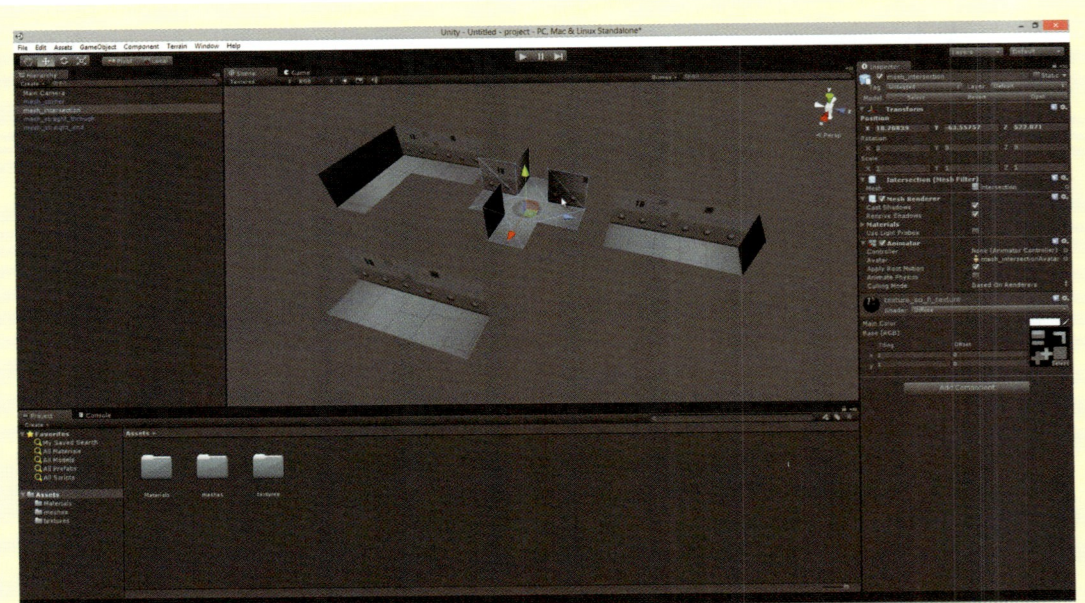

Figure 5.1 Preparing to build the space station using the Modular Building Method

1. Drag and drop each mesh asset from the Project panel into the scene only once, so each asset has exactly one instance in the scene as a game object. The scene should then feature four game objects

in total, once for each mesh; go ahead and drag and drop the imported texture into each mesh so that all meshes have a material applied. Each mesh in the scene represents an architectural *element* of the space station, a *section* of corridor. The corner L-shaped piece represents a turn in the corridor, and the intersection piece represents a point at which two corridor sections meet and intersect, allowing a turn in any of the cardinal directions: north, south, east and west. The key point to notice about each of these mesh objects is that they do not, either independently or together, represent the entire environment. Instead, each is a piece of the environment in the same way that a Lego brick is a piece of a larger construction. The environment *can* therefore be built by *duplicating* the mesh pieces and *fitting them together* to form a network of corridors. This is what we shall do here to make the environment. This technique is the Modular Building Method, so named because the environment is built from *modules* or *mesh pieces*.

NOTE: When viewing the four corridor-section meshes together from certain angles in the scene viewport, you will not be able to see all walls or ceilings at the same time (as shown in Figure 5.1). However, rotating the viewport camera around the models will probably bring some of the walls into view while causing others to disappear. This is normal. The walls are *one-sided*, meaning they can be seen only from one side – in this case, from the interior side. These walls will appear normally to the player when the game is running because the player will walk on the floor between the walls, and thus each wall will be facing the player.

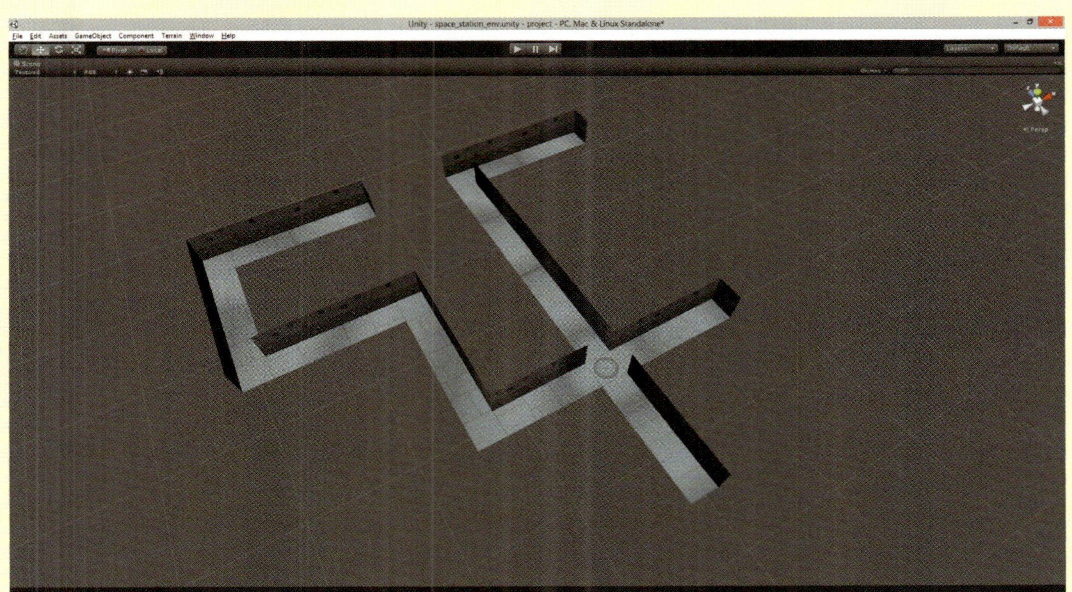

Figure 5.2 Completed environment setup, created using the Modular Building Method

2. The Modular Building method is useful for many reasons, partly because it gives level designers the ability to edit and change the layout of the environment directly from the Unity editor, rather than having to tweak the layout in the original Mesh file from the 3D modelling software. An additional benefit is that, since the environment is made up from many *duplicated* sections, the architecture of the level *reuses* and *recycles* texture space because each duplicate of the same mesh asset will use the same texture. So let's continue creating the level by arranging the pieces together to form a complete network of corridors that'll make up the space station. There's no right or wrong way to do this: I've chosen to begin by translating the intersection piece to the world origin and then by building outwards from there using the other pieces. Use the technique of duplicating meshes (*Ctrl + D*) to create copies of the sections where required; use the technique of Discrete Rotation (*Ctrl+Rotate*) to rotate pieces in fixed increments; and use the technique of Vertex Snapping (*V Key*) while translating the sections to align them together exactly. These techniques were considered in depth in chapters 1 and 3 of this book. When building the level, be sure to place proper end sections at all ends of the level – that is, make sure there's a wall at the end of every corridor section to prevent the player from falling off. Take a look at Figure 5.2 to see my completed environment setup, created using the Modular Building Method, together with Duplication, Discrete Rotation and Vertex Snapping.

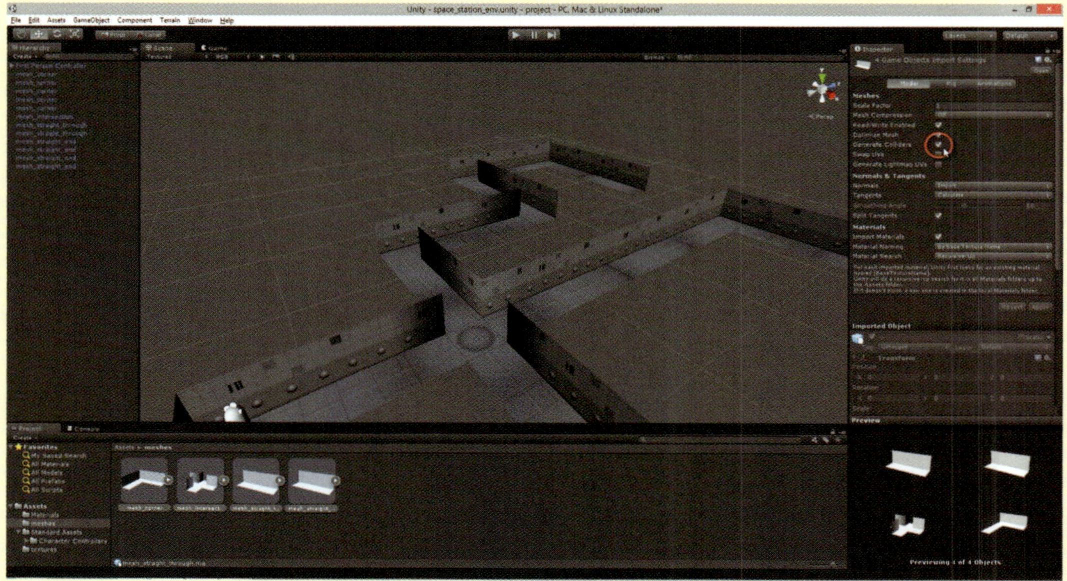

Figure 5.3 Generating Collision data for imported meshes

3. Remove the *MainCamera* from the scene and add a first-person controller to the project, just as we've done for previous projects. Insert the first-person controller into the scene and position it inside the corridor sections, at the location where the player should begin play. Press the *Play* button from the Unity toolbar to test run the scene and notice as the game runs in the *Game* tab how the first-person controller falls through the floor of the level and descends into nothingness, as though the floor were not a solid object. Stop playback of the game and select all four of the mesh assets in the *Project panel*. The problem is that Unity doesn't recognise the Mesh assets as solid objects that can be *collided* with. Instead, it thinks of them of as massless polygonal objects floating in space, through

which anything can pass. To give our section meshes mass and substance and make them the kind of thing that can accept collisions, we must adjust their collision properties in the Object Inspector. With meshes selected, use the Object Inspector to insert a tick into the check box labelled *Generate Colliders*. Then click the *Apply* button to save the changes. This will auto-generate collision data and *Bounding Volumes* for the meshes based on their vertex data. In short, it will give the meshes substance. Now test-run the game again using the *Play* button from the application toolbar and see in the *Game* tab how the camera does *not* now fall through the floor. In fact, the level can now be inspected and explored in first-person mode, although it appears very dark due to lack of lighting. If, however, you have not inserted proper end pieces at the end of each terminating corridor section, the player will be able to fall off the edge of the level and descend into nothingness again.

4. Although thankfully our player doesn't now fall through the floor, there's still a niggling little issue that's noticeable in *this* scene when the game is running – though it's not guaranteed to be noticeable in *all* scenes. It is this: the lens of the first-person camera penetrates the wall when we walk very closely to it: although we cannot *walk* through the wall, we can still *see* through it. This problem arises because of the *near clipping plane* of the camera, an optimisation technique. This specifies the minimum distance, in Unity Units, that objects have to be from the camera before they are ignored and hidden from view. This distance is currently too great and, as the player approaches close to the wall, the wall falls below this 'near-clipping' distance and is therefore hidden from view, allowing us to see the level beyond the wall. To fix this, select the camera object of the first-person controller using the Scene hierarchy panel, and examine its properties in the Object Inspector. From there, set *the Near Clipping Planes* value (in the *Camera Component*) from 0.3 (default) to 0.1. The value now appears in bold in the Object Inspector to indicate that it has been changed from its default value. Now test run the scene again to see the improvement this makes!

5.2 Lighting the Space Station – Disabling Ambient Light

The scene so far can be explored in first-person mode, but its lighting and illumination is far from ideal. The level appears dark, but not in any stylistic or interesting way such as the 'dark look' associated with Cyberpunk or Neo-noir styles. It appears sombre, uninteresting, plain and crude. This dullness is attributable not to scene layout or lack of mesh detail but to generally to lighting. So now it's time for us to concentrate on creating lighting for the scene, lighting that'll convey mood and atmosphere. This process should begin by disabling the scene's 'ambient' lighting. Consider the following steps.

1. If you play the scene now, you'll notice in the *Game* tab that, although it's dark, it can still be seen. The scene is not, for example, so dark that it appears to us as completely black. This may seem strange initially because a scene that has no lighting *should* appear completely black. Indeed, it's true that when there are no lights to illuminate anything, then nothing should be visible. But things are visible here. This suggests therefore, that there *is* actually light somewhere in the scene, and indeed there is. Every Unity scene features a default **Ambient Light**, not selectable or visible from the Scene hierarchy. It's a light that doesn't throw shadows but casts a subtle low-level illumination throughout the scene, equally in all directions. It illuminates every polygon with the same amount of light at a single intensity. The result is that Ambient Light acts like a brightness or gamma control, bumping

up the brightness of all scene objects. This light can be useful during the *development* of a scene, allowing us to test and explore it prior to adding our own lights. But when the time arrives for us to light the scene manually, then it's usually convenient to disable Ambient Light completely so it does not affect our manual lighting. To access the Ambient Light settings choose *Edit > Render Settings* from the application menu.

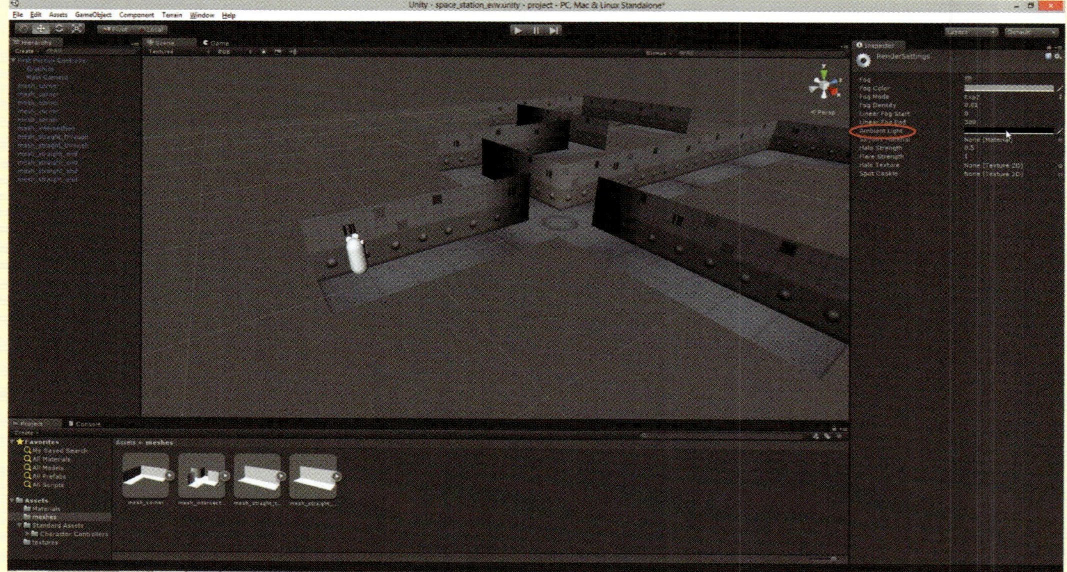

Figure 5.4 Controlling Ambient Light through the Render settings

2. The *Render Settings* menu, shown in the Object Inspector, displays a range of global settings affecting the render system for a scene. The Ambient Light for the renderer is controlled by the *Ambient Light* colour picker box. This controls the colour and intensity of the Ambient Light by way of RGB values – the *hue* controls the light colour and the *value* controls the light intensity. Set the light colour to black RGB (0, 0, 0) to deactivate Ambient Light completely. Now press the *Play* button from the application toolbar to play the scene, noticing that the scene is now entirely black. Note: the scene appears black not because the Ambient Light is black but because Ambient Light is disabled *and* there are no other lights in the scene.

5.3 Lighting the Space Station – Adding Point Lights

The process of disabling Ambient Light for the renderer does, in many ways, represent the 'tabula rasa' or starting point for creating customised lighting for a scene. The scene is now completely black and whatever visibility emerges will be the result of lights that we add and not by lights that are there by default. Unity offers a range of different light types or light primitives, which we can add to a scene as game objects and use creatively in order to simulate real-world light and its effects. What matters most for the purposes of creating our scene is not whether the lights we add truly resemble or behave as real-world lights, but only whether they produce the kind of real-world *effects* that real-world lights would if they were in our scene. When working on the lighting for our scene we can follow the simple maxim: if it *looks* correct, then it *is* correct. Consider the following steps.

Figure 5.5 Point Light positioned in the scene to simulate a ceiling light

1. Let's start by adding a *Point Light* to the scene. This light is computationally the cheapest light after the *Directional Light*. It can be used to simulate light bulbs, candles, magical glitters and other artificial light sources where light begins at an infinitesimally small point and radiates outwards in all directions for a specified radius. Mathematically, it represents a ball of light. A Point Light will be used here to simulate artificial light from ceiling or wall lights in the corridor. To create a Point Light, select *Game Object > Create Other > Point Light* from the application main menu. Alternatively, you can select *Create > Point Light* from the Scene hierarchy panel. Whichever method you choose, it will create a Point Light game object in the scene, although initially it will probably not position itself where you want it to be. Consequently, use the Translate tool to position the light source in the corridor to simulate either a wall or a ceiling light. See Figure 5.5.
2. Select Point Light in the scene viewport, if it's not already selected, and notice the spherical-shaped gizmo surrounding the light source centre representing the range of the light. If you don't see the gizmo, then make sure: 1) you're viewing the scene in the *Scene* tab and not the *Game* Tab; 2) your viewport camera is zoomed out and away from the light source far enough to see the spherical gizmo; and 3) you have Gizmo Viewing enabled for the viewport. You can enable Gizmo Viewing by clicking the *Gizmo* button at the top-right side of the scene tab to show a context menu. From there, ensure the option *Light* is enabled.
3. With the Point Light selected and its spherical range gizmo in view, use the mouse to grab the sphere handles and drag them to grow or shrink the spherical range of the light, controlling how far the

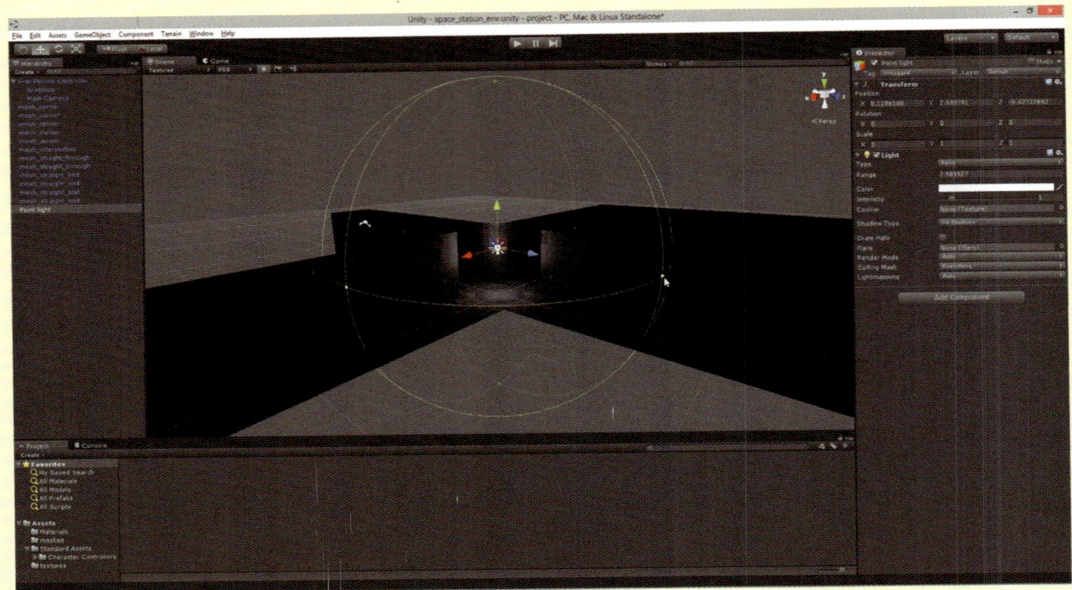

Figure 5.6 Point Light position, range and colour are specified to convey atmosphere. This light will be duplicated regularly throughout the scene to provide illumination

light's illumination extends. Adjust the range of the light to mimic a believable ceiling or wall light. You can also control the range parametrically from the Object Inspector by entering a numerical value into the Range field, or interactively by clicking and dragging the mouse while hovering over the Range field title. Examine Figure 5.6 to see how I've set the light for the scene. I've also given the light a subtle blue tint using the *Color* field from the Object Inspector, to convey a cold and sinister mood. You can also use the *Intensity* slider to control the brightness of the light, if required. Notice, however, that any areas of the scene beyond the range of the light are *completely black,* even if the light has an otherwise clear path to that location. This is certainly not how real-world lights behave. More on this important subject shortly.

4. One light has now been created. Go ahead and illuminate the rest of the scene using light duplication (*Ctrl+D*). You *could* instead create a new light and set its properties each time, but introducing new lights into the scene on the basis of the original light is quicker. Move the duplicates into place, leaving enough space between each light to distribute the light believably throughout the scene, trying to keep in mind the position of the light sources – whether ceiling or wall lights. Actively seek to minimise the number of lights overlapping where possible, as this can lead to performance improvements. Take a look at 5.7 to see the duplicated light arrangement I created.
5. Select all the lights at the intersection sections of the corridor and change their colour to red to simulate an emergency light and enhance the tension of the scene. Now select a light near one of the corner sections and change its *Shadow Type* property from *No Shadows* to *Hard Shadows*. On doing this you'll probably see an error message appear beneath that reads: "*Only Directional Lights have shadows in Forward Rendering*". This message appears because, by default, Unity uses the *Forward Renderer*. Renderer refers to an internal component of Unity responsible for drawing graphics to the screen. Unity 4 ships with three renderers, namely: *Vertex Lit*, *Forward* and *Deferred*. The specifics and details of Vertex Lit vs. Forward vs. Deferred Rendering are beyond the scope of this introductory

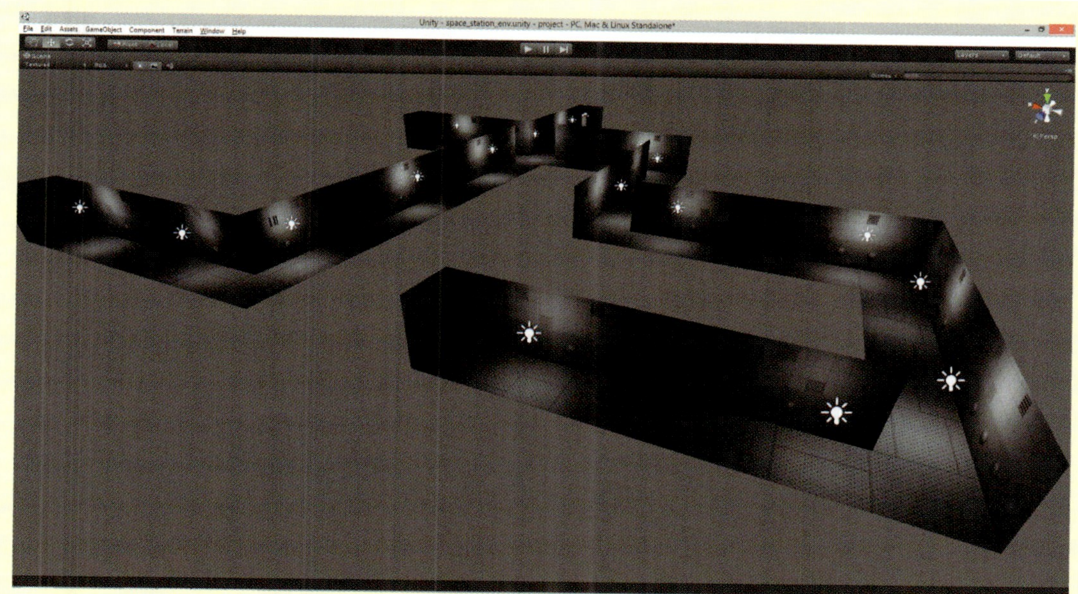

Figure 5.7 Space station corridors with Point Lights added throughout for illumination

book. But to summarise: Vertex-Lit and Forward rendering are typically used when developing games for mobile devices and legacy hardware, or when your game needs to run on a wide range of systems, including legacy hardware such as old PCs and previous-generation consoles. If, however, your aim is to create an 'AAA grade' title with the 'best' in graphical effects that Unity has to offer, then

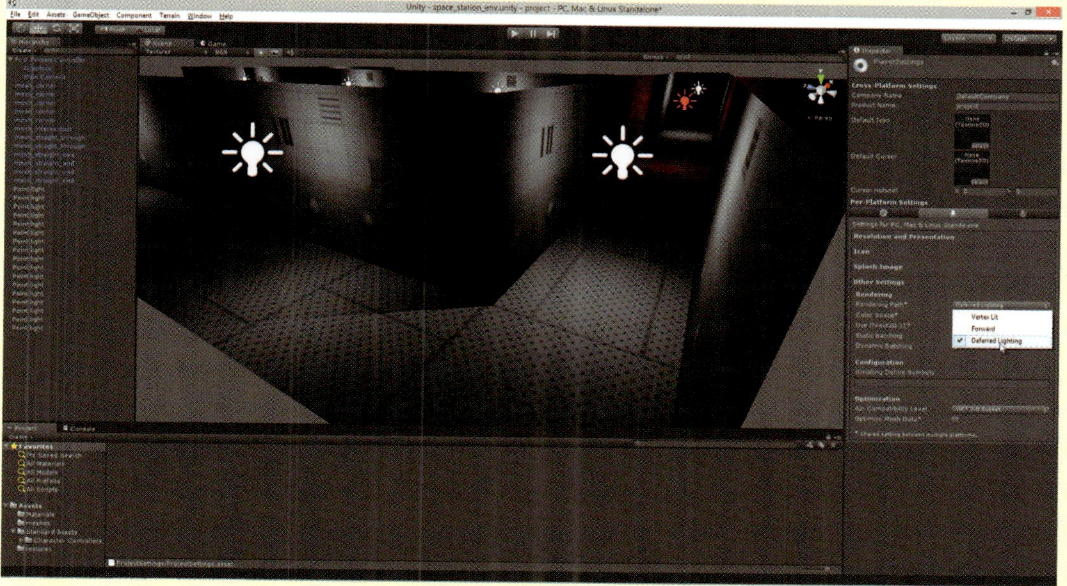

Figure 5.8 Hard Shadows created from Point Lights in real-time using the Deferred Lighting path. Notice the hard shadow cast by the wall on the floor

a Deferred Renderer should be selected. Using a Deferred Renderer will allow the Point Lights to cast shadows. To switch from the Forward Renderer to the Deferred Renderer, select *Edit > Project Settings > Player* from the application main menu. Then, from the Object Inspector, select *Deferred Lighting* from the list for the *Rendering Path* field.

NOTE: The Deferred Renderer is available only in the professional version of Unity and not in the free version. If you're using the free version, you can skip to the next section and still continue with the project.

5.4 Dynamic Lighting vs. Static Lighting

The lights created for the scene so far are 'dynamic' lights, as opposed to 'static' lights: the scene so far is illuminated by dynamic lighting only. This means the lighting and its effects, including shadows, are calculated in *real time* on a frame-by-frame basis, for each light, *as the game is running*. This method of lighting ensures shadows and illumination will continually update to reflect changes in the level, especially for moving objects. The trade-off, however, is that it is both computationally expensive and lacks a whole range of real-world lighting properties, such as indirect illumination, which would typically be too expensive to calculate in real time. For our purposes and for convenience, lighting in the real world can be conceived of in terms of rays – namely, *rays of light*. Rays are emitted from a light source, such as the sun or a bulb, and they travel in straight lines until they strike surrounding surfaces. The rays bounce from those surfaces and continue to travel until they eventually enter the eye of an observer, where they are 'decoded' by the brain to produce the sensation of sight and vision. Light that travels directly from a light source to a nearby surface before being seen is called **direct illumination**: anything that is directly exposed to a light source is said to be lit by direct illumination. However, the light that bounces will also strike and illuminate surfaces, albeit with less intensity, and this bouncing/illuminating continues with each object it hits. This explains why, in the real world, even surfaces not directly in the path of a light source can still be seen. For example, walk into your bedroom, open the curtains or turn on the light if you have a ceiling light, and then take a look under the bed. Notice you can see the floor underneath the bed even though the ceiling light or the sun light is not directly shining on it. This is because rays from the light source have previously bounced from other surfaces before finally reaching the floor under the bed. Because the underside of the bed is less exposed to the light source than other parts of the room, fewer rays actually find their way there, which accounts for why the floor – though it can be seen – appears darker. The floor under the bed is said to be illuminated by **indirect illumination** – that is, it is illuminated by light that has previously bounced from other surfaces, rather than by light that has travelled directly from a light source. Direct and indirect illumination are the two main forms of lighting in the real world, but only the former can be achieved using dynamic lights in Unity. For this reason, areas beyond the range of all Point Lights will appear completely black, because no indirect bounces are calculated to illuminate those areas. The result is that scene lighting looks more artificial than it might, given Unity's complete range of lighting tools. We can improve the lighting for the scene by making some adjustments. Specifically, we can use Unity's **static lighting** and **lightmapping** to create indirect illumination. The next section considers how this is achieved.

5.5 Static Lighting with Lightmapping

To improve the realism and atmosphere of the scene lighting we need to achieve something called **Global Illumination**. Specifically, we need to add: A) softer and more believable shadows, B) indirect illumination for areas of the scene not directly exposed to light sources, and C) **Ambient Occlusion** to add thin shadows to corners of the corridor and areas where two surfaces, such as the wall and floor, come into contact. Ambient Occlusion adds a certain embedded quality to objects in the level, as we'll see. The demands of these effects on processing resources make them generally prohibitive for real-time renderers on most consumer hardware. For this reason, they cannot be achieved using dynamic lighting. They can, however, be achieved through static lighting. Static lighting is created in Unity through the **Beast Lightmapper**, an internal system used for a process called lightmapping. Lightmapping is the process of calculating the lighting for a scene *once* using the Unity editor at development time, then saving the lighting information in the form of textures (lightmaps), and finally blending those textures onto the surfaces of objects, at run time, to make the objects *appear* to be affected by lights in the scene in real time. The job of the Beast Lightmapper then is to perform all the expensive lighting calculations for the scene, including those for Indirect Illumination and Ambient Occlusion, and to render that lighting into the textures for the game. Its job is to *pre-calculate* scene lighting. Consider the following steps for working with lightmapping.

1. Open the Lightmapping window by selecting *Window > Lightmapping* from the application menu. By default the Lightmapping settings appear in a free-floating window, but I typically prefer to dock the window into the Object Inspector panel as a separate tab. To do that, click and drag the Lightmapping window title tab into the Object Inspector, and the window automatically docks as a separate tab. It can be returned to the free-floating window style again by a similar technique: ripping the window from the Object Inspector. When the Lightmapping window is active, you should also see a small 'Lightmap Display' diagnostic window appear at the bottom right-hand side of the Scene viewport. Note that the Lightmapping window has three main panels or tabs: *Object*, *Bake*, and *Maps*. When the *Object* Tab is selected, the Lightmapping window is context-sensitive, meaning its contents will change depending on the object selected in the scene.
2. The purpose of the Lightmapper is to output a set of Lightmap textures encoding the Global Illumination for the scene. These textures can be produced whenever we click on the *Bake Scene* button at the bottom of the Lightmapping window. When this button is pressed, the lightmapper will generate the textures across several stages of processing: first, it calculates the lighting on the basis of lights in the scene and the position of objects, as well as their materials. Then it outputs the result into Lightmap textures, and finally it configures and automatically applies the textures to objects in the scene, making

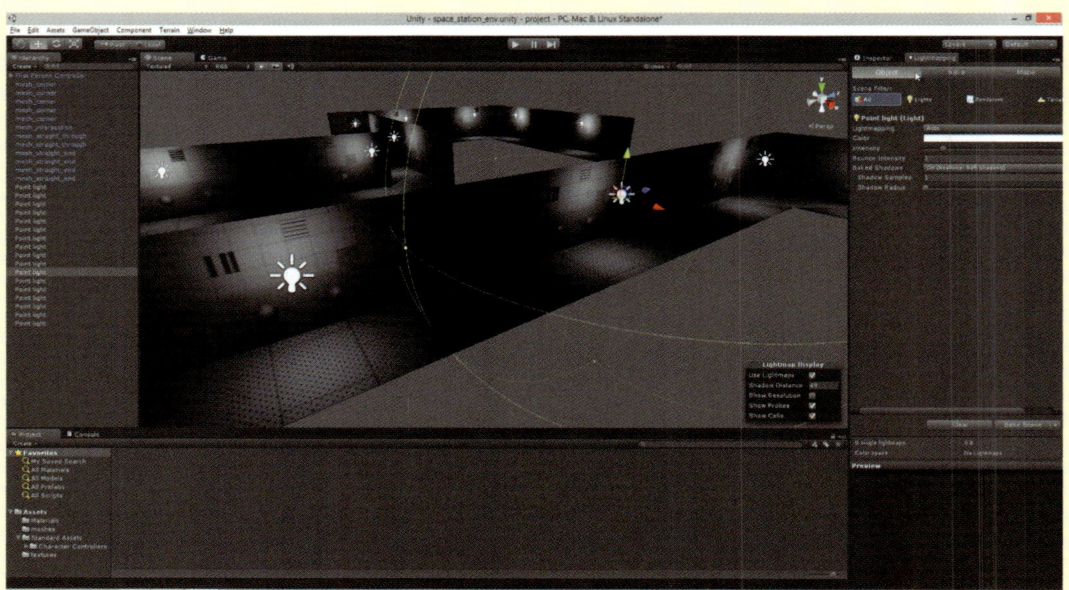

Figure 5.9 The Lightmapping window is docked into the Object Inspector. It features three main tabs: *Object*, *Bake* and *Maps*. Together these can be used to pre-bake Global Illumination (GI) for the scene

them appear illuminated by the lights. To get started, click the *Bake Scene* button. An error message appears saying: 'Nothing to Bake'. This error appears because only GameObjects explicitly marked as *Static* can factor into the lightmapping calculations. See the next step for further details.

Figure 5.10 Lightmapping will produce messy and unpredictable results when meshes do not have appropriate lightmap UVs. Notice the nonsensical diagonal-shaped shadows along the walls

3. Because lightmapping is about *pre-calculating* lighting, lightmaps can only be calculated for objects that do not move or change in the scene at run time. In short, lightmapping can only be calculated for **static** and unchanging objects, such as architectural elements like walls, floors, ceilings, statues, tables, chairs, lampposts, trees, rocks and so on. It cannot be calculated for **dynamic** objects such as enemies, the player character, flags rustling in the wind, moving machinery and the like. To calculate or approximate Global Illumination for dynamic objects, we must use the feature **Light Probes**, which are beyond the scope of this book. Here we will focus on calculating Global Illumination for the architecture of the scene, which is static. To mark all of the scene meshes as static, select all corridor sections in the scene using the *Scene hierarchy*, and enable the check box *Static* in the Object Inspector. All static and non-moving objects in the scene should be marked with the *Static* flag. Do not mark moving objects as Static.

NOTE: UVs are mathematical instructions that define how a texture wraps around the surface of a 3D model.

4. Now return to the Lightmapping window and open the *Bake* tab. Ensure *Single Lightmaps* is selected in the *Mode* drop-down list (more on this later). Then click the *Bake Scene* button, using the default settings. On clicking this, lighting will be calculated and rendered to Lightmaps. The progress of lightmapping is visible from a progress metre shown at the bottom right-hand side of the editor in the status bar. Note: Lightmapping is an expensive process and can take from minutes to hours – *or even days* – depending on the size of the scene, number of objects, number of lights, and the developer hardware. Some settings in the *Bake* tab can be adjusted to improve lightmapping speed and detail, as we'll see. Once our initial lightmap has completed, the generated maps can be previewed in the *Preview Pane*, at the bottom of the Lightmapping Window. The lightmaps will also have been applied as textures to the objects in the scene. The results in the viewport will probably not look good at all – see Figure 5.10. Shadows will be messy, appear in the wrong place as a jumbled mess – and overall the lighting will not seem to make much sense to a rational mind. I've purposefully missed an important step because I want to show you what kinds of effects lightmapping produces when that step is missed out, to help you identify this problem if it occurs in your own projects and help you see how it can be solved. See the next step.
5. The problem with the lightmapping of the current scene is that none of the meshes have lightmap UVs. The meshes *do* feature *standard texture coordinates* in the form of UVs so the appropriate parts of their diffuse texture are mapped to the correct places on the meshes themselves – the walls are mapped with the wall pixels from the diffuse texture, and the floor with the floor pixels, etc. However, lightmapping expects each static mesh to have its own unique lightmapping UVs. It uses these both to unwrap and project the results of lighting from the meshes onto a Lightmap texture, and to apply the Lightmap texture back onto the mesh at run time. If the mesh lacks suitable lightmap UVs, then lightmapping is not guaranteed to look correct for that mesh. To fix this issue and ensure each of the four-mesh corridor sections have suitable lightmap UVs, select all four meshes in the Project panel. In the Object Inspector, enable the *Generate Lightmap UVs* check box, and then click the *Apply* button. The meshes are now given lightmap UVs, but the lightmapping for the scene must be baked again in order to look correct. So return to the Lightmapping window and click *Bake Scene* to regenerate it.

5.6 Lightmapping – Controlling Lightmap Resolution

The lightmapped scene is looking much better now that each mesh has appropriate lightmap UVs. The scene might still not look dramatically different from how it appeared before, but there is a critical difference: the lighting is pre-baked and not calculated in real time. This offers a considerable performance benefit. To prove the lighting is truly baked, try the following. Select all lights in the scene using the Scene hierarchy, and then use the Translate tool to move them up and out of the scene. You'll notice that, as you do this, the scene lighting doesn't change at all: the shadows and highlights remain just as they are on the walls, ceiling and floor. This is because the illumination is now baked into their texture through the lightmaps and is not coming from the lights. You could, in theory as well as in practice, even delete the lights without affecting the illumination of the scene. This is not recommended, however, because the lights will still be needed to illuminate dynamic objects, and will also be needed by the lightmapper in the future to regenerate lightmaps. The presence of lights in the scene after lightmapping does not cause a performance hit for lightmapped objects because Unity is smart enough to distinguish between lightmapped and non-lightmapped objects. Try moving the corridor sections and see how the lighting travels with the meshes.

In this section I will further refine some of the lightmapping settings to generate lightmaps quicker and more simply. See the following steps.

1. If you tried moving the lights and geometry to see the effects of lightmapping as discussed above, then undo your changes now to return the scene back to its proper state, with lights and meshes in the correct positions. Let's improve the speed of lightmapping: this is achieved by reducing lightmapping quality – but doing that can help us to preview the results of lightmapping more easily before creating a final, higher-quality lightmap. Take a look at the Lightmap settings that appear above the preview pane of the Lightmap window (mine read *12 single lightmaps 12x1024x1024px 16.0MB*, though yours may be different). These settings indicate the number and size of each lightmap currently being applied to the scene. In this case,12 Lightmap textures were generated and each image was 1024x1024 pixels (or **texels**). This means that, based on the current Lightmap settings, 12 textures had to be generated to produce enough pixels to cover the surface of all meshes. The size and number of textures generated is controlled by the **Lightmap resolution**. These textures can also be viewed and inspected from the Project panel – all lightmaps are stored inside a folder whose name matches the scene name. In my case, they appear in the folder 'space_station_env'. See Figure 5.11.
2. Switch to the Lightmapping window and select the *Bake* tab. Then enable the checkbox *Show Resolution* in the *Lightmap Display* diagnostic window, in the bottom right-hand side of the Scene viewport. Enabling this might appear to have no effect at first sight, if your Scene camera is zoomed away from the Scene geometry. But zooming in closer to the meshes will make it clear that a chequer pattern has now been tiled over the surfaces of all static meshes in the scene. The chequer pattern can be toggled using the *Show Resolution* checkbox. The pattern illustrates the *Texel density* of the lightmap; that is, the density of the Lightmap texture that would be generated if lightmapping

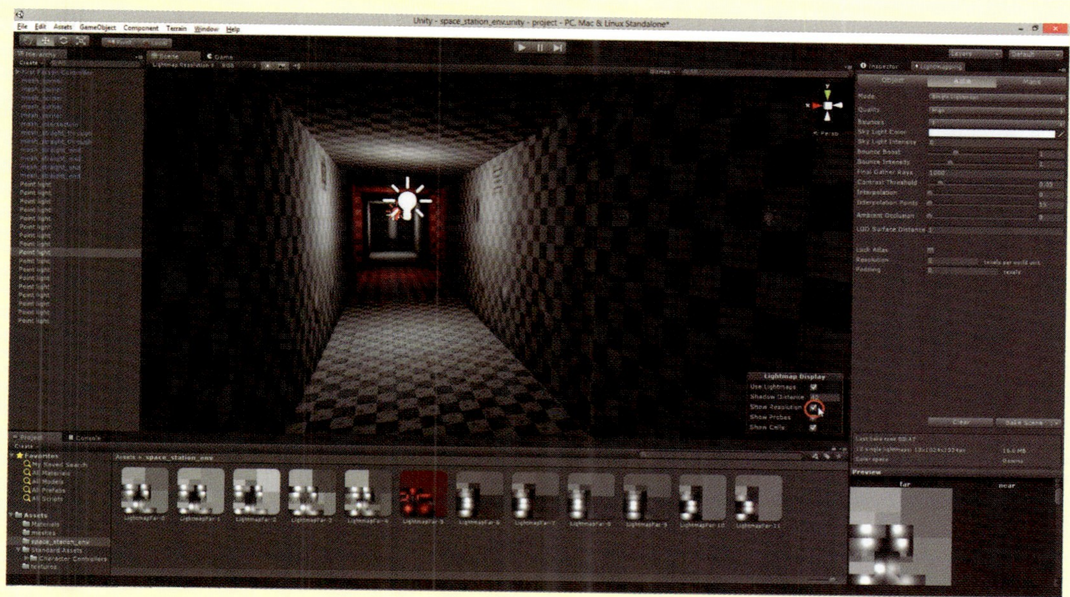

Figure 5.11 Previewing the Lightmap resolution of the scene

was baked now with the current settings. You can adjust the size of the chequer pattern by editing the *Resolution* setting from the *Bake* tab of the Lightmapping window. Change this setting from its default of *50* to *5*.

3. Decreasing the *Resolution* setting on the Bake tab *reduces* the texel density of the lightmap, and increases the size of the chequer pattern. Each square of the pattern represents 1 pixel in the lightmaps. Thus, by reducing the *Resolution*, you effectively reduce the number of texels (texture pixels) that will be needed in the lightmaps to cover the surfaces of the level. Thus, *Resolution* directly influences both the size of the generated lightmaps and their number. Click the *Bake Scene* button now with the *Resolution* set to *5* and see the difference in quality and size of the lightmaps generated. You should see a significant decrease in the calculation time for lightmapping, and perhaps little appreciable difference in the quality of the Lightmap textures themselves. Feel free to tweak and adjust the *Resolution* setting until you find a value that works well for your level.

5.7 Lightmapping – Indirect Illumination and Ambient Occlusion

Both Indirect Illumination and Ambient Occlusion have the *potential* to increase the realism and atmosphere of scenes. Indirect Illumination is especially important for adding brightness to regions beyond the direct influence of lights to simulate bounced light. Ambient Occlusion can add **Contact Shadows** to regions where two meshes meet, to add a certain 'embeddedness' and volume to the scene. The following steps improve the existing Indirect Illumination settings and add Ambient Occlusion to the scene.

NOTE: Both Indirect Illumination and Ambient Occlusion are only available in the professional version of Unity. Users of the free version should skip to the next section.

1. Let's begin with Ambient Occlusion. When two objects come into contact – for example, when a coffee mug rests on a tabletop – a small crevice usually forms between the objects. In the case of the mug and the table this is because neither of them is perfectly flat. The crevice formed at their meeting point is typically more inaccessible to light than surrounding regions because it is less exposed to the light source. Thus, the occluded space becomes darker. This effect is called Ambient Occlusion. For our level it will add a soft darkening where the walls meet the floor and where the walls meet the ceiling. To add Ambient Occlusion to the scene, start by selecting the *Bake* tab of the Lightmapping window, and change the *Ambient Occlusion* slider from *0* to *1*. This slider acts as an Opacity setting for the Ambient Occlusion effect: at 0 the effect is not visible, and at 1 the effect is fully active.
2. Once the *Ambient Occlusion* slider is set to *1*, two additional options come into view beneath. These are *Max Distance* and *Contrast*. In practice, *Max Distance* controls the size or thickness of the Ambient Occlusion shadow formed, with larger values producing thicker and wider shadows. The *Contrast* value controls the softening or blurring of the shadow – that is, the sharpness or contrast of the

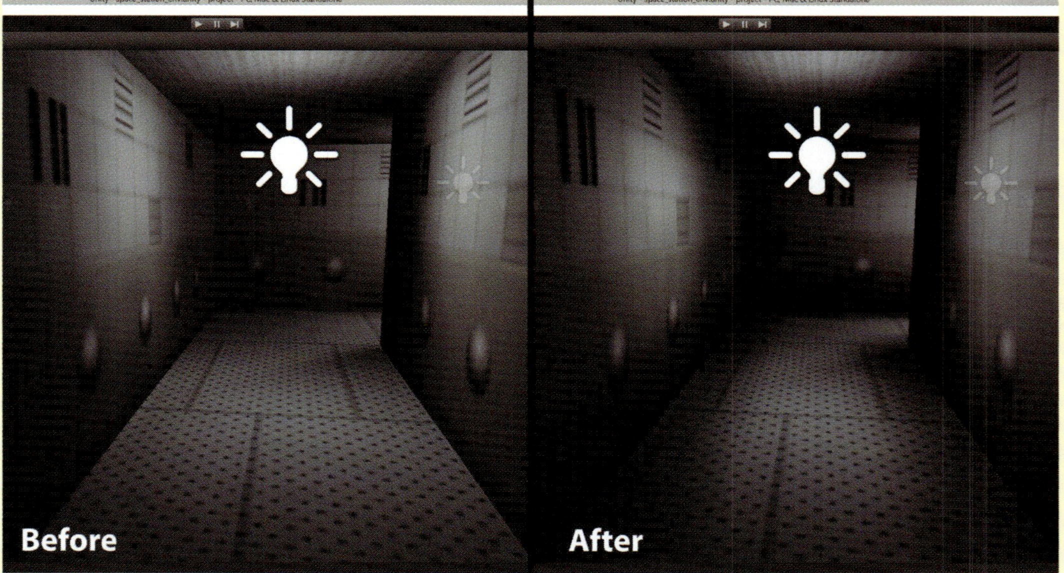

Figure 5.12 Before and after Ambient Occlusion

shadow edge. Lower values produce sharper shadow edges and thus greater contrast. I have set *Max Distance* to *0.94*, and *Contrast* to *0.39*. Take a look at Figure 5.12 to compare the before and after effects of the scene. Remember, the Ambient Occlusion settings will not be visible until lightmapping is re-baked by pressing the *Bake Scene* button.

3. The scene could benefit from some general brightening from Indirect Illumination. The Indirect Illumination settings are represented primarily by the *Bounces*, *Skylight*, *Color*, *Skylight Intensity*, *Bounce Boost* and *Bounce Intensity* settings, all available from the *Bake* tab of the Lightmapping window. The *Bounces* setting refers to the total number of times any single light ray may bounce from a surface after being 'emitted' from a light source. In the 'real world' the total number of bounces is potentially infinite, though not necessarily infinite in practice. A value of 0 for this setting disables Indirect Illumination entirely since no bounces are permitted, and any value above 1 typically increases lightmap calculation time considerably. For this project, and for most projects, a value of 1 is acceptable; a value of 2 can sometimes offer significant benefits for outdoor scenes, but – alas – I have hardly ever seen 3 or 4 bounces produce appreciable improvements. But whether or not the extra calculation time for a *Bounces* value above 1 is really worth the benefit to the scene is largely a judgement call for the developer and their specific project, as opposed to a matter of right and wrong. Remember, if it *looks* correct then it *is* correct, no matter which value you use.
4. The Skylight Color and Skylight Intensity values are typically used for outdoor scenes, though not always because some indoor environments make use of a lot of natural light. Together these settings specify a subtle and all-pervasive indirect illumination that originates from sunlight but which has bounced many times and inherited much of the colour of the surrounding environment. Skylight Color controls the colour of the light and Intensity the strength. I have left these values at their defaults for this project. It *could* be disabled since this is an indoor scene of a space station and one which has no windows, but I am satisfied with the results it is producing.
5. The *Bounce Boost* and *Bounce Intensity* settings *will* be changed for our scene, however, to strengthen the Indirect Illumination and thereby brighten the scene. These settings can effectively be used to

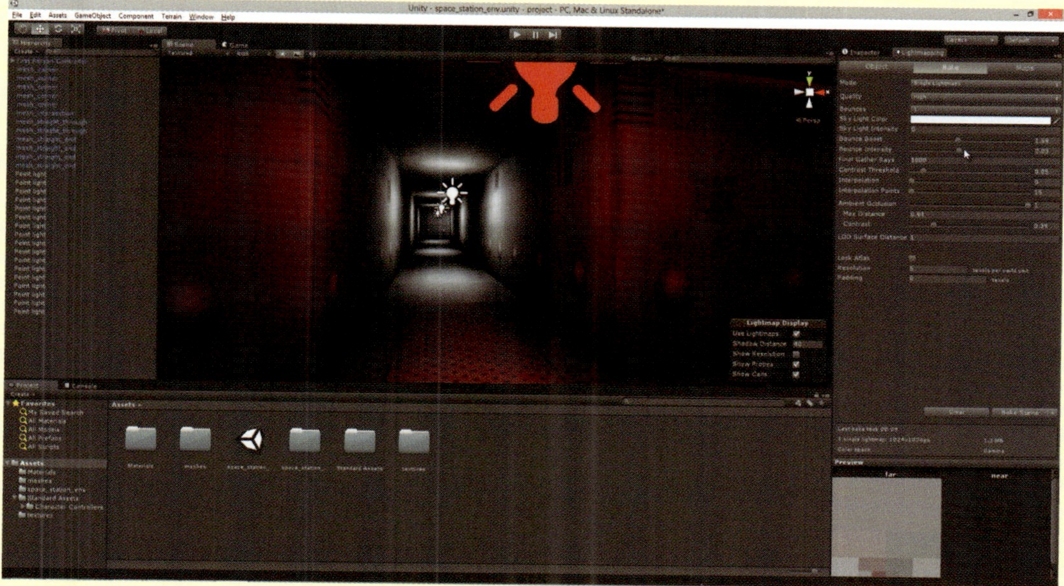

Figure 5.13 Indirect Illumination has been used to brighten the scene

simulate extra bounces from Indirect Illumination *without* incurring heavy penalties when rendering the Lightmaps, as might be incurred by increasing the *Bounces* value. Sometimes these settings can be tweaked to achieve Lightmap results that are almost indistinguishable from the results produced by an increase in the *Bounces* value. The *Bounce Boost* setting simulates an increase in the number of light bounces, and the *Bounce Intensity* setting strengthens the brightness of the bounced light. For this project, I have set *Bounce Boost* to *1.59*, and *Bounce Intensity* to *2.03*. The result can be seen in Figure 5.13.

NOTE: To remove lightmapping from a scene completely, deleting all Lightmap textures without generating new textures, click the *Clear* button at the bottom of the Lightmapping window.

5.8 Lightmapping – Dual Lightmaps

Imagine now that we wanted to add a flickering or flashing light somewhere along the corridor, to add an extra degree of creepiness. We'll not actually do that in this chapter since its implementation would lead us away from the subject of lighting, but we can imagine it all the same. Adding a light like this would create an *animated* light effect – the light would flicker on and off either randomly or at specified intervals, creating *illumination* one moment and then leaving us with *darkness* the next. This kind of effect would, however, be problematic for us to create with our level lightmapped as it is currently because, as we've seen, the scene lighting is *hard-baked* into the geometry *by way of its textures*. The result is that even if all lights in the scene were deleted to remove their illumination, the lighting effects would remain unchanged because the Lightmap textures remain in place. The same would also hold true for a flickering light; its 'off' state would really have no appreciable effect on scene lighting. This problem arises because we are using *Single Lightmaps*, a setting specified through the *Mode* field of the Lightmapping window – via the *Bake* tab. This field can accept two other values, namely: **Dual lightmaps** and **Directional lightmaps**. Dual lightmaps are designed to solve exactly the kind of problem we've been considering here with flickering lights, as well as others. In contrast, Directional lightmaps are essentially a method of baking Normal mapping effects into lightmaps. The subject of Directional lightmaps is beyond the scope of this book and we shall here consider only Dual lightmaps. Consider the following steps to convert our scene from 'Single Lightmaps' to 'Dual Lightmaps'.

NOTE: To use Dual lightmapping, you must be using Deferred lighting for the Rendering path. See Section 5.3 for further details.

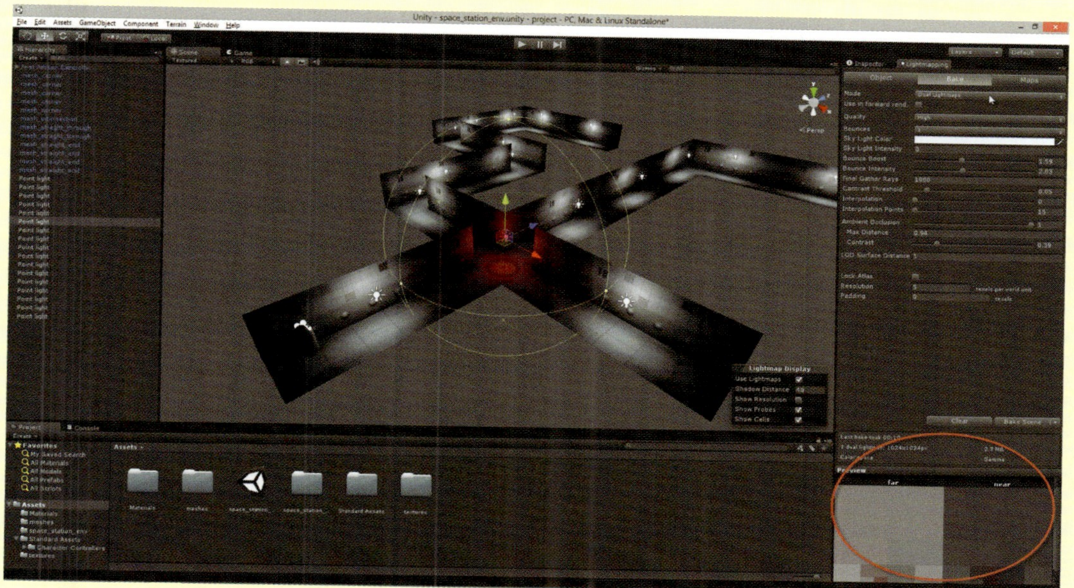

Figure 5.14 Generating Dual lightmaps

1. Open the Lightmapping window in the Object Inspector, and select the *Bake* tab. From the *Mode* drop-down list, select the option *Dual Lightmaps*. Once selected, re-bake the lightmapping for the scene by clicking the button *Bake Scene* at the bottom of the Lightmapping window. The lightmapping for the scene is now baked, and this time two sets of lightmaps have been generated as opposed to one set, as can be seen from the Lightmapping Preview pane. These sets are labelled *Near* and *Far*. The *Single Lightmaps* mode generates only the *Far* set of lightmaps. See Figure 5.14. You will notice that the *Near* lightmaps are darker than the *Far* lightmaps.
2. Now that Dual lightmaps have been generated, let's try an experiment: first, centre the viewport camera on the central corridor section of the level. Select the mesh object in the scene and press *F* on the keyboard to frame the camera on the mesh. This corridor section should also have a Point Light very close by. For me, the centre mesh (or as close to centre as is meaningful) is an intersection section with a red emergency light, as can be seen in Figure 5.14. The main reason for doing this is so that you can use the mouse scroll wheel to easily dolly the camera forwards and backwards, moving closer and further from your target. This will be useful for our experiment.
3. Now select the Point Light for the section and raise it up and away from the meshes, or delete it from the scene entirely; make sure that, whatever you do, the light can no longer affect the meshes in real time (we will be undoing this step later). Then use your mouse scroll wheel to slowly zoom the viewport camera in and out from your target mesh: zoom a long distance away and then zoom in close; zoom away again and then zoom in close again. You should notice that, as you move away beyond a certain horizon or point, the mesh appears fully illuminated, just as it did with *Single Lightmaps*. But, as you zoom closer, the mesh appears less illuminated, though probably not entirely black. See Figure 5.15.
4. So what is happening here? In short, Dual lightmapping generates two sets of lightmaps, *Near* and *Far*. The distance between any object and the viewport camera determines which set of lightmaps is applied to the object at run time. The Far Lightmap textures are applied to all static objects when the linear *distance between* the objects and the camera is *greater* than the *Shadow Distance* setting,

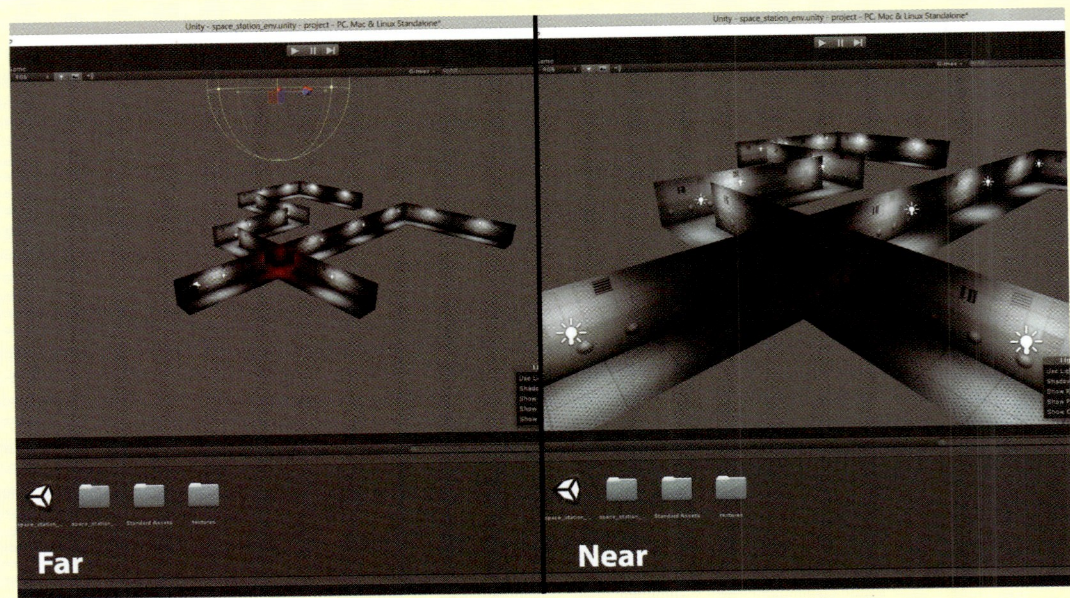

Figure 5.15 Transitioning between Near and Far lightmaps with Dual lightmapping and the Shadow Distance setting

which can be found on the *Lightmap Display* diagnostic window. Shadow Distance is measured in Unity Units – which typically equates to metres. When the distance between the camera and the target is less than the *Shadow Distance*, then the target is assigned the Near lightmap. This accounts for there being a change in the appearance of the object as the viewport camera moves. Specifically, the change in appearance is due to a change in the lightmaps being applied and there currently being no real-time light affecting the target mesh. But what is the difference between the Near and Far lightmaps? The difference is this: Far lightmaps encode all scene-lighting information featured with Single Lightmaps. The Near lightmap, in contrast, encodes *Indirect Illumination* and *Ambient Occlusion* but not direct illumination – that is, not illumination from nearby light sources. With Dual lightmapping, direct illumination is supposed to be provided by scene lights in real time. In our case, there is no real-time light present near the mesh since we moved or deleted it in Step 3. So let's undo that step and return the light to its original position in relation to the mesh. Now zoom the viewport camera in and out of the Shadow Distance again, as before, and see now that there is no difference in the appearance of the mesh, even though 'under the hood' the lightmaps assigned to the mesh still continue to change according to the Shadow Distance.

5. The upshot of Dual lightmapping, and its general intention, is that we get 'the best of both worlds' regarding static and real-time lighting. The illumination of objects distant from the camera (that is, objects beyond the Shadow Distance) receive their lighting entirely from inexpensive, pre-baked textures in the form of the Far lightmap, including their (various forms of) direct illumination, Indirect Illumination, Ambient Occlusion and shadows. Static objects within the Shadow Distance (objects close to the camera), however, continue to receive their Indirect Illumination and Ambient Occlusion from the Near lightmap, just as distant objects receive theirs from the Far lightmap, but they also receive real-time direct illumination and shadows from nearby lights. This means that nearby objects can now be affected by real-time changes in lights (such as flicker effects, shadows and colouration) while still receiving pre-baked Global Illumination from lightmaps. Of course, the benefits of Dual lightmapping are not restricted to the creation of flickering lights; they apply all real-time lighting

effects: moving lights, throbbing lights, real-time shadows, normal mapping, specular highlights and more. Before proceeding to the next step, play around a little with the scene lights and Shadow Distance settings to explore the implications of Dual lightmapping further.

5.9 Exclusion, Culling Masks and Self-Illumination

We could now call the space station project completed if we wanted to. But there's one additional problem I would like to describe to show you how it can be overcome, and in so doing we'll see still more lighting features of Unity at work. Let's imagine that a level designer approaches us after reviewing our level and says, 'It looks good, but I want one of the intersection pieces of the corridor to be totally immune from lighting. I don't want it to appear completely black in the way most objects would when not affected by light. Instead, I want it to appear at *full brightness*, minus all the effects of lighting, such as shadows, darkening, indirect illumination, lightmapping, ambient occlusion, etc'. In short, the level designer wants us to render the intersection piece in 'old-school 3D', as though the scene were devoid of lighting except for a bright white ambient light. How can this be achieved without affecting the lighting of the remaining mesh sections? The following steps demonstrate how, using the features of *Exclusion*, *Culling Masks* and *Self-Illumination*.

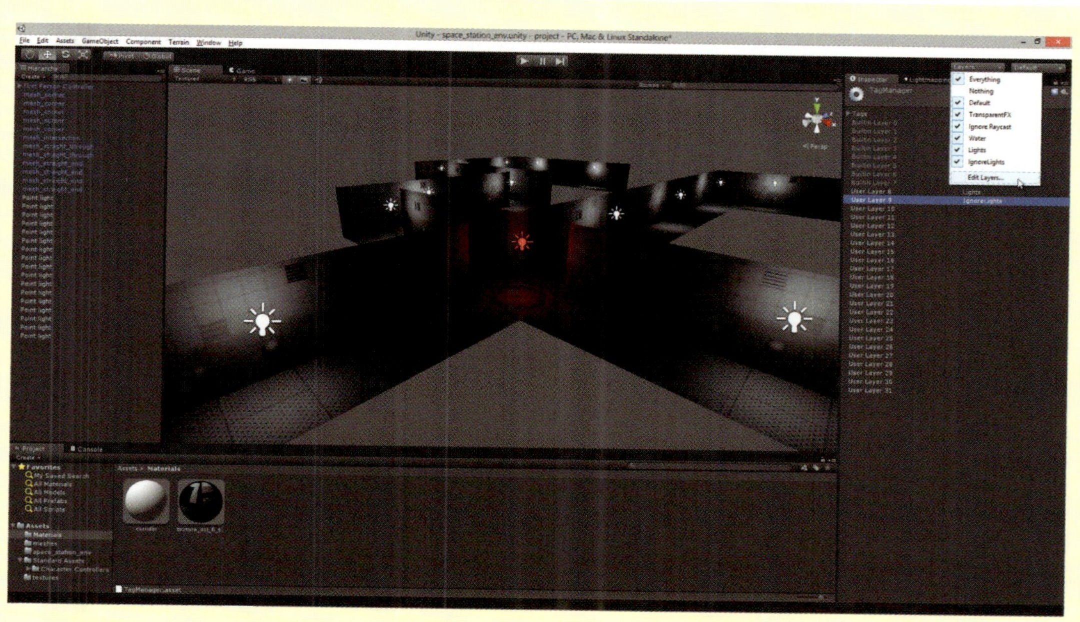

Figure 5.16 Creating a lighting exclusion layer

1. First, let's exclude the selected intersection mesh from all lighting calculations in the scene. Start by clearing the lightmaps for the scene. To do this, open the Lightmapping window and press the *Clear* button. The Lightmaps are now cleared from all scene objects. Then create a new layer for the scene. This layer will be used to contain all scene objects excluded from lighting calculations – more information on layers was featured in Chapter 3. Create a new layer by clicking *Layers > Edit Layers* from the application toolbar. Then name the new layer *IgnoreLights* – this name is not essential, of course; it can be named anything you choose. See Figure 5.16 for more details on layer creation.
2. Select the intersection mesh in the scene or from the hierarchy panel and attach it to the newly created layer *IgnoreLights*. To exclude the mesh from Lightmapping, disable the *Static* check box. To exclude the mesh from dynamic lighting, select all lights in the scene using the hierarchy panel and, for the *Culling Mask* field, select the layer *IgnoreLights* – the field will then appear with the value *Mixed*. This excludes all meshes on the *IgnoreLights* layer from the effects of all lights with the specified Culling Mask. The intersection piece should now turn black since it is no longer affected by any lights in the scene. See Figure 5.17 for further details.

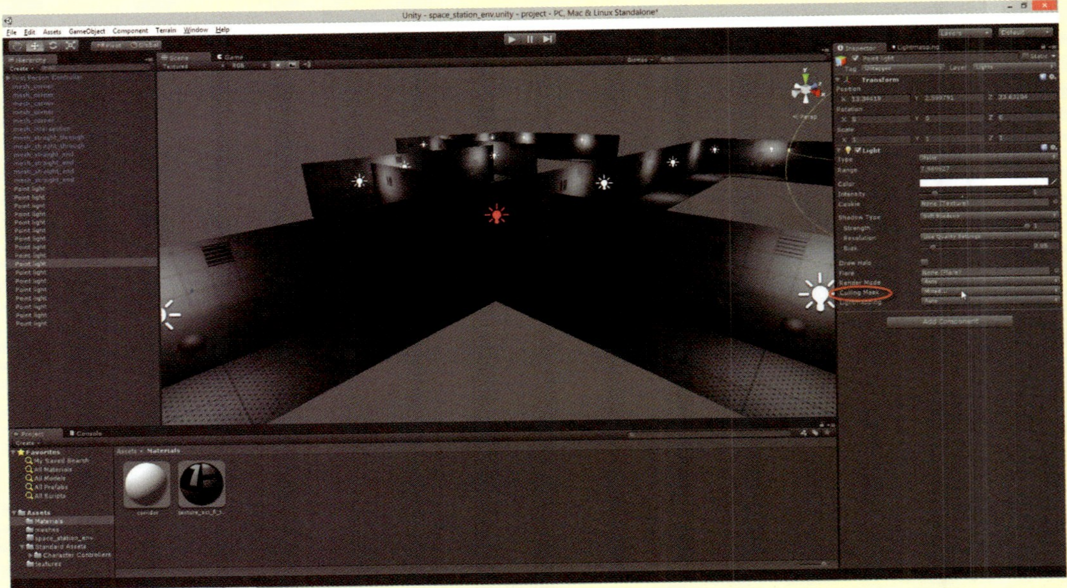

Figure 5.17 Creating a lighting exclusion layer

3. The intersection piece now appears completely black since it is excluded from illumination by the Culling Mask feature of lighting, which can exclude geometry on the basis of the associated layer. The final step is to have the intersection piece illuminate itself – that is, to display at full brightness and illuminate itself independently of scene lighting. To achieve this, a Self-Illumination material will be used. To create the Self-Illumination material from the Project panel, click *Create > Material*. With the newly created material selected in the Project panel, select *Self-Illumin/Diffuse* as the *Shader* type for the material, from the Object Inspector. Click the *Diffuse* slot and select the *texture_sci_fi_texture*. Then assign the material to the intersection mesh to complete the self-illumination process. The intersection mesh will be illuminated at full intensity, based on the brightness of the texture from the file, even though it is still unaffected by all scene lights. Now re-bake the Lightmapping and view the completed scene. See Figure 5.18.

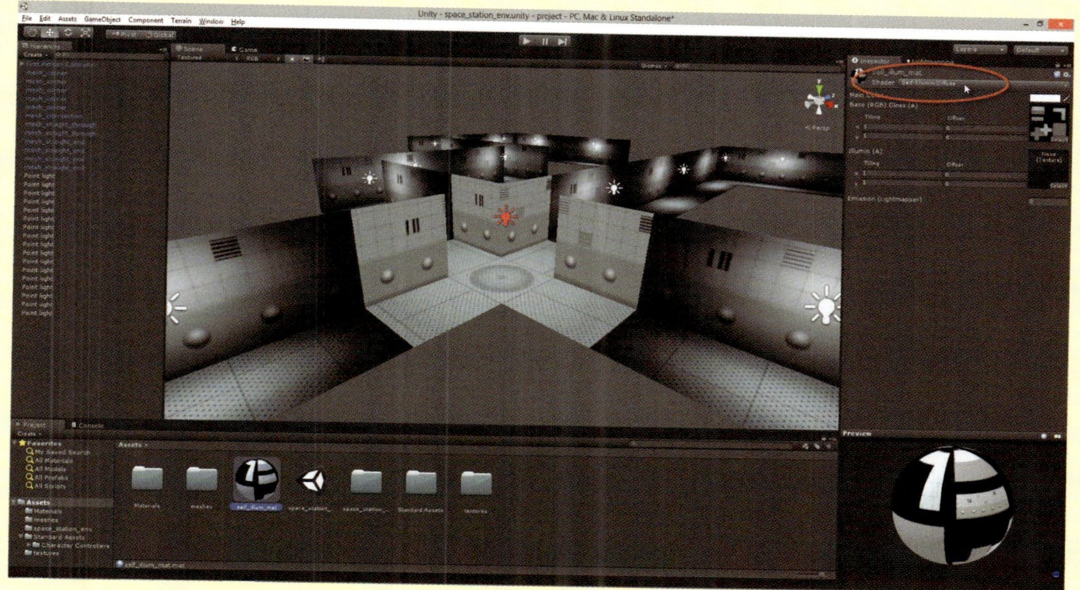

Figure 5.18 Using a Self-Illumination material

5.10 Lighting – Q&A

Lighting is one of the single most expensive ingredients involved with real-time rendering, hence the reason much of it must be delegated to static lighting in the form of pre-baked Lightmaps. Unity offers a powerful set of features for lighting scenes and increasing their realism. This chapter can at best only hope to offer a summary introduction to those features, important though they are. Rather than write another chapter focussing on further lighting details, I've attempted to address some more advanced issues or general 'gotchas' in a brief 'question and answer' (Q&A) section. Below are some answers to commonly asked questions; questions that often arise from students once they begin playing around with scene lighting and Lightmaps.

Q. Shadows do not appear in my scene and Lightmaps for all or most lights, even though the illumination and colour of those lights do. How is this fixed?

A. For shadows to feature with lights in the lightmaps, the shadow-casting ability of each and every light must be enabled *before* the Lightmap is baked. You can enable the shadow-casting ability for all lights in the scene in one operation. To do this, select all lights in the scene from the Scene hierarchy. In the Object Inspector, choose *Hard Shadows* or *Soft Shadows* from the *Shadow Type* drop-down list. You can control the strength or boldness of the shadow using the *Strength* slider, which ranges from *0* to *1* and acts much like an *Opacity* setting where 0 is transparent and 1 is full-strength. The *Resolution* setting for Shadows refers to shadow detail and smoothness, and this can significantly impact on performance for real-time shadows. By default, this value is set to *Use Quality Settings*, which means its value will be read from the Quality Settings window. This can be

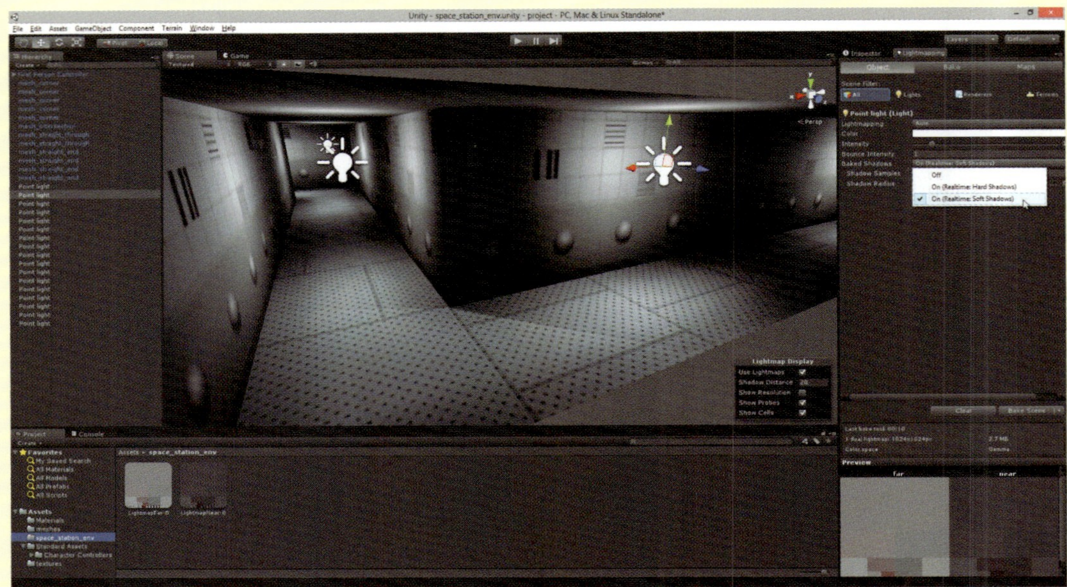

Figure 5.19 Enabling Shadow Casting for scene lights

accessed by selecting *Edit > Project > Quality* from the application main menu. Shadow resolution is read from the field *Shadow Resolution*, available in the Object Inspector. The Shadow Casting settings can also be edited and set for selected lights from the *Object* tab of the Lightmapping window. When Shadow Casting is enabled, the light will cast shadows during lightmapping, provided there is at least one surface that can *receive* shadows. Be sure to check all meshes and objects in the scene for their *Cast Shadows* and *Receive Shadows* settings in their Mesh Renderer component in the Object Inspector. If an object is to receive shadows from either dynamic or static lighting, then it must have the *Receive Shadows* setting enabled.

Q. Can I manually create Lightmap UVs for meshes, as opposed to generating them in the Unity Editor via the Mesh Asset settings?

A. Yes, and in some cases this will be preferable. The exact steps for doing this do vary according to the modelling software used to produce the mesh – whether it is 3DS Max, Maya, Blender or a different package. In short, however, it's achieved by assigning the mesh a second UV channel in the modelling software, in addition to the standard UV channel used for specifying the UVs for Diffuse textures. Please consult your software documentation for instructions on how to create the second channel. Once imported into Unity, however, ensure the mesh does *not* have *Generate Lightmap UVs* enabled from the mesh asset settings.

Q. I've heard of a Cookie Light. What is this and how does it work?

A. In Unity, 'cookies' work for lights much as Gobos do for real-world stage lighting. The Light Cookie is a greyscale texture that can be, metaphorically speaking, slotted in front of the light source to control the shape and intensity of the illumination. A noise-like texture, for example, can be used to simulate the shadow effect of clouds or leaves. Consider Figure 5.20. To configure an imported texture to act as a cookie, select *Cookie* from the *Texture Type* drop-down

Figure 5.20 Light Cookie texture configured and used to create cloud-like detail and variation in light intensity

list, available in the Texture Settings menu in the Object Inspector. Be sure to specify the type of light by which the cookie will be used in the Light Type drop-down. Typically, you will also want to enable *Alpha From Greyscale*. Figure 5.20 demonstrates the settings used for a cloud-like effect cast in a cube environment.

Q. Can I configure a light to be an exclusively real-time light or an exclusively Lightmapped light? I have one or more lights I want to exclude from Lightmapping and apply only in real time, or vice versa.

A. Yes, this can be achieved using the *Lightmapping* setting for a light, available from the Object Inspector when a light is selected in the scene. To exclude a light from lightmapping, set *Lightmapping* to *RealtimeOnly*. To exclude a light from real-time lighting, set *Lightmapping* to *BakedOnly*. This setting can also be accessed and changed for a selected light from the *Object* tab of the Lightmapping window.

Q. Each light has a *Render Mode* field, which can be one of three values: *Auto*, *Important*, *Not Important*. How does this field work, and when should I use a value other than the default, *Auto*?

A. This value controls whether the light is rendered in *per-pixel* mode (Important) or *per-vertex* mode (Not Important). If the setting is Auto, then Unity makes a decision about which of these two values should be used, based on the position and brightness of the light in the scene. Lights marked as *Important* are calculated on a per-pixel basis – that is, for each pixel of every surface affected in the scene. Lights marked as *Not Important* are calculated on a per-vertex basis – that is, for each vertex of each surface they affect. *Important* mode produces a computationally more expensive light than the *Not Important* mode, but it can result in greater detail when an affected surface has a Normal Map associated with its material. In practice, mark lights as *Important* if you know they play a key role in your scene visually. The brightest, largest and most prominent light sources are typically marked as *Important*.

5.11 Conclusion

Here we must conclude our whirlwind tour of Unity's lighting features. There is a lot to see and do regarding lighting; so much so that this chapter should be considered more of a 'first word' rather than a 'last word' on the subject. However, one principle stands out – regardless of the game engine being used – and that is: keep it simple. This advice does not mean that the lighting for a scene should look simple to the gamer, but only that developers should strive for simplicity in their lighting workflow, regardless of the complexity that is ultimately produced by that workflow. Here, as elsewhere, the principle of simplicity can make our working lives a lot easier. For lighting, simplicity often means: use static pre-baked lighting wherever possible to reduce all unnecessary run-time calculations. For dynamic lighting, take care to reduce the number of shadow casters and, as far as possible, the Shadow Distance, while still achieving the results you need. Here, however, we must leave lighting – at least as the primary subject matter. The next chapter moves into the important world of Particle Systems and Special effects. If your game needs effects such as rain, snow, dust, fog, smoke, fire, hordes of bees, magical spells, fireworks, explosions, and the like, then the next chapter will certainly be of significance.

CHAPTER 6

Particle Systems and Shuriken

By the end of this chapter you should:

1. Understand what a particle system is.
2. Be familiar with Unity's Shuriken particle system.
3. Understand the concepts of particle and emitter.
4. Be able to create your own particle systems.
5. Understand interpolation and how to graph parameters.

This chapter is primarily about particle systems and the effects they create. You may already have some idea about what a particle system is and what it is used for, or it may be completely new to you. Whatever the case, this chapter considers particle systems from the ground upwards and explains how to get started using them in Unity. Technically speaking, in Unity, a particle system refers to *any* game object that has a *Particle System* component attached, and since many different game objects could have such a component, a scene can therefore contain potentially many different particle systems. Making a particle system is a simple process: simply select *GameObject* > *Create Other* > *Particle System* from the main application menu – and that's it: you have a particle system. But what exactly is a particle system and why would anybody use it? In short, a particle system is a specialised object used to create special effects – in particular, special effects that simulate swarm- or horde-like behaviours involving many tiny pieces. For example, particle systems have been used to create rain, sparkles, flocks of birds, magic dust, rushing water, asteroid fields, flames, plasma cannons and chains of smoke. The main feature that unites all of these otherwise divergent examples is horde-like behaviour: all of the above effects involve lots of small elements (a bird, a rain drop, an asteroid) working in unison with many other similar pieces to produce a larger and more complex system. Take the case of a flock of birds: as a whole the system *is* a particle system. Each bird within the system is a unique **particle**. Each bird begins its life somewhere within the system and maintains a flight and course throughout its existence until, at some point, the bird leaves the system – perhaps it dies or perhaps it leaves to join another flock. The entity or 'thing' responsible for controlling when the bird enters the system (controlling when particles are generated) is known as the **emitter**. Thus, a particle system is formed from two main ingredients: the particle and the emitter. On the basis of these fundamental concepts, all kinds of complex and awe-inspiring special effects can be created. These effects and their creation in Unity are what this chapter is about.

6.1 The Amazing Trail of Magic Dust

In this chapter we are going to create a simple but elegant particle system in Unity. To do this, we will create a game object with a Particle System component attached, and then use Unity's **Shuriken editor** interface to customise that particle system to our requirements. Specifically, we will create a trail of 'magical dust' – something that could come from a magic wand, or from a spell book, or from any similar spell-casting entity. Though the system itself will be 'simple' it will nonetheless use a wide range of Shuriken features, demonstrate the power of the editor and equip you with the crucial knowledge you need to build your own systems for your own projects. Like many issues in game development, there is no 'single correct way' to create and configure a particle system. For this reason, don't be afraid to experiment and to deviate from what I am creating here, especially if you prefer your edits and amendments. The basis to work on is: if it looks right, then it is right. So let's get started.

1. Create an empty Unity project and save it, naming the current scene. Details on how to do that can be found in Chapter 1. Following this humble beginning, let's import some graphical assets that we can use for creating our particle system. To import these, select *Assets > Import Package > Particles* from the main application menu. From the Import Dialog, accept the default values and click the button *Import* to add the assets to the current project in the *Standard Assets* folder, viewable from the Project panel. It should be noted that these imported assets are not essentials or prerequisites for creating particle systems generally – particle systems can be created without them. Nonetheless, the imported assets do feature a range of convenient pre-made textures and materials that we will use here for creating our particle system.
2. Create a new Particle System object in the scene. This can be achieved in at least two main ways. The first method (the one-step method) is to select *GameObject > Create Other > Particle System* from the application menu. The alternative two-step method is to first create an empty game object with *GameObject > Create Empty*, and then to add a Particle System component to the object with *Component > Effects > Particle System*. Either of these two methods achieves the desired end result of creating an object in the scene with a Particle System component attached.
3. You should see that when the particle system is created and then selected in the scene viewport it will run automatically – that is, the particles will be in motion. Further, a Particle System panel will appear at the bottom-right side of the viewport window in the Scene tab, showing a range of playback controls for the selected particle system. The Object Inspector also shows a range of editable properties for the selected particle system, listed and arranged under the *Particle System* component – the grey horizontal tabs in this component can be clicked on and expanded to reveal more options. Although it is correct to call the attached component a Particle System component, the menus, tools and options available from this component are generally termed the **Shuriken**

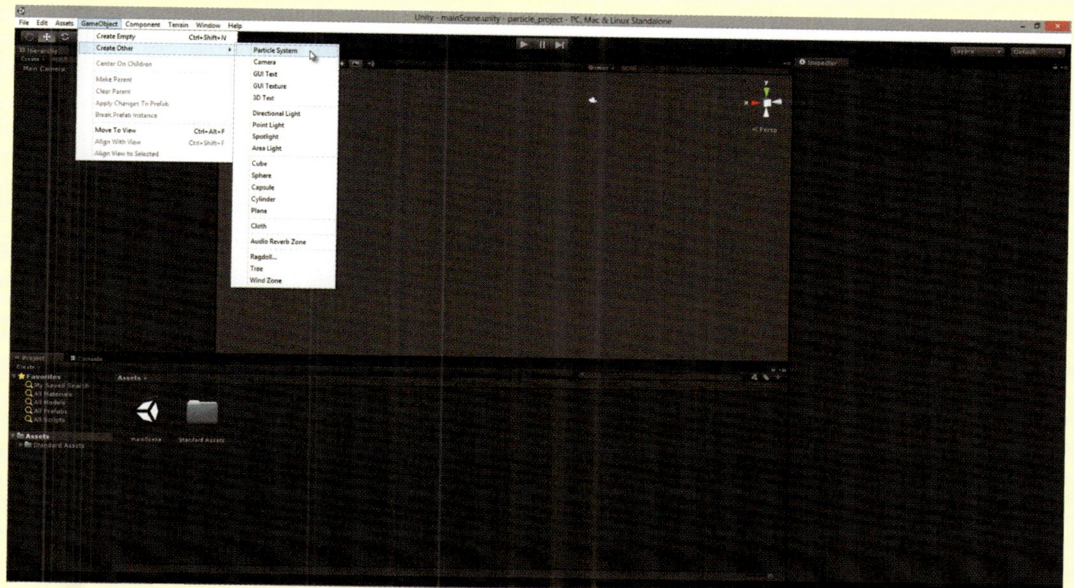

Figure 6.1 Creating a new Particle System object in the scene with *GameObject > Create Other > Particle System*

editor. The fact that a separate name has been coined here signifies the extensiveness and comprehensiveness of the tools and options available for editing particle systems. If you prefer to view the properties of the Shuriken editor in a separate and dedicated window, as opposed to inside the Object Inspector, you can click the *Open Editor* button at the top right-hand side of the Particle System component. See Figure 6.2

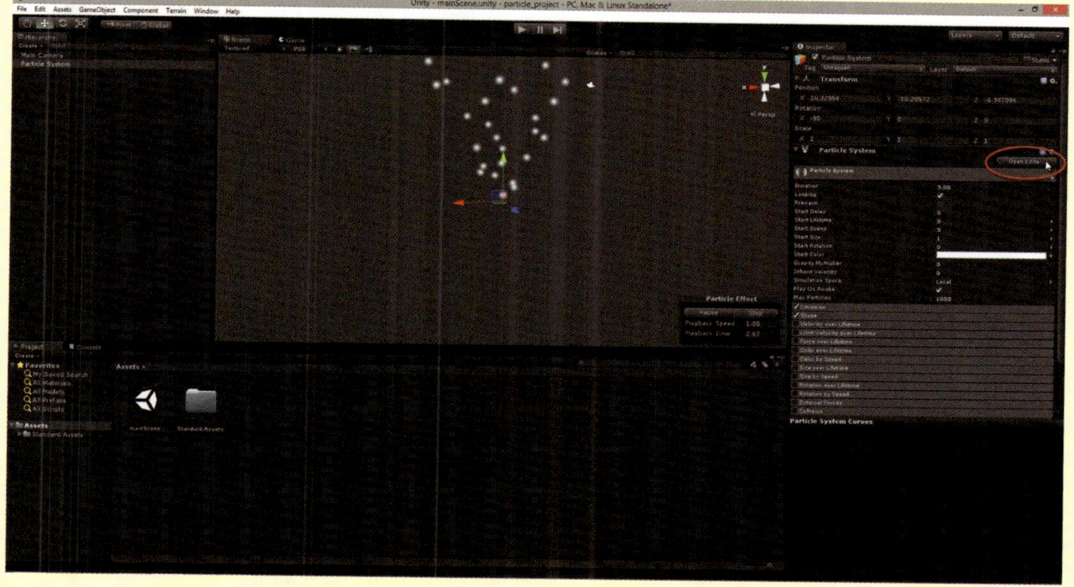

Figure 6.2 Opening the Shuriken editor in a separate and dockable window

4. The options of the Shuriken editor are arranged into tabs or panels, each with a unique heading. Only the main, overarching options are shown by default: others can be revealed by clicking the horizontal tabs. These tabs include: *Emission*, *Shape*, *Size over Lifetime*, *External Forces* and *Collision*. Figure 6.2 demonstrates the main options of the particle system, ranging from *Duration* to *Max Particles*. These options control the particle system overall, as we shall see. To get started, let's tweak some options: change the *Start Speed* value from *5* to *2* and change the *Start Color* from *White* to *Red*. Observe the real-time result in the viewport – the particle system should change immediately. If it doesn't change, check that the system is not paused from the *Particle Effect* panel in the viewport. If the leftmost button of this panel is listed as *Simulate* rather than *Paused*, then the system is paused. In this case, click the *Simulate* button to preview the particle system in the scene viewport. It should be noted that the *Particle Effect* panel controls only the playback of the system for previewing in the viewport, not the playback of the system during the game. For this reason, the settings of *Particle Effect* panel will not affect the particle systems when shown in *Play* mode.

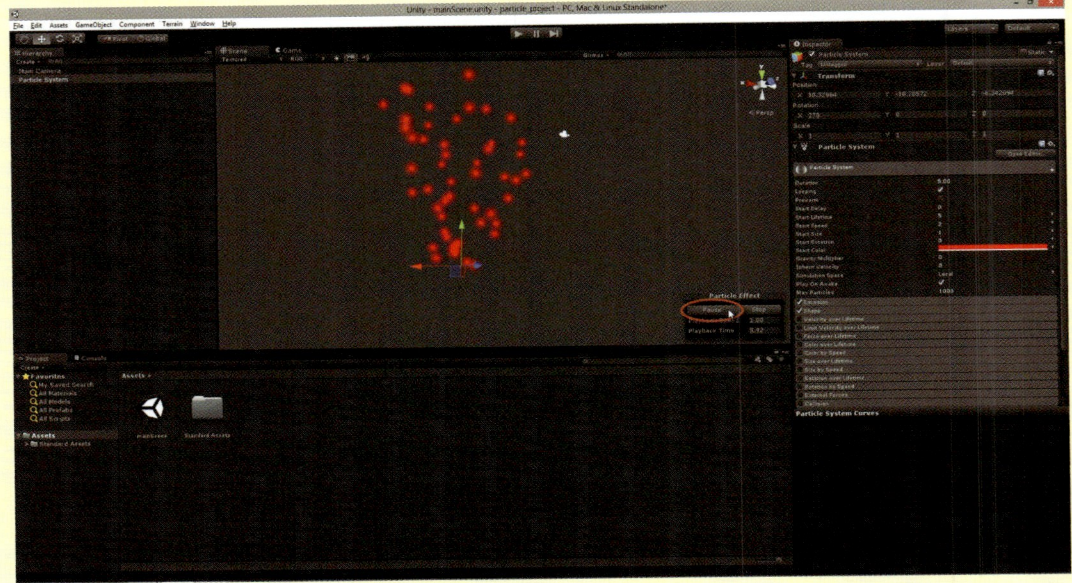

Figure 6.3 Previewing the particle system in the Scene viewport

6.2 Setting the Particle Appearance

The changes we have just effected in the previous section by changing Particle Speed and Start Color are not really suitable for our system – so let's change them back with the *Undo* (Ctrl + Z) command – or you can simply set the *Start Speed* back to *5* and the *Start Color* back to *White*. The first problem that our system faces is that the particles themselves could much better resemble magical dust. True, we might be able to tweak the default particle as it stands to meet our needs, but our imported Particles asset package already contains a material that is more suited for this effect. In Unity, a particle is typically a textured quad. That is, each particle in the system is a rectangular and planar mesh with four vertices, one at each corner, forming two triangles aligned together along their diagonal. We can confirm that this is so by simply enabling the *Wireframe* check box at the bottom of the Shuriken editor. Doing this shows the wireframe for all particles in the system inside the Scene viewport – although the hypotenuse of the two joined triangles might not be visible. In this view, each particle is seen as a mesh whose appearance is based entirely on its material. Thus, the appearance of a particle is changed by adjusting its material. The following steps demonstrate how to adjust the material for all particles in the system, plus some other things too.

1. Select the particle system in the scene, if it is not already selected, and open the *Renderer* tab in the Shuriken editor to display the renderable properties for all particles in the system. The Renderer tab is the bottommost tab in the Shuriken editor. This tab collects together a range of properties, each of which influences how the system particles are rendered. Consider, for example, the *Render Mode* property. This controls the mesh used for each particle, which is a textured quad by default; the default setting being *Billboard*. However, select the other Billboard values, including *Stretched Billboard*, *Horizontal Billboard* and *Vertical Billboard*. Notice that each affects the quad mesh used for the particles: stretched will scale the particles non-uniformly, while the horizontal and vertical settings change the default alignment of each particle in relation to the camera. The value of *Mesh*, however, can dramatically change how particles are rendered. Select *Mesh* from the list and observe the results in the viewport – see how each particle changes from a quad to a cube. You can also change particles to any valid mesh – but beware: high-res meshes for particles can incur a considerable performance hit. For our system, however, we can switch this value back to *Billboard*. See Figure 6.4.

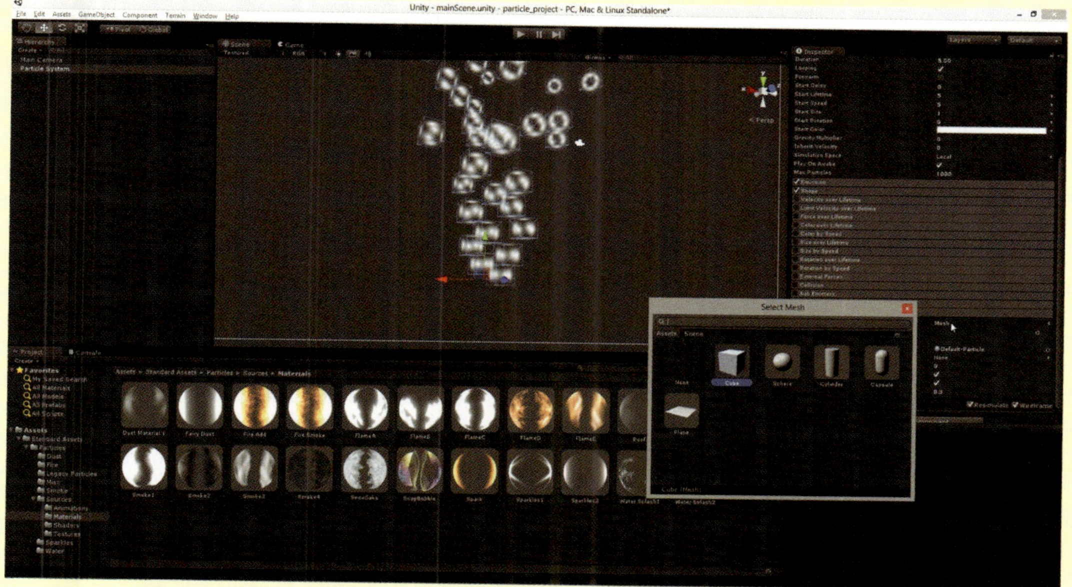

Figure 6.4 Selecting Cube mesh from the Mesh drop-down for a Particle renderer

2. Now let's change the material for the particles using the materials provided from the Particles asset package. To access these, open the *Standard Assets* folder in the *Project panel*, and navigate to *Particles / Sources / Materials*. Drag and drop the *Fairy Dust* material from the *Project panel* into the *Material* slot of the *Renderer* group in the Shuriken editor. This assigns the *Fairy Dust* material to the particles. Their appearance should change in the Scene viewport. As a result of the material change, all particles now exhibit a glow and aura appearance. This is a good beginning . . . but we can do better.

6.3 Fading out Particles over Time

Every particle that is emitted into the system has its own lifetime, as specified by the *Start Lifetime* property in the main properties of the Shuriken editor. The *Start Lifetime* property is specified in seconds, and represents a timer or counter that is assigned to each particle when emitted. When the counter expires, the particle is destroyed and removed from the system. To see this in action, zoom the Scene viewport camera outwards to take in a full view of the particle system while it's running and notice that all the particles simply disappear and pop out of existence when their lifetime expires, even though the emitter continues to generate new particles into the system. Despite particle lifetime and emitter behaving as they should, the effects look rather contrived and unrealistic, especially considering that our system should be simulating fairy dust. It seems strange that our dust should vanish so sharply – there one moment and gone the next. It would look better, or more believable, if the particles *gradually* vanished, beginning fully opaque and ending fully transparent. In addition, it would also be an improvement, I think, if we could change the colour of the particles – and even vary their colour over their lifetime. Shuriken allows us to achieve all these kinds of effects from the *Color over Lifetime group*, available from the Shuriken editor. Consider the following steps.

1. Select the particle system in the scene and expand the *Color over Lifetime* group from the Shuriken editor. This group features only one property, namely *Color*. This option is accessible as a colour swatch and can be used to control the colour of all particles over their lifetime. It is, essentially, a means of graphing a relationship between colour on the one hand and lifetime on the other. Click the swatch and a *Gradient Editor* window appears in response. See Figure 6.5.
2. The Gradient editor offers us control over both the colour and the alpha values of particles over time. The editor features a horizontal colour bar that acts like a timeline. It corresponds to particle colour at specific points in its lifetime, ranging from 0% at the leftmost extreme (particle birth) and 100% at the rightmost extreme (particle death). The editor also features *handles* or *thumbs* (or *markers*) that appear both below and above the colour bar; these mark 'keyframes' or hard-coded points at which the particle colour is set. By default, the Gradient editor features a total of four markers, two at the top and two at the bottom. Top markers correspond to Particle Alpha (Transparency) and bottom markers correspond to Particle Color. The default markers, as seen in Figure 6.5, appear at the extremities of the colour bar, marking the colour and alpha for particles at both the beginning and end of their lifetimes. Our aim is two-fold: to change the colour of particles over time and change the alpha so that particles gradually fade out until their death. Let's start with colour. Click the left and

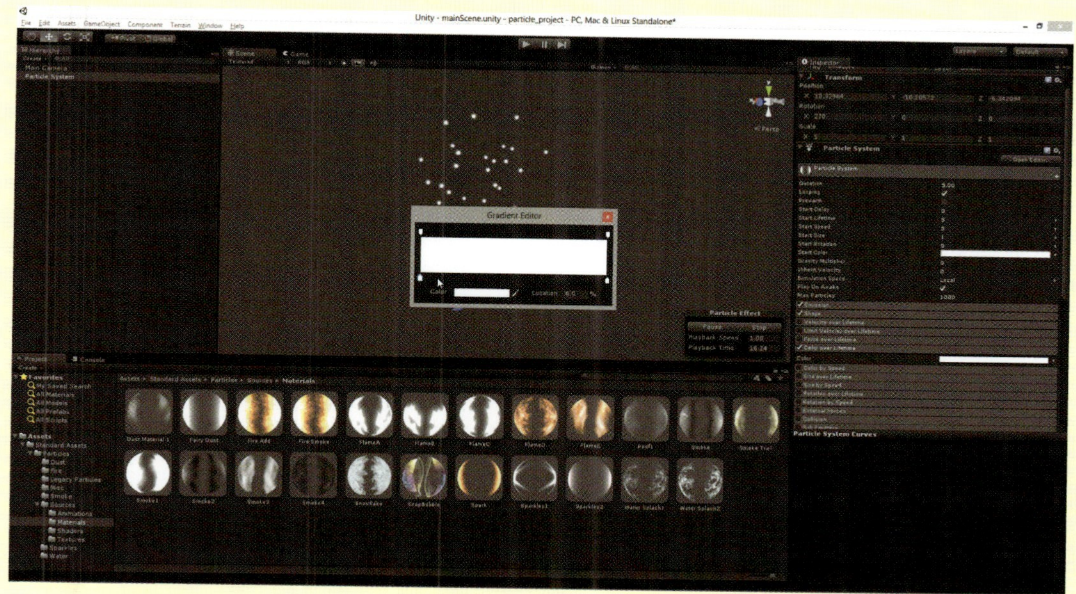

Figure 6.5 Using the Gradient editor to map particle colour to lifetime

bottommost marker in the Gradient Editor at position 0%. If there is no marker listed there, a new marker can be inserted by simply clicking directly below the colour bar. Markers can also be removed from the colour bar by selecting the marker directly and pressing the *Delete* key on the keyboard. The position of markers along the colour bar can also be changed through clicking and dragging. Select the leftmost marker and set its colour to a reddish hue – RGB (255, 135, and 135). Once the marker is selected, its colour can be set by clicking the colour swatch that appears in the Gradient Editor.

3. Select the bottom rightmost marker along the colour bar at position 100% to set the particle colour at the end of its lifetime. Set its colour to a bluish hue: RGB (125, 118, 255). This completes the colouration for the particles. From the Scene viewport, and with the particle system selected, the transition between the start and end colours should now be visible. If there appears to be no change in the colour of the particles or if the change does not appear as intended, check the markers at the bottom of the colour bar in the Gradient Editor. Overlapping and 'Doubled-Up' markers close together are easily created unintentionally and lead to unpredictable colour changes. Be sure that only one thumb exists at each position.
4. The changes made so far do successfully lead to a change in colour over the particle lifetime, from pinkish-red at birth to bluish-purple at death. However, the particles do not change over time in terms of transparency – that is, they do not fade to nothing. They continue to pop out of existence at the end, just as they did before. To fix this now, open the *Gradient Editor*, if it is not already open, and adjust the transparency using the top markers over the colour bar instead of the bottom markers. The transparency of the particle is controlled using greyscale values, where white represents fully opaque and black represents fully transparent, with values between encoding intervening degrees of transparency. The top marker at position 0% (particle birth) should be set to white, indicating that a particle is born fully visible, and the top marker at 100 per cent (particle death) should be set to black, indicating that a particle terminates fully transparent. These transparent colour values are specified using the *Alpha* edit box in the Gradient Editor, using numeric values from 255 to 0. The values in this box express the transparency values for the selected alpha marker in the gradient editor. The value

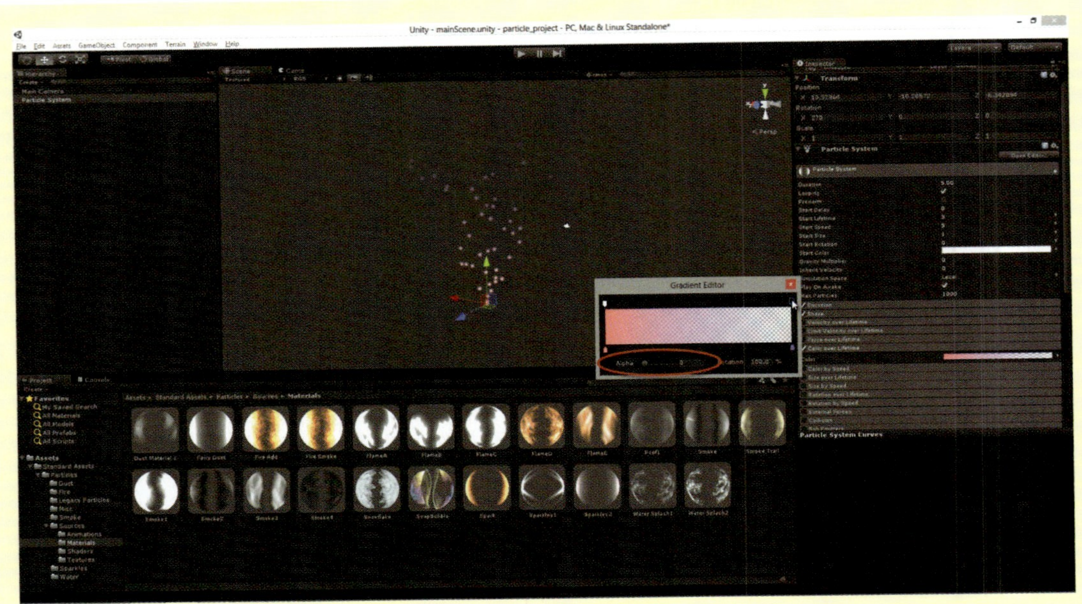

Figure 6.6 Controlling particle colour and transparency using the Gradient Editor

255 represents white and 0 black. Figure 6.6 demonstrates the completed Gradient Editor. Observe the changes in the viewport – all particles should now fade out before their death. If they do not, be sure to check for those doubled-up markers, which can cause confusion.

6.4 Shaping the Particle Emitter

If you carefully study the particle system in motion in the Scene viewport, you will see that particles are not always generated in exactly the same spot. Their point of generation seems to vary subtly with each particle, as though the point generation can be anywhere within a particular radius. This variation is principally due to the shape of the particle system's Emitter component. The emitter refers to the hose or outlet of the system which is responsible for spewing or spawning new particles into the system at a specified rate. The default shape for every emitter of a new particle system is a conic volume – that is, a cone shape. This kind of emitter volume, with its default settings, might work well for some systems, depending on their purpose. In our case, however, the aim is to create a trail of magic dust – the kind that might be left behind a swooping wand or a witch's magic broom. To create this effect successfully, further customisation and changes of the defaults will be required. Let us now look at how to customise the shape and settings of the particle emitter using the Shuriken interface. Consider the following steps.

1. Select the particle system in the viewport and expand the tab named *Shape*, which features beneath the *Emission* tab. The properties of this tab allow us fine control not only over the shape and volume of the emitter but also over how particles are generated within that volume. By default the emitter

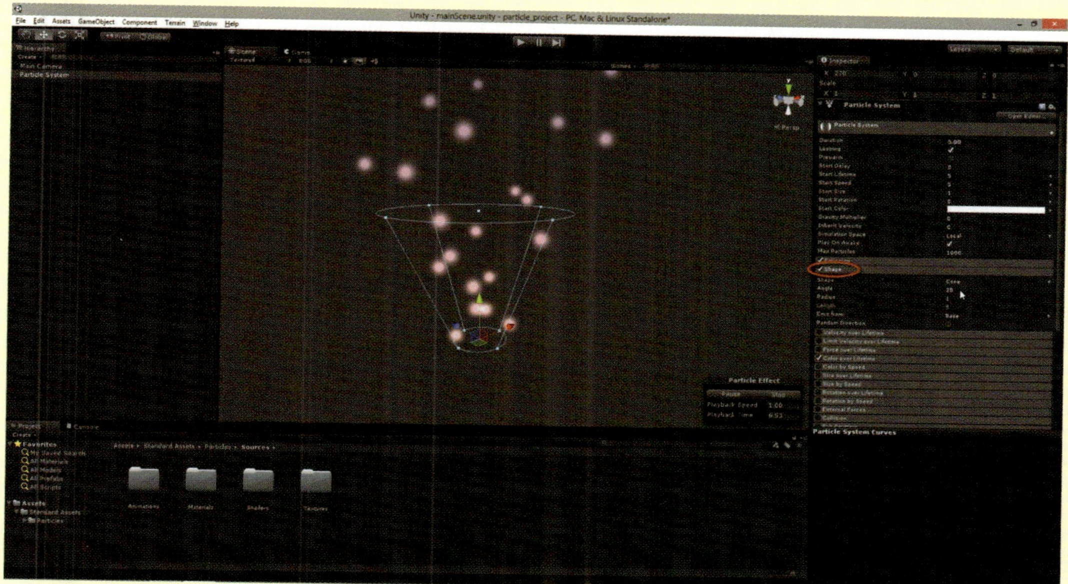

Figure 6.7 Previewing the shape of the particle emitter from the Shape tab

shape is a cone, and when the *Shape* tab is opened and active in the Object Inspector, a cone-shaped gizmo appears around the system in the Scene viewport to offer us a better visualisation of the emitter and how it affects the system. See Figure 6.7.

2. The shape of the emitter is controlled primarily by the Shape property, and this can be one of several values. Specifically, these are: *Sphere*, *Hemisphere*, *Cone*, *Box* and *Mesh*. Cycle through all of these values in turn to see the effect each has on the particle system as it updates in real time in the Scene viewport. The *Sphere* setting shapes the emitter as a sphere, casting particles outwards in all directions from the sphere centre in the scene, a setting that could be particularly useful for creating explosions, supernovas or even sporadic sparks streaming out from open wires. The *Hemisphere* works much like the *Sphere* setting except that it casts particles outwards from only half rather than a whole sphere. Again, this setting could be useful for explosion effects, especially those that occur close to or on the ground plane of the scene. The *Cone* setting, as we have seen, shapes the emitter like an ice-cream cone, casting particles outwards within a narrower field than either the *Sphere* or *Hemisphere* shapes. The cone shape is useful for effects in which the flow or stream or particles must be more focussed and directed than those cast from sphere or hemisphere shapes. It is consequently useful for smoking chimneys, fireball trails, exhaust fumes, blood splatters, magic forces, and other kinds of directed effects. The *Box* shape can cast particles from the faces of a cube and is useful for creating effects in which particles must originate from a plane-like surface. In short, it can be useful for creating effects such as rain, snow, waterfalls, dust, force fields, magical barriers and teleportation devices. Finally, the *Mesh* value allows us even greater control over the emitter shape: we can select any valid mesh asset in the scene – including custom meshes imported from our modelling applications – and have particles generated from its surface. This emitter is typically more expensive than other kinds, computationally speaking, and should therefore be used with frugality in the interests of performance. However, it can be useful for creating particles and effects that appear to surround objects, such as glowing auras around enchanted swords or electrified sparks running across the surface of an alien creature. Disregarding these options, however, we shall here stick with

the standard cone emitter – although as you will see we will tweak some of its properties. Thus, select the *Cone* emitter for the *Shape* setting.

3. If we try to imagine how the particle system might look when emitted from the tip of our hypothetical magic wand, we might reasonably conclude that the cone emitter was generating particles within too wide an area. It seems the cone's focus, or field, should be narrowed. We can do this easily using a combination of the *Angle* and *Radius* settings. The *Angle* setting controls the extent to which the cone opens outwards along its length as measured from its base, and the *Radius* setting determines the size of the cone base in terms of Unity Units. See from Figure 6.8 that for this project I have set the *Angle* to *7.79* and the *Radius* to *0.6*. As with all numeric settings in Unity, these values can be specified by typing them into the edit field or with the mouse by dragging (*scrubbing*) over the field title. Either way, the result is a narrowing of the volume in which particles are emitted and then exist. Now the system is beginning to look more like a trail or stream than it did before. Notice how reducing the *Radius* of the emitter base constrains the area in which new particles are generated.

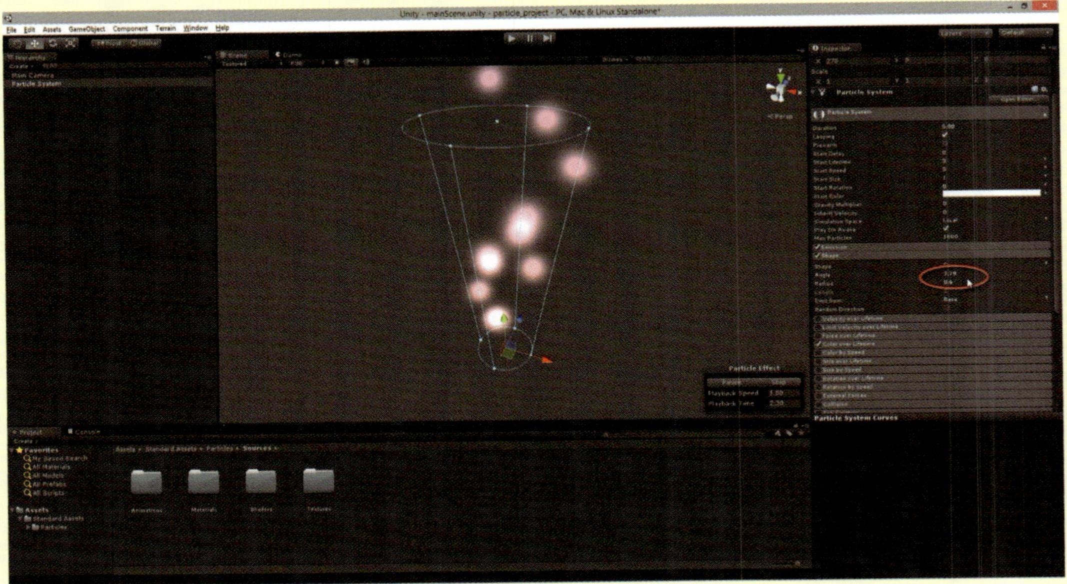

Figure 6.8 Controlling the shape and size of the Cone emitter

4. The Cone emitter, as well as most other emitters, has an *Emit From* setting, which offers us even further control over how particles are spawned into the system. For the cone specifically, this setting can be one from among the following values: *Base*, *Base Shell*, *Volume*, and *Volume Shell*. For other emitter shapes and volumes different values will necessarily apply, but all have the effect of adjusting the location of particle emission within the volume. In the case of Cone emitters, the *Base* value ensures that particles are spawned into the system from a random point within the circle at the base of the volume, and this position varies over time for each particle. The *Base Shell* value, like all other values suffixed with *Shell*, constrains particle generation to the *edge* or *surface* of the volume as opposed to *within* the volume. The *Volume* and *Volume Shell* properties work similarly, generating particles into the system from within any height range inside the emitter volume, rather than just at the base circle. For our project we can use the default *Base* value.

5. Just for fun let's preview how our particle system looks when played at double speed using our current settings – or perhaps even triple speed. We can do this by using the *Playback Speed* setting, which appears in the *Particle Effect* dialog window. This window is visible in the Scene viewport only when the particle system is selected. The default value for this property is 1, meaning *Normal Speed*. Half-speed is represented by 0.5, 2 means double-speed, 3 means triple-speed, and so on. See Figure 6.3 for more information on this window. Previewing the system at different speeds can be helpful for several reasons: first, it can help you fast-forward to specific timed effects within the complete animation, saving you from having to wait the full length of time for them to appear. And further, it can also help you visualise the general motion and flow of particles in the system, to more accurately gauge and understand whether the system is correctly configured to achieve the results you want. Remember, however, the Playback Speed setting does not affect the final speed of the particle system in-game, only the playback preview in the viewport. To control the final speed of the system you can use a combination of the properties *Start Speed*, *Start Lifetime* and *Duration*. You can also control Playback speed from script using *ParticleSystem.playbackSpeed*. Scripting in Unity is considered in a later chapter.

NOTE: It is very common in game development to find settings, like the *Playback Speed* setting, that are based around the value of 1, where 1 means *default* or *normal* or *standard*. In such cases, 0.5 means half the standard and 2 means twice the standard, and so on. These kinds of values, which are typically used as a kind of multiplier or master setting, are known as **normalized values** or **normalized properties**, or sometimes they are more loosely called **scalars**. They are powerful because they allow us to change numeric values independently of units of measure and without our having to know what the actual minimum and maximum values are in absolute terms. They are especially common for specifying transparency, volume, scale, time, distance, direction, health, damage and the like. Normalised properties will appear again and again in Unity, and especially when we visit scripting in the next chapter.

6.5 Graphing, Curves and Interpolation

We are certainly making progress with the particle system now. But there is yet another feature that I think we should add to improve realism and be consistent with what we have already made. The particles are emitted into the system and fade out over time towards their eventual termination, but the particles always remain constant in size. From the moment they are born to the moment they die the particles never change in size, and this does not truly accord with the fade-out behaviour we have given them. The fade-out behaviour is supposed to suggest a gradual weakening and decay of particles over time, and this implies that particles should not only fade out but also grow smaller in size as they age and move further from the emitter source. We can achieve this shrinking behaviour by several different methods. One of the most powerful and flexible is using the graphing features of the Shuriken editor. These features can be used not only to control and animate particle size but also to control most of the other changeable and numeric properties of particles, including *color*, *rotation*, *speed* and *velocity*. Once we learn how to use the graphing features to control size, we will know how to use them in practically all cases. Further, an understanding of how they work generally – including grasping the concept of interpolation – will open up a whole new world of power and control. The following steps demonstrate how to adjust the size of particles over time with graphing.

1. Select the particle system in the Scene viewport, if it is not already selected, and expand the *Size over Lifetime* tab from the Shuriken editor. Be sure to put a check mark inside the *Size* group or module to enable it: the check mark can be toggled on and off to enable and disable its effects – this applies to all other modules too. By default, the *Size* group does not change or affect the particle size at all, even when enabled. Or to put it more accurately, the group *does* affect the particles, but it is configured by default to ensure they retain their size over time. This might be fine and even desirable for some systems, but since we want our particles to shrink over time, we must change these settings from their defaults.
2. Changing the size of a particle over time brings two quantities into a relationship with each other, namely *Particle Size* and *Time*, both of which are expressed in terms of numbers. Because of this, the two values can be plotted on a standard line graph to help us visualise their relationship: 'particle size' on one axis, and 'time' on the other. In our case, size is mapped to time because we want to shrink the particles in proportion to their age: the older they are, the smaller they become. The Unity Shuriken editor offers us a set of graphing features to express these kinds of relationships – tools to build line graphs and curves in which we can map two quantities in relation to each other. Consequently, in the case of size, Unity will be able 'read off' the size values for each particle at any time, based on the curve we draw on a graph. To create a graph, click the drop-down arrow besides the graph swatch for the *Size* setting and select *Curve* from the drop-down list. Once selected, click inside the graph swatch to open up the *Graphing Editor*, which is visible inside the preview panel of the Object Inspector. See Figure 6.9.
3. By default, the curve graph that is generated in the Object Inspector is configured to retain particle size over time; this can be seen by examining the straight red horizontal line that appears in the graph, reaching across from left to right and maintaining a constant value of 1. In this graph, *Size* is mapped to the vertical Y axis and represents a normalised value from 0 to 1, where 0 refers to no-size and 1 to standard particle size. On the horizontal X axis is *Time*, again a normalised value ranging from 0 (particle birth) to 1 (particle death). So at Time 0 (*t0*), Particle Size is 1 (*p1*) – this translates to mean that at its birth the particle will be full-size. Again, at *t1* we find *p1* and, in fact, for *tx* we always find *p1*. See Figure 6.9 for confirmation of this.

   It should be noted that both of these normalised values, size and time, will eventually be multiplied with other settings specified in the general Particle System properties specified at the top of the Shuriken editor. The normalised Particle Size value will be multiplied with Start Size to produce a final particle size, and the normalised Particle Life value will be multiplied to Start Lifetime. In short, Start Size expresses the maximum size a single particle can reach, and Start Lifetime represents the total time in seconds that a single particle lives. Since the graph deals only with normalised values as opposed to absolutes, we do not need to concern ourselves with what the actual Start Size and Start Lifetime settings are. Further, we can know that even if the Start Size and Start Lifetime properties change after we build the graph, the graph settings will continue to apply and work just as they did before.

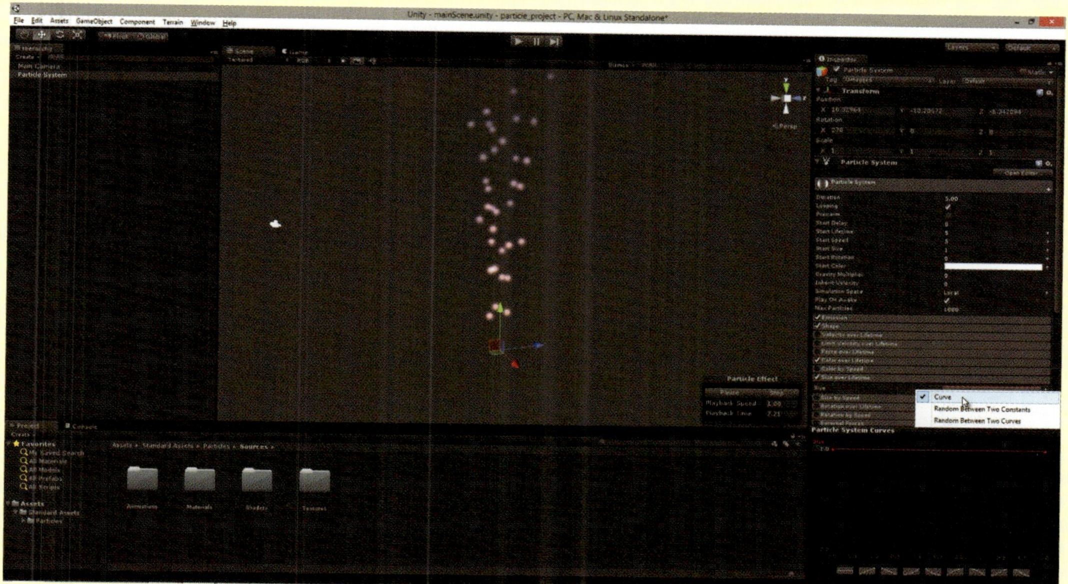

Figure 6.9 Creating a curve graph for interpolating particle size over time

4. Before we start editing the graph in more detail, let us consider the **graph presets** that are available. These can be viewed at the bottom of the graph as a horizontal list of thumbnail images, representing common graph configurations. Clicking these thumbnails will change the line of the graph according to the preset. Notice that, as you click the presets and change the line of the graph, the particles in the viewport also change and update in real time to reflect the changes. Click between the presets and notice the effect each curve shape has on the size of the particles: ascending curves increase particle size over time, and descending curves decrease particle size over time. This makes sense because the curve is creating a mapping relationship between *Size* on the vertical axis and *Time* on the horizontal axis. Notice also the fall-off or ease-out effect that results from using curved lines instead of straight lines.
5. Let's play around with this graph for a while to see what kinds of effects we can achieve and understand better how it works. Select the leftmost line preset to reset the graph line back to a straight horizontal. The vertical position of the line, after pressing this preset, will vary depending on which preset was selected previously, but we can easily control the position of any point on the line if we need to. To select a point (**anchor point** or **key**) on the line from among the start and end points, simply use the mouse to click on one of them in the graph. Once selected, the point changes from its default red colour to a highlighted orange colour, and a further grey point or line might be seen sticking out from it tangentially – this point is called a **Bézier handle**, named after the engineer and mathematician Pierre Bézier. You can also move the anchor point by clicking and dragging it to a new position. Try adjusting the vertical position of the anchor point on the graph and observe its effects on the particle system in the Scene viewport.
6. The line created so far has two points: the start and end points. Together these define an unbroken line that reaches linearly across the entirety of the graph, from time t0 to time t1. The points on the line are called anchor points because they mark specific moments in time where we, as developers, have explicitly positioned and fixed the value of the point. In positioning the point on the graph we have stated what size the particle should be at *that* particular time. Whenever this time is reached in the particle lifetime, we can know that the particle will be at the size we have specified. But what

about the size of the particle at other times in its life when there is no point on the line to tell the system its size? Well, the points are joined by a line, and the line reaches continuously across the graph covering *all* times from start to end. Therefore, the size value for particles at the *intervening* time is read from the graph using the connecting line. When the two axes of the graph intersect along the line at any time, that point will be used as the size for the particle at *that* time. This process of 'filling in' the size values for all times between the anchor points is known as **interpolation**, because the size values are calculated or generated on the continuous curve generated between the points we manually set down. This makes it possible for a graph to feature just two points and still control the size of particles at every time in the animation. To see this at work in more detail, let's create a third anchor point on the line. This will fix the particle size at a different time, and we'll also see how this adjusted line will continue to interpolate sizes at other times. To create a new point, right-click the mouse button at a different place on the line where a new point is to be inserted – let's say the middle of the line. Then select *Add Key* from the menu.

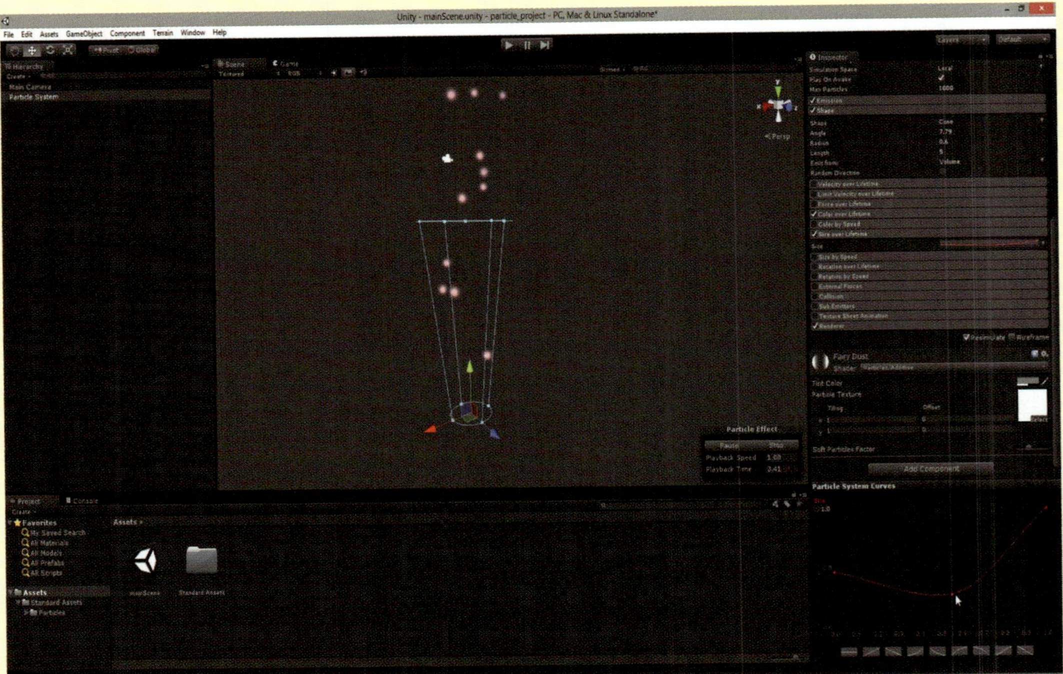

Figure 6.10 Creating a Smooth curve through an additional point

7. Selecting *Add Key* from the context menu inserts a new point on the line, and this point can be moved and adjusted in the graph like all other points, using the mouse. Notice that as the third and middle point is moved, the line curves and bends to match it – always moving to ensure the line passes through all points. It is should also be noted that the third point causes the line to curve *smoothly* by default as the point is moved, as seen in Figure 6.10. It does not cause the line to bend *sharply* as though the point were a hinge, leaving only straight edges on either side, although this is another way the graph *could* have looked with the same points. The curvature of the line, whether straight or rounded, is controlled by the points themselves, and the curvature affects how values between points

are interpolated. Points on the line can be of different types, and these types affect the curve. By default, newly inserted points are *smooth*, but they can be changed to other types to change the curvature of the line. The type can be changed by right-clicking the selected point and selecting a type from the menu. The options are: *Auto*, *Free Smooth*, *Flat* and *Broken*. The default is *Auto*, which represents an Automatic point, the simplest kind. Using automatic points, you simply position the point on the graph and Unity handles the rest: it adjusts the curve *automatically* and controls how the curve blends and moulds on the basis of the point. *Free Smooth* offers an additional level of control: it provides access to the Bézier handles of the point, which appear as a dull grey line gizmo perpendicular to the point. In this mode, we can not only move the point but also drag the Bézier handles to change the angle and shape of the curved line as it passes through the point. *Flat Mode* flattens out the Bézier handles into a fixed, horizontal line allowing curved sections of the line to flatten out into straight sections. And finally, the *Broken* settings gives us independent control of the Bézier handle on either side of the point, allowing us to create sharp and right-angle-style edges in the path. See Figure 6.11.

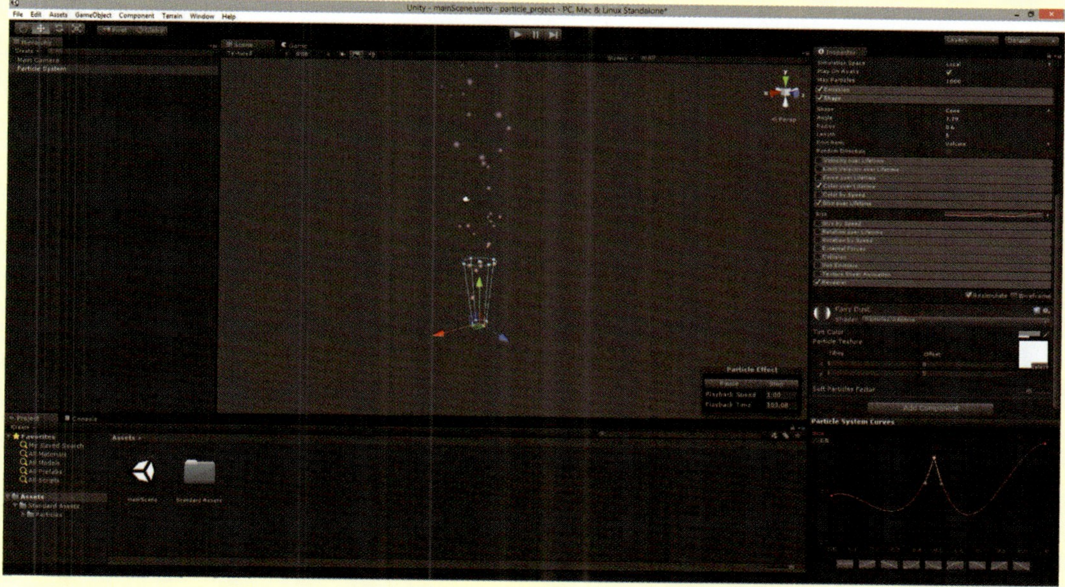

Figure 6.11 Adding sharp corners to a line using the Broken point settings

NOTE: Points on the line can also be removed and deleted. To do this, select the point, then right-click it with the mouse and use the context menu to choose the *Delete Key* option. The point is removed and the line automatically 'healed' or repaired back into a shape that accounts for the removed point.

8. Despite the extensive control we have over points on the line, our aim for this project requires us to use only one of the line presets. The intention is to reduce the size of particles with age to create a fizzling-out look: the older a particle is, the smaller it becomes. To create this effect, we can use the

third graph preset from the left – the presets are listed horizontally from left to right at the bottom of the Object Inspector preview panel. This preset features a two-point descending line, which has a size value of *1* at time *t0*, and a size value of *0* at time *t1*. On the graph these look like a straight line travelling from the top-left corner of the graph to the bottom-right corner. Select this preset and take a look at the changes in the viewport on the selected particle system – see how particles all reduce in size the further they move away from the emitter. This effect, combined with the changes in particle transparency, help to give a sense of 'weakening in strength or potency'. This now completes the customisation of particle sizes for our magical trail system – but not only that, we have seen more generally how graphs can be a powerful visual tool for controlling size over time. See Figure 6.12 for the completed graph controlling particle size.

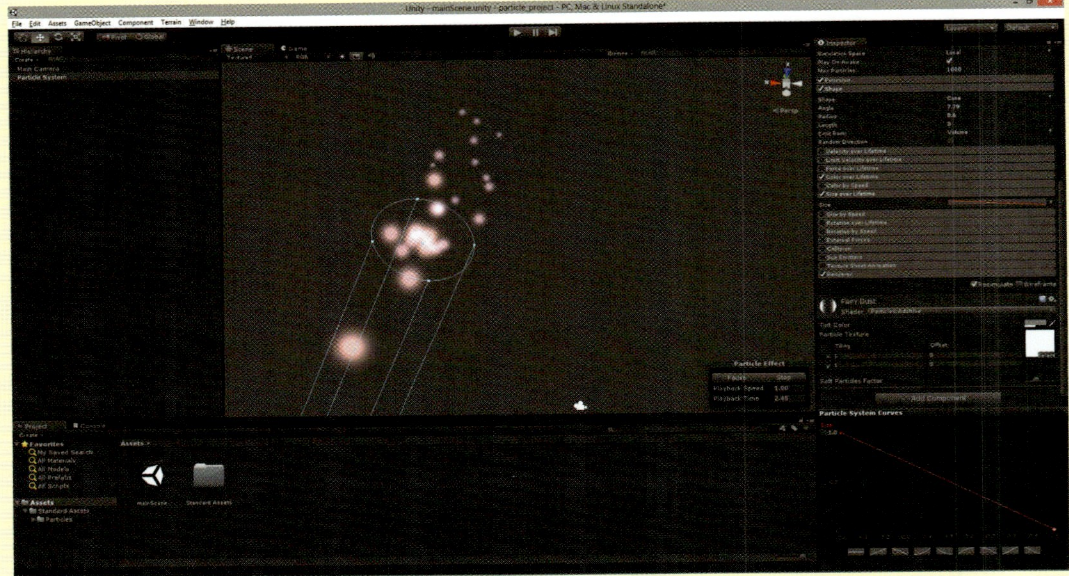

Figure 6.12 Creating a graph to reduce particle size over time

6.6 Emission Rate

The next issue to address in our particle system is the emission rate, which is a ratio defining how often or frequently the emitter spawns new particles, and this ratio is typically specified in terms of *Particles per Second*. The emission properties are controlled through the topmost tab in the Shuriken editor, the *Emission* tab. Here, our aim is to simulate a magic trail effect: a trail of magical dust particles left behind by a waving wand. Right now our system fails still to create this effect despite the edits we have made with colours, transparency and graphs. The setback we face now is now largely due to the emission rate for our system. Specifically, it is too low. There are simply not enough particles being generated for the bold look we are seeking and the system looks sparse and underwhelming. In this section we shall not only increase the emission rate to intensify the particle density of the trail but also consider the *Bursts* setting to add some variation to the system, breaking up its uniformity. Consider the following steps.

1. Select the particle system in the scene viewport, and then expand the *Emission* tab in the Shuriken editor to see the settings relevant to the particle emitter. There are two settings listed, namely *Rate* and *Bursts*. By default Rate specifies a relationship between particles and time: defining how many new particles will be generated into the system by the emitter for each second. Rate can also be measured in terms of particles and distance – but this section considers only the particle and time relationship. Set the *Rate* field to *70*, and ensure the value of *Time* is selected in the drop-down box beneath the *Rate* field. This specifies a particle emission rate of 70 particles per second. Take a look at the particle system in the Scene viewport to see an overall increase in particle density – already the system is looking much better. Feel free to tweak the emission rate further.
2. *Bursts* is a fun parameter that has genuine relevance to our system, too. Imagine: a wizard or witch waves their magic wand, casting a spell, and (poof!) magic dust gushes from the wand like smoke from a chimney, indicating both forces at work and physical activity. Thinking about this, though, it is likely that particles will not be emitted at a *constant* rate but rather emitted non-uniformly. Specifically, at the height of intense magical activity, when the spell is cast, there will be a burst or surge of magical dust from the tip of the wand. Further, this emission of magical dust will gradually taper out to a more constant rate as the magical energies fade. Creating this initial surge of particles is something we can create with the *Bursts* setting. *Bursts* is essentially a list of ad hoc emission rates. Let's create a Burst now and see how it works. To do this, click the circular + button listed under the Bursts settings, which creates a new Burst entry. See Figure 6.13.

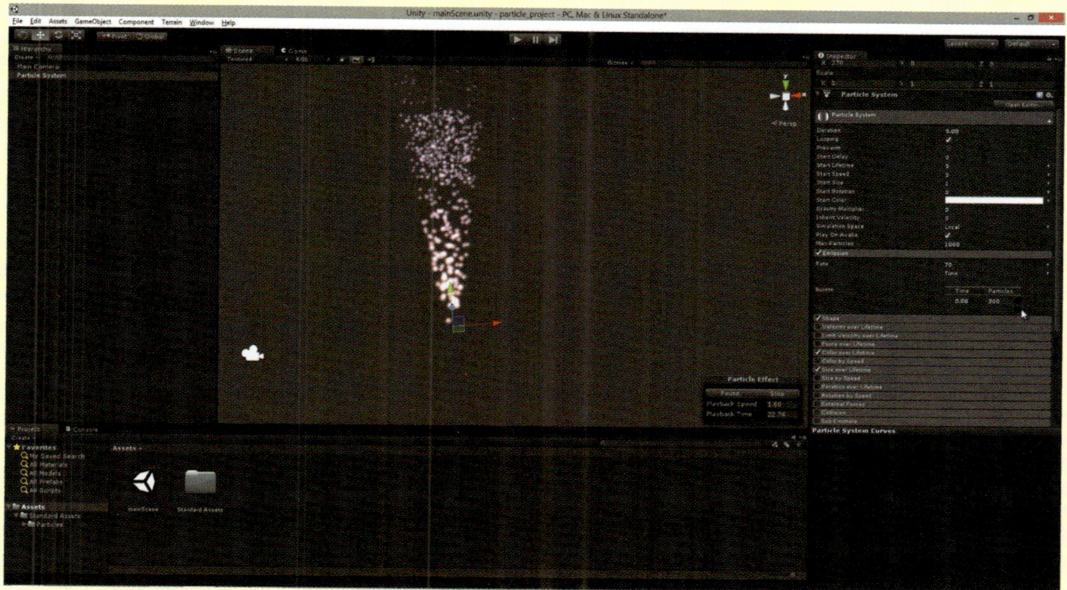

Figure 6.13 Creating a Bursts entry to produce a surge of particles at a specified time

3. You can add as many *Bursts* entries as you need to your particle system to add different levels of bursts at different times. However, our system for this chapter requires only one. Each *Bursts* entry specifies a *Time* value and a *Particles* value. The Time value is absolute rather than normalised, meaning it does not range from 0–1 but specifies actual times in terms of seconds. This value can range from 0 to *Duration* – the setting *Duration* – can be specified in the main and general Particle System properties in the Shuriken editor. Duration represents *not* the total time for which the particle system is visible and working, but the total time for which the emitter is spawning new particles. After this duration expires, the emitter will either stop generating new particles completely, or will loop around and repeat its generation process again – if the Particle System is set to loop using the *Looping* property. The system we have created so far uses the default duration of *5* seconds; meaning the Time value for Bursts can range from *0* to *5*. Here, we should insert a particle burst at the beginning of the system, when the magical energies are at their most intense. Consequently, the Time value can be left at 0. The *Particles* value specifies how many *extra* particles, *in addition* to those generated using the standard emission rate, should be added to the system at the specified time as part of one big burst. I have set this value to 300 to create the necessary burst effect (See Figure 6.13). Feel free to tweak these values; but overall things are looking better.

NOTE: When working with the *Emission* and *Bursts* settings it is important to be aware of the global *Max Particles* setting, which is accessible on the main Particle Systems tab in the Shuriken editor. *Max Particles* specifies the total number of individual particles that can exist (be alive) in the system at any one time. If the emission rate or the bursts settings cause the number of particles to match or exceed this total, then *all* further emissions and bursts will be stopped *until* a sufficient number of particle deaths occur, after which emission and bursts will automatically resume. Thus, if your system is not emitting or bursting as intended, be sure to check the *Max Particles* setting to see that it is not unintentionally limiting particle generation. If it is, you can either decrease the emission rate or raise the maximum number of particles. If the latter, always keep in mind run-time performance: *use as few particles as necessary to achieve the effect you need*. It could make the difference between a game that 'sinks or swims'.

6.7 Gravity and Physics

We are now approaching the end of our particle system project. I say 'approaching' because we have not finished yet! This highlights an important workflow characteristic that applies in practice when building particle systems in Unity, as well as in most other game engines. Specifically, creating particle systems typically involves a lot of *tweaking*; a lot of editing numbers, then previewing the results, then returning to tweak the settings to further refine their effects, and so on, until the results match what you want and perform in the way that you need them to for your target hardware – whether that hardware is a high-performance desktop gaming system or a comparatively low-powered mobile platform such as iOS, Windows 8 or Android.

In this section we must apply further tweaks to our system in order to modify the way particles behave and make our system look more realistic. Specifically, we will transform the particle system into a more appropriate orientation in the scene, and we will also tweak the gravity setting to increase the believability of particle motion, making the particles appear to be affected by gravity.

1. In Unity, particle systems are classified as game objects, simply game objects with a special kind of component attached – namely a *Particle System* component. Consequently, Particle System objects can be moved, scale and rotated in the scene just like any other game object, for example a mesh. Since our system should be a trail of magical dust emitted from the tip of a wand like smoke from a moving steam train, it will typically not be emitting particles in an upwards direction. The system should be orientated to cast particles *horizontally*. This can be achieved simply by rotating the particle system in place. That is, select the rotate tool by pressing *E* on the keyboard, hold down the control key to constrain rotation to discrete increments, and then use the gizmo to rotate the system into place by 90 degrees. In short, rotate your system to look like Figure 6.14.

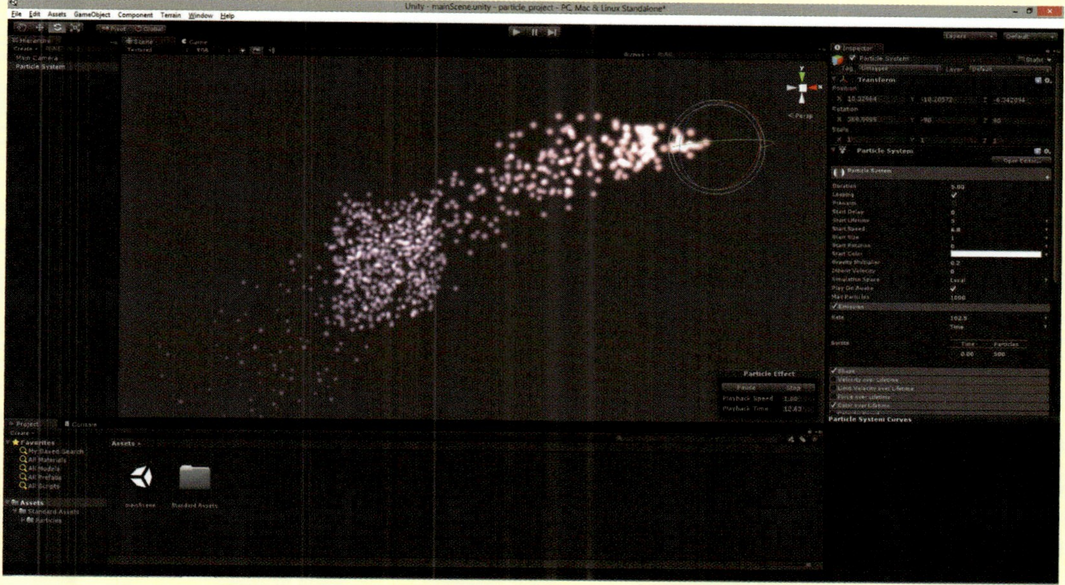

Figure 6.14 Using the Gravity Multiplier value to tweak the motion of particles. Notice the drop or fall effect of particles after emission

2. The system is now rotated into place and, so long as it is selected in the viewport, it can be seen to cast particles outwards horizontally as opposed to vertically, which more closely accords with our design. Notice also that rotating the system does not in any way corrupt its existing settings; particles are still generated from the emitter and continue travelling along their predetermined course, just as they did before, except now at a different angle due to the rotation. One of the chief obstacles facing us now pertains to the motion of the particles when arranged horizontally. In particular, the particles are generated at the emitter and continue moving in a horizontal line, completely unaffected by environmental factors – such as gravity. In the 'real world', particles such as sparks and fireworks do

not follow a perfect straight course. Rather, their motion over time tends downwards towards the ground because of the influence of gravity. The extent to which they incline downwards depends on the nature of the environment and the substance of the particles themselves, and here we have some creative room for manoeuvre in our system, but nonetheless the particles should incline downwards to some extent. We can achieve this effect using the *Gravity Multiplier* setting, featured on the main Particle System properties tab in the Shuriken editor. This value ranges from 0 to 1; 0 and 1 leave the particle system at its defaults. Values in between, however, influence the motion of particles. Higher values represent stronger gravitational pulls and lower values weaker gravitational pulls. Play around with the values for this setting and check out its effects. For this system I have specified a value of 0.2. The results of this can be seen in Figure 6.14.

See **Video**: *Chapter06_Vid01_UnityParticles* for a video tutorial on how to build the project in this chapter.

6.8 Particle System Tips

The amazing trail of magical dust is now completed, sporting a range of colourful features that demonstrate some of the core functionality of Shuriken. Nevertheless, this project only touches the surface of a whole range of effects which the particle system can be used to create. The extensiveness of particle systems and the full range of features which Shuriken offers, as well as the creative uses to which it can be put, is worthy of a whole book in itself. Rather than delve deeper into the refinements of Shuriken, this section offers some high-level tips and techniques that are worth keeping in mind when working with particle systems in Unity.

One particle system does not always equal one effect

Initially, it is easy to assume in Unity that *one* particle system object is supposed to create *one* complete particle effect, like the effect we have created in this chapter. In this case we *were* indeed able to successfully create the look we wanted on the basis of only one particle system. But not all effects are so comfortingly simple to create. Consider the case of a whirling tornado travelling across miles of landscape, wreaking havoc and disaster wherever it goes. It rips up soil, rocks, debris, even wooden houses, and carries them all inside itself, swirling them upwards and around in a dangerous air-based vortex. Based on this it is easy to think that the tornado is one particle system and that, when we come to make it in Unity, all its qualities and features will therefore be created through one particle system object. Thinking in these terms, however, can prevent us from creating convincing particle effects. The tornado in this case is better thought of not as one system but as a collection – or *Prefab* – of particle systems. We can identify at least three different systems at work in this effect: 1) the chaotic cloud of dust and smoke that gathers at the base of the twister as it strikes the soil; 2) the twister itself, an elongated and spinning cone of dust and dirt that moves independently of the cloud at its base; and 3) the debris, rubble and rubbish the twister has collected within its vortex, which look and behave differently from the other two elements of the system. In short, when creating a particle effect, always seek to break down the effect into its smallest constituent pieces; this will often mean thinking of a particle-based phenomena not as one complete system but as a collection of different particle systems working together in loose synchronicity.

Pre-warming Particle Systems

Have ever you noticed with your particle system projects that, whenever you play your game and start in view of a particle system, it takes a while for the system to get going? You press *Play* from the toolbar and the scene opens empty of any particles; you have to wait for the emitter to generate new particles before the system begins to look remotely as you intended. This happens because, prior to your pressing the *Play* button, the scene was not created and there was no pre-established particle system running. For some effects this might not matter in the least, but with others it can devastate the realism of your game. Consider particle systems for creating fiery torches on the wall of a medieval castle: imagine how preposterous it would be if, every time the player entered the castle, it looked as though all the torches lit at that moment. In these cases, it would be great if the particle system looked as though it had been running before we arrived. Thankfully, the Shuriken editor offers us the *Prewarm* setting for achieving exactly this, available from the main Particle System panel. Simply tick that *Prewarm* box and the particle system will always look as though it has been running prior to being seen.

Texture Sheet Animations

It was mentioned earlier in this chapter that particle systems could be used to create not only natural or supernatural phenomena like tornados or magical dust but also more organic complexes like a flock of birds flying together through the sky. The flock-of-birds effect is interesting because it places a very specific demand on a particle system: namely, it requires not just particle textures but *animated* particle textures. Birds, as they move through the sky, will inevitably flap their wings. Observers who look up to see the birds fly past see not only the flock itself in motion but each individual bird (or particle) moving its wings. Implementing a system like this requires us not only to animate the motion of particles in unison but also to animate the textures of the particles themselves. This effect, and others like it, can be achieved through the *Texture Sheet Animation* panel in the Shuriken editor. This panel assumes that the particle texture has been created as an **Atlas texture**, a texture in which all the frames of animation are neatly stacked together in rows and columns of equal size, all within the *same* image. With this arrangement, each frame of animation can be given a unique index and each particle only displays one frame of animation from the texture at any one time. In this way, the frame index assigned to each particle can be changed and animated over time through graphing to create a flip-book animation effect. Atlas textures are beyond the scope of this book. More information on how to generate them can be found in my video course *2D Games for Unity*, available at *3DMotive.com*

6.9 Legacy Particles

The term 'legacy' is used in computing generally to refer to 'outdated', 'outmoded' or 'superseded' features or software. Thus, the term 'legacy particles', when applied to Unity, refers to all the older, surpassed features of particles and particle systems – all the particle system features that were once used in the software but which are not used anymore. The main reason for their disuse is that they have been surpassed by the features of the Shuriken particle system, first introduced in version 3.5 in 2012, which replaced the system that came before it. Despite this, however, the *Particles* asset package, which was imported into our Unity project at the beginning of this chapter, ships with a number of useful pre-made particle systems for common effects like fire and water. These systems were made using the older particle system features of Unity prior to Shuriken, but they nevertheless could be helpful to you and your projects. Just drag and drop them into the scene from the Project panel. Let's take a brief look at some of the systems available, even though we will not be considering any of the specific features of the legacy system itself.

Fire

The Particles asset package ships with two fire-based particle systems that are ready to be dragged and dropped in your scenes. These can be found in the folder Standard *Assets / Particles / Fire*. The first system *Fire 1* can be used for simulating raging infernos, magical force fields and dangerous firey barriers. The second system is named Flame, and this can be used for creating candles, burning oil drums, gas lighters, oil maps and

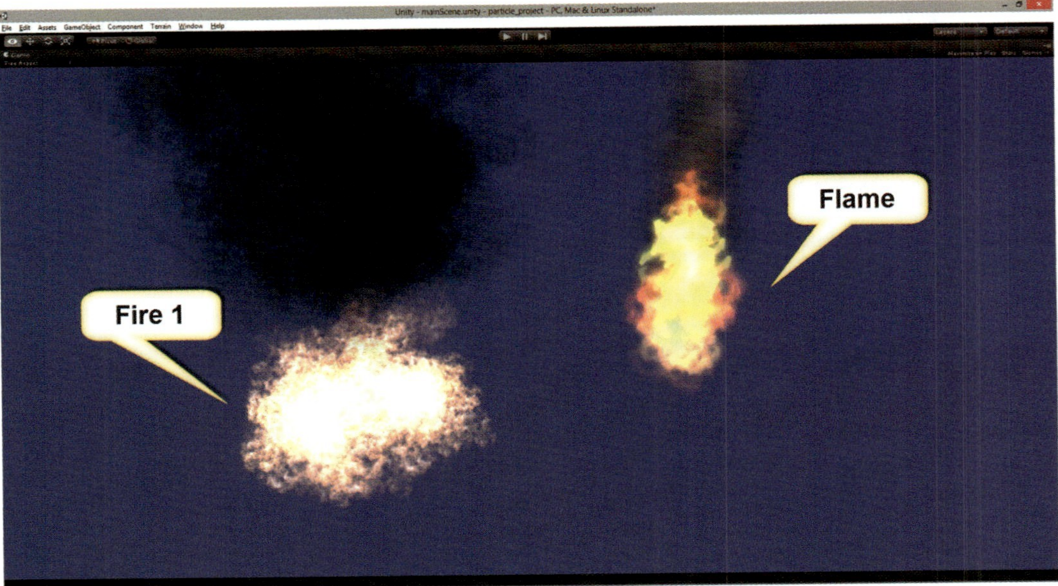

Figure 6.15 Legacy Particle Systems at work

other flame-based rather than fire-based effects. Consider Figure 6.15 featuring both *Fire 1* and *Flame*.

Misc

The folder *Standard Assets / Particles / Misc* features a collection of miscellaneous particle systems – disparate systems with no firm connection lumped together as a group. These systems are diverse in look and use and could prove useful in a range of different cases. These systems include: *Fireworks*, *Light Snow*, *Soap Bubbles*, and *Sparks*. Consider Figure 6.16.

Figure 6.16 Fireworks, Light Snow, Soap Bubbles and Sparks all at work together

Smoke

Smoke receives special attention from the Particles asset package. There are a total of four different smoke systems to be found at *Standard Assets / Particles /Smoke*. These are: 1) *Detailed Smoke*, useful for creating a thick, dark, noxious-looking smoke that might arise from bonfires or other burned items; 2) *Fluffy Smoke*, useful for simulating chimney smoke from chugging steam trains, industrial factories and steam releases on pipes; 3) *Fluffy Smoke Large*, which is similar to *Fluffy Smoke* but larger, and useful for creating the impression of large fires in the distance; and finally 4) *Smoke Trail*, which is an elongated chain of smoke – useful for creating effects like aircraft after-burners, car exhaust, small, travelling explosions and other smoke trails. Take a look at Figure 6.17.

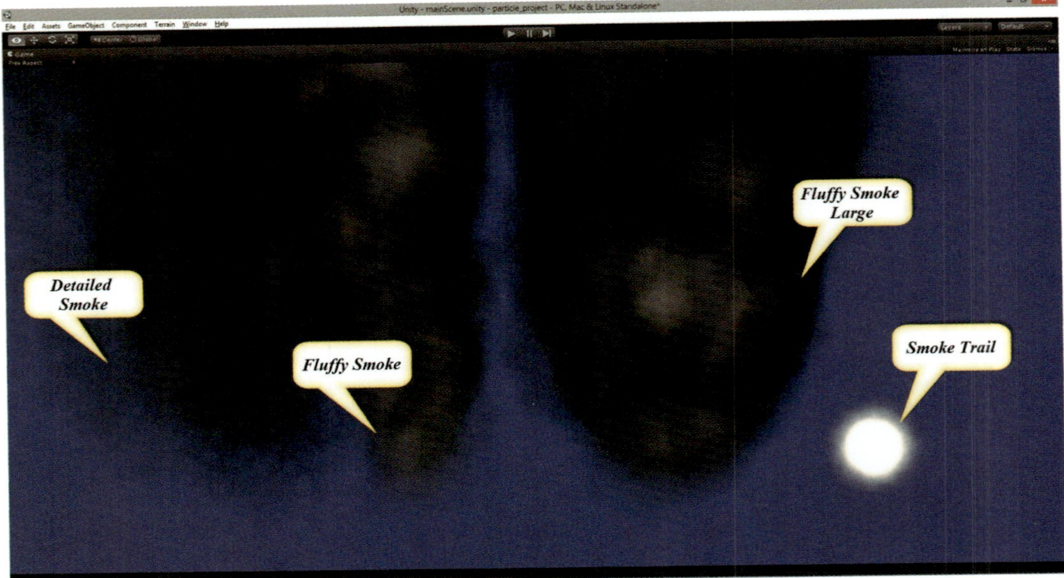

Figure 6.17 The Particles asset package features four Smoke particle systems

NOTE: This section has highlighted just some of the main systems available pre-made from the Particles package. There are more to discover and I recommend you take a look at them all at the soonest opportunity. Other systems include: *Dust*, *Sparkles*, *Water* and *Explosions*. You never know when these systems could come in useful and save you a lot of time.

6.10 Conclusion

If you are reading through this book chapter by chapter, it should have become clear by now just how much depth there is to the Unity engine; how much there is to learn. The subject of particles and particle systems is just one facet of the Unity engine and, like all the others – terrain, lighting, scripting and so on – it is extensive, detailed and diverse. In fact, so extensive and diverse is it that no single chapter of a book could hope to do justice to the subject, for it is a subject which really demands a whole book of its own. What I have tried to offer here is not a comprehensive look at everything there is to know about particles but an introduction to particle systems in general, a first taste of a fascinating world of special effects. In this chapter we saw how to create particle systems as components attached to game objects, and also how to edit their properties using the Shuriken editor. This editor offers us features for controlling the emission of particles, their colour, lifetime, size, animation, motion and more. Finally, we closed by stepping back in time to the legacy particle system to see how, despite the fact that it has been superseded by Shuriken, we can still rely on it to produce useful pre-made particle effects that can be dragged and dropped into our projects to enhance the realism of our scenes. In the next chapter we visit one of most extensive, versatile and comprehensive features of Unity: scripting.

CHAPTER 7

Scripting with C#

By the end of this chapter you should:

1. Understand what scripting is and its importance for game development.
2. Learn to how create C# scripts for Unity games.
3. Appreciate the coding, debugging and component-based workflow.
4. Understand singletons and inter-component communication.
5. Understand event-driven programming.

If there is one fundamental idea that has been repeated throughout this book, it is this: practically all Unity projects, as they move from drawing board to completion, follow a distinctive six-stage process. Step 1 involves creating and naming a new project that is to house all game files and act as the main container for everything that is to follow. Step 2 requires us to import game assets like meshes, images and sounds into the project from independent files on disk – that is, to add those assets to the Project panel, from where we can add them to our scenes and levels. Steps 3 and 4 require us to create the scenes and game environments, and then to populate those environments with instances of our assets: this stage effectively equates to 'level building'. Here we add meshes to the level, as well as sounds, animations, particle systems, lights, cameras and more. Step 5 comes next and it is here that we breathe life into the level we have created in former steps. We do this by creating **script files** using a programming language such as C# or JavaScript or Boo; these will define logic and patterns of behaviour that will govern how the game objects in our scenes should act and respond to user input and other game events. If our game features elevators that should go up or down when the player stands on them, we need script. If we are to have 'intelligent' enemies that chase or attack the gamer or instead run for cover and hide, we need script. If we are to keep track of player ammo – score and health – we need script. There is simply no getting round scripting and its importance for making interesting games in Unity. Once you accept that objects in your game should do something more than just sit there motionless, then you have already begun to think of a game where scripting will be needed – even if you do not realise it at the time. Specifically, scripting is needed to define exactly what that 'more' should be: exactly how your game objects are to behave and do things. This chapter and the next consider the issue of scripting from slightly different perspectives. The general importance of scripting cannot be understated for making Unity games – your ability to write script, and especially optimised script, is in many respects the chief measure of your power as a Unity user. This chapter will help get you started on the road to becoming a powerful user.

7.1 Getting Started with Scripting

In this chapter we will use scripting to create a coin collection game. It will be a first-person game where the player must run around an environment collecting as many coin power-ups as possible before the timer expires. Before getting started on this project, however, it is important to discuss a couple of preliminaries – specifically, some assumptions and decisions that I, as the author, have had to make to ensure the book is written to length, contains only relevant information and is generally as useful and accessible as possible to the majority of readers. The first issue that arises is exactly *where* I should begin to explain scripting in Unity, because there are many places where I *could* begin. I could, for example, assume that you had no knowledge of programming at all in any language – that you were, essentially, completely new to programming. In this case, I would have to start by explaining the basics of programming, including basic concepts such as variables, loops, if-statements, object orientation, and a lot more besides. However, this explanation, while interesting in itself, would be quite apart from Unity-specific topics – in fact, I would have to spend practically the whole book discussing the basics of programming before we could even return to Unity. For this reason I will not take that approach here. Since this is a Unity book, such programming basics would be a preposterous digression, the repetition of introductory information amply detailed in other books. Instead, I am going to assume that you already *have* programming knowledge, preferably in C# or JavaScript, and that your aim is simply to learn how to use your language of choice *in Unity*. I will assume that you can already program but have simply not programmed before in Unity. Thus, if you are a programmer looking to get started at coding with Unity specifically, then this is the chapter for you. On the other hand, if you are here to learn how to get started at programming more generally, then I strongly advise reading some of the introductory materials in the note box below before proceeding further.

NOTE: For those completely new to programming looking for introductory material, I can recommend the following books: for C# programming, *Head First C#* by Andrew Stellman and Jennifer Greene (ISBN: 978–1449380342), and for JavaScript programming, *JavaScript: The Definitive Guide* by David Flanagan (ISBN: 978–0596805524).

The second issue that arises relates to the choice of language used in this book. Unity supports three completely separate and very different languages, namely C#, JavaScript and Boo. The name JavaScript should be used here with some qualification because the language Unity actually supports is a modified form of JavaScript, not the JavaScript used for web development; for this reason, some Unity users refer to it as *UnityScript*. However, this book focusses on only one of these three languages, and that is C#. As a result, all code samples in this book, and all code used in associated projects, will be in the C# language. For some developers, the choice of language is controversial. There are developers who hold that one language is intrinsically 'better' than another for game development – and argue in this vein across forums and chat channels. I take a different view, which is: different languages offer different benefits in different circumstances. My choice of C# here largely reflects my personal preference and experience rather than any sense of 'language superiority'. C#, UnityScript and Boo are *all* powerful languages for game development; they all have advantages and disadvantages which vary from project to project and in the eyes of different developers. True, it can be easier for new users to learn Unity programming using either C# or UnityScript, because most documentation and tutorial materials use these languages rather than Boo. However, none of that changes the fact that all three languages have been used successfully in commercial games. When it comes to language choice, I recommend taking a look at all three, seeing which one you prefer and then using that consistently throughout your projects where it is appropriate. For this book, I could have chosen UnityScript or Boo – either of which would have led us to the same destination with generally equal performance. I chose C#.

7.2 The Coin Collection Game in C#

The rest of this chapter will focus on creating a coin collection game. This game will be played in first-person perspective and the aim is for the player to collect as many coins as possible within a specified time. The environment will be filled with floating coins that spin in situ, and the player collects a coin by simply running through it, as though collecting a power-up. If the player collects enough coins before the time expires, they successfully complete the game. Otherwise, they lose the game. This project will require us to use script to create the time limit and all checks that the player has collected the required number of coins. Scripting will also be used to determine when collisions occur between the player and coin objects – detecting the collisions between these two objects is necessary in order to know when the player collects a coin. To help us get a head start in this project with its focus on scripting and save us from having to repeat things we have already learnt, I have created its bare bones – a project with a space-station tunnel-like environment using the modular mesh assets from Chapter 5. This project contains no scripting at all – it will be our job to add it. I have assembled the meshes and assets into a level, complete with illumination and lightmapping as well as a first-person controller and some particle system effects. This environment will represent the level for our coin collection game and it is from this point that we will begin. The associated project files can be found in the folder */Chapter07/Project_Files*. Simply load up that project and you're ready to begin. The level should look something like Figure 7.1. Now try the following steps.

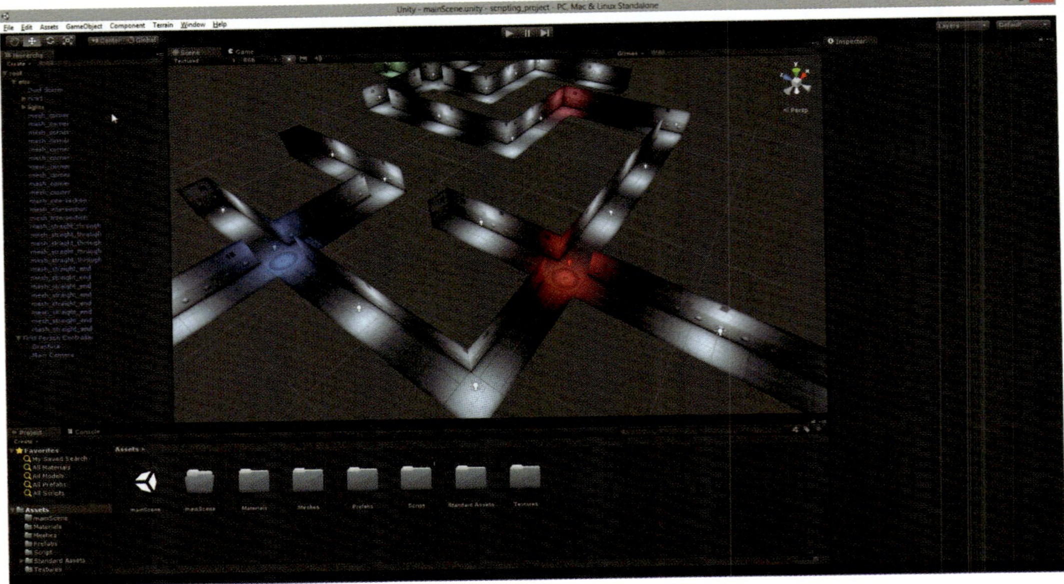

Figure 7.1 Project starting point. From here we will make a coin collection game with C#

1. The starting project that we have features an empty level environment inside which our coin collection game will take place. The first issue that we need to address is the lack of coins. Our starting project contains walls, floors, ceilings and corridors – but no coins. This is a problem because coins are essential in a coin collection game. So let us create a coin object from among the basic primitives available to us from within Unity. We'll start by creating only one coin object and then, much later in the project – when we are satisfied everything is correct with the coin – we will make a prefab from it and duplicate it around the level. To create our first coin object, select *GameObject > Create Other > Cylinder* from the main application menu. Selecting this creates a cylinder in the scene that does not initially resemble a coin. However, it can be made into a coin through scaling non-uniformly the cylinder depth with the Scale tool (*R* key on the keyboard). Give that a try. Take a look at Figure 7.2 for more details. Don't forget to give the object an appropriate name from the Object Inspector – such as *Coin*.
2. When selected in the Scene viewport the scaled cylinder can be seen to be surrounded by a green wireframe sphere or an elongated sphere: this represents the collision data for the object. This shape is attached to the object because of the *Capsule Collider component*, and it mathematically approximates the overall mass and shape of the object so that collisions between this object and others can be detected. When two collision shapes or volumes intersect, a collision occurs between those two objects. When creating colliders it is sensible to ensure the shape closely matches the shape of the mesh in order to achieve accurate collision detection. The default capsule collider attached to the cylinder object was most suited when the cylinder was at is default size and depth, but since scaling the collider looks awkward – the flattish coin nothing like its spherical-shaped collider. Consequently, let us remove the *Capsule Collider* from the object. To do this – or to remove any component from an object using the Object Inspector – click on the *Cog* icon with the downwards point arrow at the top-right corner of the component to reveal a context menu. From the menu, choose *Remove Component*. The Capsule collider component is now removed from the object.

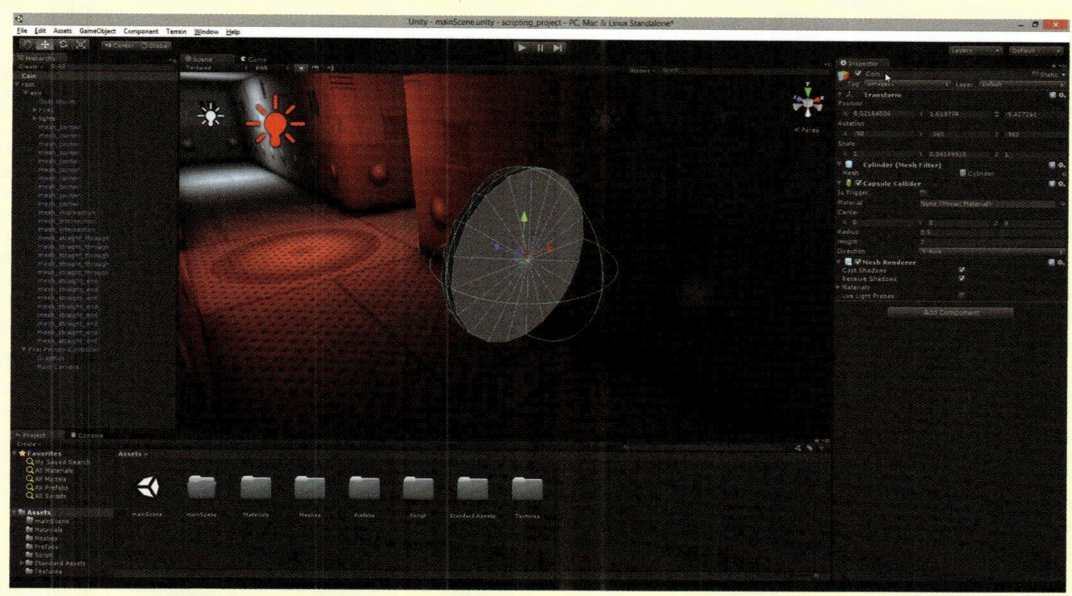

Figure 7.2 Creating a coin object from a scaled cylinder primitive

3. The coin object currently has no collider attached. In this state, the object can never detect when collisions occur, meaning that we cannot know when the player has collected a coin. To fix this, we will attach a new and more suitable collider to the object, namely a Box collider. Ensure the coin object is selected, and from the application menu choose *Component > Physics > Box Collider*. A Box

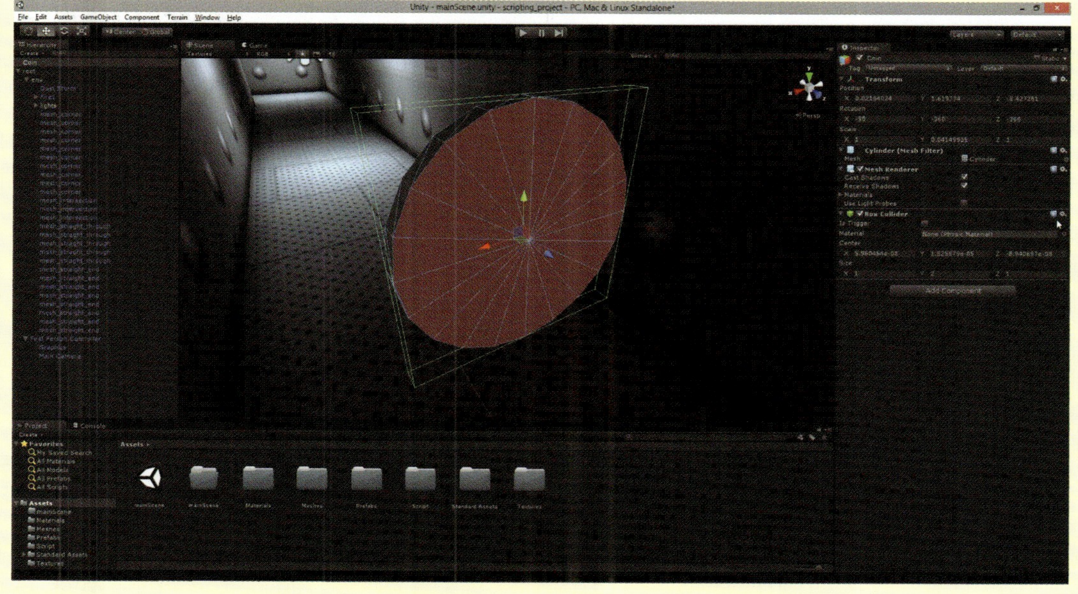

Figure 7.3 Attaching a Box collider component to the coin mesh

collider component is attached to the object and should be auto-sized to tightly hug the shape of the mesh, more closely approximating the shape of the coin; see Figure 7.3. If the Box collider is not auto-sized then its size can be changed manually from the Object Inspector by adjusting the *Size X, Y* and *Z* properties.

4. How about adding a material to this coin to make it look like a shiny gold or silver coin? We can do this by creating a new material in the Project panel. Open the *Material* folder, and right-click inside the *Project Panel*. From the Context menu, select *Create > Material*. Or you can choose *Assets > Create > Material* from the main application menu. Name the material *gold_coin* and, from the material properties in the Object Inspector, set the material *Shader* to *Specular*. Specular materials allow objects to exhibit shininess. Leave the Specular *Color* and *Shininess* settings at their defaults and set the material *Diffuse* colour to gold *(R: 223, G:182, B: 42)*. Then finally assign this material to the coin in the scene by simply dragging and dropping the material from the Project panel onto the coin mesh. The resultant coin will look gold and shiny. Take a look at Figure 7.4 to see the effect in action.

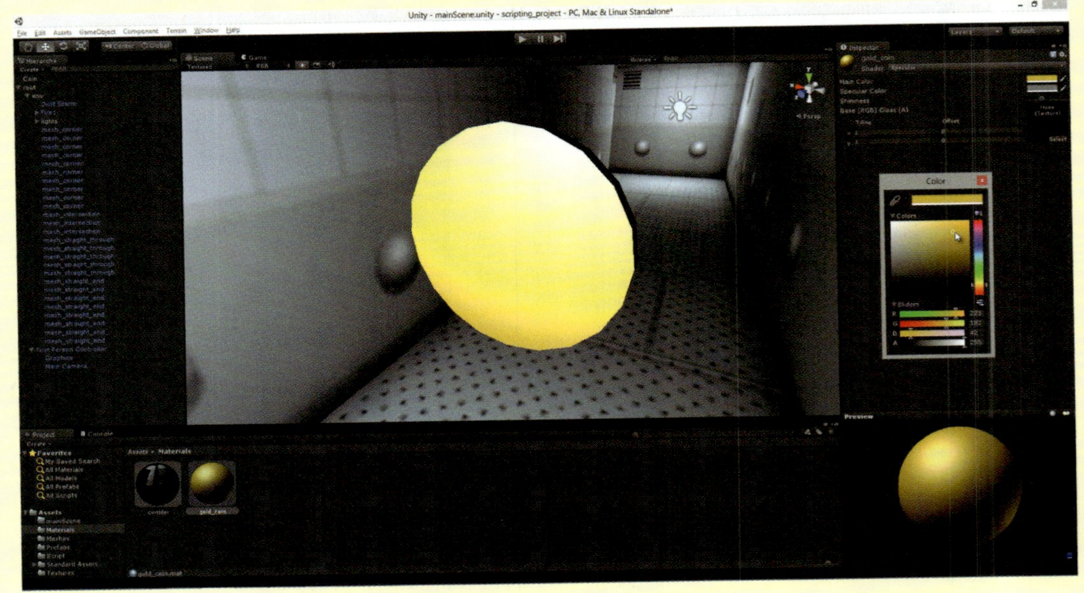

Figure 7.4 Creating a gold material for a gold coin

7.3 Scripting the Coin – Part 1

Some of the most fundamental properties for the coin object have already been created: the coin now has a mesh, a size and shape, a collider volume, and also a material. But there are still crucial ingredients as well as nice touches missing. If you press the *Play* button on the application toolbar to test your level in the *Game* tab, you will first see that we cannot walk through the coin as though it were a power-up. This is because the coin's collider volume blocks the first-person controller from passing; the default behaviour is not to allow solid objects to pass through one another. We will correct this issue later. In addition, the coin is motionless – it sits there doing nothing. It seems to me that the coin's general appearance could be greatly enhanced by a spinning motion. That is, the coin would look decidedly better if it were continually spinning on its own central axis. This would both emphasise that it is a coin to be collected and visually distinguish it from static objects like the walls and floor. Notice that the coin object should not be marked as *Static* in the Object Inspector, unlike the environment which *is* static. This is because the coin will rotate and transform during gameplay. In this section we will add that spinning behaviour, and we will do this through script. Of course, scripting is not the only option available to us for spinning the coin: we could use the animation editor. Unity often offers us more than one solution to a problem. But in this chapter we will explore the scripting option. Consider the following steps.

1. To add spinning behaviour through script we must first create a C# script file, sometimes called a *source file* because it contains source code. Inside the file we must create a C# *Class* – that is, a class in standard object-oriented terms. Unity recognises a script file as an asset in just the same way it recognises meshes, materials, movies, textures, animations, sounds and other imported files as assets. The *filename* of the script file should match the name of the *class* you intend to create; so a file named *MyClass.cs* will feature a class called *MyClass* (C# files have the extension *.cs* to represent *C-Sharp*). Though each script *can* contain more than one class, many script files contain only one, and the name of the file should match the name of that class. If there is more than one class in the file, then the filename should match the name of the main or most important class in the file. For our purposes we will be creating a single class to define the behaviour of the coin object, as well as all other instances of the coin when they are added to the scene. Thus, we will create a new C# script

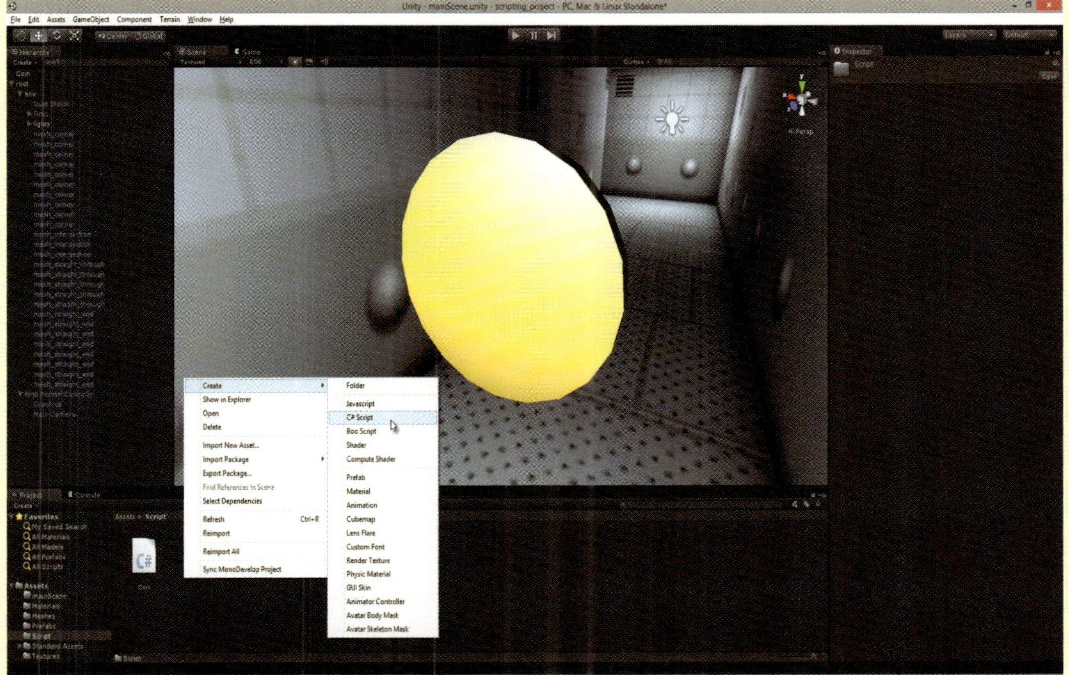

Figure 7.5 Creating a C# script file for the gold coin. Script file names should match the name of the main class in the script file

file for a *Coin* class and the name of the file will be *Coin.cs*. To create this file, right-click in the Project panel and from the context menu choose *Create > C# Script*. Name the file *Coin* (Unity adds the .cs file extension automatically). Once created, double-click the file in the Project panel to open the file inside *MonoDevelop*, a third-party code editor that ships with Unity for writing code. See Figure 7.5 for the created file in the Project panel, and Code Sample 7.1 to see what the auto-generated source code will look like.

Code 7.1 *Coin.cs*

```
using UnityEngine;

using System.Collections;

public class Coin: MonoBehaviour {

       // Use this for initialization

       void Start () {

       }


       // Update is called once per frame

       void Update () {

       }

}
```

NOTE: When a new script file is created, Unity auto-generates some class code inside the file. It generates this code on the basis of the filename that was specified. Specifically, it names your class to match the filename. This means that if you originally mistyped the filename or if the filename is not what you intended it to be, then you will have a similarly misnamed class. You can, of course, rename the script file, but if you do so, be sure to also rename the class inside the file to ensure the filename and class name correspond.

2. The auto-generated class is named on the basis of the filename and is derived from *MonoBehaviour*, which in turn traces its class ancestry back through a lineage of classes including class *Component*, and then finally back to the ultimate ancestor class *Object*. The classes *MonoBehaviour*, *Component* and *Object* are all pre-defined Unity classes that form part of the

built-in Unity API, and they offer methods and properties which can be accessed and changed, if required, to get things done. We will examine these classes in further detail as this chapter and the book progress. The source code and implementation specifics of these classes is not publicly available as Unity is not an open source engine, but comprehensive documentation for their properties, methods and general use can be accessed online in the Unity documentation at http://docs.unity3d.com/Documentation/ScriptReference/. In summary, the default behaviour of Unity when creating a new script file is always to derive its class from *MonoBehaviour*, because *MonoBehaviour* is essentially the base class from which all components are derived – components such as *MeshRenderer*, *BoxCollider* and *ParticleSystem*. In effect, by creating a class that descends from *MonoBehaviour*, we are creating an object that can be dragged and dropped from the Project panel onto an object in the scene, where it will be added as a component. Try that now: minimise the MonoDevelop editor window, if it's open, and then drag and drop the newly created *Coin.cs* script file from the Project panel and onto the coin object in the scene. Then select the coin in the viewport and notice the newly added *Script* component attached to the Coin in the Object Inspector. See Figure 7.6.

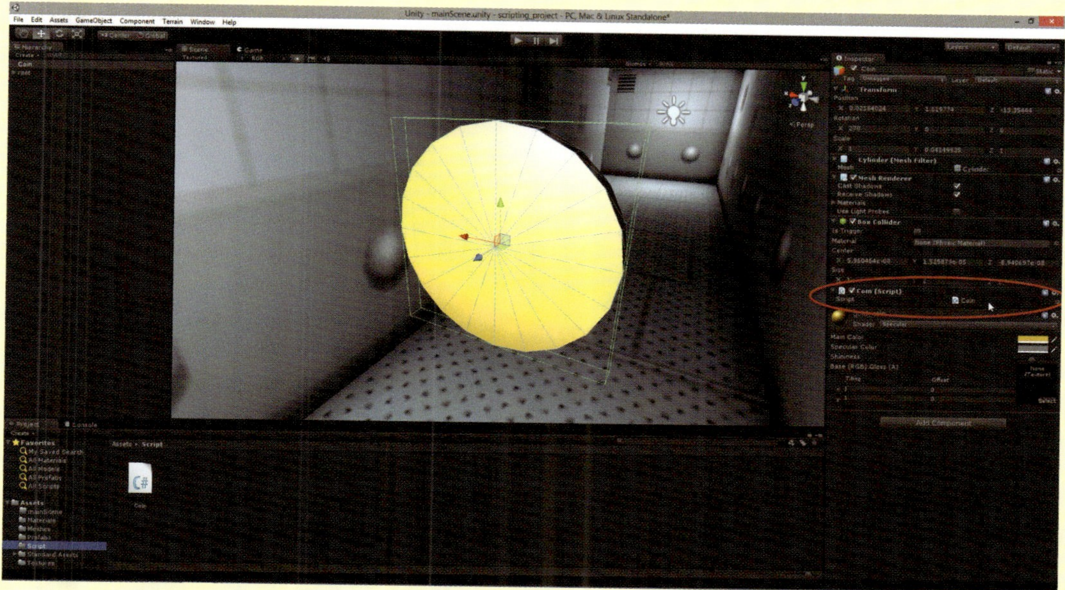

Figure 7.6 Attaching a script to an object as a component

3. The newly created script is now added to the coin object as a component, and doing this brings the object into a *subject-predicate* relationship with the script. This relationship means that the class *acts on* the object; the class *applies to* the object. If you run the game now by pressing the *Play* button on the toolbar, nothing will appear to change, even though the coin object now has a script attached. Nothing changes, of course, because the script as yet does nothing, featuring only empty functions. We can, however, customise the behaviour of the coin by returning to *MonoDevelop* and adding some code to our class. The default auto-generated code features two empty methods, *Start* and *Update*, and these methods can be seen in Code 7.1. These methods are essentially *virtual functions* that can be *overridden* in descendent classes where they act as

events: the *Start* function is called automatically by Unity when the object is first created and added to the scene, which for the coin means 'as soon as the game is run', because the coin object exists in the scene from the very beginning. This function is useful for running any initialisation code we might have that applies to the object. The *Update* function is called once per frame or 'update cycle'. This essentially means the function is called many times per second – possibly even 100+ times per second depending on the system, the hardware and the frame rate settings. Though the exact number of times this function is called cannot be known or predicted with certainty, we can rest assured that it is called 'a lot', and for this reason it is useful for defining behaviours of the object that must change, update or apply across time – such as the movement of a missile or the spinning motion of a coin! Let's quickly see this function in action right now. Edit the *Update* function to look like Code 7.2 below. Once amended, save the source file in *MonoDevelop* with *Ctrl+S* on the keyboard, minimise *MonoDevelop*, and then return to the Unity editor. When you return, Unity detects the changes to the script file and automatically recompiles and validates your code – you can see Unity doing that in the status bar at the bottom right-hand side of the editor interface: a spinning compilation icon turns to indicate a compilation is in progress. When the icon disappears, you can safely press the *Play* button on the toolbar and Unity will be using the latest code changes. Coding in Unity really is that simple: we edit code in MonoDevelop, save the file, switch back to Unity, let it recompile, and then run to test. So, now go ahead and run the game. When the game is running, check out the status bar at the bottom of the Unity interface or switch to the *Console* Tab besides the Project panel to examine the text output of the code we just created. On every frame it prints the amount of time in seconds that have elapsed since the game started running. Congratulations! You have just written your first script.

Figure 7.7 Use Debug.Log to print the elapsed game time to the Unity console

Code 7.2 *Editing the Update function of Coin.cs*

```
// Update is called once per frame
void Update ()
{
    Debug.Log(Time.time);
}
```

NOTE: The statement *Debug.Log(Time.time)* relies on the Unity API. The function *Debug.Log* is equivalent to a Print statement and is used for printing messages at run time to the debug console. The expression *Time.time* is used here to print the *time* floating-point member of the *Time* class. The Time class is a Unity API class for keeping track of time within the game. It features a range of other properties and methods, including the very useful *deltaTime*, which specifies the total time in seconds that have elapsed since the *previous frame*. This property will be used later to calculate the spinning motion of the coin at a constant speed.

TIP: Always try to minimise both the amount and complexity of code inside the Update functions of objects. Unity executes *all* Update functions for *all* scripts on *all* objects in the scene many times per second. Consequently, lengthy and intensive operations in this function can severely impact on game performance. For this reason, when a Unity developer experiences poor performance in their game on their target hardware, they often begin looking for the problem in the Update functions of scripts. Thus, when coding and designing your games, always be on the lookout for ways of arranging or redesigning your code to lessen its computational complexity in the Update functions. It can make the difference between a game that 'sinks' and a game that 'swims'.

1. Let us now remove the *Debug.Log* statement from the *Update* function of the Coin class, because it is not really doing us any good at all. It was helpful, certainly, to demonstrate how the *Update* function works and to introduce the code-editing and compilation procedure, but it does not actually get us any nearer to creating a spinning coin in the scene. We want the coin to continually spin around its own axis at a constant **speed** over time. To do this, we will start by adding a floating-point global variable *SpinSpeed* to the Coin class, which we can use to customise the spinning speed of the

coin in terms of *Degrees per Second*. In adding this variable we will also see one of the most useful, versatile and impressive features of Unity coding, namely the exposure of public class properties in the Object Inspector. Code 7.3 lists the updated Coin class with the *SpinSpeed* member added as a public variable. Save the changes to this code in *MonoDevelop* with *Ctrl+S*, return to the Unity editor, wait for compilation, and then select the Coin object in the scene. With the object selected, examine its script component in the Object Inspector. See that the public member variable *SpinSpeed* is now visible in the component as an *editable* property: that is, that the value of *SpinSpeed* can be edited in the Object Inspector, directly from the Unity Editor, to set its initial value without ever having to return to the source file at all; see Figure 7.8.

Figure 7.8 Editing global class properties from the Object Inspector

Code 7.3 *Editing the Coin Class to have a SpinSpeed Property*

```
using UnityEngine;
using System.Collections;
public class Coin: MonoBehaviour
{
        public float SpinSpeed = 100.0f;
        // Use this for initialization
        void Start () {}
```

```
    // Update is called once per frame
    void Update () {}
}
```

NOTE: The values for global variables that are specified in the Object Inspector will always override any defaults specified in the source file. Code 7.3 assigns *SpinSpeed* a default value of *100.0f*. In Unity this means that the variable *SpinSpeed* will begin initialised to a value of 100.0f, *unless* a *different* value is specified in the Object Inspector. In that case, the Object Inspector value will always take precedence.

5. The *SpinSpeed* variable now offers a way to control the spinning speed of the coin both from code and, more interestingly, from the Object Inspector. But the coin itself still does not spin when the game is run. We will address this now by accessing the coin's *Transform* component in script. Every game object has a Transform component, which features properties for *Position*, *Rotation* and *Scale*. In previous chapters we set the values of this component for objects directly, via the Unity editor and using the GUI transformation tools of *Translate*, *Rotate* and *Scale*. Now we will set the *Rotation* property through script inside the Update function, to ensure the property changes over time on a frame-by-frame basis. To do this, return to *MonoDevelop* and edit the *Update* function to match Code 7.4. Notice from the listing that the *Transform* component is accessed through a member variable inherited from the *MonoBehaviour* class, the *transform* member (lowercase *t*). This member is of type *Transform* (uppercase *T*) and, as with other classes, more information about it can be found in the Unity documentation at http://docs.unity3d.com/Documentation/ScriptReference/Transform.html. This class offers the *Rotate* function to turn an object around any of its three cardinal axes: *Right*, *Up* and *Forward*. Compile this code and give the scene a test run to see the coin spinning. Now try editing the *SpinSpeed* value from the Object Inspector and see how it affects the spinning speed in the game: higher values result in faster spins.

Code 7.4 *Editing the Coin Class Update Function to Spin the Coin*

```
void Update ()
{
    //Rotates coin
    transform.Rotate(0,0,SpinSpeed * Time.deltaTime);
}
```

NOTE: Here is an incredibly powerful and exciting feature: you do not have to stop running the game in order to change the *SpinSpeed* value in the Object Inspector! This applies not only to the *SpinSpeed* value but also all others in the Object Inspector. You do not have to use the traditional debugging framework of stopping the game, editing the value and then starting playback again to observe the effects of the change. With Unity, *while the game is running*, you can select the coin object in the scene, change its *SpinSpeed* value (or other values) and see the results update in real time in both in the *Scene* and *Game* tabs! Using this technique you can try out all kinds of values for different properties and see the run-time results immediately. You can even select transformation tools such as Translate, Rotate and Scale and use them to adjust the transformation properties of objects in real time during gameplay.

NOTE: If you do change an object's properties during gameplay like this, it is important to note that those properties will always *reset back* to their former values when gameplay ends: the effects of property changes during gameplay are only temporary, they last just as long as the gameplay session. This handy feature of making run-time changes works both ways too: you can not only *set* properties during gameplay from the Object Inspector, you can also *see* and *read* their values in the edit fields as they update and change in real time. This makes the Object Inspector one of the most powerful and versatile tools in Unity's debugging arsenal. Not sure if your object is behaving as it should during gameplay? Are you in doubt whether its properties are being set to the correct values at the correct time? Well, if those properties are public then you can use the Object Inspector to find out: run the game, select the object and keep a watch on the Object Inspector. Take this opportunity to explore these debugging features – have a play around with them and get to grips with their awesome debugging potential.

6. Since we are on the topic of debugging, let's see how Unity reacts to coding mistakes and compilation errors, because errors and slip-ups are something every programmer makes, whether new or veteran. Return to MonoDevelop and remove the terminating semi-colon (;) symbol from the end of the *transform.Rotate* statement in Code 7.4. Save the file and return to Unity to recompile the changes. In response, Unity will detect the errors, prevent the game from being run and, further, print red-coloured error messages to the Console tab, one message per error, describing the nature of the problem. Double-clicking on an error message from the console will open up MonoDevelop and focus the cursor on the line of code suspected of being related to the problem – although MonoDevelop's diagnosis is not always correct. Of course, don't forget to correct your error by re-inserting the semi-colon at the end of the statement.

7.4 Creating a Game Manager Component

The result of our work from the previous section is a spinning coin; a coin that rotates continually around its own local axis during gameplay. This effect was achieved primarily by creating a *MonoBehaviour* component from a C# script, a script in which we continually call the *transform.Rotate* function in the *Update* event to change and update the orientation of the coin object on each frame. This works fine so far, but our needs do not end there. The game we intend to create should feature not only spinning coins but also the ability of the player to *collect* those coins, and there must be some kind of time limit to determine whether the game is won or lost. In this section we will address the issues of a time limit and a coin counter – required, respectively, to keep track of how much time has elapsed in the game and see how many coins the player has collected. Specifically, as the game begins a countdown must commence. During this time the player is free to explore the scene and collect what coins they may find. When the countdown expires, the game will check the number of coins collected. If the coin count *exceeds* a specified minimum then the game is *won*, otherwise the game is *lost*. The developmental question that faces us now is: where and how do we code this behaviour? We could return to the Coin class we have started and code in some extra features and functions to implement a time limit and coin counter. But this approach does not seem appropriate because the scene will feature *many* coins. For our game, we require only one time limit and one counter for the *whole level*, not one for *each coin*. This suggests that the time limit and coin collection counter do not belong in the Coin class, but in a higher-level class that will have only one instantiation in the scene. Therefore, we need to create an additional C# script class, and this class will be called the *GameManager* because of its overarching and managerial role in determining the main gameplay logic. The following steps get us started at creating this manager.

1. Create a new C# script file from the Project panel and name the file *GameManager* to create a new *GameManager.cs* file asset with an auto-generated class inside named *GameManager*. The generated class will look like Code 7.5. By default this class is derived from class *MonoBehaviour*, although it is not currently attached to any game object in the scene as a component.

Code 7.5 *GameManager.cs*

```
using UnityEngine;
using System.Collections;
//————————————————————
```

```
public class GameManager : MonoBehaviour

{

     // Use this for initialization

    void Start () {}

    // Update is called once per frame

    void Update (){}

}
```

2. The GameManager class will maintain three public properties that we will add, all of which we want to be able to tweak, if required, from the Object Inspector, as opposed to tweaking in code. These three properties are: 1) *CoinsCollected*, to keep track of the actual number of coins the player has collected in the scene; 2) *WinCollect*, defining the number of coins the player must collect by the expiration of the timer in order to win the game; and 3) *TimeLimit*, the time limit itself which expresses in seconds the total time for which the player may actively collect coins in the scene, measured from the beginning of the game. These three properties can be added as public member variables to the class, as shown in Code 7.6. Save this code and then return to Unity and compile.

Code 7.6 *Adding the CoinsCollected, WinCollect and TimeLimit public members*

```
public int CoinsCollected = 0;

public int WinCollect = 10;

public int TimeLimit = 10;
```

3. The *GameManager* class works a little differently than the *Coin* class. The Coin class encapsulates a discrete and physical object in the scene, namely a coin, which can potentially be instanced any number of times throughout the level for however many coins we need. The *GameManager,* in contrast, does *not* encapsulate any tangible thing that exists in the scene, such as a coin, monster, wall or car. Rather, it acts as a non-physical, invisible law enforcer, ensuring the game runs as it should. Further, unlike the Coin class, the GameManager should be instantiated only once in the scene, to act as a single and authoritative overseer. This makes sense because instantiating multiple versions of the GameManager would lead to conflicting coin collection counts and conflicting time limits. There are multiple solutions available to us for implementing this kind of class, where only one instance can be made: one popular method is to use the *Singleton design pattern*, but this approach and its details are beyond the scope of this book. The method used here will be to create an empty non-visible game object in the scene and to assign the *GameManager* class as a component of that

object. This method will serve our purpose for this game. True, it does not really limit the number of instances of this class that we could potentially instantiate; it is still *technically* possible to create multiple instances. For example, if we added more game objects with a *GameManager* component there would be no class or functionality to prevent this from happening. But as long as we resolve to create only *one* game object with *one GameManager* component in the scene, and as long as we adhere to that resolve, we can be safe in the knowledge that nowhere else in our code or game will additional instances of this class be created. On that basis, we can know that our scene will have only one *GameManager* component active – and that is enough for us in this project. So let's now create a new and empty game object by selecting *GameObject > Create Empty* from the application menu. Name this object *GameManager* and then attach the *GameManager* class to it as a component, by dragging and dropping the script file from the Project panel to the game object in the scene. Now, when the GameManager object is selected in the scene, the GameManager class properties are shown for the object in the Object Inspector. The scene now contains one GameManager object, with a GameManager component attached, and this component displays the three public variables we have added.

NOTE: If you are interested in the Singleton design pattern, check out the source code for this project. There I have coded the GameManager as a Singleton class. This class cannot be instantiated more than once in the scene at run time. You simply cannot do it. Don't believe me? Try and create several GameManagers in the Scene view and then press the *Play* button from the toolbar to see what happens when the game runs: all instances of GameManager but one will be removed.

7.5 Coroutine and Yield Statements

The GameManager class created so far has three public properties that are intended to record the total number of coins collected, the total number needed to win, and the total time in seconds that must expire before the game is over. These properties can be tweaked and edited directly from the Object Inspector, via the GameManager component. However, our class is still missing the key functionality that makes use of these properties: at present, nothing increments the coin counter and nothing applies the time limit. In this section, the time-limit functionality will be implemented, and to do this we will call upon a powerful and versatile Unity feature, known as the CoRoutine – which, for readers familiar with these concepts, is functionally equivalent to a thread or asynchronous function. Before considering the thread further, however, let us consider an alternative route that we could take for creating the time limit, a method that is open to us entirely on the basis of code and functionality that we have already seen in this chapter. In short, we could use the *Update* method of the GameManager class, called once per frame, to check the *Time.time* value to see how long has elapsed in seconds since the game began, and then terminate gameplay when the time limit expires based on a simple conditional statement: if (*Time.time* > = *TimeLimit*). While this method is perfectly acceptable, I will use a different method here for the purpose of demonstrating CoRoutines. Consider the following steps to create and use a CoRoutine.

1. The term 'CoRoutine' in Unity is the name given to any function that has a specific form and structure. Coroutines are distinct from other functions in that they work like background processes and their execution can span multiple frames. Typically, when a standard function is called, the execution of the program waits until the called function has completed before moving onto the next line and executing the next statement – this is standard *Synchronous* workflow, where functions are executed in sequence, one at a time. Coroutines, however, have the power to work 'in parallel with' or 'at the same time as' other processes: you can start them running and 'off they go'. It should be noted that Coroutines are not truly a form of parallel processing because they do not *really* execute at the same time as other functions. Nevertheless, Coroutines are functionally equivalent to such a process, and they appear to execute in parallel because of the way the Unity engine has been designed. To create a CoRoutine you need to declare a function using the form given in Code 7.7 below.

Code 7.7 *Declaring CoRoutines*

```
public IEnumerator MyCoRoutine()
{
        yield break;
}
```

NOTE: In C#, all Coroutines have the return type **IEnumerator** and at least one **yield** statement, which can be post-fixed with expressions such as *break*, *return null* and *new WaitForSeconds()*. In essence, the yield statement, as we shall see, acts like a specialised return statement. If a function has an IEnumerator return type *and* a yield statement, then it is a CoRoutine – at least, it is in *C#*; the specifics of other languages such as JavaScript and Boo are different. Please consult the Unity documentation for more details on Coroutines in languages other than C#: *http://docs.unity3d.com/Documentation/ScriptReference/index.Coroutines_26_Yield.html*

2. For our GameManager class in this project, a CoRoutine will be started as the game begins, and it will continue to execute 'in the background' or 'in parallel' to keep track of the game countdown and timer. When the timer expires, the CoRoutine will 'interrupt' general execution and end the game,

checking to see whether the player won or lost the game based on the number of coins collected. To create a CoRoutine to do this, add the following CoRoutine *StartCountDown* as a member function of the class. See Code 7.8 below. Notice it features the return type *IEnumerator* and a *yield* statement, this time post-fixed with a *new WaitForSeconds* expression.

Code 7.8 *Declaring CoRoutines*

```
using UnityEngine;
using System.Collections;
//————————————————
public class GameManager : MonoBehaviour
{
        public int CoinsCollected = 0;
        public int WinCollect = 10;
        public int TimeLimit = 10;
        public IEnumerator StartCountDown()
        {
                //Wait until time has expired
                yield return new WaitForSeconds(TimeLimit);

                //Time  has expired
                if(CoinsCollected >= WinCollect)
                {
                        print ("Game Won");
                }
                else
                        print ("Game Lost");
        }
}
```

CoRoutines and yield in depth. The yield statement of a CoRoutine is like a pause button for the function. It will cause the function to exit at the line of the yield statement and the function will pause execution *for that frame*. But the function will *resume* again, and when it does, execution *continues on the line after the yield statement*. The expression following the word 'yield' controls exactly *when* the function will resume. The statement *yield break* will terminate the CoRoutine completely. The statement *yield return null* will pause the CoRoutine for this frame, and it will resume again, from the line after, at *the next frame*. The statement *yield return new WaitForSeconds(time)* will pause the CoRoutine and resume its execution, from the next line, after the specified time has elapsed in seconds. The StartCountDown function in Code 7.8 uses this latter method. Here, the CoRoutine waits until the time limit has expired and then resumes the CoRoutine at the next line, which checks the win condition for the game.

3. The problem that now exists is this: if you add that CoRoutine to the GameManager class and play the game, the CoRoutine is not executed. In fact, even if you edit the *Start* event of the class to explicitly call the function with *StartCountDown(),* the CoRoutine will still not start. This is because a specialised convention must be used to start CoRoutines. To be specific, CoRoutines can be started using the *StartCoroutine* function. There are two versions of this function available: the first (Method A) allows you specify the CoRoutine by name, for example: *StartCoroutine("StartCountDown").* The other (Method B) allows you to specify the CoRoutine by function reference, for example: *StartCoroutine(StartCountDown()).* Of these two methods, I recommend Method A in almost all cases. This is because all CoRoutines started by Method A can be stopped manually, if necessary, by calling the function *StopCoroutine(),* for example: *StopCoroutine("StartCountDown").* CoRoutines initiated with Method B cannot be stopped manually and must complete their course. Thus, the Start Event for the GameManager class can be amended as in Code 7.9 below. Add this code to your GameManager class, then save it, compile it, and take it for a test run. Wait until the timer expires and then see the debug messages printed to the console to confirm that the CoRoutine is up and running.

```
Code 7.9 Declaring CoRoutines
// Use this for initialization
void Start ()
{
        //Start game count down
        StartCoroutine("StartCountDown");
}
```

7.6 Collecting Coins

With both a *GameManager* class and a *Coin* class created, it is now time to implement the coin collection functionality; specifically, the ability to *detect* when the player has collected a coin and to *increment* the coin counter whenever this happens. Achieving this will require interclass communication. That is, it requires the Coin class, which will detect when a coin is collected, to communicate with the GameManager class to make it increment its coin counter. There are several ways interclass communication like this can be achieved in Unity, including static member access for Singleton objects and using the Unity API functions. This chapter will focus on the latter method. Consider the following sections.

1. The first step in implementing the coin collection functionality is to detect when the player collects a coin. Collection should occur when the player walks through the coin, or more accurately, when the player walks through the coin's *collision volume*. By its default settings, however, the Box collider component attached to the coin object does not allow the player to pass through the coin. Instead, it acts like a solid and impassable obstacle, requiring the player to walk around the coin. This behaviour can be changed, though, by enabling the *Is Trigger* property of the Box collider component. Enabling this setting causes the collider to change its behaviour: it ceases to act as a solid and impassable thing and becomes simply an invisible volume that detects collisions and intersections with other objects in the scene. Go ahead and enable the *Is Trigger* property and give the scene a test run. You should now be able to pass through the coin, although – at present – nothing happens when you do.
2. Once the property *Is Trigger* is enabled for the coin's collider, detecting a collision is simple and can be handled in script. Open up the *Coin.cs* script file in *MonoDevelop* and add to the class the function *OnTriggerEnter*. This function acts as an event and is called each time an object collides with or enters the Trigger volume, including the first-person controller object. See Code 7.9 for the full OnTriggerEnter function, and then consider the following note for a code discussion.

Code 7.10 *Detecting Collisions*

```
void OnTriggerEnter(Collider other)
{
    //If player collided
    if(other.CompareTag("Player"))
    {
        //print current score
        print("Coins Collected");
```

```
            //Destroy coin

            Destroy(gameObject);

        }

    }
```

NOTE: The function *OnTriggerEnter* is called for the coin object whenever an intersection occurs on the attached box collider volume. This collision could occur when the player collides with the volume, or when any object collider intersects the volume. The colliding volume is passed into the *OnTriggerEnter* event as the function argument *Other*. This object is of the base class *Collider*, from which all other colliders are derived, and this class – like most others in Unity – is part of the built-in Unity API. The Unity documentation lists all of the functions and members of this class at: http://docs.unity3d.com/Documentation/ScriptReference/Collider.html.

Since we only want to detect collisions between the player and the coin (as opposed to collisions with other objects), it is necessary to check which volume has collided with the coin, to verify that it is the player. The function performs this check using the *CompareTag* function – checking to see whether the *tag* of the game object, which owns the Collider volume, matches that of 'Player'. If you select the first-person controller object in the scene, you will see that it has the 'Player' tag assigned to it. Once the tag is verified, a message is printed to the debug console and the coin object is removed from the scene using the *Destroy* function. This destroys an instance of the selected Game Object. The coin is destroyed immediately on collection to prevent the player from collecting the same coin again, because that would severely skew the coin collection counter. Notice, however, that the code does not (yet!) increment the counter itself on the GameManager class.

3. Give the game a test run now to confirm that the coin is indeed deleted from the scene whenever the player passes through the coin's collider volume. When this event occurs, however, it is also important to notify the *GameManager* to increment the coin collection counter. Unless the counter is incremented on this object, the *GameManager* will not officially recognise that a coin has been collected when it comes to figure out whether the game has been won when the timer expires. To increment the collection counter on the *GameManager*, the *OnTriggerEnter* function of the coin class can be amended as in Code 7.11 below.

```
Code 7.11 Incrementing the Coin Collection Counter
void OnTriggerEnter(Collider other)
{
        //If player collided
        if(other.CompareTag("Player"))
        {
              //Find Game Object in Scene
              GameObject GM = GameObject.Find ("GameManager");
              //Get Game Manager Component on Object
              GameManager GM_Component = GM.GetComponent<GameManager>();

              //Increment Counter
              ++GM_Component.CoinsCollected;
              //print current score
              print("Coins Collected:" + GM.CoinsCollected);

              //Destroy coin
              Destroy(gameObject);
        }
}
```

NOTE: Three statements have been inserted into the *OnTriggerEnter* function. These increment the coin counter on the GameManager class. The first statement calls the static function *GameObject.Find* to search the scene hierarchy for an object whose name matches "GameManager". If no object of matching name is found, null is returned. But since our *GameManager* object has been assigned the name "GameManager", it will be returned from the GameObject.Find function. *GetComponent* is then called on the *GameManager*

object. This is to get a reference to the *GameManager* class, which is attached to the object as a component. Using the GetComponent function, a reference to any attached component – including colliders and mesh renderers – can be retrieved if required. Once the GameManager component has been retrieved, its coin collection counter can be incremented through the statement *++GM_Component.CoinsCollected*.

4. Splendid work! Give the game a test run to see that, now, not only does the coin disappear from the scene when collected, but the GameManager coin collection counter is incremented. Of course, at the moment the scene contains only one coin. To fix that we can create a prefab from the selected coin, complete with its Coin component and Box collider, and then instantiate more of those prefabs around the level to represent different coins. To do that, create a new *Prefab* folder in the Project panel, and then new add a new Prefab asset to the folder with *Assets > Create > Prefab* from the application menu. Assign the prefab the name *Prefab_Coin*. Then finally drag and drop the coin object in the scene onto the Prefab object in the Project panel to add that object to the *Prefab_Coin* prefab.
5. Now simply drag and drop the coin prefab into the level wherever you want another coin. Each separate drag and drop operation will add a new coin to the scene for collection when the game is played. Though each coin is separate in that each one can be independently collected, they all still *share* the common coin behaviour that was coded in the *Coin* class. Consider Figure 7.9 for the completed level in action.

Figure 7.9 Completing the Coin Collection game

7.7 Conclusion

Excellent work! The coin collection game is now soundly functional through C# scripting in Unity, though not, of course, without being open to substantial improvements. In this chapter we examined not only how to create C# scripts in MonoDevelop, but also how to code and debug applications using a range of Unity specifics features. Using the Object Inspector we can edit and tweak values for global variables on classes, and we can also edit and tweak the same properties while the game is running. Further, we examined the Unity API, class structures, CoRoutines and yield statements, and also how to achieve inter-object communication using the *GameObject.Find* and *GetComponent* functions. Combining these features we have succeeded in creating a coin collection game in which the player must race against the clock to collect as many coins as they can. When the time limit expires, the game tests the collected coins against the target and displays a win or lose message accordingly. This sample does not actually terminate the game or lock player input when the timer expires, neither does it present a window or fancy graphics to indicate the game has ended. It does nothing beyond print a message to the console. Now, while this does serve its purpose, it seems a bit underwhelming compared to what we could achieve. Specifically, the game would be much improved with a GUI – a graphical user interface. It would be improved if we could show a text message on screen displaying the number of coins the player has collected while the game is running, and it would also be improved if we displayed a 'Game Won' or 'Game Over' graphic when the timer expired. The next chapter implements these GUI features into the game, and more. In it we shall take our knowledge of scripting further as we consider the process of creating graphical user interfaces in Unity.

CHAPTER 8

GUIs and Scripting

By the end of this chapter you should:

1. Understand what a GUI is and the GUI workflow for Unity.
2. Understand the challenges of aspect ratio and resolution.
3. Be able to prepare and import Alpha texture for GUIs.
4. Be able to create and render GUIs for your games.
5. Understand GUI content and GUI styles.

The acronym GUI (often pronounced *gooey*) stands for *Graphical User Interface*. In practical terms the GUI of a game refers collectively to all the 2D and on-screen graphical elements that either give the gamer information – about, for instance, their health status – or allow access to specific game features such as save and restore. GUI elements include main menus, buttons, scores, progress bars, health bars, avatar pictures, icons, status indicators, messages boxes, windows, inventories, mini-maps and a lot more besides. Although GUIs do sometimes make use of 3D graphics or 3D space, typically they appear in two-dimensions only – that is, in *screen space* as opposed to *world space*. Visually then, GUIs appear to exist on a separate layer in front of everything else on the screen. Of all the aspects of game development, it is perhaps the GUI that is most commonly underestimated by both new and veteran developers, some of whom overlook the GUI's technical complexities and regard it as simply an afterthought, a secondary feature to be tacked on quickly at the end without much foresight or design. For developers who take this line, the GUI soon becomes one of the biggest sources of aggravation in their everyday work. The overall purpose of this chapter is two-fold: first, to emphasise the importance of the GUI and its associated concepts, so that you create GUIs for your games without falling into the dangerous trap of underestimating GUI-work. And second, to show you the powerful range of features Unity offers us for creating GUIs – as well as the features Unity does *not* yet offer us! Alongside the consideration of these important aspects we'll pursue a fun project: specifically, we'll create a GUI for the coin collecting game we began in the previous chapter when exploring scripting. Consequently, this chapter picks up where the previous one left off and assumes you're already familiar with that content. If you're reading this book non-sequentially (perhaps as a reference), then you should read Chapter 7 before continuing with this one.

8.1 Getting Started with GUIs

This chapter could have begun with a lot of theory and discussion about concepts such as resolution, aspect ratio, pixel perfection, Atlas texturing and dynamic and static fonts. But instead we'll focus on a creating a practical project that features a GUI. In doing this we'll be visiting and exploring almost every one of the above concepts but in a practical context, just as in previous chapters. We'll create a GUI for the coin collecting game, which will involve adding three main GUI features: a FPS-style console where we can print debug messages to the screen as though it were the standard Unity console in the Editor; a HUD (Heads-Up Display) coin counter to show the gamer how many coins they have collected – this will be on screen permanently while the game is running; and finally, 'game win' and 'game over' graphical messages. These will display when the game timer expires and the game is won or lost respectively. Once the project is completed and looking good, complete with its GUI, we'll then play Devil's advocate. We'll start pushing the limits of our game to see the different ways our interface can break and go wrong, and we'll close the chapter by considering various techniques for fixing these problems. These techniques, like almost all of them in this book, apply not only to the project in the chapter but to practically all Unity games, whether they are desktop games, console games or mobile games. So let's get started: either open up the project you completed in the previous chapter, or open the project I have provided for you from the project files, in the folder *Chapter8*. This project represents the coin collecting game so far: the gamer is able to run around an environment in first-person mode, collecting coins under time pressure. Before we get started at coding anything, let's configure our project to run at a predetermined resolution or screen size – in this case 1024x768 pixels. Consider the following steps on how to do this.

1. If you press the *Play* button on the toolbar right now, the game will run and play as it did before. The rendered view of the game from the camera will take up or fill the entire contents of the *Game* tab. If you maximise or shrink the Game tab, the rendering will resize and expand or shrink to fill the whole of that tab. This behaviour happens because the Game tab is by default in *Free Aspect* mode – it doesn't 'care' about screen size. Consider Figure 8.1. Free Aspect behaviour is fine in many cases when testing 3D games; it has, for instance, worked flawlessly for us so far. But games are typically made with specific screen sizes and resolutions in mind, not just any sizes or resolutions. For this reason there inevitably comes a point in development when it is essential to see what the game will look like at its intended resolution. Being able to see this is *especially* important when creating GUIs, for reasons that will become clear as we progress.

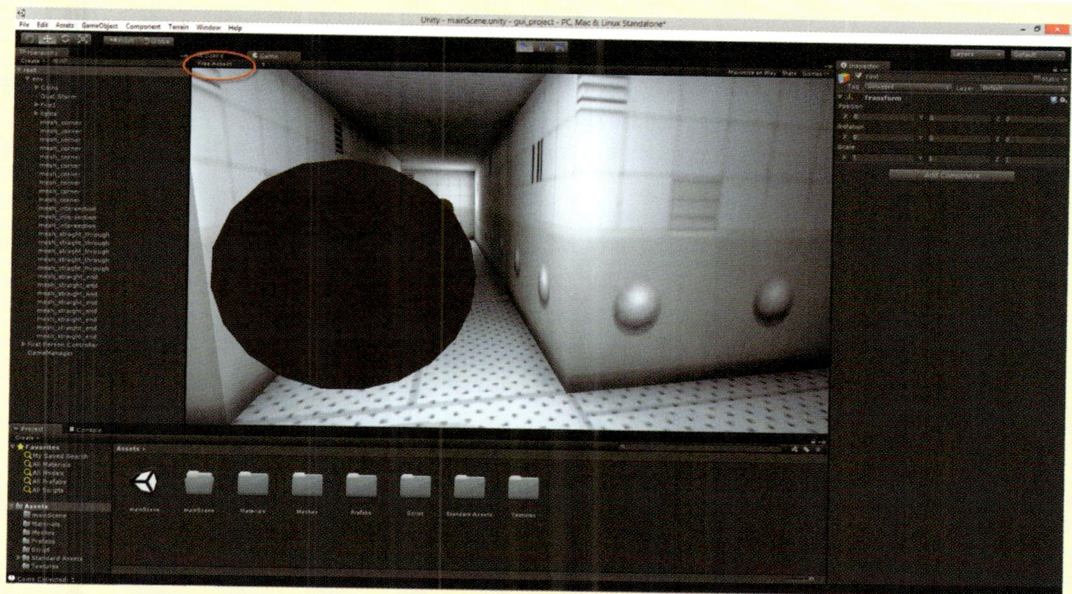

Figure 8.1 The coin collection game running in the Game tab with Free Aspect mode

2. Unity can be configured to lock or fix the size of the Game tab to a specific resolution and size; any size that we choose. We'll now fix the resolution of this game to 1024x768 pixels, a standard screen size for many older desktop and PC games prior to the HD era, which includes the sizes 1280x720 and 1920x1080. To do this, first access the Player Settings menu by choosing *Edit > Project Settings > Player* from the application menu. The player settings are displayed in the Object Inspector. From here,

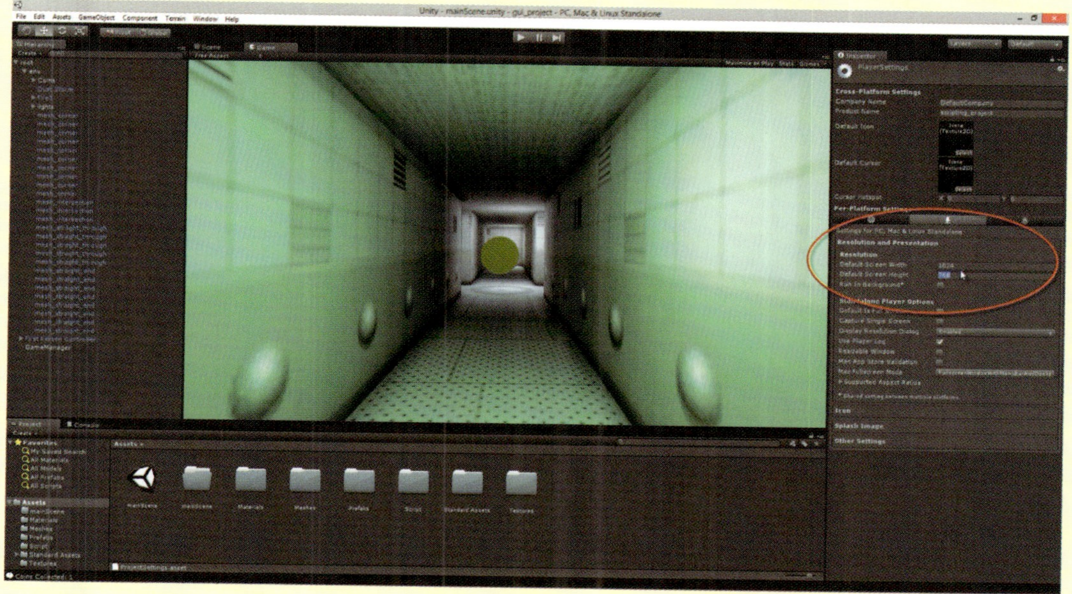

Figure 8.2 Setting the default resolution for the project from the Player Settings menu

expand the *Resolution and Presentation* tab, and for the *Resolution* setting, specify a Width and Height of 1024 x 768 respectively, as shown in Figure 8.2.

3. Once the default resolution for the project is specified, the *Game* tab can be locked into this resolution by clicking the *Resolution* drop-down list (currently *at Free Aspect*) and changing it to 1024x768. This will resize the Game tab rendering area, filling excess areas of the screen with empty space and ensuring the rendered area matches the default resolution. Consider Figure 8.3 below. Having now configured the Game tab in this way, we are ready to start coding the first part of the GUI: namely, the console window.

Figure 8.3 Fixing the Game tab into the 1024x768 resolution

8.2 Getting Started with the FPS Console

Many of the famous FPS games, such as Quake, Unreal Tournament, Team Fortress and Duke Nukem, feature a *Console* or *Command Window*. This refers to a panel component in the GUI that can be made to slide into view during gameplay, typically by pressing a dedicated key combination on the keyboard, and used to type in special commands to change the behaviour of the game or query specific details – even to input cheat codes. It can also be used to view outputted debugging information from the game, information such as the frame rate, the number of players connected to the session and the amount of time spent playing the level. Here we will code the beginnings of a similarly styled console feature for our coin collecting game: our console will not allow the player to input text instructions but will allow the developer to view on-screen any text statements and outputted debug information we may wish to show.

It will effectively act like the Unity console that we have seen already, except that our console will not reside within the Unity Editor interface but will be a graphical part of the game. In creating this feature we will see the core elements of the UnityGUI system at work and gain an appreciation of its general form and structure. Consider the following steps.

1. Start by creating a new C# class in the project named *ConsoleWindow.cs*. This class will contain all our code for the console window and will ultimately be attached as a component to the existing *GameManager* object in the scene. Create the class now, and also attach the script as a component to the GameManager. Refer to the previous chapter, Step 1 of section 7.3, for specific instructions on how to create C# source files. Remember, the class name generated inside the script file will be based on the name of the file: if you mistype the file name then the class will also be misnamed. You can also go ahead and delete both the *Start* and *Update* functions of the class, as we will not need them for the console. The generated source file, after edits, should appear as follows.

```
Code 8.1 ConsoleWindow.cs
using UnityEngine;
using System.Collections;

public class ConsoleWindow : MonoBehaviour
{
}
```

2. In Unity, GUIs are created almost entirely through scripting. Each class descended from *MonoBehaviour*, as our ConsoleWindow class is, inherits a special function and event named *OnGUI*. Like most other inherited functions, this function is optional in that a class does not *need* to provide any implementation for it but *should* do so if it intends to provide GUI functionality. The *OnGUI* function, similarly to any other functions it might call, is used for separating and containing all the GUI code for a class from other functions that might be concerned with standard game behaviour: it is to help us ensure the GUI code does not leak or spread into other game-related functions like *Update* or *Start*. The *OnGUI* function is called automatically by the Unity engine *at least* once per frame but often more frequently: this means it's typically called even more frequently than the *Update* function! For this reason it is practically never a good idea to use this function for performing expensive calculations or work that could just as easily be carried out in functions called less frequently. The more code and functionality that is added to *OnGUI*, the greater the computational overhead for your game. So with that advice in mind, let's go ahead and add the *OnGUI* function to our newly created ConsoleWindow class in preparation for building our GUI. See the code sample 8.2. Right now this function is empty and thus does nothing productive, but that will soon change.

```
Code 8.2 ConsoleWindow.cs, with OnGUI Added
using UnityEngine;
using System.Collections;
public class ConsoleWindow : MonoBehaviour
{
        //Called to render GUI elements
        void OnGUI()
        {
        }
}
```

3. The newly added function *OnGUI* is intimately associated with a specific Unity class that is part of the API – this class is called *GUI*. The documentation for it can be found online at https://docs.unity3d.com/Documentation/ScriptReference/GUI.html. The basic idea is that whenever the *OnGUI* function is run, we call upon the functions and methods of the *GUI* class to tell Unity how to draw the GUI for our game *in that frame*. Unity conceives the GUI as composed from a range of different elements, each element being called a *control* – though sometimes the term *widget* is used instead. A text box, a button, a label, a window, a scroll bar and a progress bar are all examples of controls (*plural*), each one being termed a control (*singular*). This means: each time *OnGUI* is called, we must tell Unity about the controls in our interface *for that frame*. The console window we must create here is basically a box with text in it. Luckily, the Unity *GUI* class offers a function for adding such boxes with text to the GUI. This function is called *Box*. It is one among many functions for creating and drawing GUI controls, all in one statement; others include: *Label*, *Button*, *Toolbar*, *Window*, *TextField* and *DrawTexture*. Consider the following code and its associated comments for creating a box in the GUI.

```
Code 8.3 ConsoleWindow.cs — Rendering a Box control
using UnityEngine;
using System.Collections;

public class ConsoleWindow : MonoBehaviour
{
        //Called to render GUI elements
        void OnGUI()
```

```
        {
            GUI.Box(new Rect(10,10,500,50), "hello world");
        }
    }
```

NOTE: Notice that the Unity GUI framework is in a fundamental sense *not* object-oriented: it doesn't require us to declare and instantiate classes and objects representing specific controls, like boxes and buttons. We do not need to code Box or Button classes and then instantiate them in the *Start* function and then use them elsewhere, such as in *Update*. Rather, using only one statement through the *GUI* class in the *OnGUI* function, we can create and show a Box control as part of the GUI. It uses a *Render* paradigm as opposed to a *Class* paradigm; we tell the GUI class what it should render – that is, what it should show on screen. The Box control can be shown using the *Box* function, and in this example we have passed two arguments to this function. The first is a *Rect* structure (meaning *rectangle*). This defines the size and extents of the box to draw. In the Unity GUI system, all measurements and sizes are specified in pixels and are measured from the top-left corner of the screen, which is the origin of screen space. The form of the Rect structure is: left, top, width, height. Thus, the values 10 for *x* and 10 for *y* mean that the box will be positioned inwards from the origin (top-left) by 10 pixels horizontally and vertically. The width and height of the box will be 500 pixels and 50 pixels respectively. Lastly, the string argument "Hello World" simply defines the text that will be shown inside the box.

4. Let us now test the code we have written. Be sure to save the source file in MonoDevelop and attach it as a component of the GameManager – or any other GameObject; it doesn't *have* to be a component of the GameManager. However, since this class, like the *GameManager* will be a singleton object (there will be only one instance of it in the scene), I have chosen therefore to keep the *ConsoleWindow* class and the *GameManager* class as part of the same GameObject. Consider Figure 8.4.
5. So we should now have a box 'up and running' in our game, and it looks a promising basis for our GUI console. You can of course return to the code and change the box dimensions and position if you want. Here, let's amend the class in two ways. First, expose the *Rect* properties as a **public** member of the class so they can be edited and customised in the Object Inspector and the size of the box controlled without our having to recompile the code. This is very useful! Second, change the default values of these properties to better size the console and position it at the bottom of the screen. See code sample 8.4 and also Figure 8.5. Be careful running the game from this code and arrangement:

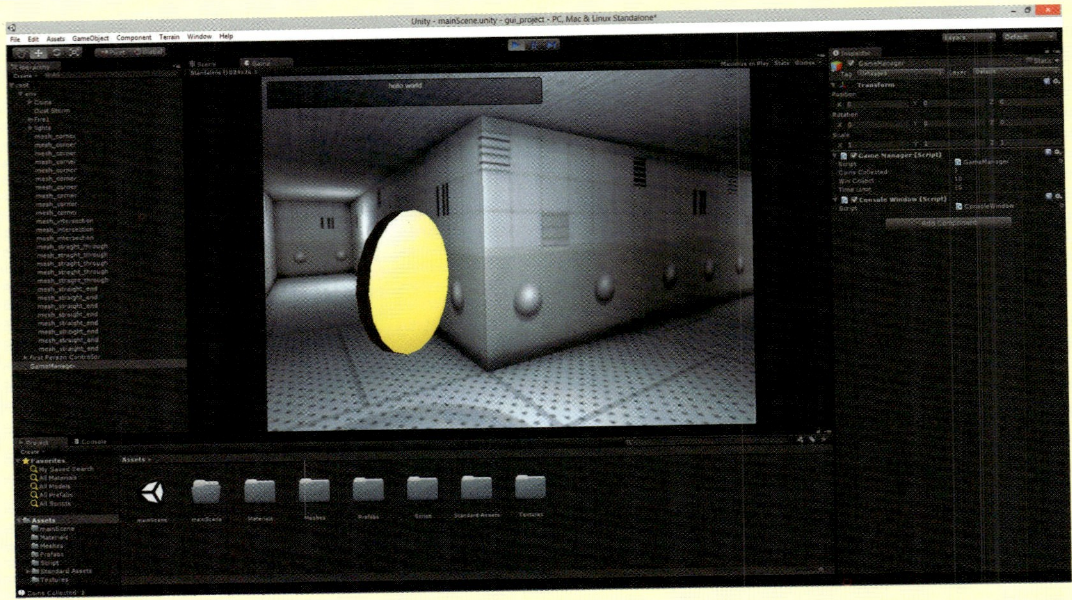

Figure 8.4 Running the coin game with the beginnings of a console, using GUI.Box

you may need to maximise the Game tab to its fullest extents (with a space bar press) to see the GUI elements correctly – more on why this is so will be discussed later. Alternatively, you could detach the Project and Console panels from the editor – changing them into free-floating windows – to increase the size of the Scene and Game viewport. Either method works.

Code 8.4 *ConsoleWindow.cs – Tweaking the Box control*

```
using UnityEngine;

using System.Collections;

public class ConsoleWindow : MonoBehaviour

{

      //Dimensions of console

      public Rect ConsoleDimensions = new Rect(10,708,1004,50);

      //Text of console

      public string ConsoleText = "hello world";

      //Called to render GUI elements
```

```
        void OnGUI()
        {
                GUI.Box(ConsoleDimensions, ConsoleText);
        }
}
```

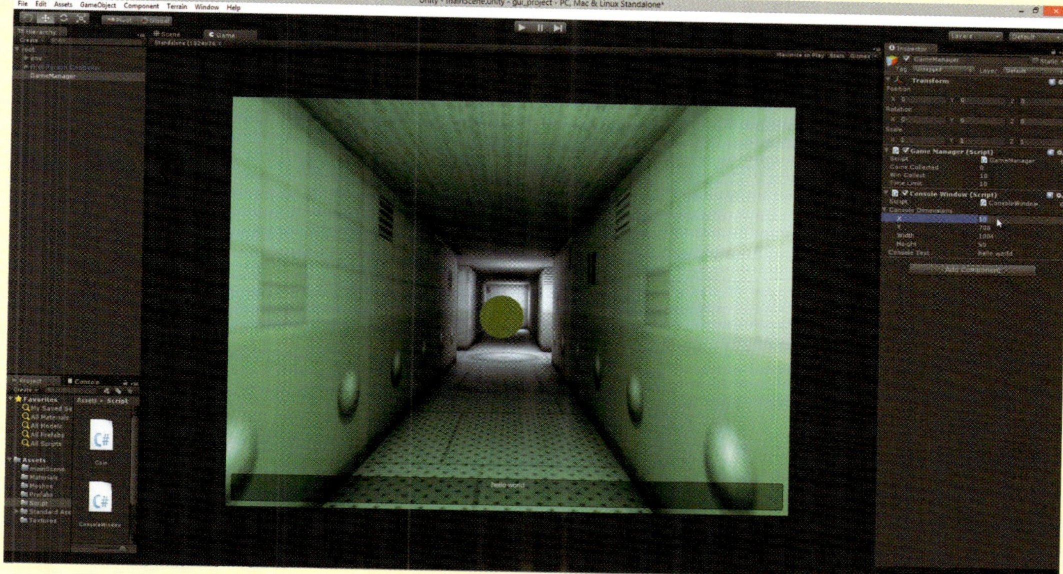

Figure 8.5 Controlling the size and position of the console. Notice the temporary rearrangement of the interface panels to get a larger view of the Scene and Game tab and see the 1024x768 interface at full size

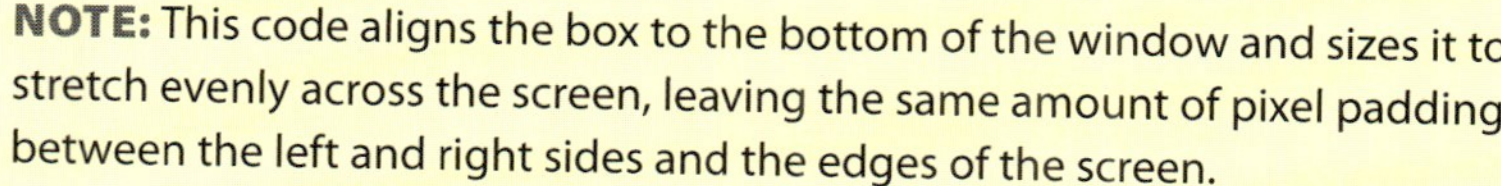

NOTE: This code aligns the box to the bottom of the window and sizes it to stretch evenly across the screen, leaving the same amount of pixel padding between the left and right sides and the edges of the screen.

6. One irritation that arises (for me) in relation to the default Unity workflow for coding GUIs like this involves visual feedback, or the lack thereof. Specifically, each time we change the dimensions of our GUI console we must replay the game using the *Play* button from the toolbar to see the result.

We must do this *even if* we change the console size from the Object Inspector. We do not get a real-time WYSIWYG preview of the box from the editor in either the *Design* or *Game* viewports. We can 'fix' or improve this issue by adding a line of code to the top of our Console class that forces Unity to run the code in *Editor Mode* – that is, to run it regardless of whether or not the game is playing. In C#, this line is *[ExecuteInEditMode]*. Add this line to your ConsoleWindow script file, above the class declaration line, and then save the changes. This line will not prevent your code from running in game mode, but it will also run normally when game mode is *not* active. Consequently, your ConsoleWindow becomes visible in the Unity editor viewport as soon as the code is saved and recompiled. Further, changing the ConsoleWindow size and position from the Object Inspector will update the console in real time, meaning you can preview your edits immediately. Be careful with this command, though: any logical errors and bugs in your code will manifest themselves in editor mode too. If your code runs into infinite loops or causes a freeze, this can affect your ability to save your work in the editor.

7. FPS consoles are not always visible on screen during gameplay. Typically, the player can show or hide the console on demand by way of a button press or keyboard shortcut, often by using the *Tilde* key (~). Use of this key acts a toggle: pressing it once will display the console, pressing it again will hide the console, and so on. Here, we'll integrate this behaviour into our console, except we'll show and hide the console based on a *C* key press – *C* for console. To do this, consider the following code in Code 8.5 and then consider the code comments. Once coded, take it for a test run to see the console toggle functionality in action.

Code 8.5 *ConsoleWindow.cs – Showing and hiding the console with keyboard presses*

```
[ExecuteInEditMode]

public class ConsoleWindow : MonoBehaviour

{

	public Rect ConsoleDimensions = new Rect(10,10,1004,50);

	public string ConsoleText = "hello world";

	private bool bShowConsole = false;

	void OnGUI()

	{

		if(bShowConsole) {GUI.Box(ConsoleDimensions, ConsoleText);}

	}
```

```
        void LateUpdate()
        {
        bShowConsole = Input.GetKeyDown(KeyCode.C) ?
        !bShowConsole:
        bShowConsole;
        }
}
```

NOTE: This code sports some interesting features. First, it includes the [ExecuteInEditMode] statement at the top of the class. Second, it adds a new private Boolean variable, *bShowConsole*, to keep track of whether or not the console should be visible on screen and uses the *LateUpdate* event, called at the *end* of each frame, to detect a keypress for the C key. Notice that *GUI.Box* is now conditional on whether *bShowConsole* is set to true; the box is rendered only if the user has pressed the *C* key to activate the console. Lastly, as an aside, notice that I've used the convention known as **Hungarian Notation** for naming the private *bShowConsole* variable. That is, I have prefixed the variable name with the lowercase letter *b* for *Boolean*. This convention has its promoters and detractors, like all conventions, but it can be useful for explicitly indicating the data type of a variable in its name, saving the programmer from having to return and reread variable declarations to ascertain a variable's type; other data types can lead to other prefixes, such as *i* for integer, and *f* for float. Why not give it a try?

8. The console can now be shown and hidden on demand during gameplay, but it can still only display the default 'Hello World' text message, which means the console is not especially useful for us as a debugging tool. It is now time to code two functions: one that will allow us to print and add a text message to the console from anywhere else in our code, and another that allows us to clear the console of all printed messages. These two functions will rely on the Unity concept of functions as *Messages*, as we shall see. Consider the code in 8.6: this does not reproduce the code from previous samples, it just shows the functionality that has been added. It is not supposed to replace any of the crucial code that came before.

Code 8.6 *ConsoleWindow.cs – Adding functions for printing messages to the console*

```
public void PrintMessage(string Message)

{

        ConsoleText+ = "\n"+ "Time: " + System.DateTime.Now.
        ToString("hh:mm:ss") + " Date: " +
        System.DateTime.Now.ToString("MM/dd/yyyy") + ": " + Message;

}

public void ClearConsole()

{

        ConsoleText = "";

}
```

NOTE: The ConsoleWindow class features two new functions, *PrintMessage* and *ClearConsole*. The former adds a new message to the console, including the time and date the message was printed, and the latter erases all text data in the console. Nothing yet in our code explicitly calls or initiates these functions and therefore they are never run. But the functionality does exist, and the question is now how can we call them and use them. See the next step.

9. For any other class or component to call upon the functionality of our console window for printing messages, it needs only a reference to the *GameManager* object – or to the object to which the ConsoleWindow is attached if it is not attached to the GameManager object. Once you have that object reference, however, you can call upon the native Unity function *SendMessage* to do the rest of the work for you. For example, the Coin class, created in the previous chapter, can be amended to print a message to our custom console by the simple one-line change to the *OnTriggerEnter* event listed in Code 8.7.

Code 8.7 *Coin.cs – Editing the Coin class to print a message to the console*

```
void OnTriggerEnter(Collider other)
```

```
{
    if(other.CompareTag("Player"))
    {
    GameObject GM = GameObject.Find ("GameManager");
    GameManager GM_Component = GM.GetComponent<GameManager>();
    ++GM_Component.CoinsCollected;
    //print current score to unity console
    print("Coins Collected: " + GameManager.Instance.CoinsCollected);
    //print current score to our custom console
    GM.SendMessage ("PrintMessage", "Coins Collected: " +
    GameManager.Instance.CoinsCollected);
        //Destroy coin
        Destroy(gameObject);
    }
}
```

NOTE: The GameObject *SendMessage* function takes two main arguments. The first is the string name of a function name to run and the second is the argument to be passed to that function. Whenever *SendMessage* is run on a GameObject, *every* function of a *matching name* is run for *every* component attached to the object. Thus, calling *SendMessage* to run "*PrintMessage*" on the GameManager object will call the *PrintMessage* function for the *ConsoleWindow* class, because that class has a *PrintMessage* function and is attached to the GameManager object. If the GameManager had multiple components and all of them featured a *PrintMessage* function, then all of those functions would be run from the single *SendMessage* call. Give this code a test run to see it in action: as you collect a coin in the level a message is printed to the console. Notice that by default Unity applies a limit to the total amount of text that can be shown in the GUI console: for this reason you may want to call the *Clear* function before printing a message. You can call *Clear* just as you called *PrintMessage*, using the *SendMessage* function of the GameObject class. Congratulations! You just created the basics for a debug console. See Figure 8.6.

Figure 8.6 Printing messages to the GUI console

8.3 Creating a HUD Coin Counter

The acronym HUD stands for Heads-Up Display, and HUDs are pervasive in both video games and augmented reality applications. They are typically used to display graphical elements that must remain on screen during gameplay and which should be overlaid on top of all other graphics. In games they are used to show health bars, character avatars, status indicators, mini-maps, and more. For the coin collection game we will create a HUD to show a real-time coin collection counter – that is, a number in the corner of the screen to indicate how many coins, if any, the player has collected so far. This number will begin at 0 as the level starts and will increment each time a coin is collected. Creating this counter will demonstrate two important features of GUIs in Unity, namely *Fonts* and *GUI styles*. Consider the following steps.

1. There are many ways we could approach the task of creating a HUD coin collection counter: one of the beautiful qualities of the Unity engine, and game development tools generally, is that there is a multitude of ways the tools can be used to solve any one problem. Here, we *could* create a completely new class, such as *GUICollectionCounter*, and then begin to code the collection functionality inside that class. But I shall instead edit the *GameManager* class we created in the previous chapter, simply adding an *OnGUI* function to that class to render the counter on screen each frame. So go ahead and add *OnGUI* to the GameManager, or create a new class if you prefer.

2. To display the counter we could use a *Box* control, as we used for the console. But again, let's deviate from the approach we took before and use a *Label* control in this case. The Label control refers to text: it displays text on screen – as before, we can choose the position and size of the text, as well as the text itself. Consider Code 8.8 below to see the *OnGUI* function for the *GameManager*, which, in only one line of code, displays a fully functional coin counter. Compile this code and take the game for a test run in the Game tab. Consider Figure 8.7 to see the initial coin counter at work in our application.

Figure 8.7 The coin counter is visible but small!

Code 8.8 *GameManager.cs – Adding an OnGUI function to render a Coin counter*

```
void OnGUI()

{

        GUI.Label(new Rect(Screen.width-100,10, 100, 50),
        CoinsCollected.ToString());

}
```

NOTE: See how this function specifies the leftmost position of the label in *relative* as opposed to *absolute* terms, as a pixel offset from the right-hand side of the screen. To do this, it uses the native Unity variable *Screen.width*, which expresses the width of the screen in pixels no matter what size the game

window might be. There is also a *Screen.height* value to express the screen height in pixels. These variables are accessible everywhere and at any time to your application and can be relied upon to express the exact pixel dimensions of the *game window,* not the monitor dimensions – although the window and screen dimensions will match if the application is exclusively full screen.

3. The label counter created so far is functional in that it is visible and accurately shows the coin collection count as it changes in real time. But arguably it is far from aesthetic, far from 'looking good'. Its *content* and *functionality* are correct, but its *style* is in need of a make-over. The Unity GUI, like the web technologies of HTML and CSS, separates the GUI content from the GUI style, meaning that we have control over both and that control is independent: we can apply different styles to the same content. Here, we want to keep the content and functionality of the label control just as it is, because it is correct, but we want to change its appearance. We can do this using the class *GUIStyle* and the *Skin* feature. The *GUIStyle* class is a data structure specifying how a control is to look: with it we can specify the fonts for labels, the colour of text, the alignment of controls, and other properties. All the GUI functions, such as *Box* and *Label*, accept an additional and optional argument to a *GUIStyle* class, which can be used to override the default style that is applied to controls whenever this parameter is absent, as it is in our code. So let's try, just for fun, a basic style here that will change the text colour of the coin counter from its default of white to red. The following code will do this: consider sample 8.9.

Code 8.9 *GameManager.cs – Setting the Label text colour to red using GUIStyle*

```
void OnGUI()

{

      GUIStyle MyStyle = new GUIStyle(); //Create style

      MyStyle.normal.textColor = Color.red; //Set color to red


      GUI.Label(new Rect(Screen.width-100,10, 100, 50),
      CoinsCollected.  ToString(), MyStyle);

}
```

NOTE: This code creates a GUIStyle named *MyStyle* and assigns the colour red via the constant *Color.red* value to the *TextColor* member of the *Normal* state. Each style offers a range of states, including *Normal*, *Hover*, *Focussed*, to define different appearances for a control based on user input. Take this code for a test run and see the counter now appears in red. You can also make *GUIStyles* global properties of a class and edit their values from the Object Inspector.

4. The code above works fine and serves our purposes for setting the colour of a label. That is, it works fine so long as all we want to do is set *just* the colour of *this particular* label. But this is presumably not all we want to do: it would also be good to set the size of the font and perhaps its boldness. To do this we could of course add more lines of code to the *OnGUI* function, setting more of the properties available to us from the *GUIStyle* class, such as *GUIStyle.fontSize* and *GUIStyle.fontStyle*. The total range of properties for this class can be found in the Unity documentation at http://docs.unity3d.com/Documentation/ScriptReference/GUIStyle.html. The problem with adding additional lines of code in this ad hoc way is that at a later stage we might want to add still more labels and controls to the GUI and have all of them *share* a consistent style. We might want all labels to have one style, all buttons to have one style, all boxes to have one style, and so on. We could achieve this by creating additional *GUIStyle* classes and managing all these separate instances ourselves in code, one for each control instance. But Unity offers a simpler method for streamlining the styles of controls in the form of 'skins'. A skin is, essentially, a collection or list of *GUIStyle* objects defining how each Control type should look, one *GUIStyle* for each type. By applying a skin globally to a GUI, we consistently style all its controls. We'll now create a skin for our application to have high-level power over the style of controls in our GUI. To do this, create a new folder in the *Project Panel* named *Skins*, and from the application menu select *Assets > Create > GUISkin*. Name this skin *CoinGameSkin*. See Figure 8.8.

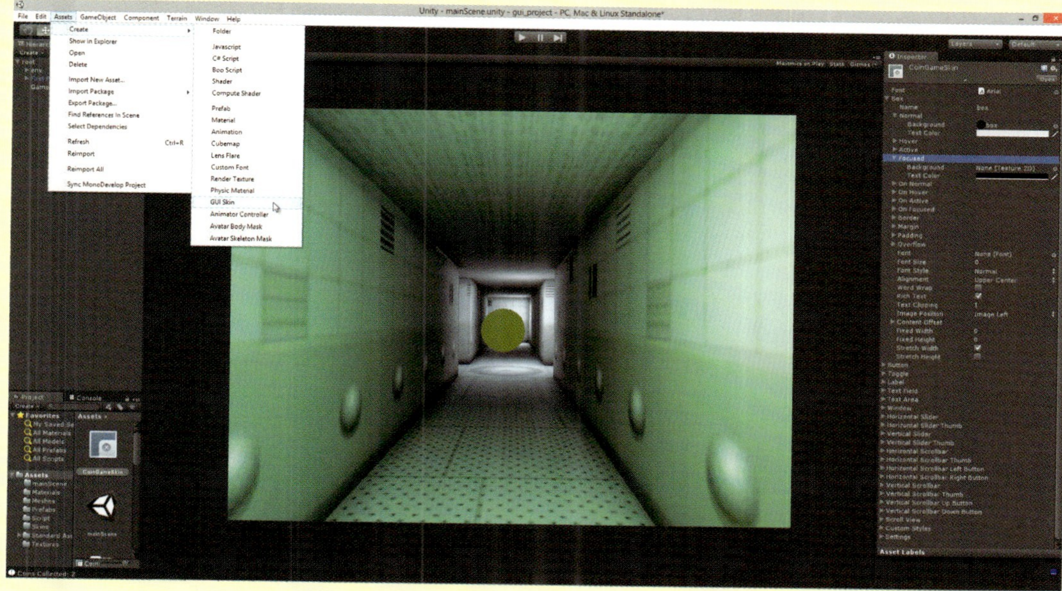

Figure 8.8 Creating a GUI skin to stylise the interface

5. A *GUISkin* object has now been created to define a collection of styles for the GUI controls. Select the skin in the Project panel and from the Object Inspector take a browse through its different options and properties. Then expand the *Label* group, and set the text colour (*Normal.TextColor*) to a golden brown colour, to imitate the coin look. Also set the *Font Style* to Bold and change the *Font Size* to 40. Notice the *Font* property is set to *None*, which means the default font of *Arial* will be used. You can import your own font files (.TTF and .OTF) to use for font rendering – but this chapter will remain with the default Arial font. See Figure 8.9. Now give your game a test run and notice that none of the

Figure 8.9 Configuring the default skin for the coin game

settings applied to the skin have taken effect on the Label control. This is because we must also make a change in code.

6. Since a project can potentially contain more than one *GUISkin*, Unity does not make assumptions about which skin, if any, to use to stylise the GUI controls. For this reason, Unity must be explicitly told in code which *GUISkin* to use. To achieve this, the *GameManager* class should be amended to feature a public *GUISkin* member. This can then be specified from the Object Inspector, and the class will set this skin as the active skin in the *OnGUI* function. See Code 8.10.

Code 8.10 *GameManager.cs – Setting the GUI Skinb*

```
void OnGUI()

{

        GUI.skin = Skin;

        GUI.Label(new Rect(Screen.width-100,10, 100, 50),
        CoinsCollected.ToString());

}
```

NOTE: Notice that the earlier GUIStyle code, featured in sample 8.9, has been removed to accommodate the newer GUISkin code. Take this code for a test run and see the coin counter in action. Congratulations! You now have a completed coin counter, as well as a working console. Now it's time to add *Game Won* and *Game Over* graphics.

8.4 Preparing Game Won and Game Over Graphics

The GUI elements considered so far deal primarily with text and text rendering: the console displayed text messages and the coin counter showed a text indication of the coin collection status. These elements rely chiefly on Unity to provide the graphical raw materials for showing the GUI controls. We had parametric control over the size, colour and style of text, but it was Unity that generated the final pixels shown on screen to represent the text. However, most games do not rely so heavily on text alone for their GUI elements – they take advantage of additional graphical features and images. They display progress bars, status indicators, maps and charts and icons. All these elements make use of pixel-based graphics that we import in the form of textures. In this section and some of those that follow we'll work with graphical images to display them as GUI elements for our coin game. Specifically, we are going to import two images: a *Game Over* image and a *Game Won* image. The *Game Over* image will be shown on screen when the timer expires and the player has failed to collect enough coins to win, and the *Game Won* image will be shown when the timer expires and the win condition is satisfied. Each of these images will be imported as a separate texture.

Before we 'rush in' and import these textures into our project, it is worth pausing to consider a number of technical issues that arise often in the case of GUIs and their graphics. GUI textures are in many respects different from textures used for standard 3D models. First, GUI textures are not applied directly to geometry and meshes through UV mapping; rather, they are drawn directly and orthogonally in screen space. Second, GUI textures feature a lot of transparent pixels: button graphics, icons, sprites, and even the *Game Won* and *Game Over* images in Figure 8.9. Those two images have large regions of pixels outside of the main star shapes that should render as transparent during the game – we do not want to see the background pixels of the sprite. Third, GUI textures come in all shapes and sizes; their dimensions need not be a power-2 size (such as 256, 512, or 1024) – they can be any size at all. These three considerations combine to make GUI textures potentially expensive computationally for most real-time render systems and graphical hardware – for a variety of technical reasons that we need not go into here. To avoid a lot of these problems there are specific guidelines we should follow both when saving and exporting GUI textures from our content-creation applications, like Photoshop, and when importing and configuring those textures in Unity. In short, there is an optimal way to save GUI textures from Photoshop and an optimal way to import them into Unity.

8.4.1 Saving and Exporting GUI Textures from Photoshop

In Unity, textures featuring transparent regions are known as *Alpha textures*. This is because they contain an extra greyscale channel in addition to their RGB channels, a channel known as the Alpha Channel – the term 'alpha' having come to denote transparency. In the Alpha Channel, black pixels mark out transparent regions and white pixels mark out fully opaque regions, and values between denote varying strengths of transparency. You might have already tried creating transparent textures for your games, in either Unity or other engines and systems. In doing this you may have found that effects like fog, mist or glass never turned out quite right when shown in-game even though the image looked fine in Photoshop, and you may also have found that the edges and outlines of sprites looked rough or sometimes 'artefacted' and discoloured. These sorts of problems are common and usually the result of not correctly saving and exporting transparent images. Just because an image looks fine in GIMP or Photoshop, it does not mean that it will translate 1:1 when shown in a real-time engine like Unity, because these engines apply further sampling and processing to images and this may change how they look.

Since this is a Unity rather than a Photoshop book, I shall not devote much space to all the steps for exporting an Alpha texture, but I will refer you to material that does fully explain the process. For more information on exporting Alpha textures, please consult the following URL: http://docs.unity3d.com/Documentation/Manual/HOWTO-alphamaps.html

8.4.2 GUI Textures in Unity

Importing textures into Unity is frequently just a drag and drop process; drag from Windows Explorer or Finder into the Unity Project panel, and that's it! For importing GUI textures, however, although we *do* drag and drop them into Unity, the import process doesn't end there. There are *additional* settings we must apply to the texture after it has been imported if we want it to appear correctly as a GUI graphic. Once we have configured the textures appropriately, we can then go ahead and integrate them into the GUI. Consider the following steps.

1. Drag and drop the *GameWon.psd* and *GameOver.psd* files into Unity as textures and arrange them into the *Textures* folder – remember good organisation. Once imported, select both textures in the Project panel, and in the Object Inspector change the *Texture Type* from *Texture* to *GUI*. This explicitly notifies Unity that the imported texture is to be used for GUIs as opposed to standard meshes. Doing this prevents Unity from forcibly up-scaling or down-scaling the texture to the nearest power-2 size, leaving its original dimensions intact. In addition, go ahead and change the *Texture Format* from *Compressed* to *True Color*. Doing this improves texture quality but at the expense of memory footprint and render performance. Ultimately, judgements about which formats and sizes to use for textures depends on the needs of the project and the target hardware. Given all factors relevant to performance, developers must seek the optimal balance between quality and performance. For this project, *True Color* will be acceptable. Once configured, click the *Apply* button to confirm and accept the settings. The texture is now configured for use as a GUI texture. See Figure 8.10.

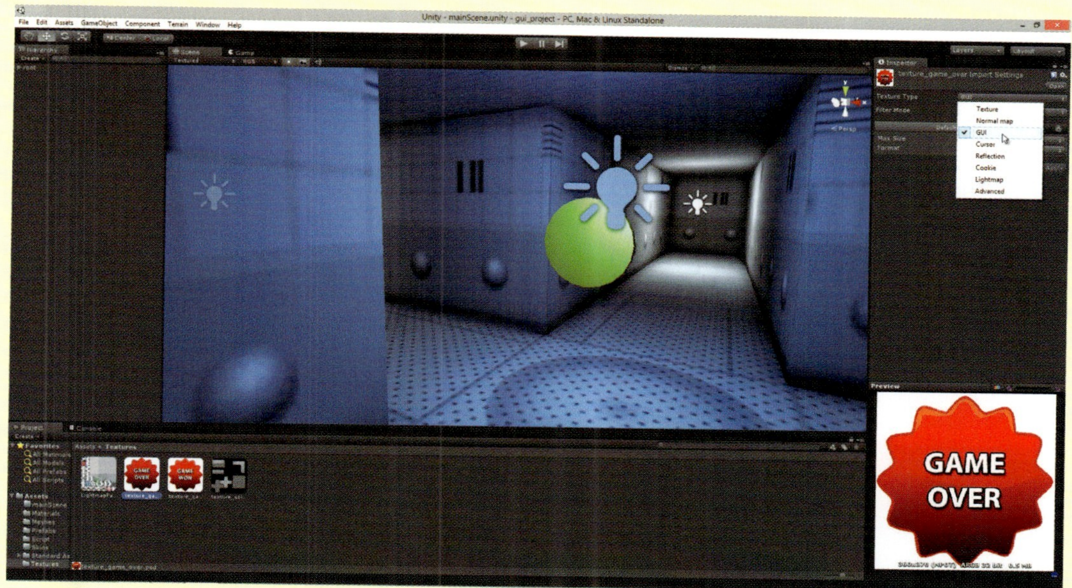

Figure 8.10 Configuring GUI textures

2. Now let's jump back to our source code for the *GameManager* class. This class will now be amended to draw our textures to the screen, in addition to drawing the coin counter. To achieve this, first add three additional variables or properties to the class. One, a reference to the Game Won texture; two, a reference to the Game Lost texture, and three; a final Boolean variable representing the status of the timer – whether or not it has expired. These members can be added to the *GameManager* by adding code highlighted in Figure 8.11 – this is also the code featured in sample 8.11. The purpose of adding the first two texture members is to allow the *GameManager* class to access the texture assets. By adding this code we gain the ability to specify (and change) our Game Won and Game Lost textures from the Unity Object Inspector if we wish. Add these variables now, and then select the *GameManager* object in the scene to examine its *GameManager* component in the Object Inspector. Notice the variable slots for the textures – and now you can drag and drop the *GameWon* and *GameLost* textures from the Project panel into them.

Code 8.11 *GameManager.cs – Adding Texture variables*

```
public bool GameOver = false;

public Texture2D GameWonTexture = null;

public Texture2D GameLostTexture = null;
```

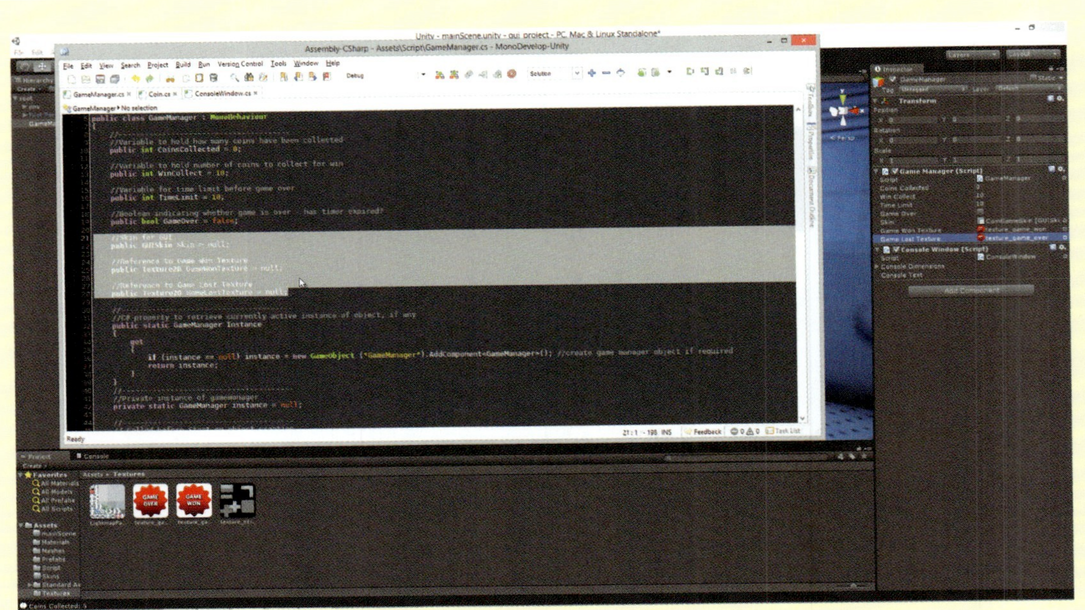

Figure 8.11 Editing the GameManager to support GameWon and GameLost textures

NOTE: See from Figure 8.11 that the MonoDevelop editor has a dark colour scheme applied to it: meaning the editor background is dark and the text is low contrast. Dark colour schemes are popular and used widely among developers for at least two reasons: first, the darkness of the interface makes it easier for us to shift our attention or focus away from the interface and onto the content we are creating: whether it is the code we are writing, the texture we are making or the scene we are designing. Second, the darkness dulls the brightness and luminance of the screen – it reduces the harshness for our eyes, which must focus for long periods on the screen. If you feel the brightness of your screen is hurting your eyes or limiting your concentration, you may want to change MonoDevelop's default settings and default colours of whites and light grays. To do this, select *Tools > Options* from the MonoDevelop file menu. From the Options window that appears, select *Text Editor > Syntax Highlighting* from the List box, and then choose a colour scheme. I have used the *Oblivion* colour scheme.

3. Let's now recode the *StartCountDown()* Coroutine of the GameManager, a routine determining when the timer has expired. Here we're just going to add one line at the end of the Coroutine to set the Boolean *GameOver* flag to *true*, indicating that the timer has expired. This value will be used shortly by the *OnGUI* method for conditionally drawing the GameWon or GameLost textures. Take a look at the recoded *StartCountDown* Coroutine in Code 8.12.

Code 8.12 *GameManager.cs – Setting the GameOver flag*

```
public IEnumerator StartCountDown()
{
      yield return new WaitForSeconds(TimeLimit);
      if(CoinsCollected >= WinCollect)
            print ("Game Won");
      else
            print ("Game Lost");

      GameOver = true;
}
```

4. Now we can code the *OnGUI* function to draw our Game Won and Game Lost textures on screen after the timer expires. Add the code in sample 8.13. However, before running this code to see its effect, be sure to specify the *GameWon* and *GameLost* texture properties for the class in the Object Inspector – by dragging and dropping the textures into their appropriate slots – otherwise these values will be set to *null* when the game runs. Consider the code comments in the note following the sample for more information.

Code 8.13 *GameManager.cs – Editing the OnGUI function to draw textures*

```
void OnGUI()
{
      GUI.skin = Skin;

      GUI.Label(new Rect(Screen.width-100,10, 100, 50),
      CoinsCollected.ToString());

      //If timer expired then show won or lost message
      if(!GameOver) return;

      //If won
      if(CoinsCollected >= WinCollect)
```

```
        {
            //Show game won texture
            GUI.DrawTexture(new Rect(0,0,GameWonTexture.width,
            GameWonTexture.height),GameWonTexture);
        }
        else //Game lost
        {
            GUI.DrawTexture(new Rect(0,0,GameLostTexture.width,
            GameLostTexture.height),GameLostTexture);
        }
    }
```

NOTE: In Code 8.13 the GameWon and GameLost textures are drawn to the screen on each frame using conditional logic and the *DrawTexture* function of the GUI class. Like many GUI functions it expects two main arguments: a *Rect* marking the size of the texture as it should appear on screen and a reference to the texture itself. Notice that the width and height dimensions of the Rect are read directly from the texture, ensuring the texture is shown at its default pixel dimensions. Higher or lower values will cause Unity to stretch or shrink the texture to fit the specified size.

5. If you run and test the game now you will see the textures are always drawn from the top-left corner of the screen; this is because their X and Y Rect values are both 0. We want to draw the textures at the screen centre. We can calculate this position as shown in sample code 8.14. We divide the screen width and height by 2 to calculate the screen centre, and from there we offset the texture position by half its width and height to fix its centre pixel at the screen centre. See Figure 8.12 for the effect this code has on the application.

```
Code 8.14 GameManager.cs – Centre-aligning screen textures
if(CoinsCollected >= WinCollect)
{
```

```
        GUI.DrawTexture(new Rect((Screen.width/2)-(GameWonTexture.
width/2),(Screen.height/2)-(GameWonTexture.height/2),GameWonTexture.
width, GameWonTexture.
height),GameWonTexture);

        GUI.DrawTexture(new Rect((Screen.width/2)-(GameWonTexture.
width/2),(Screen.height/2)-(GameWonTexture.height/2),GameLostTexture.
width, GameLostTexture.
height),GameLostTexture);

}
```

Figure 8.12 Display textures at screen centre using Width and Height values

8.5 The Problems with GUIs

Congratulations! You've now coded a game that displays both text and GUI elements conditionally, using the *OnGUI* function of classes. These elements consist of a Console panel for printing debug messages to the screen, a label as a HUD element for showing the total number of coins collected in the game, and centre-aligned

GameWon and GameOver graphics for notifying the gamer about Game Won status. In creating this application you may have noticed two main, and potentially major, problems concerning GUIs, both of which shall be considered here in summary. The first problem relates to screen size and the second to performance.

8.5.1 Absolute and Relative Measure

The first 'problem' is that both the position and sizes of GUI elements in our game were almost always specified in *absolute* as opposed to *relative* terms. The position of the console, for example, was set to a specific screen location in pixels, and its width and height were also measured in pixels. This is not itself a problem, so long as we run the game in *full screen mode*, showing the screen at its full screen size of 1024×768 pixels. If we use the Unity editor to stretch or shrink the game window or if we want to change the game resolution or display the game at a different size or on a mobile platform, then all of our absolute measurements are invalidated because the screen shows a different number of pixels from the size we originally had in mind. If this limitation was binding on us and there were no possible workarounds, it would mean our game could only run at 1024x768. If a platform, screen or device could not show 1024x768 then it could not run our game. Thankfully there are solutions for this problem, but all of them involve extra steps and additional techniques, and these add greater complexity to the implementation of user interfaces. The first and simplest solution that Unity offers us is a **scaling** system: this technique allows us to stretch and scale a GUI of any original size to fit any intended resolution. Using this technique you can be sure your GUI will always fit the intended resolution. There is, however, a significant limitation to this method, as we'll soon see. First, however, let's look at the code to scale our GUI to any size we want. Consider code sample 8.15. Simply add this code to the top of any *OnGUI* function to see it in action, resizing your GUI to any size. Notice this code uses the absolute values of 1024 and 768: if your interface is a different resolution, you can simply plug your own dimensions into the formula.

Code 8.15 *GameManager.cs – Resizing the GUI*

```
Vector3 scale = new Vector3((float)Screen.width/1024,
(float)Screen.height/768, 1.0f);

GUI.matrix = Matrix4x4.TRS(Vector3.zero, Quaternion.
identity, scale);
```

This solution will apply any necessary stretching or shrinking to every GUI element in the interface to ensure it displays at the intended resolution – and it will work for practically any resolution you choose. Therein lies the source of the problem, however. The problem relates to 'aspect ratio': the relationship between the width and height of the screen. For example, the resolution 1024x768 has a different aspect ratio to the resolution 1920x1080. The AR (Aspect Ratio) of 1024x768 is 1.333 (because 1024/768 = 1.333), and the AR for 1920x1080 is 1.777 – sometimes expressed as 16:9. This means the distribution of pixels across the width and height of an image differs across these two resolutions. Stretching a 1024x768 image to the resolution 1920x1080 involves non-uniform scaling, meaning the image will be stretched more in the width than in the height, making the image look wider than it should be. So what is the solution to this problem? How is it possible to create *one* interface that appears correctly across *all* possible resolutions and aspect ratios? How is it possible to create a *resolution-independent* GUI? The answer to this problem, if there is one at all, is one of the 'Holy Grails' of interface development: continually sought and worked for. Different developers come up with different solutions or workarounds: for example, some design completely different interfaces for each aspect ratio and code their game to choose the appropriate version for the screen. Perhaps the most common method, however, is to design a more intricate hierarchical and anchor-based system of controls and positioning. In brief, this system works by scaling all GUI components, but scaling them uniformly on the basis of the screen height or the screen width but not on the basis of both. This ensures all controls are scaled uniformly, but their positioning on screen might still be inaccurate. To remedy this, a system of relative positioning is introduced, known as anchoring, because controls can become locked or aligned to fixed points such as the left side or right side or the top, bottom or centre of the screen. The details of implementing this system, however, are beyond the scope of this book.

8.5.2 GUI Performance

The second problem that frequently arises relates to performance. This issue becomes especially pronounced for lower-powered hardware, such as hardware for mobile platforms, and for GUIs that are 'complex', such as those for RPG games, which must show character statistics, skills, inventories, items and spell lists. In these cases the game must potentially draw many textures, graphics and text, and also offer the user the ability to input information through text boxes, buttons and drop-down lists. In some cases, GUI elements must rotate, stretch and shrink, animate and change. To meet these requirements and produce numerous other kinds of GUI effect, developers need not abandon the Unity GUI system entirely. In theory at least they can probably keep using it to produce a GUI that matches their needs, provided its features are used inventively and optimally every step of the way. However, in practice it can be troublesome to get 'good' performance from the Unity GUI system for complex interfaces of this kind, especially on mobile devices like iOS and Android. Interfaces that rely on multiple textures, graphics and dynamic fonts frequently increase the number of *Draw Calls* required on each frame, which increases the amount of renders and processes the graphics hardware must perform to draw pixels to the screen. This increase in Draw Calls raises the heaviness or burden of the application and can lead to a reduction in Frames Per Second (FPS). The result is that many developers ultimately abandon the default Unity GUI system to develop a home-made version, or use third-party systems available from the Unity Asset Store; systems such as *EZ GUI* and *NGUI*. These systems typically offer significant performance benefits. For this reason, if you're making a Unity game with a complex GUI, then rolling your own interface solution can have a powerful appeal. Developing a custom interface solution is beyond the scope of this book. However, readers interested in this issue can find out more about developing custom GUI and 2D systems through my online video course *Creating 2D Games in Unity*, available at 3DMotive.com.

8.6 Conclusion

This chapter focussed on GUIs (Graphical User Interfaces) in Unity. It explored how a range of customisable GUI controls are accessible to us in script via the *OnGUI* function of any class. Using this function we can call upon the methods of the *GUI* class to present GUI controls to the user, for example text controls such as labels and graphical controls such as textures. Here, we made use of these features to add a GUI system to the coin collection game. In doing this we also explored problems with our interface, the problems of resolution, aspect ratio and performance. These problems apply not only to the sample game created in this chapter but to any game we choose to make in Unity, as well as other games in other engines. The issue of resolution can be solved using scaling: Unity offers us features to scale GUIs to destination resolutions. The issue of aspect ratio requires us to rethink how our sizes and measurements are made in the GUI. And finally, the issue of performance leads us to ask questions about whether to use the built-in Unity GUI system or to code our own. Together this chapter and the previous one also offered an introduction to Unity scripting and related transferable skills that can be applied to almost every Unity project. The next chapter moves on from scripting in general and explores *Post-production* and *debugging*.

CHAPTER 9

Debugging and Post-processing

By the end of this chapter you should:

1. Understand how to debug games using the Object Inspector and Stats panel.
2. Understand how to use the Profiler window for assessing performance.
3. Understand what post-processing is.
4. Be able to use post-processing effects such as Blur and Bloom.
5. Be able to use cell shading.

The final stage of the six-stage workflow to making a Unity game is about building, testing and refining the game. It is a cyclic stage that comes after the core functionality has been created. It's cyclic because a developer typically tests the game to find errors, glitches or routes to improvement, and then makes changes based on that testing, and then tests some more and makes more changes, and so on until no more changes are needed or a point is reached where development must simply stop. The result of this stage should be a completed game ready to distribute to the gamer. This chapter considers this stage in some detail. Specifically, it looks at how to *Play Test* and *Debug* a game to find errors or problems, how to use the *Profiler Window* to make the debugging process simpler, how to refine and improve the look of a game through *Camera Effects*, and how to finalise and *Build* a game for a specific platform. By the end of this chapter you'll be equipped with all the fundamental knowledge required to create a Unity game from start to finish using the six-stage workflow. Unlike previous chapters, this chapter is not project-based; we will not be working step by step to create a project. Instead, we'll open up an existing project and see how the debugging and post-processing features relate to it. For simplicity, I'll assume you're working with the *AngryBots* sample project that ships with Unity, but really you can work with any project you like, including the coin collecting game created in the last two chapters. Whatever the project, open it up in Unity now and let's get started.

Debugging and Post-processing

By the end of this chapter you should:

1. Understand how to debug games using the Object Inspector and Stats panel.
2. Understand how to use the Profiler window for assessing performance.
3. Understand what post-processing is.

The final stage of the six-stage workflow to making a Unity game is about building, testing and refining the game. It is a cyclic stage that comes after the core functionality has been created. It's cyclic because a developer typically tests the game to find errors, glitches or routes to improvement, and then makes changes based on that testing, and then tests some more and makes more changes, and so on until no more changes are needed or a point is reached where development must simply stop. The result of this stage should be a completed game ready to distribute to the gamer. This chapter considers this stage in some detail. Specifically, it looks at how to *Play Test* and *Debug* a game to find errors or problems, how to use the *Profiler Window* to make the debugging process simpler, how to refine and improve the look of a game through *Camera Effects*, and how to finalise and *Build* a game for a specific platform. By the end of this chapter you'll be equipped with all the fundamental knowledge required to create a Unity game from start to finish using the six-stage workflow. Unlike previous chapters, this chapter is not project-based; we will not be working step by step to create a project. Instead, we'll open up an existing project and see how the debugging [illegible]

Whatever the project, open it up in Unity now and let's get started.

Code 9.1 *Using the ToString Function*

```
Vector3 scale = new Vector3((float)Screen.width/1024,
(float)Screen.height/768, 1.0f);

print (scale.ToString());
```

9.3 Debugging with the Object Inspector

By now the Object Inspector should be one of your most familiar tools in Unity. In fact, it may be so familiar as to be part of your 'muscle memory': you instinctively move your mouse or attention to that area of the screen – even accidentally when you're in full screen mode and the Object Inspector isn't even there. However, many believe the Object Inspector is only important at design time, for setting the properties of selected objects, and nothing else. This is not true, though, because the Object Inspector is also a powerful debugging tool, along with other scene-editing tools such as the Translate and Rotate tools. How is this so? To understand better, open up the AngryBots project in the Unity editor, select the player object in the scene, and then run the game but not in full-screen mode. Run the game with the default Unity panels visible, including the Object Inspector. Now, while the game is running, take a look at the Object Inspector and its properties as you also move the player around the level. It requires a bit of brain multi-tasking, but don't worry about playing the game properly: just move the player around with one eye on the Object Inspector. Take a look at Figure 9.1.

Figure 9.1 Reviewing object properties at run-time with the Object Inspector

The Object Inspector gives us a view of all publicly accessible properties for all components attached to the object. As the object changes and moves at run-time, the properties in the Object Inspector update to reflect the changes, giving us a real-time view of those properties. This is significant because it means we can see in real time the values for all public properties for a selected object in the scene, and we can do this simply by looking at the Object Inspector – we don't need to create print statements in code or set breakpoints or other kinds of code watches used in traditional programming. Take a look at the player's Transform component and see his position values update as he moves; and then look at the player's health property to see it change as he takes damage. Furthermore, if we finish watching an object and decide to investigate a different object (perhaps an enemy character), we don't have to stop playback of the game and start over again. We can just hit the *Pause* button from the toolbar, switch over from the Game tab to the Scene tab, select a new object in the scene, and then resume playback while watching the Object Inspector as before. In short, the Object Inspector offers us a real-time status report for the selected object during game play.

The debugging benefits of the Object Inspector don't end there either! Not only can we see and *read* the properties of selected objects, but we can also *set* and change them to observe their effects in real time, just as though we had set them while in design mode. As I write this, AngryBots is playing in the background and my character is taking damage from the gunfire of enemies. So, I'll just jump back into Unity, select the player object and cheat by changing his health value back to maximum again from the Object Inspector. I could also change his position, rotation and other properties using the same technique. This ability to set properties at run-time is immensely powerful because it allows us to experiment with values and settings and receive live updates and previews of them. For example, we can test how enemies react to the player when he is standing at particular locations; we can see how his gun behaves when it is emptied of ammunition; we can manipulate time limits and counters to save us having to wait in real time, plus much more. The debugging potential of the Object Inspector is almost limitless and it will typically be your first point of call when you want to find errors or test out scenarios in your game. But the Object Inspector is not the only editor tool with debugging potential: we can also use the transformation tools of *Translate*, *Rotate* and *Scale* to transform any objects in the scene while the game is running – using these tools is really just another way of editing the Transform component of a game object. Simply press the *W*, *E*, or *R* keys (Translate, Rotate or Scale) from the Scene tab during game play to transform the selected object using the mouse.

NOTE: Take care when editing an object's properties at run-time, however. The changes made are not permanent. All run-time changes will be reset or undone when the game returns from *Play* mode to *Design* mode.

9.4 Debugging with the Stats Panel

If you switch to the *Game* tab and scan its toolbar buttons, you'll see the Stats button in the upper right-hand corner; this is a toggle-able button (see Figure 9.2). Press it once to show the Stats panel and again to hide it, and so on. The Stats panel, also known as the *Rendering Statistics Window*, is useful not so much for diagnosing specific errors or issues with your game, such as the location of a particular bug in code, as for assessing a game's overall run-time *performance* on your target hardware. It's useful for measuring game frame rate, assessing the number of vertices and polygons being displayed, seeing how much memory is being consumed for textures, and learning the total number of draw calls required to show a frame on-screen. The Stats panel answers performance questions about a game that is otherwise working as intended, to help developers identify system requirements and work out where to make changes to improve performance, if improvement is feasible. The Stats panel can typically help you if you have questions such as: 'Will my game run on mobile devices?', 'Are there too many polygons?', 'Which scene is the most computationally intensive to render? Why?, 'Where can I make optimisations to improve performance?'. The Stats panel breaks down this performance information into categories, most of which are discussed below.

FPS and Time Per Frame

The upper right-hand corner of the Stats panel shows the averaged FPS (*Frames Per Second*) count for your game, and the average time in milliseconds (ms) for Unity to calculate a single frame (*Frame Time*). In short, the FPS is calculated through 1000ms/Frame Time. This

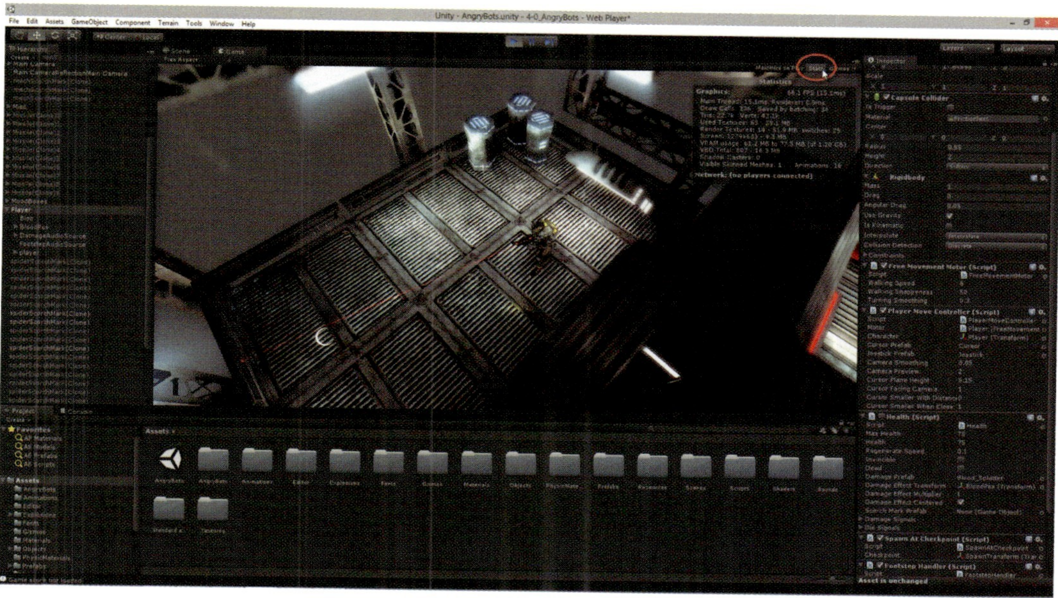

Figure 9.2 Accessing the *Stats* panel from the Game tab

count will change during game play because each frame has different render requirements and complexities to the frame that came before. For most games this typically means the FPS and Frame Time fluctuates between a minimum and maximum, tending towards the mean. The question frequently arises as to what the FPS *should* be, or what constitutes a 'good' FPS. The answer, however, varies across platforms, games, systems and even between different scenes within the same game on the same system; in short, the answer (if there is one) is case-specific. It is perhaps easier and more practical to say what the average FPS should *not* be: it should not be less than 15 frames per second on practically any device, game or system because frame rates below this value generally appear to the human eye as lag or jitter. Many developers and studios set 30FPS as an acceptable minimum for the average, but sometimes this is not practically possible on mobile devices. In short, experience as well as a solid understanding of your target hardware, combined with the content of your game, can help you reach reasonable decisions about what kind of minimum FPS for your game is appropriate. Be sure to play-test your games with the Stats panel open in the Game tab and keep an eye on the FPS, observing when it rises and falls and how these fluctuations correspond to what you know is happening in the game. If a drop in FPS to unacceptable levels always coincides with a specific event, use that as a starting point for diagnosing where performance improvements can be made in code or content. Generally speaking: the higher the FPS, the better the performance.

Draw Calls and Batching

The *Draw Call* and *Batching* values appear next on the *Stats* panel. The Unity engine uses a 'render system' to draw graphical data to the screen on each frame. This system makes it possible for objects in our scenes, and everything else, to be visible on screen when required. To draw these graphics, the renderer internally issues a *Draw Call* to the graphics hardware, typically one draw call for each object to be rendered. Each *Draw Call*, however, involves significant processor overhead and demand. This means draw calls are directly related to performance: the more there are, the more demanding a game is to render. Performance can be improved therefore by reducing draw calls. To help achieve this, Unity operates a 'batching' scheme, allowing draw calls to be 'batched'. This means Unity can internally group specific objects together and draw them in one call as opposed to multiple. The batching technique comes in two forms: static batching and dynamic batching; both have the effect of consolidating objects into fewer draw calls. Batching is largely an internal and automatic process in Unity, meaning Unity makes decisions on its own about how to batch objects and when. But it makes these decisions on the basis of properties and settings applied to the objects through the Object Inspector. Consequently, this places *requirements* on game objects, meaning not all kinds of objects can be combined and batched. It also means that we have some degree of control over how batching works if we understand how Unity makes batching decisions from these properties and settings. In summary, the following advice applies and can help reduce draw calls for your game.

NOTE: In general, taking steps to reduce draw calls to their minimum is sound practice. But take care to observe a 'balance' in the performance optimisations you make. Optimisations made to one aspect of your game can adversely impact other areas: reducing draw calls, for example, often involves the combination of meshes, and this can increase the vertices rendered on each frame.

Figure 9.3 Marking objects as Static can be held towards batching

1. Mark as Static

If you know a mesh will *never* move during game play, then *always* mark it as *Static:* insert a check mark into the *Static* check box that appears in the Object Inspector when the object is selected in the scene (See Figure 9.3). This advice will typically apply to walls, floors, ceilings, windows, tables, chairs, rocks, mountains, crates, and other motionless props and set-dressing items. Marking objects as Static is not in itself sufficient to make Unity batch the objects into a single draw call, but it is a good first step when combined with other properties.

2. Share Materials

Share the *same* material across as many objects as you can. Only objects with the same material can be batched: two objects with different materials cannot be batched. If you have two or more objects with different materials, identical to each other in every respect *except* for the textures they reference, then with a little more work you can make these objects compatible for batching. To do this, use an image-editing application (such as Photoshop) to merge the separate texture files into one larger texture, known as an *Atlas texture*. Then use your 3D modelling application and remap the UVs of your meshes to align with the Atlas texture, and then re-import into Unity, assigning them all the same material referencing the Atlas texture.

3. Batching applies only to MeshRenderer and ParticleSystem Components

Only standard meshes and particle systems can be batched. Unity does not currently support batching for Skinned meshes (animated character meshes), Cloth objects, Trail renderers and object specialist mesh objects. For this reason, plan your batching optimisations only on these objects.

NOTE: Further information on Render Batching and Optimisations can be found in the Unity documentation at: http://docs.unity3d.com/Documentation/Manual/DrawCallBatching.html

Tris and Verts

The Stats panel also lists the total number of triangles and vertices. This count refers not to the total number of triangles and vertices across all meshes in the active scene, but only to the total number currently visible in the Game tab, based on the position and viewing angle of the cameras. This count will change if cameras and objects move in the scene. Furthermore, this count will not necessarily have any direct correspondence to the vertex and triangle count for your meshes as they appear in your 3D modelling application. The Tri and Vert count in Unity will typically be higher, because Unity will double-up vertices at UV seams as well as in other areas of your meshes. For this reason, always use the Unity Tri and Vert stats for your final analysis of triangle and vertex counts. These counts are often dismissed by developers as being something that mainly applies to legacy hardware, because contemporary hardware and render systems have become adept at crunching vast quantities of vertices. Nevertheless, the principle still stands that lower vertex and polygon counts are associated with better performance, since there is less data to process. Consequently, make your counts as low as possible without sacrificing the quality you need.

Used Textures and VRAM Usage

The *Used Texture* setting offers a real-time view of the total amount of pixel data, in megabytes, being used to display the current frame, given the position of the camera and the texture data for all visible meshes. Again, the principle of simplicity applies: the lower this value, the better for performance – but take care not to sacrifice quality for performance. The VRAM setting displays both the total amount of Video RAM being used on the graphics card for the current frame and the total reservoir of memory available on the graphics card for your system. These latter settings are useful especially when testing your game on your target or minimum hardware.

9.5 Debugging with the Profiler Window

NOTE: The Unity Profiler is available in the professional version only, and not in the free version. Users of the free version can safely skip this section.

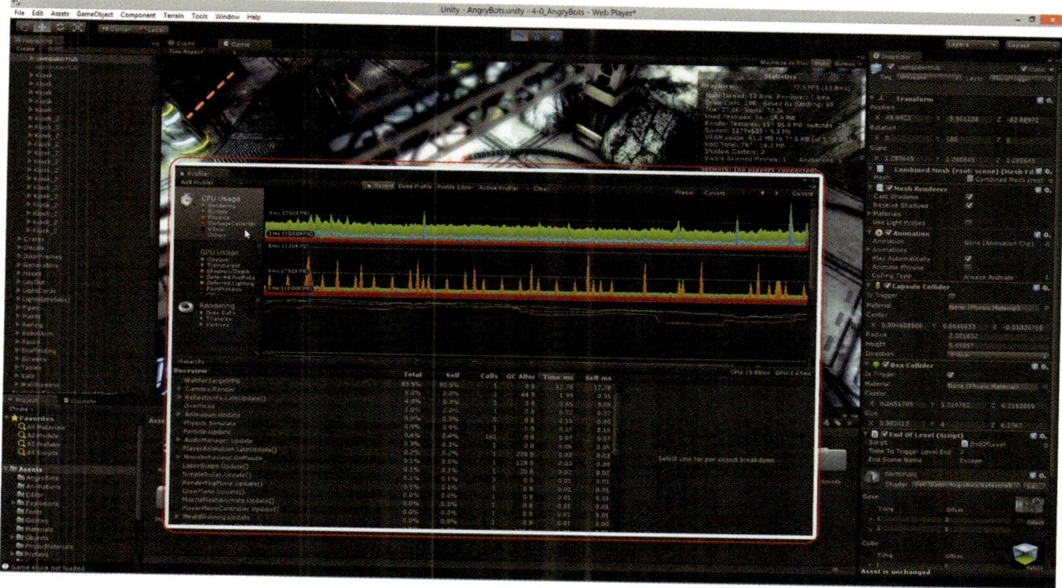

Figure 9.4 Unity Profiler at work on the AngryBots sample project. It can be used to monitor performance-critical fields of data to identify and diagnose issues

If your game is performing badly on your target hardware and you simply cannot identify the cause using the traditional debugging techniques and the Stats panel, then you may need to 'roll out the big guns'. One of the most powerful tools in Unity's debugging and diagnostic armoury is the Profiler tool, which is accessible via the Profiler window. This tool is a dream come true for almost every developer who has a statistician living with them, one who loves to measure and compare and read graphs. In this section we'll take a look at the Profiler window in depth through an example. Let's work from the AngryBots project. So go ahead and open up that project, if you haven't already, and let's get started looking at the Profiler.

1. With the AngryBots Project open in the editor, access the Profiler window by selecting *Window > Profiler* from the application menu, or press *Ctrl + 7* on the keyboard. Pressing this displays a window featuring numerous graphs and sources of information. This information is divided between two main panels or groups, an upper panel (A) and a lower panel (B) – see Figure 9.5. The upper panel is a graph view, and the lower panel offers expanded and further details, as we'll soon see. Your Profile panel might appear differently to Figure 9.5. If this is the first time you've opened and used the Profiler, its graph and panels will appear clear of information, since no data has yet been recorded. Don't worry, we'll start recording soon.

NOTE: If your Profile is not clear of all data, then you can clear it manually by pressing the *Clear* button, from the top toolbar of Panel A.

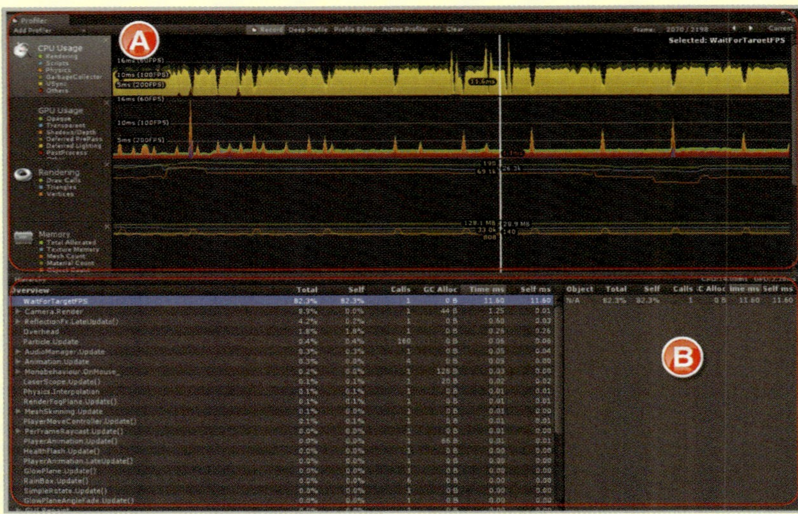

Figure 9.5 Unity Profile Window is divided into two main panels, an upper panel (A) and a lower panel (B)

2. The Profiler works by recording performance data for each frame while your game is running. This data is then collected by the Profiler and arranged and sorted into a graph where it can be viewed and examined by us to search for potential problems. To start using the Profiler, however, we need some data to work with. So let's record some data now from the AngryBots game. To do that, ensure the *Record* button is pressed and activated from the top toolbar of *Panel A* in the Profiler window. Now press the *Play* but, keeping the Profiler window open in the editor. While the game is running you should immediately see the Profiler spring to life, recording data and compiling a graph. Keep playing the game for a while until the Profiler graph is filled from left to right with frame data, and then end play to stop recording. The Profiler window should now look similar to Figure 9.5, although the exact values and data will vary from system to system.
3. Panel A of the Profiler features two histograms and four line charts. Each graph spans from left to right across the window in Panel A. The horizontal (X or left-right) axis of these charts refers to *Frames*, and the vertical (Y or up-down) axis refers to *Time*. Thus, each graph plots *Frames* against *Time*. Try clicking and dragging the mouse horizontally within the range of a graph. When you do this, and as you move the mouse, a vertical line bisects all graphs, showing the currently selected frame and some time values for that frame printed along the line. Take a look at the top-right corner of the profiler window to see the number for the currently selected frame in the graph – you can also use the left and right arrow buttons to step through the frames one by one. Consider Figure 9.6.
4. Each graph shows Frame to Time information for different dimensions of data. The topmost histogram in the Profiler window charts *CPU* Usage for the processes of *Rendering (Green)*, *Scripts (Blue)*, *Physics (Orange)*, *Garbage Collection (Dark Yellow)*, *V Synch (Light Yellow)* and *others (Red)*. That is, the graph tells us *how long* in milliseconds the CPU spent on each of those activities for *each recorded frame*. We can click to select a frame in the graph and then read the CPU values for each process on that frame. In Figure 9.6, for example, rendering for the CPU took around *16ms* for Frame *758*. For the same frame, the mesh count value for the Memory graph was around *808* – meaning that at Frame 758 there were a total of 808 meshes in memory. Notice that line graphs below the histograms compare *Frames* to values other than *Time*, such as the number of *Meshes* or *Megabytes*.

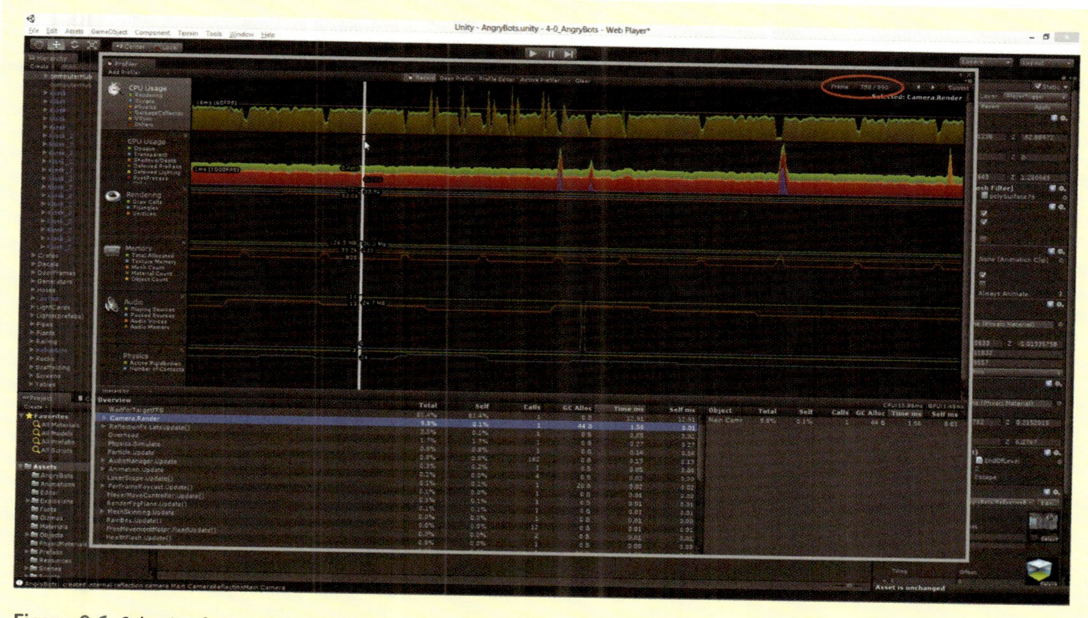

Figure 9.6 Selecting frames from the Profiler graph

Right now, the V-Sync value is probably taking up a lot of room in the CPU graph. So let's disable the V-Sync option in the graph. To do that, just click the *VSync* button in the CPU graph – yes, these are actually toggle buttons, even though they may not initially seem clickable. See Figure 9.7. Once you have disabled V-Sync, clear the graph and start a new recording by pressing the *Play* button from the toolbar. You can record and re-record as much as you need.

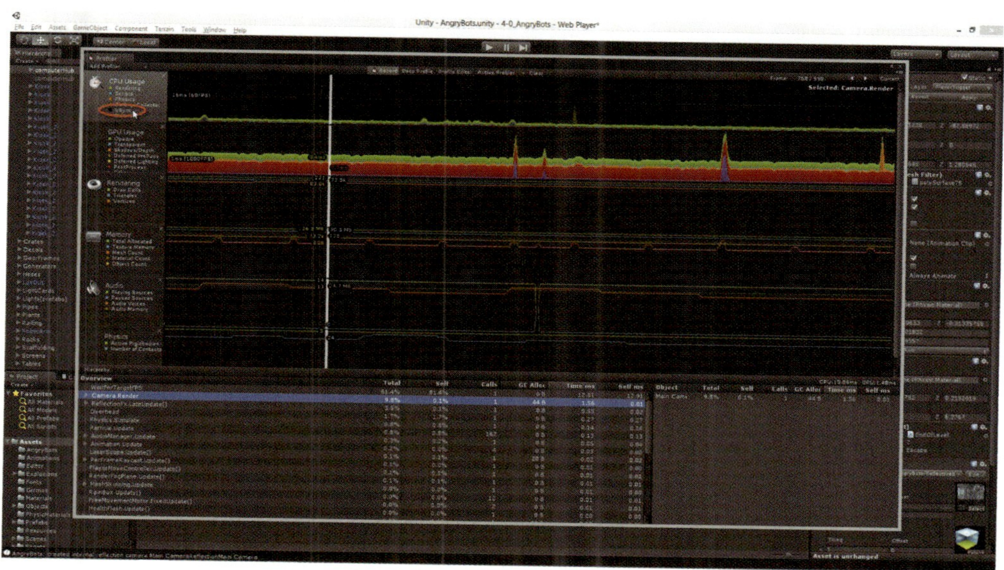

Figure 9.7 Disable V-Sync display in the CPU graph

5. Let's now take a closer look at the Panel A graphs, as shown in Figure 9.8. In these graph, the most intensive CPU process is *Rendering*, because the green data is on average the highest data in the chart. No other form of data ever appears taller than rendering data. After rendering, the next most intensive is *Scripts*, then *Physics*, then *Other*, then *GarbageCollector*. Processes fluctuate across frames, so no process appears as a horizontal line in the graph. That is normal behaviour. On occasion, the data *spikes*; that is, suddenly rises to a sharp point or mountain. This represents a sudden surge or burst of activity in that process. In Figure 9.8, rendering surges have been circled. At these moments, the render took longer than average. Such surges are often unproblematic – 'normal' behaviour – but sometimes they can signify problems or hint at places in your game where performance could be optimised. For this reason, if you're concerned about performance in your game, and want to find places for improvement, then use the Profiler tool to find *spikes* and to locate when those spikes occur during game play. If we transfer what we've learned from reading the CPU graph to the other graphs in the window, we'll see that for GPU usage, *Opaque* graphics (standard textures and meshes) were on average the most intensive process (green data). We can also see from the Audio graph that the total number of Playing Audio Sources was 14, and this value remained constant throughout the recording, hence the reason it appears as a straight horizontal line from the left to right of the graph.

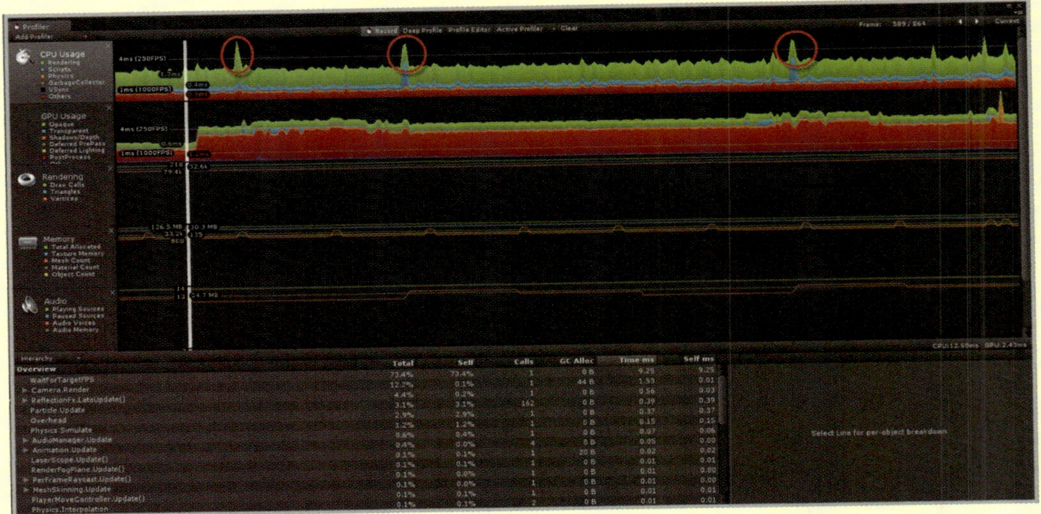

Figure 9.8 Disable V-Synch display in the CPU graph

6. Let's investigate the data spikes in the CPU graph some more; specifically the first spike, as shown in Figure 9.8 (the leftmost spike). You will likely see different spikes in your graph as you follow along, but they can be investigated using the same workflow. This workflow will introduce Panel B of the Profiler. Left-click on the data spike in the graph using the mouse to move the frame line to that point. When clicked, statistical data will appear in Panel B. Panel B is divided into two columns, the *Overview* column on the left side and the *Object* column on the right side. The overview displays a list of the all scripted functions called or run on the selected frame, and by default these are listed in order of time – that is, they're listed from top to bottom based on the time they took for the CPU to process, the most intensive listed at the top and the 'lightest' listed at the bottom. By selecting the spike frame in my Profiler, I can see that, in my case, the most intensive function on that frame is

ReflectionFX.LateUpdate. See Figure 9.9. This function accounted for around 36.2 per cent of the CPU time for that frame, which equated to 2.72 ms. By returning to the CPU graph in Panel A and clicking the frames on either side of the spike, one at a time, I can see by comparing values in the Overview list in Panel B that the most intensive function is different. This difference is suggestive: namely, it indicates the *ReflectionFX.LateUpdate* is to some extent responsible for the data spike in the CPU graph. We can investigate this further.

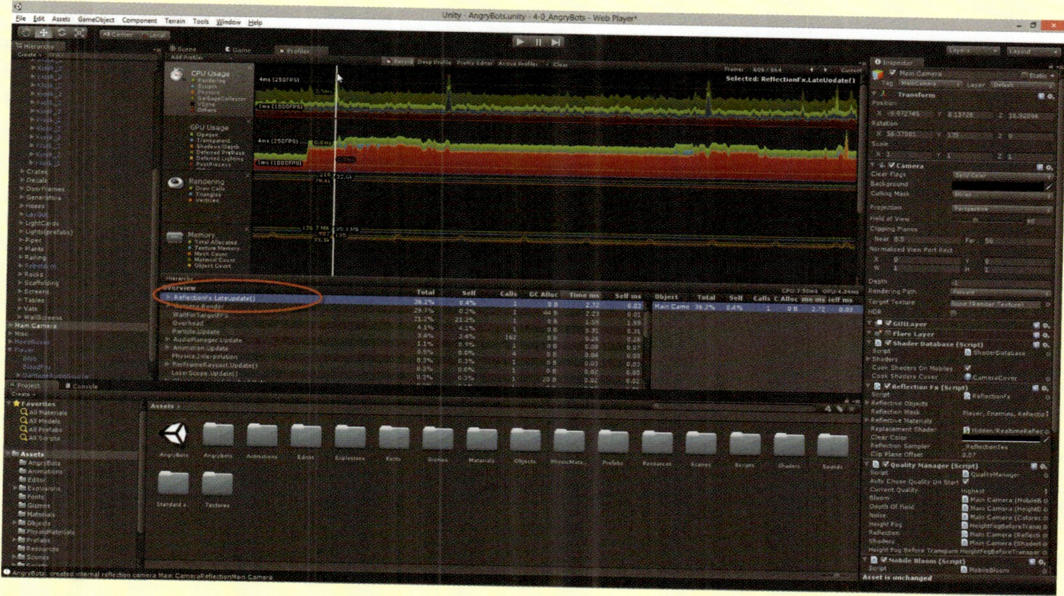

Figure 9.9 Tracing the possible cause of a spike

7. If you select the *ReflectionFX.LateUpdate* function in Panel B, or any function in this panel, the rightmost column (the Object Column) will display information about the *GameObject* associated with this script. By selecting *ReflectionFX.LateUpdate* I see it is run from the *ReflectionFX* Script, which is attached as a component to the Main Camera object in the active scene. See Figure 9.10. I can double-click the Camera object listed in the Object Panel of the Profiler to select the camera in the scene and display its properties, as usual, in the Object Inspector. At this point, notice what we have achieved. We have run the game and recorded its performance data in the Profiler. And from among the statistics and graphs there, we have examined the data to trace a spike and its performance issues to a specific *component* on a specific *game object* in the scene. From the data we have isolated and reached a concrete function, namely *LateUpdate* in the *ReflectionFX* script. True, the presence of a performance spike does *not* confirm that a problem exists. Indeed, AngryBots performs without issues on my system. Further, we cannot be certain the identified spike is actually related to *LateUpdate* – it could be the result of a different process altogether. But the Profiler has given us enough data to make some educated decisions about where to begin our search for problems. The Profiler can give us evidence and statistics that point in particular directions or to specific objects and scripts, and then it is our role to investigate the code further to see whether the evidence is justified. In short, if your game is performing badly, the Profiler is a tool which helps *guide* our search for the cause – it is not, of course, the ultimate solution for each and every problem.

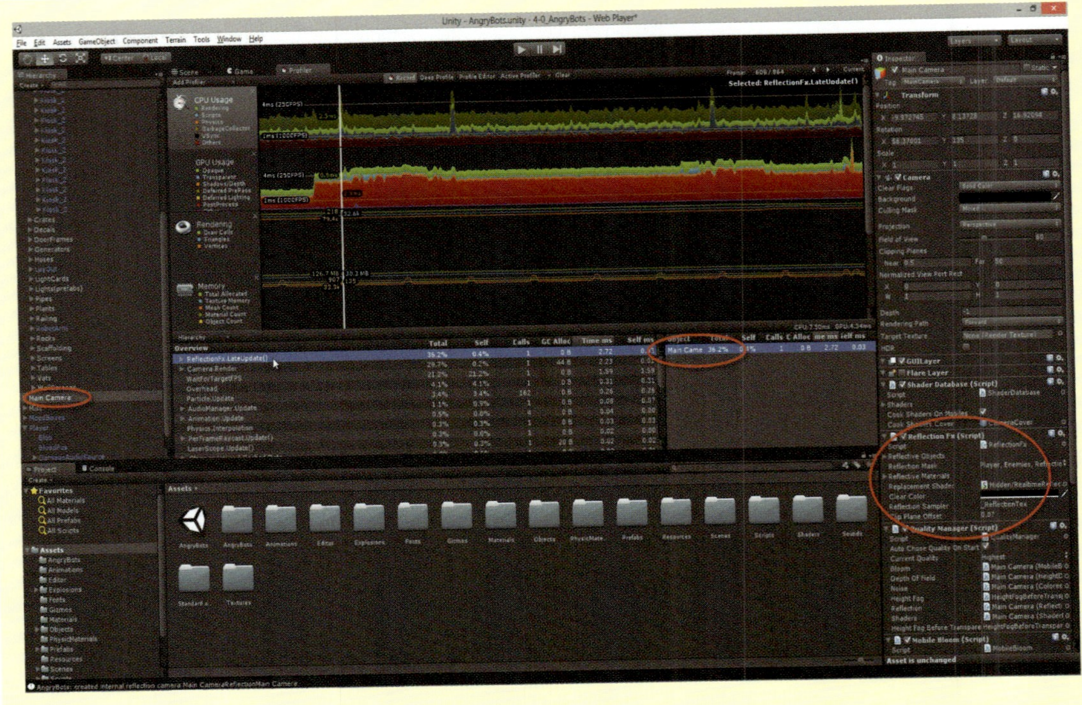

Figure 9.10 Using the Profiler to reach a game object and function

9.6 Debugging Summary

Errors and performance issues are likely to crop up somewhere in your game development career – typically in every project you work on! We don't plan for them to happen and we don't want them to happen, but issues will arise, despite our best efforts, because humans are fallible. Unity offers us a range of powerful tools for debugging and diagnosing these issues. The tools it offers range from simple debugging techniques, such as printing messages to the console, to more elaborate systems, such as the Profiler. But, despite their power, none of these tools are *ultimate* problem-solvers. Their purpose is to help developers *find* and *isolate* problems and make their *search* for issues easier. Once the problem is identified, its resolution is an issue for the developer and not something managed by the tools. For this reason, there is no better substitute for fixing and removing bugs than to create and plan your game carefully to avoid issues in the first place. There will be issues that turn out to be unavoidable, and these will arise no matter what because they afflict even the best of plans. But there are also issues that arise from bad management, poor planning, sloppy coding and weak organisation. This is one of the reasons I stressed the importance of asset management and consistency in earlier chapters, rather than jumping in with a large project straight away. By cultivating good organisational habits in the early stages and applying them then to all your project work, you can make your life exponentially easier when it comes to debugging.

9.7 Building

When you've finished developing and debugging your gaming masterpiece and it's ready to sign off and distribute to the anxiously waiting gaming masses, then it's time to start using the Build features of Unity. These features compile and package your game into an independent, stand-alone form: a form that can be distributed to the gamer and allows them to play your game without having the Unity engine installed on their own system. By using the Build features you can – depending on the add-ons you've purchased for Unity (if any) – potentially deploy your game to Windows, Mac, Linux, Android, iOS, the web, and even console systems such as the *Wii U*, *PS3* and the *Xbox 360*. The free and professional versions of Unity by default support only desktop platforms, including Windows, Mac and Linux, and the web through the Unity Web Player. Purchasing add-ons for other platforms will unlock the potential and features to build for those platforms. This section considers only the Unity native build features for distributing to desktop systems.

9.7.1 Building For Desktop Platforms

Let's build the coin collection game we completed in the previous chapter. To get started, open up the completed coin collection project from the Chapter 8 files in the Unity editor. The following steps explain how to build this project for Windows, Mac and Linux Ubuntu.

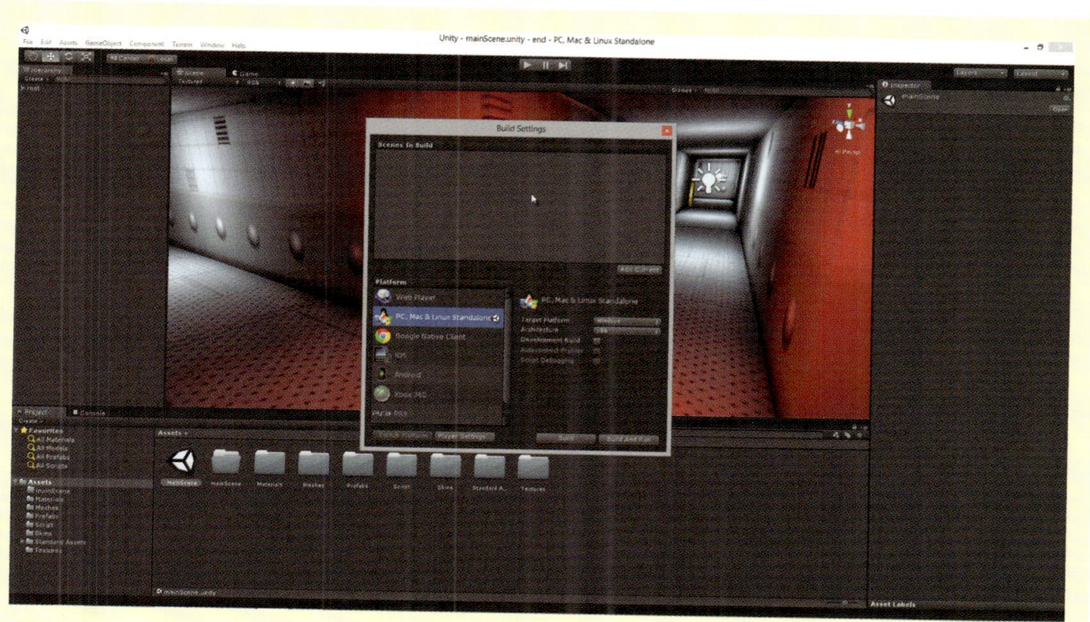

Figure 9.11 Using the Profiler to reach a game object and function

1. Before building a project be sure to save any changes, to commit all edits you have made and ensure no work will be lost if the compilation process goes wrong. Once saved, click *File > Build Settings* from the application menu. This displays the *Build Dialog*, as featured in Figure 9.11. From here, the project can be compiled to all available platforms.
2. The topmost list box of the Build Dialog is *Scenes In Build*, which is empty by default. This list should display *all* scenes in the project that'll feature in the final build. Any scene you want to include in your game should be included here. You can add scenes to the list by dragging and dropping them from the Project panel into the *Scenes in Build* list box. Go ahead: drag and drop the main scene of the project into this list. Since this is the first and only scene of the project, it will appear at the top of the list and be assigned an ID of *0*. ID values of scenes are important: specifically, the scene with an ID of 0 is classified as the *starting scene*. This is the scene which loads and displays when the game is first executed by the user. You can change the order of scenes, if you have multiple scenes, by dragging and dropping them within the Scenes In Build list to different locations. For the coin collection game we need to include just one scene, our original main scene. See Figure 9.12.

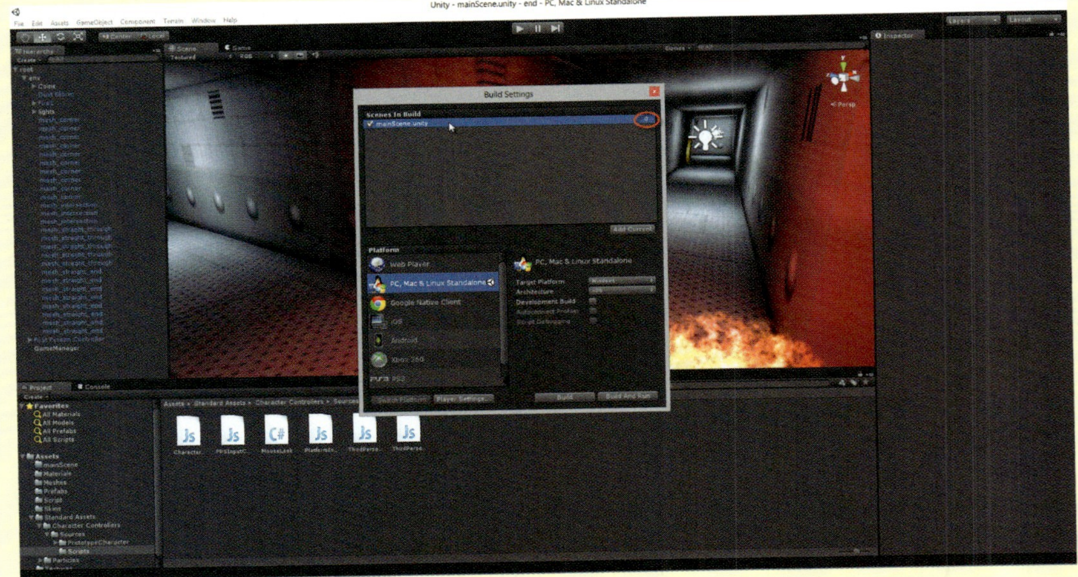

Figure 9.12 Adding a scene to the Scenes In Build list

3. When all scenes have been added, you can build straight away! But let's take some time here to customise and specify important properties for our build, such as the game title, the developer title, the screen resolutions, and whether windowed mode is permitted. To control these settings, click the *Player Settings* button from the bottom of the *Build* dialog. This displays the Player Settings menu inside the Object Inspector. This menu can also be reached by selecting *Edit > Project Settings > Player* from the application menu. From here, enter the *Company Name* and *Product Name*. Company Name is the name of your game company, and Product Name is the name for your game. You can also specify an application icon here, but for this project the icon field will be left blank. Expand the *Resolution and Presentation* group. From there, be sure the *Default Resolution* is set to 1024×768, the *Default Screen Mode* is *Full Screen* (since our game is intended to run full screen), and the only supported aspect ratio is 4:3, which is the aspect ratio for 1024x768. If other aspect ratios are supported, the gamer will be able to select other resolutions and aspect ratios for running the game. See Figure 9.13.

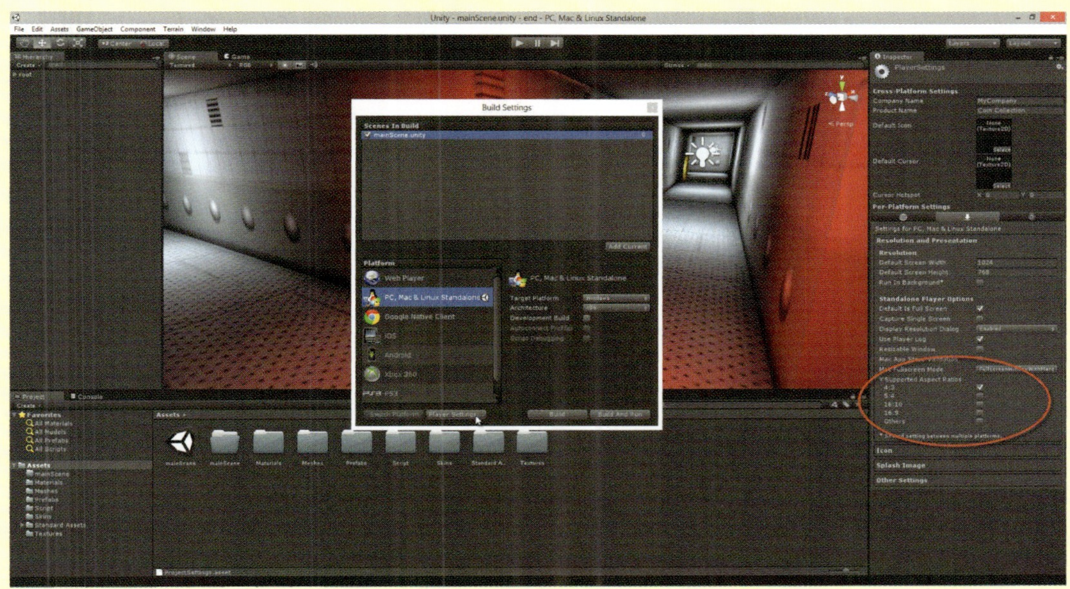

Figure 9.13 Choosing player settings for the build

4. Now create the 'builds' for our game, one for each platform. Select the *PC, Mac & Linux Standalone* option from the platform list box in the Build dialog. To build for Windows, select the *Windows* option in the *Platform* drop-down list and then click *Build*. Unity will display a save dialog for selecting a local path where the build should be saved. Once selected, Unity compiles your project and produces a workable Windows build for your game. Repeat this process for the Mac and Linux platforms, each time selecting a different local path to save the build. See Figure 9.14.

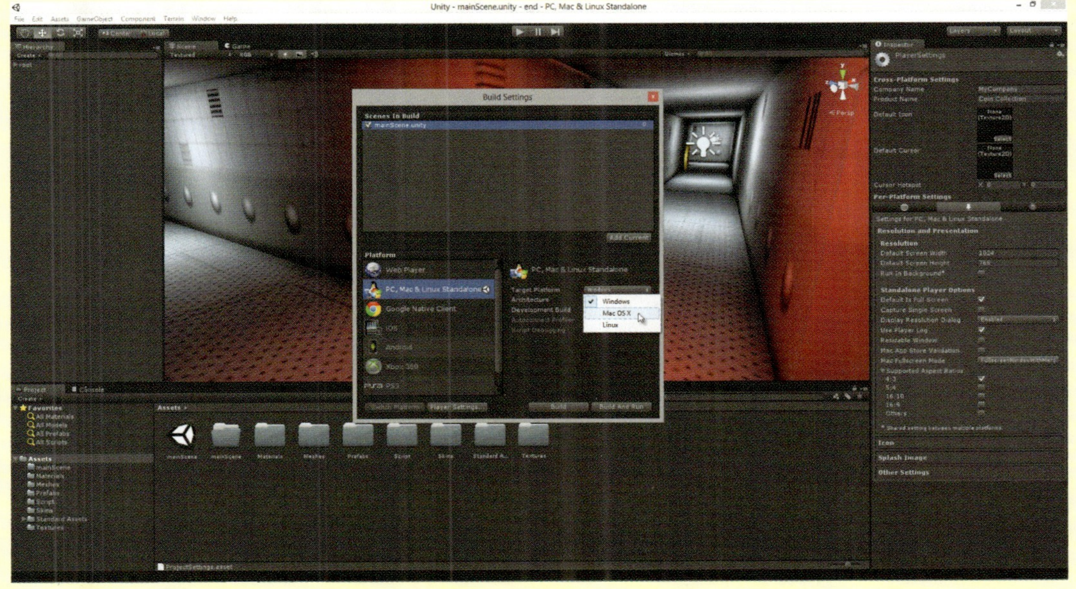

Figure 9.14 Build a project for Windows, Mac and Linux

5. Three builds have been generated and saved, one for each desktop platform. Navigate to their folders on your hard drive and take each for a test drive, if you have access to each platform – otherwise, test the build for your current platform. Each of these builds runs as a native application for their intended platforms and on a standalone basis, without the Unity engine being installed on the system. Simply copy and paste the build files to a different system, and it will run as intended, hardware permitting. Congratulations! You've just created a Unity build for the coin collection game.

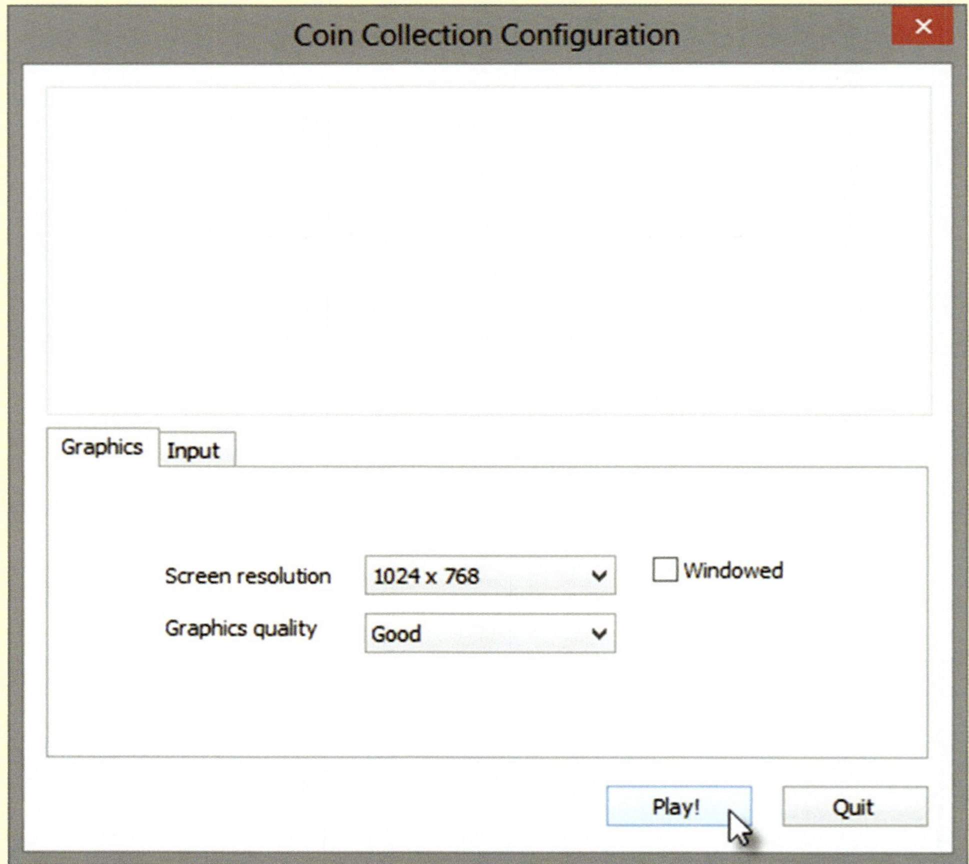

Figure 9.15 Running a Windows build. The Resolution dialog will display by default at start-up, allowing users to select resolutions and options. This dialog can be disabled from the *PlayerSettings* menu by disabling *Display Resolution Dialog*

NOTE: For Linux Ubuntu builds, take special care about whether you're building for 32-Bit or 64-Bit architectures. 32-Bit builds will not run on 64-Bit systems, and 64-Bit systems are not *by default* configured to run 32-bit builds. To run 32-Bit builds, users must install additional libraries and software. More information on this subject can be found on the Ubuntu website at https://help.ubuntu.com/community/32bit_and_64bit

9.8 Post-processing

Let's now turn our attention to 'post-processing'. This is a step that generally comes before debugging, but I am considering it here because I want to end this chapter leaving you with some fun ways to edit and tweak renders on your own. Post-processing is a generic term referring to all the additional image manipulation work we perform on a rendered image. On each processing cycle or frame, the Unity Renderer draws the active scene to the game window – and it does this many times per second. The specifics and internals of the rendering process are not relevant here. Here it is enough to think of each rendered frame as a single image: a separate and unique render of the active scene. If we think of the render as a single image, we could imagine opening up that image in an image editor, such as Photoshop, and applying edits and tweaks to it – colour correction, blurring, twirling, inverting and changing pixels, and so on. These edits would be referred to as post-processing because they are processes applied to the image *after* it has been rendered. Unity offers us a whole range of post-processing features that we can apply to rendered images on each frame, in real time, to further improve the graphical quality of our games. Using them, we can turn our game into black and white, add blurring and bloom effects, increase sharpness, add depth of field and vignettes, and much more. These effects all belong to a special Unity package named *Image Effects*, and they are restricted to the professional version. If you're using the free version of Unity, then you can skip this section and move to the next chapter.

9.8.1 Getting Started with Image Effects

In this section we'll take a look at some of the Image effects available to us for use in our games. We'll do this by pursuing a small practical project. Specifically, we'll open up an existing project available for free from the Unity Asset Store and we'll add Image Effects to it to change how it looks. In doing this, we'll see how the look and style of our game can be overhauled and changed parametrically from the Object Inspector. Consider the following steps from beginning to end.

1. Open up the Unity Editor and create an empty new project, if you have not already. Since post-processing is about applying effects to *rendered* images, we'll need an existing scene or project to render, as opposed to an empty and blank project. We could open up the *AngryBots* sample project, or one of the projects created in earlier chapters. Here, however, let's download and use an existing sample project from the Unity Asset Store: specifically the 3rd Person Shooter project. To download and access this project, select *Window > Asset Store* (*Ctrl + 9*) from the application menu to open the Asset Store. Log in to the store with your user account, if you're not logged in already, and search for the project: *3rd person shooter*. Import this project into Unity by clicking the *Import* button; see Figure 9.16. Once imported, open the default scene *Demo*. You may need to rebuild LightMapping for the project if your scene meshes and surfaces don't appear as in Figure 9.16. For more information on building LightMapping, see Chapter 5.

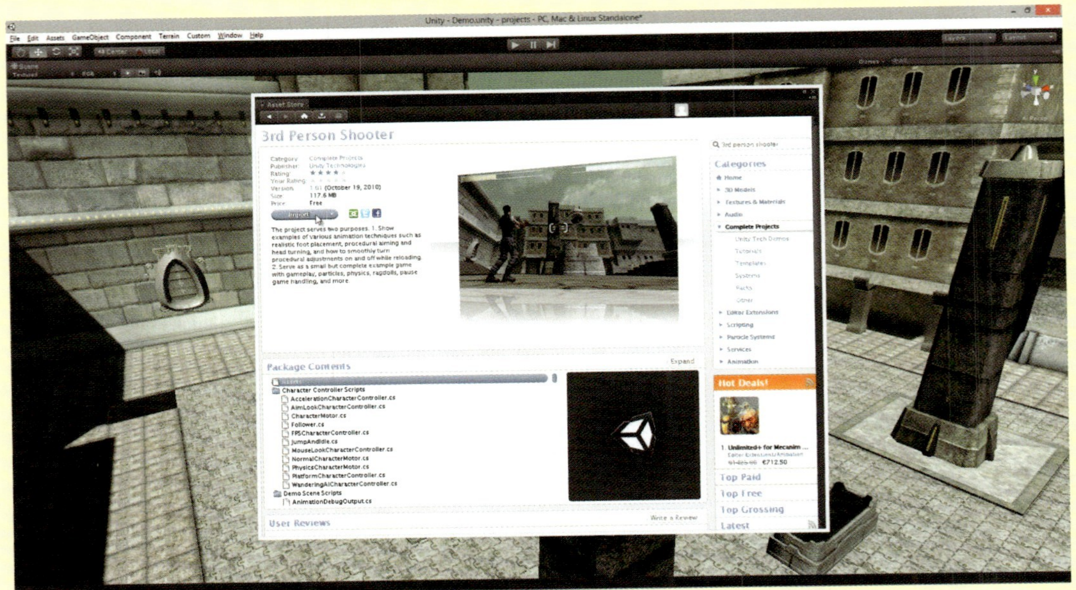

Figure 9.16 Importing the 3rd Person Shooter project, ready for using Image Effects

2. Now we have a project and a scene to work with. Give the scene a test run to play the game and see how it works. Our aim here is to apply Image Effects to this game to 'improve' or change its overall look and feel. To do this, we'll also need to import the Unity *Image Effects* package into the project. Do that now by clicking *Assets > Import Package > Image Effects* from the application menu. Accept the default settings from the *Import Package* dialog, and click the *Import* button to confirm the operation, adding the Image Effects assets to the project. Once added, a slew of new image effect options will become available from the main menu at *Component > Image Effects*.
3. For this project, let's use *Forward Rendering* as opposed to *Deferred Rendering*. To change this, select *Edit > Project Settings > Player* from the application menu. In the Object Inspector, expand the group *Other Settings*, and change the setting *Rendering Path* from *Deferred Lighting* to *Forward*. You may notice a small change in the rendering output in the Game and Scene tabs. Exit from this dialog. Now we're to get started applying some Image Effects to our game.

9.8.2 Grayscale Effect

You can add a brooding mood or old-fashioned atmosphere to your game by using the Grayscale post-processing effect. With this effect, all pixels in the rendered image retain their value or brightness but lose their hue. The result is a render that looks 'black and white' – in a loose sense: it actually features more tones than simply black and white. To add this effect, consider the following steps.

NOTE: The process of adding an Image Effect to a render is the same for *all* effects, even though the specific properties of each effect differ. For this reason, in later sections, I'll assume you know how to add an effect.

1. Select the camera in the scene (*MainCamera*) from which the game is rendered. Either select the camera in the Scene viewport, or select it from the hierarchy. With the camera selected, let's add an Image Effect component to change how it is rendered. To do this, select *Component > Image Effects > Grayscale* from the application menu. Doing this will attach an Image Effect component to the camera, and it will also convert the camera render into greyscale. The result of this effect will be immediately noticeable in the *Game* tab, but not the *Scene* tab. Give the game a test run now, pressing *Play* from the toolbar, and see how the effect applies to all rendered frames – that is, applies to all renderings from the camera in real time. This means the game continually appears in greyscale. See Figure 9.17.

Figure 9.17 Adding a Grayscale effect to the Main Camera

2. You can tweak the properties of the effect further by visiting the Image Effect component attached to the camera. The Grayscale effect accepts two main properties: *TextureRamp* and *RampOffset*. TextureRamp accepts a reference to any valid texture whose colour values can tint or shade the render, while the RampOffset controls the strength of the effect. For most Grayscale effects these settings can be left at their defaults, but they can be tweaked to add specific stylisations. When *TextureRamp* is left empty, the RampOffset setting controls the brightness, or 'gamma', of the Grayscale effect: -1 changes the render to black, 0 leaves the effect at its defaults, and 1 sets the render to white.

9.8.3 Blur

Blur is often a stigmatised term in video graphics – a 'bad thing' to be *removed* or *fixed*. However, it can be *added* to a render to create a range of interesting stylisations and effects to simulate drunkenness, dizziness, fog, speed, motion, myopia, dreaminess, heat and the like. With Blur effects, the following advice usually applies: a little goes a long way. Over-using Blur can lead to a confusing mess. You can add Blur to any camera by selecting *Component > Image Effects > Blur* from the application main menu. The main properties of Blur are: *Iterations* and *Blur Spread* (See Figure 9.18). *Iterations* controls the overall strength of the Blur; the higher this value, the blurrier the render becomes. *Blur Spread* controls how blurring is internally calculated: it controls the area over which the render is averaged and re-sampled. The best way to get a feel for blur is to try it – go ahead and experiment with these two values.

NOTE: Remember, you can *combine* image effects by adding multiple Image Effect components to the camera. Be careful, though: each image effect adds additional processing overhead.

9.8.4 Bloom

Bloom is a specialisation of the Blur Image Effect, a form of selective blurring to create the phenomenon of 'light bleeding'. If you have played the games Oblivion, Halo,

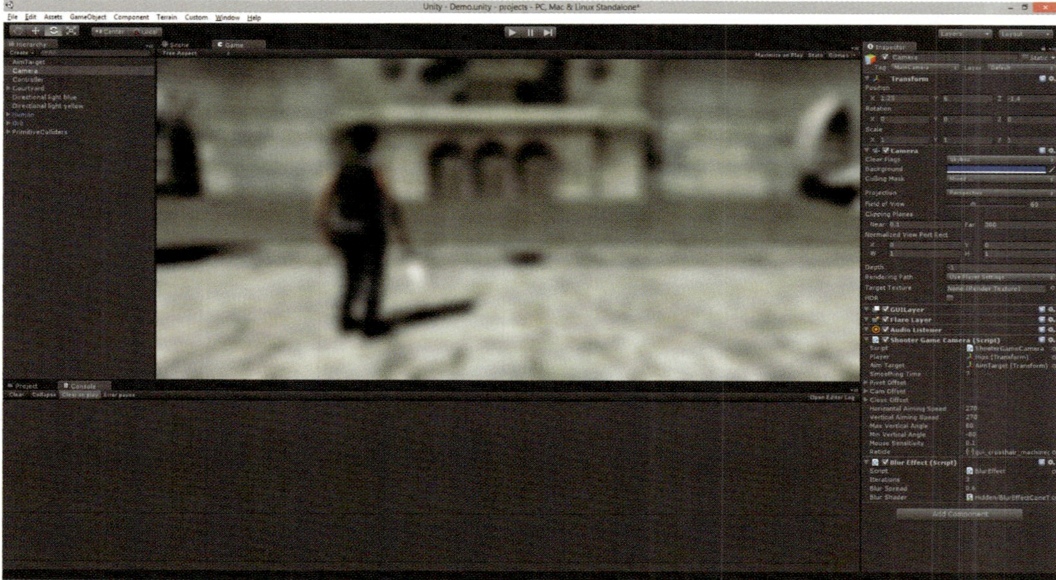

Figure 9.18 Blurring the game camera

Figure 9.19 Applying Bloom to create light bleeding for scene highlights

Syndicate or Crysis you will probably have experienced Bloom first hand. Bloom works by proportionally blurring only the highlights in the rendered image – that is, by blurring pixels with an RGB brightness typically greater than 200. The net effect is that natural lights, artificial lights, reflections and specular highlights in the scene appear to be surrounded by a faint aura or ethereal glow. This can impart a dreamy, whimsical or surreal feel to a scene. It's a graphical effect used commonly in Medieval Fantasy and Futuristic Cyberpunk games, but it is by no means limited to them. Bloom became a popular effect around 2004 and since then has been used, or over-used, in hundreds of games. You can add Bloom to a camera by selecting *Component > Image Effects > Bloom (4.0, HDR, Lens Flares)* from the application menu. See Figure 9.19. The core properties of Bloom are as below.

Intensity

Controls the strength of the effect and acts much like an Opacity value. Lower values weaken the effect and higher values strengthen the effect. Intensity does not have an effect on performance, meaning that all values perform equally.

Threshold

Threshold specifies a minimum brightness value for pixels – pixels higher than the threshold will be affected by Bloom and pixels below the threshold will be ignored. The lower this value, the more pervasive and noticeable the effect becomes.

Blur Iterations

Blur Iterations can range from 1 to 4, controlling how smooth and continuous the Bloom effect appears. Higher values produce a smoother effect but impact

Figure 9.20 Adding a darkened Vignette frame around the edges of the render

significantly on performance. Keep this value as low as possible while still achieving the results you need.

9.8.5 Vignette and Chromatic Aberration

Vignetting in video games refers largely to a framing process – surrounding the rendered image with a frame or a border or a shape. With Vignetting you can add a darkened, blurred border to the edges of the render, as shown in Figure 9.20. This effect is useful for simulating views through the lens of a camera or for creating dramatic tension or fear. It can also be complemented by other Image Effects, such as *Grayscale, Sepia Tone* and *Noise*, for simulating vintage video recordings or old movie reels. Vignette relies on two main properties, as follows.

Vignetting

Vignetting controls the overall size of the darkened circular border surrounding the render. Higher values will expand the vignette inwards towards the centre of the image. Increase this value to make the border larger and the render darker, and lower this value to make the border smaller and render lighter.

Blurred Corners and Blur Distance

The Blurred Corners and Blur Distance values work together to control the extent and size of blurring in and around the vignette. Blurred Corners can be raised to increase the radius of the blur effect inwards into the render, and Blur Distance affects the extent of blur within the Blur Corners area.

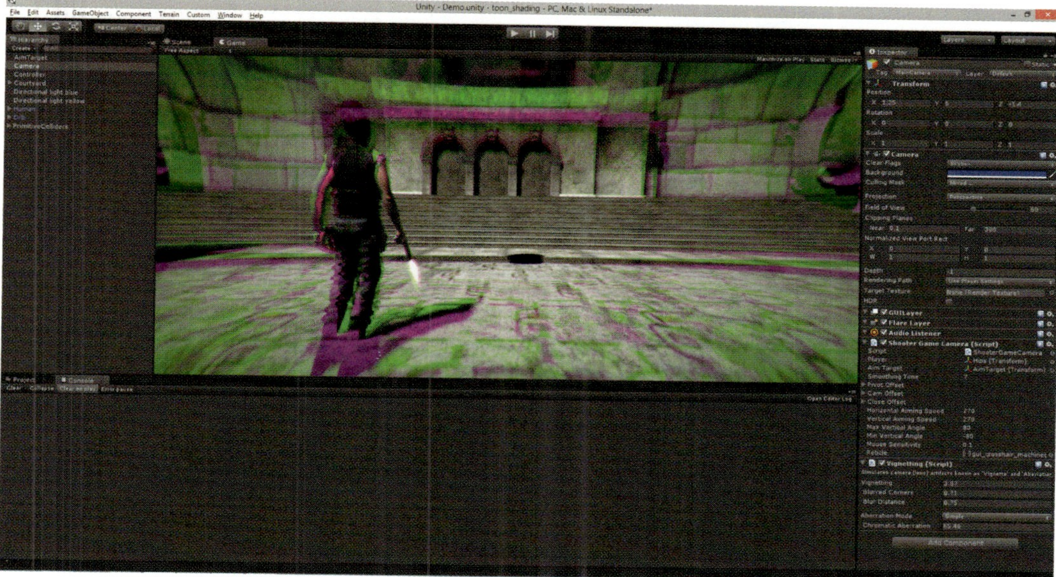

Figure 9.21 Adding surrealism with Chromatic Aberration

The Vignette effect is combined with a Chromatic Aberration effect, which not only colour-adjusts a render but pulls and stretches pixels away from the image centre. This effect is useful for simulating surreal atmospheres and first-person views of intoxication, drug-effects, dreamscapes and the like (see Figure 9.21).

9.8.6 Image Effects in Summary

Here we've considered only a subset of the many Image Effects available in Unity for customising the look of a rendered frame. Now we've seen how to import the Image Effects package into a project and add them to the camera through the *Component* menu, it's probably more fun to explore them through *practice* rather than by reading about them: so go ahead and add them to the camera, tweak their settings and see what each one does. In short, Image Effects are a powerful way to stylise the look of your renders with only a few setting and property adjustments. They don't require you to remodel or re-texture your assets: just add them to the camera, customise, and that's it! More information on all the Image Effects available and their properties can be found in the Unity documentation at http://docs.unity3d.com/Documentation/Components/comp-ImageEffects.html.

9.9 Toon Shading

A unique and especially striking 3D graphical style is *Cel* (or *Toon*) *shading*, and this method is available 'out of the box' in Unity. The chief aim of this shader model is to achieve not photo-realism or illustrative realism, which is the default model, but *implied* realism – that is, the look of a cartoon, comic book or graphic novel. Games such as *Borderlands*, *Killer is Dead*, *No More Heroes 2* and *Sly Cooper* are all examples of Toon-shaded games. Its main characteristics are inked outline borders around objects and staggered or stepped shading as opposed to continuous gradated shading. It's important to note here that Toon shading is intended to *complement* rather than *replace* cartoon textures or models – that is, to enhanced the Toon feel of 3D meshes already modelled and textured in the Toon style. It is not designed to miraculously convert your photo-real assets into cartoon versions. For this reason, the effectiveness of Toon shading depends largely on the assets for your game. This section offers a brief overview of how to get started using Toon shading in Unity. Consider the following steps.

1. Toon Shading is provided with Unity from an asset package. Consequently, to use Toon Shading, this package must be imported into our project. To do this, select *Assets > Import Package > Toon Shading* from the application menu. Accept the defaults from the Import Package dialog, and click the *Import* button. The Toon Shading assets have now been added to the project. These assets are added to the Standard Assets folder and consist of a *Demo* scene, alongside some materials, textures and shaders.

Figure 9.22 Toon Shading sample

2. Open the folder *Standard Assets > Toon Shading*, and double click the demo scene _*ToonShadingSample* to open it in the Unity editor (see Figure 9.22). These scene features four spheres, each assigned a unique Toon Shading material. Together they demonstrate all four of the Toon-shaded materials in the Toon Shading package. The materials are divided into two main groups: *Basic* and *Lit*, and within these groups there's a *Standard version* and an *Outline version*. The Basic Group

materials are immune from scene lighting, are the least expensive computationally and will use their own internal routines to shade objects. The Lit group materials are, by contrast, affected by scene lighting. The *Outline* versions display an inked outline or stroke around the border of the object, which changes and updates based on the viewing angle of the scene camera.

3. Select each of the four Toon-shaded materials in the Project panel. Notice that each material accepts a *Diffuse* texture and also makes use of a specific Toon-shaded cube-map asset. These materials are designed to be templates for customisation rather than as final materials for your objects. You should duplicate the materials and tweak their settings for your needs, assigning the duplicates to your objects rather than the originals. The Toon-shaded cube-map asset can usually be left as is for most situations, but the Diffuse texture should be assigned with the Toon textures of your game. Remember, Toon Shading is designed to enhance Toon assets and not to 'magically' convert realist assets to Toon assets. For this reason, assigning photo textures to the Diffuse slot will not necessarily lead to appreciable benefits or the intended results.

9.10 Conclusion

This chapter is not the last of the book, but it marks the end of an important section. Up to this point the chapters have covered in sequence the six steps of the Unity workflow. This chapter was concerned with the last of the six stages: debugging, building and post-processing. Together, chapters 1–9 constitute the foundation or core of our Unity knowledge. The book will now proceed to expand our understanding of that core and introduce more 'intermediate' topics to complement and consolidate your power as a Unity user. Before moving forwards it's worth taking a look back through the earlier chapters, to summarise and recap what you've learned. Next, we'll consider a form of 'artificial intelligence', made up of *Pathfinding* and *Navigation*. Knowledge of this will allow us to create enemies and characters that can move around a scene autonomously, with purpose and meaning.

CHAPTER 10

Navigation and Pathfinding

By the end of this chapter you should:

1. Understand what Pathfinding is.
2. Understand what *NavMesh* and *NavMesh Agents* are.
3. Be able to bake NavMesh objects from scene geometry.
4. Understand NavMesh bake settings.
5. Be able to configure NavMesh Agents.

Most popular video games today feature vast expansive worlds where players engage enemies in combat. These enemies, when attacking or being attacked, don't just stand on the spot and 'do nothing'. They're intelligent, or *appear* to be intelligent, depending on your definition of intelligence. The enemies seek out players in the environment, as well as power-ups and places of safety and cover. They travel to those places by walking, running, flying, swimming, jumping or other modes of locomotion. They move intelligently from one place to another, and they move with intent: not arbitrarily but to destinations according to their schemes. They run to collect health power-ups when damaged and 'critical', they take cover behind the nearest shelter when under fire, and they ambush the player passing by unawares. Furthermore, they don't take simply *any* route to their destination but the shortest or most direct route – the one you'd expect any sensible person to take in the same circumstances. As they travel from their source location to their destination, they avoid obstacles such as walls, doors, crates and boulders. They don't walk *through* these things, as though they were substance-less forms on the astral plane, but walk *around* them in recognition of their solidness and immovability. This form of NPC (Non-Player Character) exhibits *Artificial Intelligence* (AI). AI is simulated in games by many different techniques. The kind which allows NPCs to move around intelligently falls under the label of *Pathfinding* – a sub-field of graph theory, for those interested in the underlying mathematics. The Pathfinding label is appropriate because questions about where and how to travel are about finding the right path. Unity offers a range of native features for implementing Pathfinding in your games; this chapter considers them only briefly. There is a great deal to be said on the topic, but only so much may be included in an introductory title.

10.1 Getting Started with Pathfinding

The native Unity Pathfinding system is primarily mesh-based rather than node-based. This means it uses a hidden mesh object (a *NavMesh*, or *Navigation Mesh*) to help enemies and characters (*NavMesh Agents*) calculate their way successfully around a scene. The term *NavMesh* refers to all the Pathfinding or map data that is 'baked' or stored in a scene in the form of a mesh with polygons, edges and vertices. The NavMesh is to a scene what road map data is to a TomTom or other satellite navigation device. The term NavMesh Agent describes any dynamic object in a scene that can move around and calculate the correct path to its destination, based on the NavMesh data. NavMesh Agents include enemy characters, robots, vehicles, homing missiles, and more. Creating successful Pathfinding in Unity is largely a three-stage process: first, we *Bake* or generate the navigation data for a scene in the form of a Navigation mesh. Second, we configure all NavMesh Agents (or NPCs) to work with the Navigation mesh. And third, at run-time we tell the NavMesh Agents through scripting *where* to travel and then let them travel there, working out how to do it on their own. To get up and running with Pathfinding, we'll pursue a project based on the coin collecting game coded in chapters 7 and 8. However, I've amended the project, removing the first-person controller and *GameManager* class. This project is included in the course files for this chapter and represents our starting point. Once completed, we'll have a project in which a cube object (a hypothetical NPC) can successfully travel through a maze of corridors to any valid destination we specify. To get started, open up the Navigation project from the course files inside the *Chapter10* folder. Then consider the following steps.

NOTE: Though we'll be working with a cube in this project, we could use any GameObject, from the simplest to the most complex. True, a cube NPC is hardly inspirational visually when compared to grand NPCs in AAA games. But here, as elsewhere, I want to use the simplest possible assets *for a reason*. I want to distil and crystallise the concepts, features and ideas in their *purest and clearest* form so you can see them for what they truly are. This is so we're not distracted by example-specific details – bundles of meshes, animations and sounds – that won't transfer to your own projects. As mentioned in the introduction, the chief purpose of this book is to equip you with the *fundamentals* of Unity, to help nourish a solid understanding of them.

1. The first step in working with Pathfinding involves generating a Navigation mesh object, which stores all Pathfinding information about a scene. This process has parallels with lightmapping, because developers generate the Navigation mesh at design time from the Unity Editor, just like baking lightmaps, and then NPCs will use the mesh at run-time to calculate the shortest path and find their way in the scene. The Navigation mesh is a special mesh object that Unity will store as part of the scene, and it represents the total area inside which NPCs can walk. To generate this mesh from our scene objects, we must first prepare them. To do this, select all of the *static* mesh objects in the scene, the 'environment' meshes. This includes the corner sections, the intersection pieces, the straight-through sections and also the dead ends. You don't need to select lights or particle systems: these will not generally have an effect on Pathfinding. With the environment objects selected, click the drop-down arrow beside the *Static* check box in the Object Inspector. Ensure the option *Navigation Static* is checked from the list. Only objects marked with this tag may be baked into the Navigation mesh. See Figure 10.1.

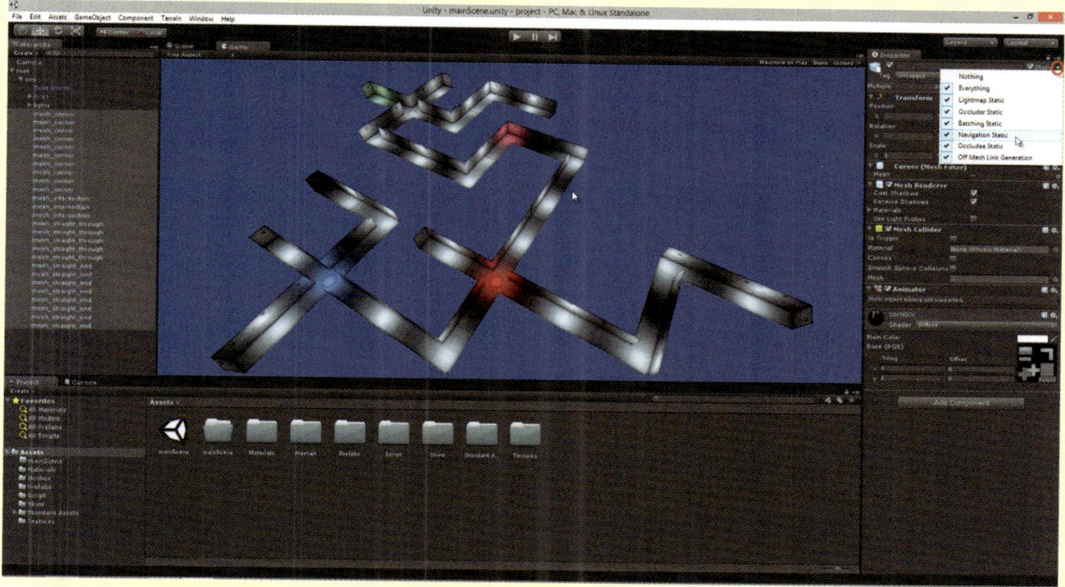

Figure 10.1 Marking objects for inclusion in the Navigation mesh

2. Let's now create the Navigation mesh. To do this, ensure the *Scene* tab is active and not the *Game* tab, otherwise the results of the bake will not immediately be visible in the viewport. Then select *Window > Navigation* from the application main menu. This displays the Navigation window, which mirrors the lightmapping with its *Object* and *Bake* tabs. Select the *Bake* tab, and click the *Bake* button. This generates the Navigation mesh for the scene by the default settings. The generated mesh appears in the viewport above the floor and is highlighted in blue. This mesh will not be visible during gameplay; it is used internally by Unity and is not a visible part of the scene, just as Light gizmos and Collider volumes are not visible. See Figure 10.2. Notice the *NavMesh Display* dialog, shown in the *Scene* Viewport. Be sure *Show NavMesh* is selected to see the Navigation mesh in the scene.
3. Take a look over the generated mesh in the Scene viewport. Notice immediately from Figure 10.3 how the Navigation mesh does not cover any of the walls, the ceiling or any objects *vertically aligned*. The NavMesh mesh is projected or flattened downwards onto the floor and horizontal surfaces from

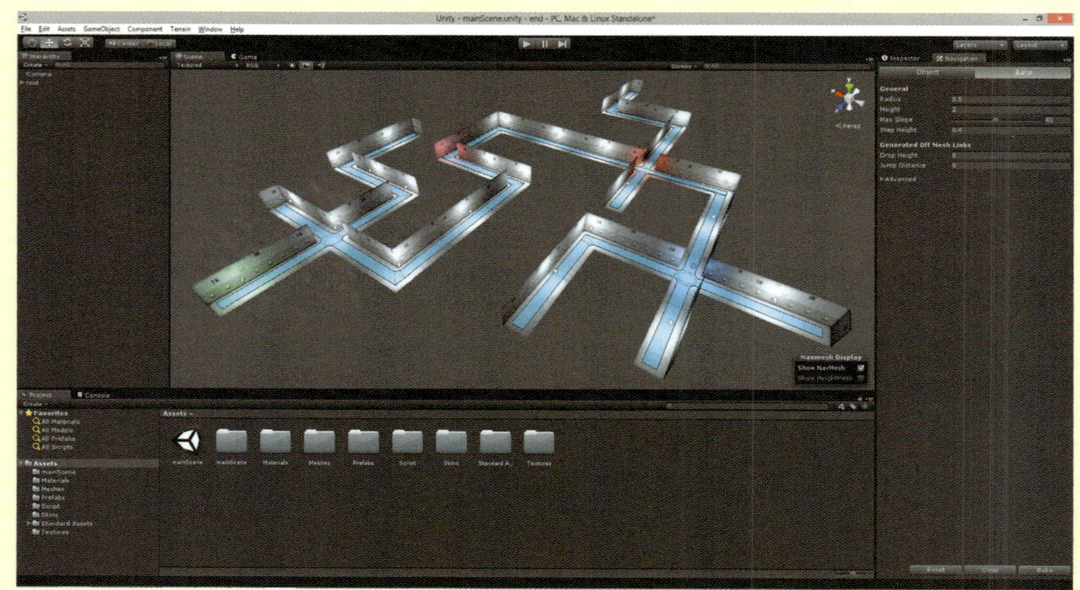

Figure 10.2 Generating a Navigation mesh (shown in blue)

an imaginary plane suspended in the air above the scene. Unity generates the NavMesh in the XZ plane, since this plane corresponds to the ground surface in most scenes – unless you're creating a scene where characters can walk on walls! Next, however, notice two potential issues: first, the NavMesh is positioned away from the floor: it does not rest *exactly* on the ground plane but above

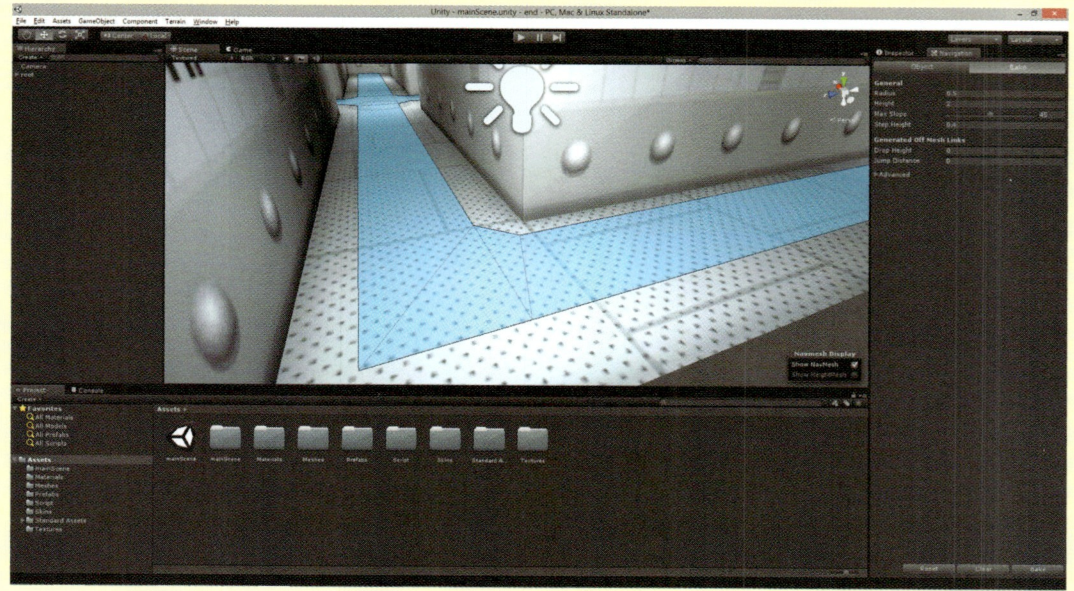

Figure 10.3 The NavMesh is generated in the XZ plane (on the floor). It is offset vertically from the floor and is inset with padding around the edges

it by a marginal distance. This is due to calculation inaccuracies during mesh generation. Second, notice the mesh does not expand outwards from the floor centre to fill the floor area completely but is inset away from the walls on each side, again by a marginal distance.

4. Let's address the first issue: the mesh is offset upwards from the floor. This offset is controlled by the *Height Inaccuracy %* setting, available from the *Advanced* tab in the Navigation window. The default value for this field is 10 per cent, allowing a Y position deviation of the Navigation mesh by 10 per cent from the source mesh position, in either direction: up or down. The appropriate value for this field differs from project to project, and developers should proceed by trial and error to generate a NavMesh in line with their floor. In this case, specify a value of *1*, and then click *Bake* again to regenerate the NavMesh. This aligns the mesh with the floor.
5. The NavMesh is also inset away from the walls, meaning there is a gap or padding between the mesh and walls on each side. This setting is controlled, perhaps surprisingly, by the *Radius* value in the Navigation window! *Radius* here refers to the radius of an imaginary bounding sphere drawn around a potential NPC that must walk on the NavMesh to find their way around. If the NavMesh were expanded to leave no padding or gap from the wall, the NPCs could walk along on the edge of the NavMesh, centred on its edge, and their extremities would penetrate the wall. For this reason, a margin of padding is inserted into the mesh at the wall. The default value is 0.5 Unity Units, which will be left as is for this project. However, the NavMesh could be expanded to meet the wall exactly using a value close to 0 – provided afterwards you press *Bake* again to regenerate the mesh.

NOTE: The Navigation mesh represents the total surface area on which NPCs can move and find paths: it's the invisible floor of Pathfinding. Larger, and more complex NavMeshes increase the area over which Pathfinding computations occur. For this reason, it's in the interests of performance for your NavMeshes to be no larger or more complex than is essential. If your scene geometry and your assets produce a NavMesh with excess – with regions where NPCs will never move or walk in any circumstances – then you have *wastage*. In these cases I recommend separating your *true* floor geometry from all other geometries; that is, separating out all surfaces on which NPCs can really walk. Or at least importing separate floor geometry, if only for generating the NavMesh. By generating your NavMesh from the simplest geometry possible you make your NavMesh as small as it can be while still consistent with your needs.

10.2 Creating a NavMesh Agent

Unity scenes can feature none, one or potentially many NavMesh Agents. Each agent is a separate GameObject that can travel around the scene using the NavMesh data. Typically, each NPC in a game will be a *separate* NavMesh Agent. NavMesh Agents, when configured with a NavMesh, have the ability to travel from their current location to any other valid location on the surface of the NavMesh, avoiding all obstacles and choosing the most direct route or the most reasonable route. In this section, we'll create a cube mesh object, with a blue material, that'll travel to the location of a second cube mesh with a red material. If the red cube moves, the blue cube will automatically update and change its course, travelling to the red cube in the scene, no matter where it is. To achieve this, consider the following steps.

1. Create two cubes in the scene, one to act as the NPC NavMesh Agent and the other to act as a moveable destination point. Select *GameObject > Create Other > Cube* from the application menu to generate the first cube, and use duplication (*Ctrl+D*) to create the second cube. Name the first cube *objNavAgent*, and the second cube *objNavDestination*. Position them at different locations within the scene. Create a new blank material by selecting *Assets > Create > Material* from the application menu, naming it *matNavAgent*, and assign it a blue colour using the *Main Color* swatch in the Object Inspector. Duplicate this material, naming it *matNavDestination*, and change its *Main Color* to red. Finally, assign the material *matNavAgent* to the cube *objNavAgent* and the material *matNavDestination* to the cube *objNavDestination*. See Figure 10.4.

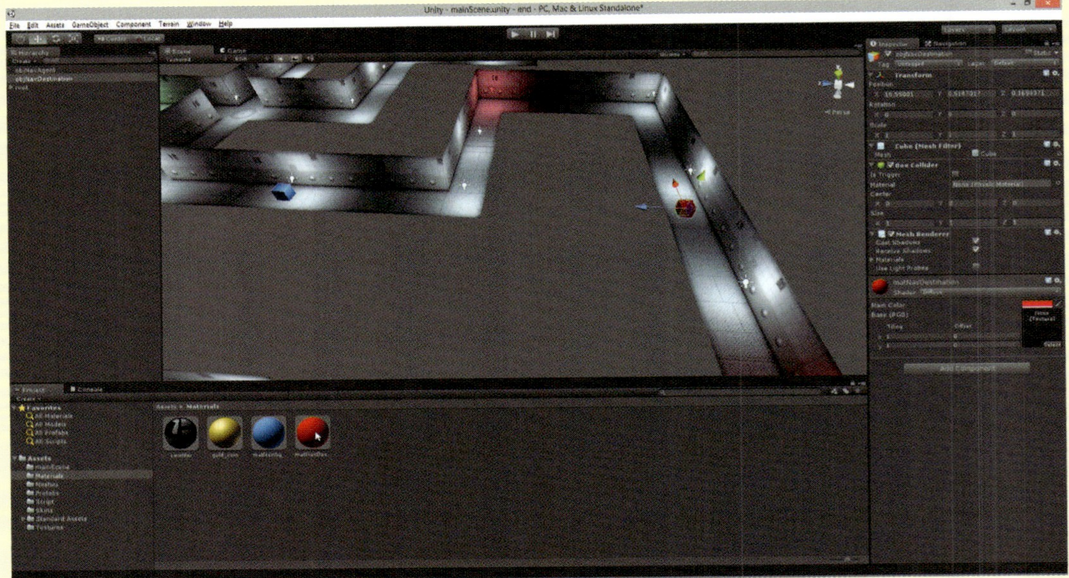

Figure 10.4 Configure the agent and destination cubes in the scene. You do not have to work only with cubes, of course. You could use any mesh assets or game objects you wish

2. The *objNavAgent* cube will be our NPC NavMesh Agent. Our level *could* contain more than one NavMesh Agent, if we wanted, but for this example I'll keep to only one. To make the cube a NavMesh Agent we must attach a *NavMesh Agent* component to the object – again, this makes use of the component-based paradigm that we explored in Chapter 3. Select the cube in the scene and attach the NavMesh Agent by selecting *Component > Navigation > Nav Mesh Agent* from the application menu. On doing this, the cube object is surrounded by a cylindrical or capsule-shaped gizmo volume and a selection of properties is available for the NavMesh Agent component in the Object Inspector. The Cylinder volume *appears* like a Collider volume, but it is not *actually* a collider. You control the size of the volume using the *Height* and *Radius* properties of NavMesh Agent, but these properties

only affect how the volume looks to *you* in the editor from the Scene tab. The volume is used internally for Pathfinding purposes and thus it can be practically any size you want. Typically, I size this volume as though it were a collider, to improve its visibility in the viewport. Go ahead and size the collider to approximate the cube object. See Figure 10.5.

NOTE: The Navigation gizmo (the collider-like volume) may not appear to surround the object. It might be smaller than and contained within your object.

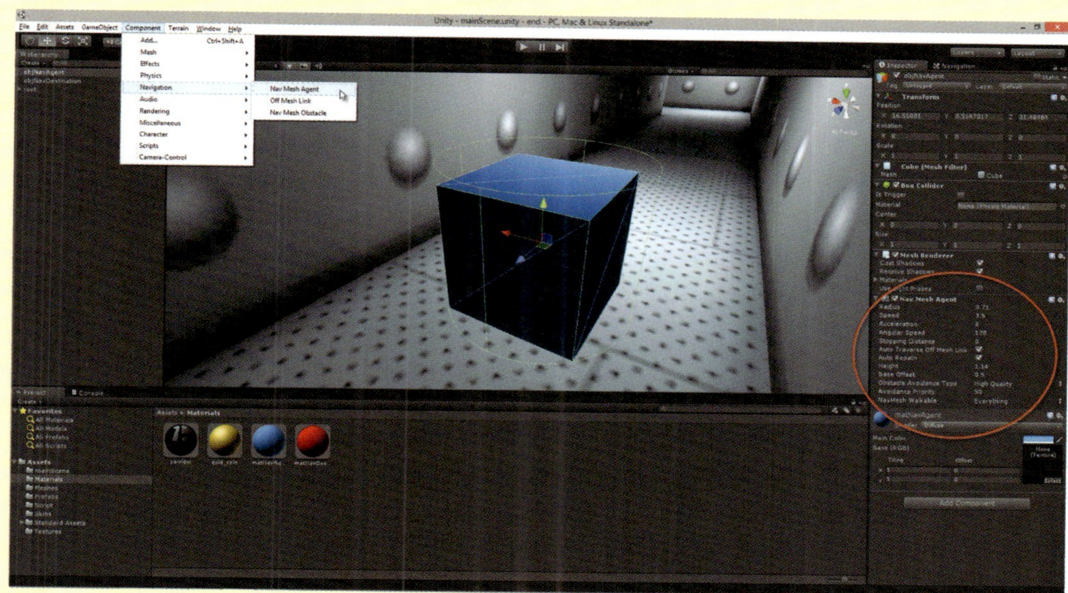

Figure 10.5 Attaching a NavMesh Agent to a cube NPC object. Agents are surrounded by a gizmo volume

3. Select the Translate tool (press *W*), making sure *objNavAgent* is selected in the viewport, and take note of the orientation of the transformation gizmo. The blue horizontal directional arrow representing the local Z axis indicates the nose or *Forwards* direction of the NPC. By default, the NPC will travel forwards. If the destination is behind the NPC, then it will turn or rotate to face its destination before travelling there, aligning the Z axis with its trajectory. Pay attention to the orientation of the Transformation gizmo. Make sure your NPC is oriented in the direction most suited for your scene; rotate it if necessary. Be sure to create your models and mesh assets so the nose, point or face of your character is aligned to the world Z axis in 3DS Max or Maya, or whichever software you use. If your objects are not Z-aligned before import, they will not travel forwards in the expected pose or alignment.
4. The NavMesh Agent features properties for Speed (speed when *translating*), Angular Speed (speed when *rotating*), and Stopping Distance. These can be left at their defaults for now, but feel free to tweak them later. Two properties critical to Pathfinding are *Obstacle Avoidance Type* and *NavMesh*

Walkable. *Obstacle Avoidance Type* defines how accurate this NavMesh Agent should be when detecting for dynamic collisions and obstacles. In other words, how clever and accurate should this agent be at avoiding obstacles? For this project, *Obstacle Avoidance Type* can be left at *High Quality*, meaning it should successfully detect and avoid all obstacles in its path in the most *believable* way. Quality, however, is related to performance: the better the quality, the more intensive the avoidance calculations. For this reason *High Quality* may not be a feasible value for larger projects such as real-time strategy games with potentially many, maybe even hundreds of, NavMesh Agents. You will need to tweak these settings on a per agent basis to see what works best for your game. The *NavMesh Walkable* property should be set to *Everything* for this project. It can, however, be other values, including *Everything*, *Default*, *Not Walkable* and *Jump*. Using NavMesh layers, developers can mark or label specific areas of the Navigation mesh to designate difficult terrain, inclines and declines, impassable zones, or any other area over which movement is not uniformly easy. The specifics of NavMesh layers are not discussed in this introduction, but more information can be found at http://docs.unity3d.com/Documentation/Components/class-NavMeshLayers.html

10.3 Making the Agent Move

So far we've generated a NavMesh from our scene geometry and created one NavMesh Agent, representing an NPC that can potentially use Pathfinding to intelligently move around the level, choosing the shortest route and avoiding obstacles. However, the agent does not yet move to any destination: it's not yet told where to go or what to follow. In this section we'll use both *scripting* and *debugging* techniques to make our cube NPC follow a moveable target around the level. The following steps explain how to do this.

1. Create a new C# script file in the project and name it *PathFinder.cs*. To do this, click *Assets > Create > C# Script* from the application menu. Consult chapters 7 and 8 for more information on scripting. Drag and drop the newly created class from the Project panel onto the NavMesh Agent in the scene, where it is attached as a new component. This component will be responsible for finding a path to the destination cube and making our agent follow that path. Once created, this script will give us the ability to move our destination cube anywhere in the scene at run-time and have the NavMesh Agent update and change its course to reach the destination.
2. Open up the *PathFinder.cs* script file and add the following code from listing 10.1. Comments on the code are provided in an upcoming note.

Code 10.1 *Pathfinder Class*

```
using UnityEngine;
using System.Collections;
//-----------------------------------
```

```
public class PathFinder : MonoBehaviour
{
    //------------------------------------
    //Reference to object to follow
    public GameObject Dest = null;
    //Private reference to attached NavMesh Agent Component
    private NavMeshAgent Agent = null;
    //------------------------------------
    // Use this for initialization
    void Start ()
    {
        //Get NavMesh Agent
        Agent = GetComponent<NavMeshAgent>();
        //Set Agent Destination
        Agent.destination = Dest.transform.position;
    }
    //------------------------------------
    // Update is called once per frame
    void Update ()
    {
        //Update Destination
        Agent.destination = Dest.transform.position;
    }
    //------------------------------------
}
//------------------------------------
```

NOTE: The PathFinder object features one main public variable, a reference to the destination object. That is the object we are to follow and reach. For our sample, this object should be the red cube *objNavDestination*. The class also makes use of the *NavMeshAgent* component which will be attached to the *same* game object using our PathFinder class; both components on the same object. For this reason, the *GetComponent* function can be used internally to retrieve a reference to that component. In both the *Start* and *Update* functions, the *destination* member of NavMesh Agent is assigned the transform position data from the destination object. In making this assignment we *automatically* assign the NavMesh Agent a destination.

3. Save and compile the changes to the PathFinder code. Select the NavMesh Agent in the Scene viewport and use the Object Inspector to assign its *Dest* variable to *objNavDestination*. To do that, just drag and drop the *objNavDestination* object from the Scene hierarchy panel into the *Dest* variable slot in the Object Inspector. Then you're ready to run the code and test the application in the Game tab. Insert a camera into the scene if you don't already have one and position it to get a good view of the scene: a view displaying both the source and destination objects. As you run the game, see the agent cube move towards the destination object!

NOTE: Notice: if you select the agent object, and then switch back to the Scene tab while the agent is still travelling, you'll see a Pathfinding diagnostic in the scene. You'll see a line gizmo drawn from the agent to the destination, or at least drawn from the agent and towards the direction he is travelling. See Figure 10.6.

4. But wait! Although this project works fine as it is – that is, the agent *does* travel to the destination – how can we be sure it will really change its route when the destination object moves elsewhere. Let's grant, for a moment, that it *will* change. But how we can test that, quickly and easily, without having to add more code? Answer: we use the Object Inspector and Scene transformation tools as debugging aids, as we saw in Chapter 9. To achieve this, click and drag the *Game* tab and 'rip' it away from its current position in the editor, then dock it into the interface side by side with the *Scene* tab, allowing a split view. This will allow us to *view* the game and *edit* the scene at the same time, moving back and forth. Now press *Play* on the toolbar and select the *Translate* tool to move the destination object in the Scene tab while the game is running. Then notice in the Game tab how the agent changes its direction and movement according to the new position of the destination. See Figure 10.7. The power of Unity debugging comes to the rescue!

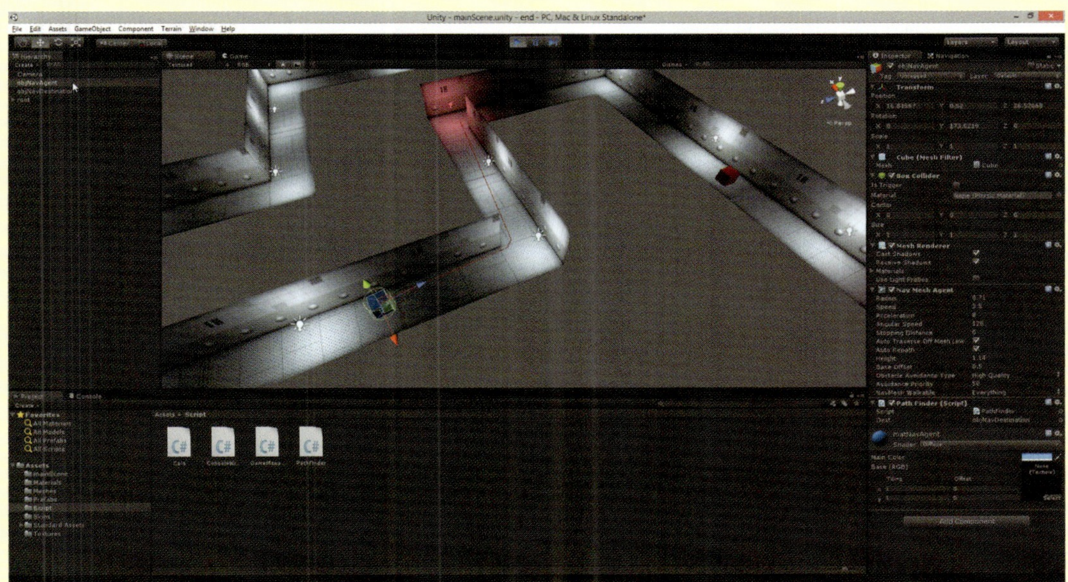

Figure 10.6 Moving the NavMesh Agent to a destination. See the diagnostic Pathfinding lines point from the agent to the destination

5. Just for fun, let's create a really quick and simple third-person camera for the cube agent. Third-Person Cameras are an alternative to first-person: they show the game world from a perspective *outside* of the player's eyes. Here, we'll create a camera that sits some distance away from the cube

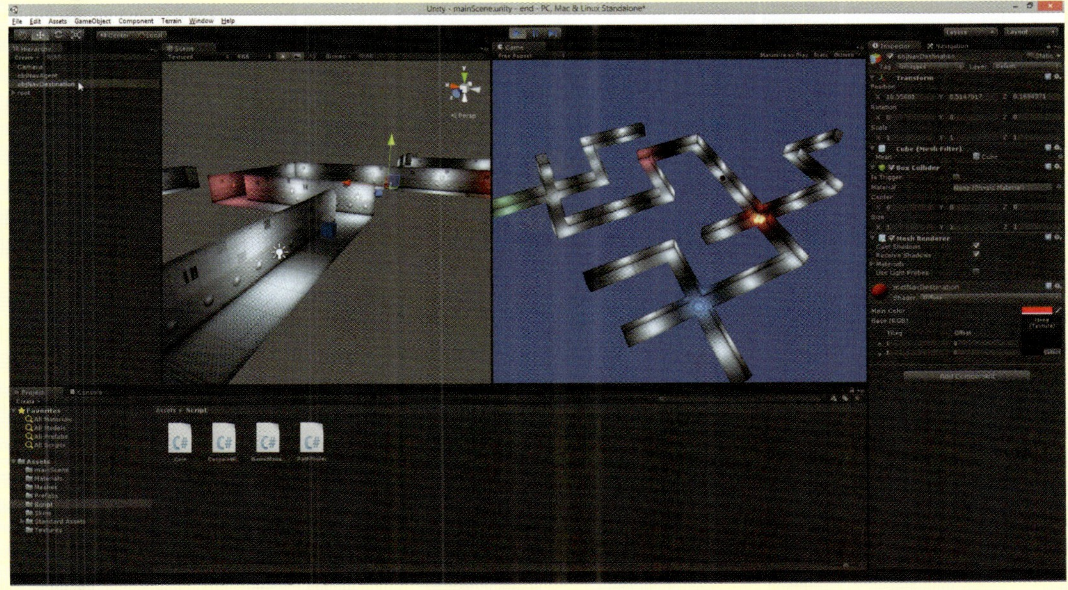

Figure 10.7 Changing the destination of the NavMesh Agent

and follows it around the scene as it travels, maintaining the same relative distance. To do that, we'll start by using the Scene viewport to align our camera. Simply move your viewport into a position close to the navigation agent in the scene. Centre your view on the agent with the *F* key (remember, *F* is for *Frame*), and zoom in or out to the distance you want for your third-person camera. Set this camera orientation as the default for the game camera by selecting *GameObject > Align with View* from the application menu (making sure your camera is selected). If the camera is not selected but a different object is, then the selected object will transform and move to the viewport position: you can use the Undo command to revert your action. Then use the concept of *parenting*, as seen in Chapter 3, to *parent* the main camera to the cube agent node. That is, make the camera a *child* of the cube agent node: specifically, drag and drop the camera from the hierarchy panel onto the Agent node. This works because transformations *cascade* downwards through the hierarchy, from parent objects to child objects. Then press *Play* on the toolbar and see an intelligent agent moving around the level during game play, followed by a third-person camera! See Figure 10.8. In just one step we created a third-person camera! Notice how the fundamental concepts of hierarchies and transformations learned from the outset have returned again to help us achieve complexity in this case.

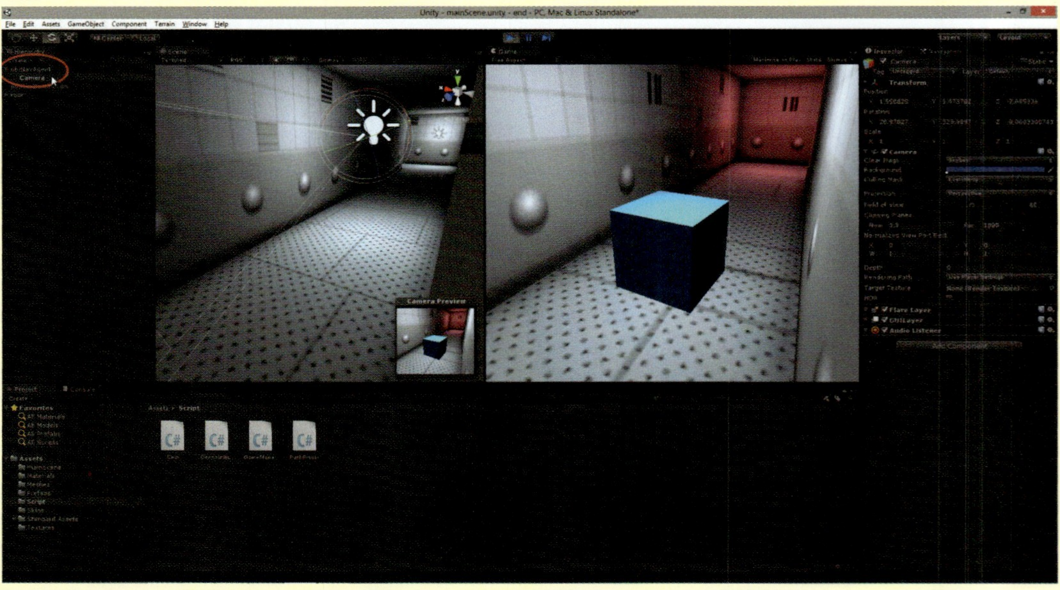

Figure 10.8 Creating a third-person camera to follow the NavMesh Agent

10.4 Conclusion

This chapter considered Pathfinding, but only briefly. For those interested, there's a lot more to this subject. If we reflect on the project created in this chapter, a number of problems, issues and potential improvements can be identified. Our project features surfaces that are flat and level throughout. Furthermore, there are no small objects scattered around the floor to get in the way of agents. There are no holes in the floor and there are no major complications. From this, a number of serious questions involving implementation can be raised. For example, how can we vary the speed of agents on different types of terrain – if our floor were divided into smooth, rough or boggy surfaces? Or how can we manage Pathfinding if the floor is not connected throughout the scene but contains gaping holes or has deep chasms separating the floor into separate parts? How can we tell an agent it must jump across disconnections in the floor to reach the other side? How can we create lava pits and other dangerous areas – walkable, but *only* if the NPC has no alternative route, even if that route is the 'longer way around'? And what about moving platforms or moving sections of floor, such as elevators and hover pads? How could we handle those? Surely we cannot produce a Navigation mesh from *moving* regions, because these cannot be *static* objects? These are all valid questions and likely to come up with projects of greater complexity. The Unity Pathfinding system provides answers to almost all these questions, but covering them in depth and with the detail they deserve would require another book. For this reason, our discussion of Pathfinding ends here and the rest is left as a project for the reader. More information on Pathfinding can be found from the online Unity documentation at

http://docs.unity3d.com/Documentation/Manual/NavmeshandPathfinding.html
http://docs.unity3d.com/Documentation/Components/class-NavMeshLayers.html
http://docs.unity3d.com/Documentation/Components/class-NavMeshAgent.html
http://docs.unity3d.com/Documentation/Components/class-OffMeshLink.html

CHAPTER 11

Animation and Mecanim

By the end of this chapter you should:

1. Understand what Mecanim is and how it relates to animation.
2. Understand how to use Mecanim.
3. Be able to import, configure and use animated meshes in Unity.
4. Use curves to customise animations.
5. Interact with Mecanim through scripting.

This chapter represents a kind of culmination of knowledge from previous chapters. It requires us to combine much of what we've learned so far and then extend it by creating a complete project with animation and user interaction. Here we'll use the skills of asset importing, scene building, scripting and more. In addition, we'll see how to import and work with animated meshes using the Mecanim animation system, one of the highlight features new to Unity 4. Using this system we'll be able to not only import animations and play them for meshes in a linear way but also configure, tweak, edit and respond to the animations at run-time. Once completed, this chapter will empower you with a foundational grasp of Mecanim, allowing you to import and use your own animations for your own projects and also offering you a firm grounding for expanding your knowledge to import more complex animations and meshes, such as Skeletal Meshes and animated characters. So let's get started.

11.1 Project Overview – what are we going to make?

This chapter is almost entirely project-based, meaning it'll chart the complete development of a project from start to finish. For this reason you're encouraged to be seated at your computer with Unity open and follow along with me, step by step. We'll make use of some assets, provided in the companion files, to create a small, simple-looking scene, one which is nonetheless filled with complexity the deeper we dig. This scene will feature a square room with a first-person controller and an elevator platform at its centre. This platform begins in a raised state, docked to a floor above. In two opposite corners of the room, on the floor, are two pressure plates, one in each corner. One pressure plate will lower the elevator to ground level when stepped on. The other pressure plate will raise the elevator back to its starting position when stepped on. On the floor directly beneath the elevators are cogs and cylindrical pistons, and these will spring to life when the elevator moves, raising or lowering, to simulate mechanics and hydraulics. See Figure 11.1. The scenario seems simple enough when stated in this way, but to create this project we'll have to call upon a wide range of Mecanim and Unity features. Consider the following steps to get started.

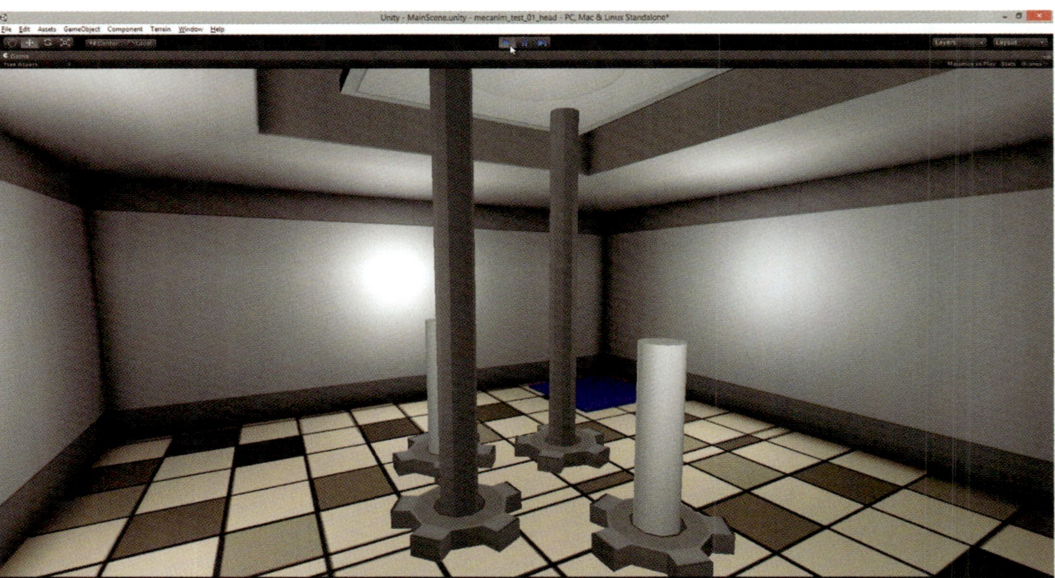

Figure 11.1 The project to be created: an animated elevator system

1. Let's create a new blank Unity project and prepare it for our work ahead. Name the project *Proj_Elevator_Mecanim*, and save the default scene as *Scene_Main*. Import the *Character Controllers* package using the application menu *Assets > Import Package > Character Controller*. Create a folder in the Project panel for organising our assets, to be imported soon. These folders will be: *animation*, *materials*, *meshes*, *textures*, *scenes* and *scripts*.

2. Now let's import the assets for this project. These assets can be found in the book's companion files at *Chapter11/assets_to_import*. Import the two meshes *animated_platform.ma* and *env_room.ma* into the *meshes* folder in the Unity Project panel. The *env_room* mesh represents all the *static*, architectural and non-moving elements of our game environment. The *animated_platform* mesh represents the elevator platform positioned at the room centre and has animation data attached. Details about how to preview and configure animated assets follow soon. Select both mesh assets in the Project pane and then select the *Model* tab from the Object Inspector to view the mesh import options. Enable the *Generate Colliders* option and click *Apply*. Further, select only the *env_room* mesh and enable the Generate *Lightmap UVs* option; click *Apply*. In addition to the mesh assets, import the texture file *Final_Texture.psd* into the textures folder of the Project panel. Be sure to configure its *Maximum Size* to 4096 from the Object Inspector if Unity defaults to 1024. All other texture settings can be left at their defaults for this project. See Figure 11.2.

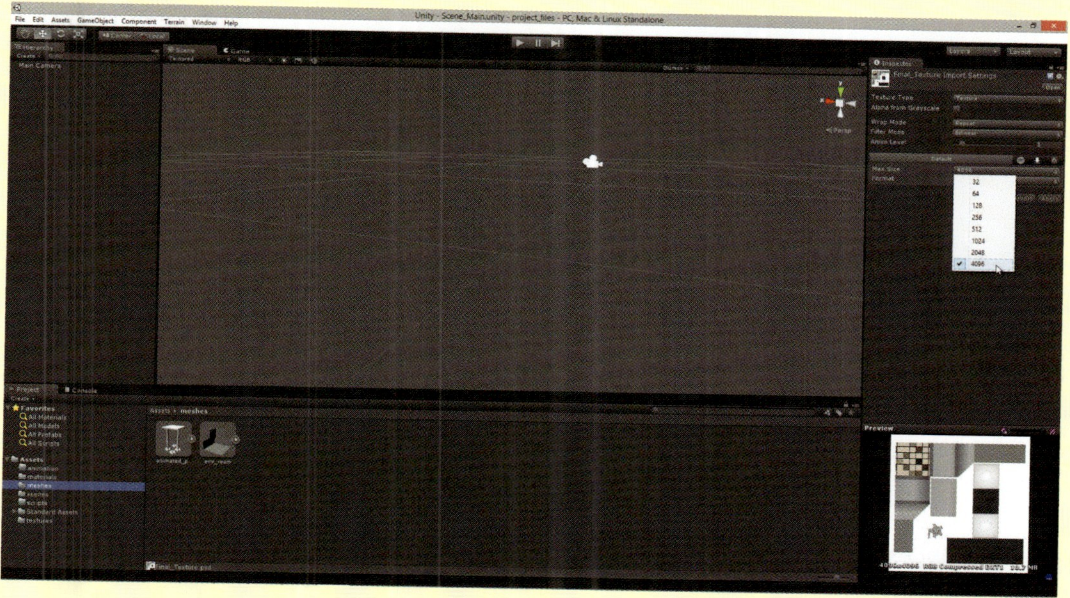

Figure 11.2 Configuring and organising imported assets for the project

3. OK, so the assets – meshes and texture – are imported! Now we'll build our scene, complete with lightmapping, in just a few steps. Drag and drop the *env_room* mesh from the Project panel to the Scene viewport and use the Object Inspector to position it exactly at the world space origin at (0, 0, 0). Name the object *env_room*, if it is not so named already, and then mark it as *Static* from the Object Inspector – because it is an architectural element it should be lightmapped and, if you remember, lightmapped objects must be static. Then drag and drop the *Final_Texture* asset onto the environment mesh to automatically apply it through a material: the mesh should now be textured in the viewport. Finally, to prepare the scene for lightmapping, disable the Ambient Light in the scene. To do this, select *Edit > Render Settings* from the application menu and set the *Ambient Light* colour to black, meaning *no light*.
4. Create a Point light in the scene, positioning it at the corner of the room. Configure its radius, colour and intensity, as shown in Figure 11.3. Then duplicate the light as many times as needed, positioning

the duplicates around the room to illuminate the whole scene, ensuring no space is left in darkness. Overall the scene should look slightly darker than intended, because it will be brightened through indirect illumination when lightmapped.

5. It's time to lightmap the scene. Select *Window > Lightmapping* from the application menu to show the Lightmapping dialog. Dock this into the Object Inspector. Switch to the *Bake* tab, and bake the

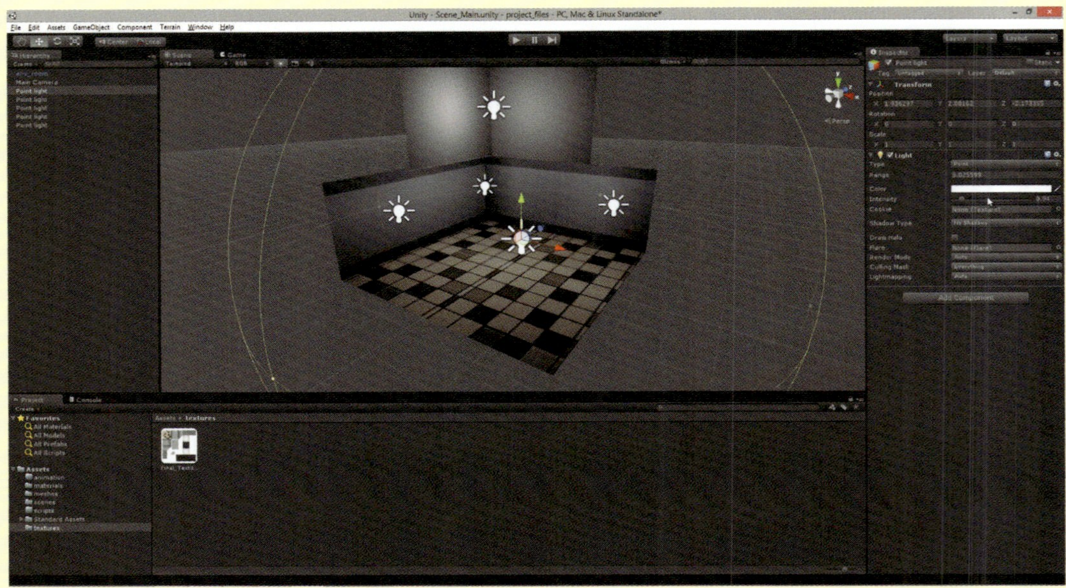

Figure 11.3 Positioning lights in the scene before lightmapping

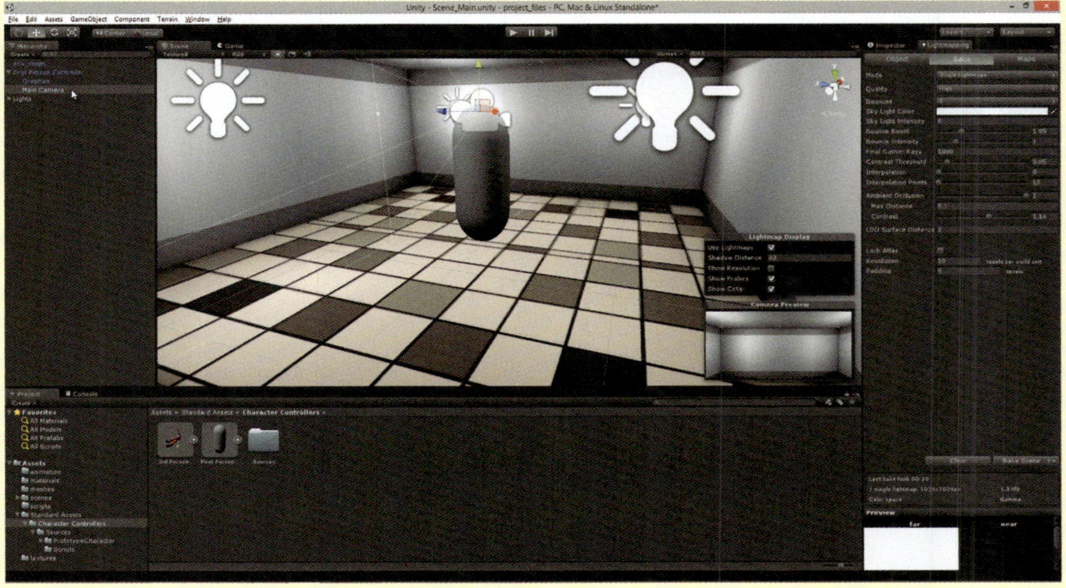

Figure 11.4 Configuring lightmapping and the Main Camera

scene using *Single LightMaps* instead of *Dual Lightmaps*. Add some *Bounce Boost* to the Indirect Illumination with a value of 1.05, enable *Ambient Occlusion* and set the *Resolution* to 10 texels per world unit. Check how the scene looks and tweak until it looks good: tweak and re-bake, tweak and re-bake, etc. Once you're happy with it, go ahead and insert a first-person controller into the scene and position it in one of the room corners, removing the original *MainCamera*. Be sure to set the *Near Clipping Distance* of the camera from *0.3* to *0.1* to protect against clipping through walls. Then take the game for a test run. If the first-person camera falls through the scene floor, then ensure you've generated colliders for the environment mesh object. See Figure 11.4.

6. To finalise the scene ready for animation work, let's add the two pressure plate objects to the level. These will be created from cube primitives and will rest on the floor. Create the first pressure plate by selecting *GameObject > Create Other > Cube*. Use the Scale tool to flatten and resize this object, positioning it on the floor as a tile, as shown in Figure 11.5. Name the object *PressurePlateDown*, because it will be used to lower the elevator when stepped on. Duplicate this object, and position the duplicate to the other corner of the room, naming it *PressurePlateUp*. Create basic Diffuse materials for these objects, choosing *Assets > Create > Material* from the application menu. Choose a red color for one material and a blue for the other – I've used blue for *PressurePlateDown* and red for *PressurePlateUp*.

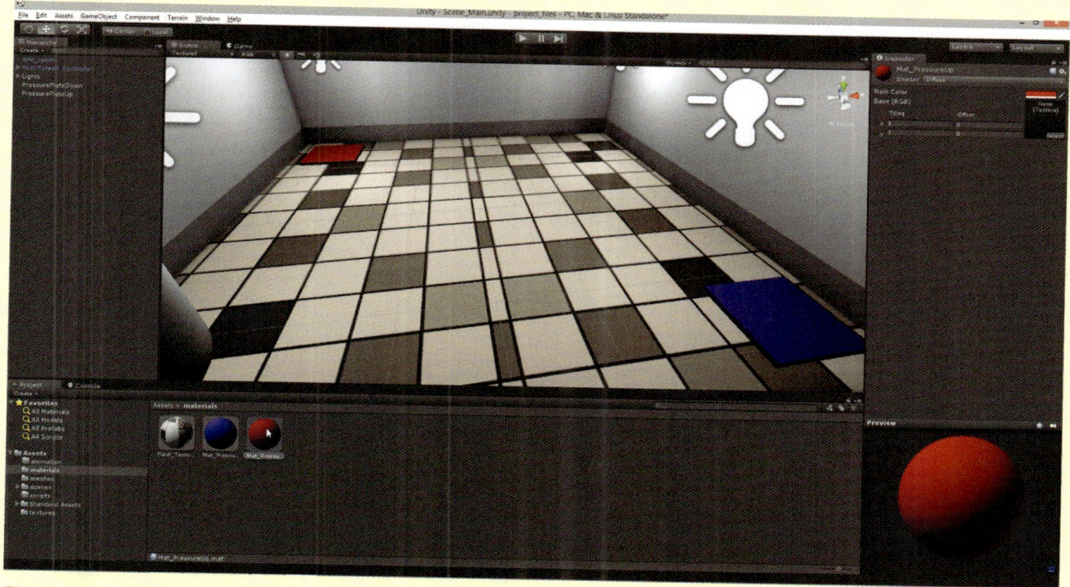

Figure 11.5 Creating pressure plates from primitive objects

Splendid: the scene is now ready and in these six steps we've combined techniques and ideas from almost every chapter of the book so far. Let's move forwards to animation now.

11.2 Getting Started with Animation

The term *animation* refers to change over time: *any* change over *any* length of time. A change in the position of the player as he or she moves around the level is animation. A change in the colour of a material or structure of a mesh is also animation. Consequently, animation can be created in many different ways in Unity: with visual tools provided by the editor and with scripting, as well as by using methods outside Unity. Aside from scripting, there are two main ways to create animation for scene assets. I'll call these **Method A** and **Method B**. Method A is to import *static* and *non-animated* meshes – such as doors, windows and cars – into a Unity project and scene and then use the *Animation Window* directly in the Unity editor to *record* animations. That is, to record the *transformations* of game objects over time to play them back during gameplay – this allows us to create sliding doors, travelling cars, falling boulders and so on. The other method, Method B, involves artists *baking* animations into their mesh assets. Here, meshes and their animations are created together in modelling software – such as 3DS Max and Maya – rather than in Unity and then imported into Unity where the mesh and animations are read from the file and applied to the mesh during gameplay. In Unity, Method A is achieved largely through the *Legacy* animation system, and Method B is achieved largely through the new *Mecanim* animation system. The stated aim of the Unity developers, as Mecanim evolves, is to entirely replace the legacy system with Mecanim, so that Mecanim can do everything the legacy system does, as well as more. However, the state of Mecanim development at the time of writing is such that if you want to record keyframe-based animations on your objects graphically *from within* the Unity editor, then you should still use the legacy system. If you've baked animations *into your mesh files* to play back in Unity, though, then Mecanim is recommended for its power and flexibility. For this project we'll be using Mecanim because our imported mesh asset already features animation data that I created using Maya. We'll also use scripting in combination with Mecanim. Consider the following steps for getting started.

1. Select the *animated_platform* mesh in the Project panel, dragging and dropping it into the scene. Position it at the world space origin at (0, 0, 0) and apply the *Final_Texture* material to all its pieces. Once added, if you press *Play* on the toolbar, the platform object will not move at all: it appears as a static object, even though it has animation data assigned. This is because Unity requires instructions as to when and how to play the animation. Providing these instructions is the primary purpose of Mecanim. Select the *animated_platform* asset in the Project panel and examine its import properties in the Object Inspector. Select the *Animations* tab. This tab lists all animation data attached to the object – where it can be previewed, edited and inspected. The platform mesh features only one *50*-frames-long animation, named *Take 001*. This is listed under the *Clips* group of the animation tab. For each imported mesh, Unity scans for animation data and encodes into an internal data structure called *AnimationClip*. Select the clip *Take 001* in the Clips group. You can preview the clip by pressing the *Play* button from the preview window in the Object Inspector. See Figure 11.6.
2. The animation clip is a way of *selecting* a frame range within the total timeline, and specifying whether it should play on a loop or only once. The default clip *Take 001* spans from frame 0 to frame 50, the total animation length. If you preview this animation, however, you'll see the elevator changes states abruptly half-way along the timeline, jumping from a downward position to an upwards or raised position at frame 25. This is because two different animations span the timeline, not one. To reflect this, Unity *should* be using two different animation clips, one for each of the animations. Because by default Unity creates only one clip, we'll need to 'fix' it. To do that, rename the *Take001* animation to *Elv_Lower* (for Elevator_Lower). Mark the *Start* frame as 0 and the *End* frame as 24,

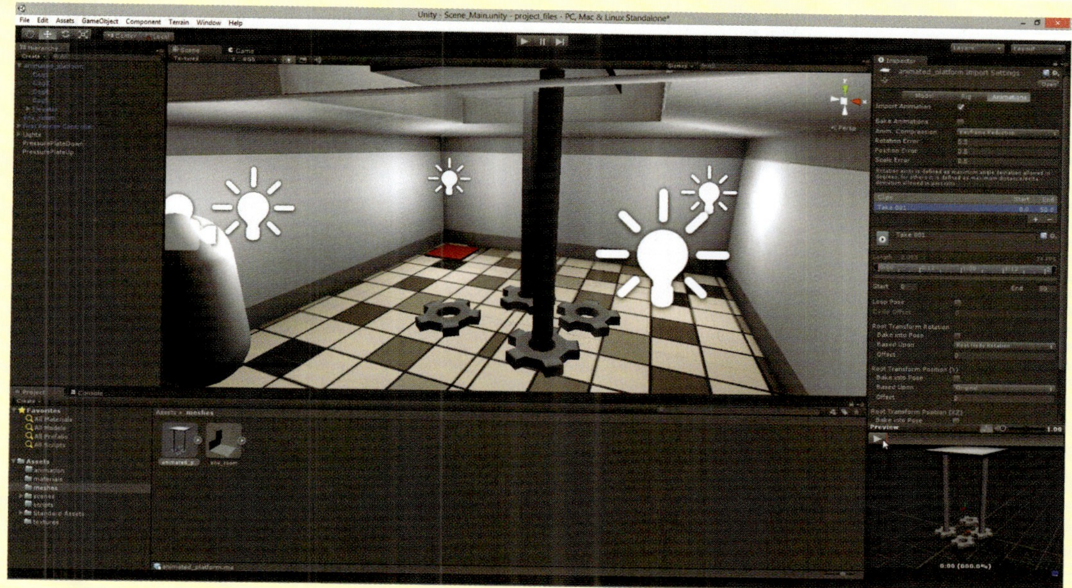

Figure 11.6 Previewing animation clips

not 50. This range represents the 'Elevator Lower' animation, in which the platform moves from an upwards state to a resting downwards state. Ensure *Loop* is not checked, since this clip should play only once. Now preview the animation; it should look 'correct'. See Figure 11.7.

3. Create a second animation clip. To do this, click the + icon in the lower right-hand side of the *Clips* list. Name this clip *Elv_Neutral* (for Elevator Neutral). Mark the *Start* frame as 25 and the *End* frame as 50, and ensure *Loop* is checked. This animation will play when the elevator is in its

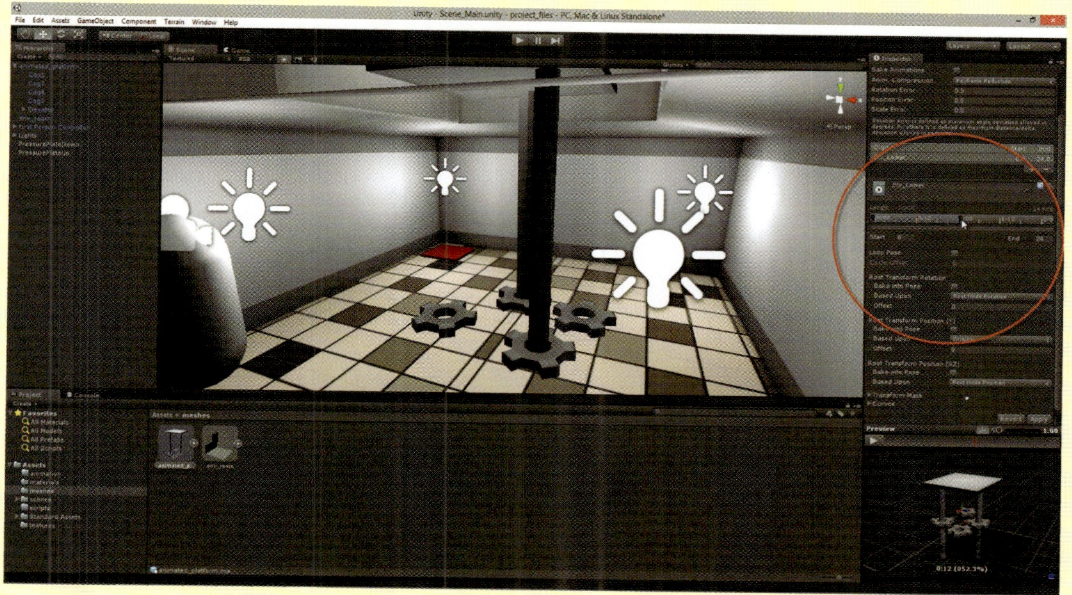

Figure 11.7 Creating the *Elevator Lower* clip

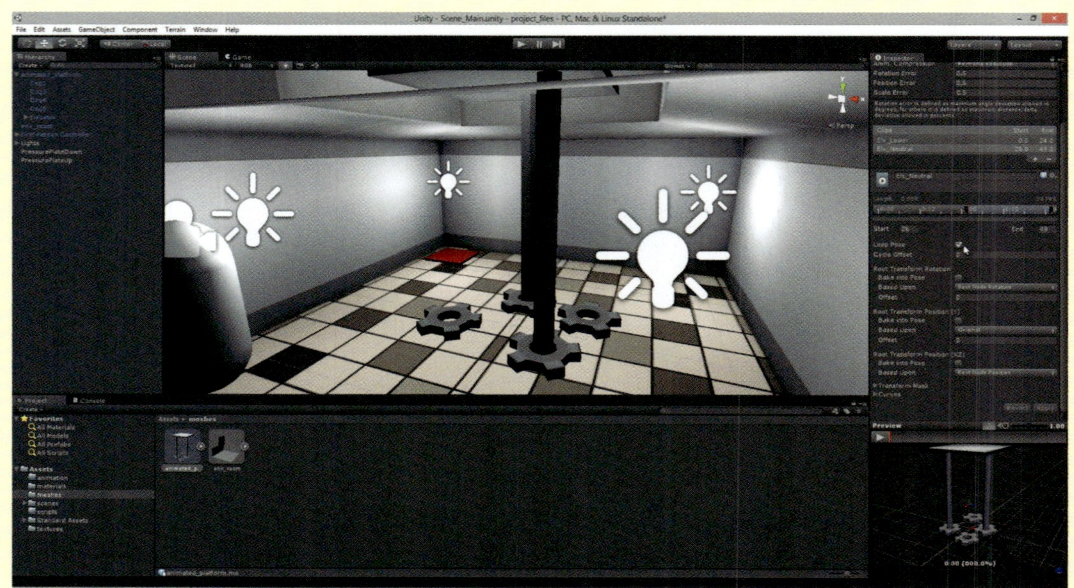

Figure 11.8 Creating the *Elevator Neutral* clip

default state on the upper floor, neither raising nor lowering. The cogs at the elevator bottom will spin continuously, looping again and again. Preview this animation in the Object Inspector. If the looping of the cogs is not seamless, then adjust the *Start* and *End* frames to 26 and 49 respectively. Remember to click the *Apply* button to confirm the changes and update the mesh asset. The mesh now has two animation clips attached, which, as we'll soon see, can be selected and played using Mecanim. See Figure 11.8.

11.3 Playing an Animation with Mecanim

The animated platform mesh now has two unique animation clips attached, one played on a loop when the elevator is in a neutral or default state, and the other played as the elevator lowers or raises to or from the floor. It might be noticed here that the *Elevator Lower* animation clip only defines movement for the elevator as it *lowers* – there is no separate clip for the *upwards* motion. This is because the lower animation will be played *in reverse* for the elevator-raising motion – and thus we get two animations from one clip! This forward-reverse technique is used almost everywhere in video games to cut down on the number of animations and increase animation diversity: doors opening/closing, trees swaying in the wind, levers turning, etc. Regardless of the clips we have, however, none of them actually play – that is, take effect on our meshes – if we test our game. Unity must be told when to play animations and how it should do so (forwards? in reverse? in slow motion?) These instructions are provided by Mecanim through an *AnimationController* asset. Consider the following steps to get the default neutral animation up and running for the elevator mesh.

1. Select the animated platform mesh in the scene and examine its component make-up in the Object Inspector. It features, by default, an *Animator* component. This is because Unity detected animations on the mesh asset for this object. The *Animator* component has an empty property for the *Controller*, which expects an object of type *AnimationController*. The Animation Controller is an asset defining all data about how and when animations should play for an object. This asset is the main *output* of the Mecanim system. Mecanim is largely used as an editor or system for creating and sustaining animation controllers. Without an animation controller, an object cannot animate. So let's create an animation controller now. To do this, select *Assets > Create > Animation Controller* from the application menu. Name the controller *ElevatorControl*. Drag and drop this controller asset into the Controller slot of the elevator's Animator component, in the Object Inspector. See Figure 11.9.

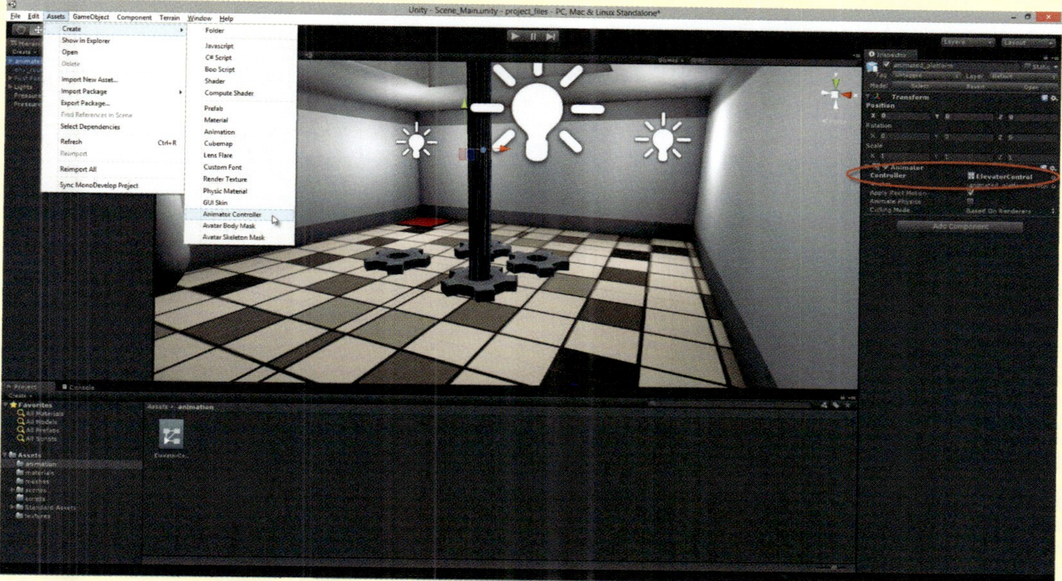

Figure 11.9 Assigning an AnimationController to the elevator Controller slot in the Animator component

2. Double-click the *ElevatorControl* asset from the Project panel to open it up for editing in the *Animator* Window. This window can also be opened by selecting *Window > Animator* from the application menu. The Animator uses a graph-building GUI interface for defining how animations are combined and work together. The *whole* of our elevator animation logic will be defined in this window – that is, we'll use the Animator window to specify when the neutral animation should play and when the raise and lower animations should play. In its empty default arrangement, the Animator window features an *Any State* node at the centre of the graph and the window is displaying the *Base Layer*, as can be seen in the top-left corner. The *Graph* refers to the entire workspace or area inside the Animator window. Each block or node inside the graph is termed a *state* or *animation state*. This is because each node defines a single animation state for an object: such as *Neutral* or *Raising* or *Lowering*. As we'll see, animation states can be connected together through links, called *Transitions*, which define how it is possible for one state to change to another. The Animator also contains *layers*, and each layer is essentially a separate graph in which a set of states are connected together. For this project we'll use just one layer: the base or default layer. Right now, the graph in this layer is empty (except

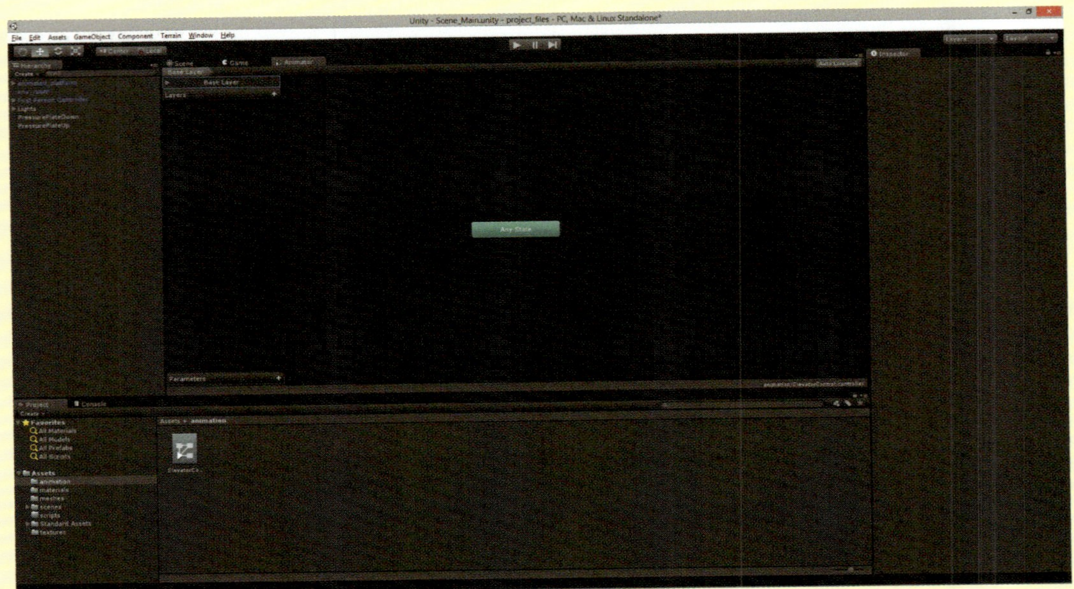

Figure 11.10 The Animator window in its default state

for the *Any State* node), and this explains why the elevator does nothing when the game is run: an empty graph results in no animation. See Figure 11.10.

3. Now we'll add a new animation state (node) to the graph, which will automatically become the *default state*; meaning that our Elevator object will enter this state when the game runs. The default state for the elevator should be the *Neutral* animation. To add this state, keep the Animator window

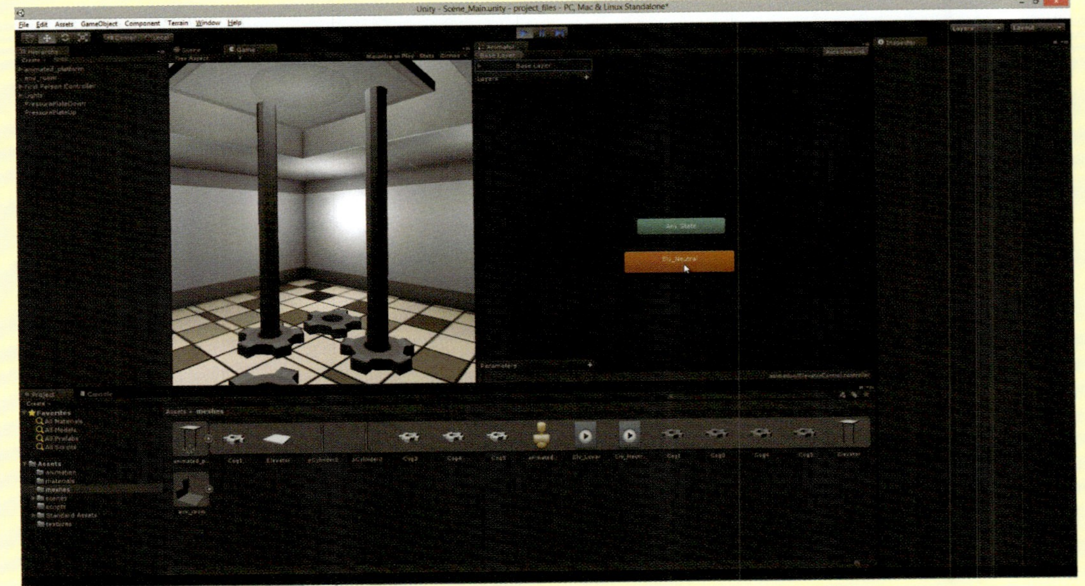

Figure 11.11 The elevator animating in its default state

open in the editor (dock it somewhere if you want) and expand the *animated_platform* mesh asset in the Project panel. Click on the arrow icon that appears on its thumbnail. This displays all the data objects belonging to the mesh asset, including its two animation clips. Click and drag the *Neutral* clip from the Project panel into the Animator window graph area where it is added to the graph as a state, coloured orange to indicate it is the *default* state. Now test-run the game and see the elevator platform in motion: the platform is suspended on the upper floor and the cogs on the ground are spinning in a loop cycle, as specified in the clip. Excellent work! If the elevator is not animating, be sure to assign the *AnimationController* asset to the Controller slot of the object's Animator component.

NOTE: You may want to dock the Animator window side by side with the Game and Scene tab windows, to keep an eye on the graph configuration and behaviour in the scene while the game is running. Consider Figure 11.11.

11.4 Default States, and Raising and Lowering

The neutral animation state now plays continuously for the elevator object whenever the game runs. This is because the *AnimationController* is associated with the elevator's *Controller* field in its Animator component, and also because the neutral animation is specified as the default state in the graph. The default state is where playback of the graph begins. The neutral Animation clip only plays *because* the graph tells it to. Thus, to play the raise and lower states for the elevator, the graph must be reconfigured. Consider the following steps.

1. Let's add the raise and lower states to the graph. To do this, expand the *animated_platform* mesh in the Project panel and drag and drop the *Elv_Lower* clip into the graph. Then drag and drop it a second time. This will create two identical *Elv_Lower* states in the graph, one for raising and one for lowering. Click on one Elv_Lower state and rename it to *Lower* using the Object Inspector. Click the other state and rename it to *Raise* (even though, right now, it represents a 'lower' animation). Both the newly added states will be shaded grey, not orange – meaning that the neutral state remains the default state. To prove this, test-run the game and see the neutral state still in action. The graph always begins with the orange-coloured state, which never changes unless there are *connections* to other states.
2. Just for fun, let's see what the elevator would look like animating in the *Lower* state as opposed to the neutral state. To do this, we make the Lower state the new default state. Right-click the mouse on the *Lower* state in the graph, and select *Set as Default* from the context menu. The state changes colour from grey to orange to signify the change. Press *Play* from the toolbar to test-run the game and see the elevator lower to the ground level. Be quick to look, though, because the animation plays only once and then stops, as specified in the *Elv_Lower* animation clip (Loop was disabled). See Figure 11.12. You can of course return to the *Elv_Lower* animation clip properties and enable looping without having to change the Animator graph.

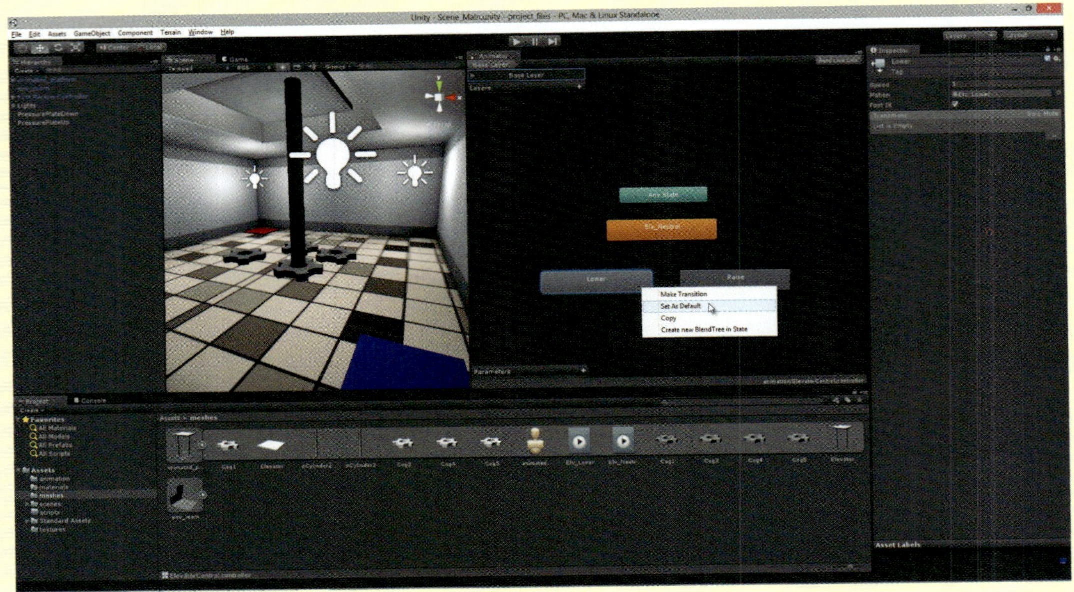

Figure 11.12 Changing the graph default state to *Elv_Lower*

3. Now try setting the *Raise* animation to default and test-run the game again. As expected, the elevator plays the *Lower* animation and not the *Raise* animation we intend, because the *Raise* state is simply a duplication of the *Lower* state. To raise the elevator we must reverse the Lower animation. We must play it backwards. We control this using the *Speed* property of the animation state. Select the *Raise* state in the graph and from the Object Inspector change the *Speed* value from 1 to -1; 1 plays an animation

Figure 11.13 Changing animation speed

forwards at its default speed and -1 backwards at its default speed. Test the game and observe the effects. We now have raise and lower animation states.

4. Change the *Neutral* animation back to the default state. Right now, the default speed of the animation is 'too fast': the cogs should spin slower. So reduce the speed from 1 to 0.6. Then visit the raise and lower states and change their speed to -0.6 and 0.6 respectively. See Figure 11.13. All states are now configured. But the graph still only shows the default state. We'll consider how to change that next.

11.5 Changing States – a First Look

In Mecanim, the Active State refers to the animation clip currently being applied to an object in the scene. Though it is possible, using *layers* and *blend states*, to play more than one animation state on an object at the same time, this project will only be playing a single animation state at any one time. The graph must be configured to create this behaviour. By default, the elevator begins in a raised and neutral state. When working properly, it can be shifted to a lowered state and then back to a raised state again. To change between states in Mecanim, we use *transitions*. These appear in the graph as links between states. These links are assigned properties defining how one state changes to another. The following steps will configure linkages between the elevator states.

1. For test purposes and to see transitions at work more clearly, let's temporarily change the default state in the Animator graph from *Neutral* to *Lower*. Then right-click on the *Lower* state, and select *Make Transition* from the context menu. This activates the Transition Drawing mode: now just left-click on the Neutral state to create a directed Transition link between *Lower* and *Neutral*. This link is drawn on the graph as an arrow. Notice that it is *one way*, not *bi-directional*. The link is from *Lower* to *Neutral* and does not work or apply in reverse. See Figure 11.14.

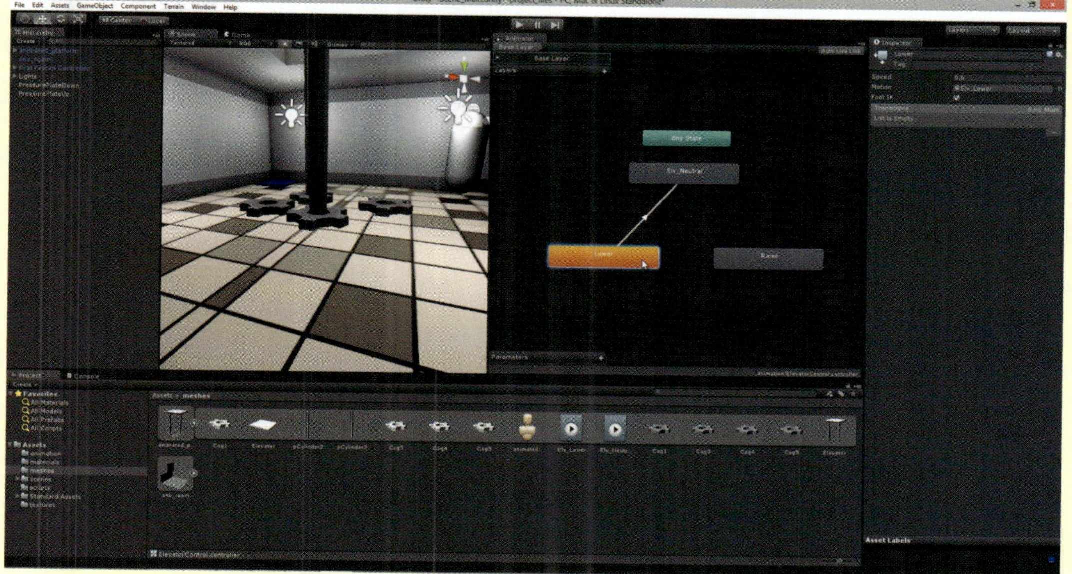

Figure 11.14 Changing the default animation state to *Lower*

2. Select the transition in the graph (just click on it) and examine its properties in the Object Inspector. The Object Inspector lists all transitions for this state in the *Transitions* list, which currently features only one transition. The transition can be previewed on the preview pane at the bottom of the inspector. Click the *Preview* button to see the transition in action. See how playback of the transition in the preview window updates the timeline view in the inspector. The timeline is created from a horizontal bar chart, describing how one state blends to another. Drag the slider in the timeline to step through and examine the Transition preview. Below the timeline is a *Conditions* panel. This lists *all* the conditions or events that must be satisfied in the scene for the transition to happen. Right now, this list features only one condition marked as *Exit Time*. This condition has a value of *0.75*. This means that when 75 per cent (0.75) of *Elv_Lower* animation has completed playback, a transition towards *Elv_Neutral* will begin, until eventually the state has changed from *Elv_Lower* to *Elv_Neutral*. Thus, after 75 per cent of Elv_Lower has played, there will be a smooth change in the motion of the elevator towards the neutral state, as illustrated in the preview. See Figure 11.15.

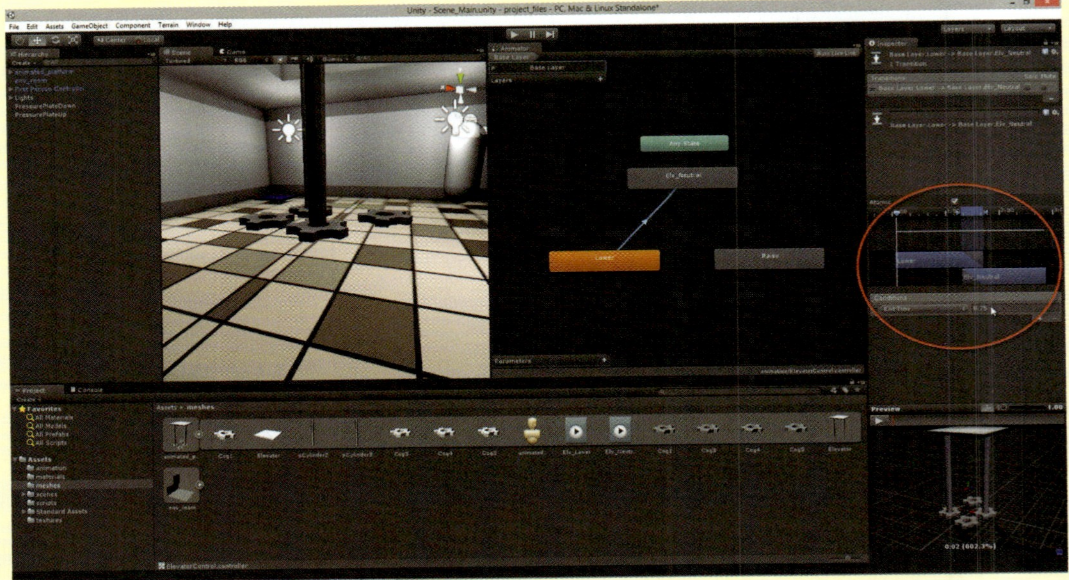

Figure 11.15 Configuring a transition

3. Change the *Exit Time* from *0.75* to *1.0* and take the game for a test run. This time the *Elv_Lower* animation is allowed to finish entirely before *Elv_Neutral* begins. Notice also that you can adjust the start and end range handles in the timeline to increase or decrease the speed of the transition.
4. The central problem we have right now with our elevator and its animation states concerns transitions. A transition occurs between *Lower* and *Neutral*, but it does not occur *when* we want it to. We need the elevator to *begin* in a neutral state and to change to a lowered state *only when* the player explicitly calls the elevator by stepping on a pressure plate. Similarly, the elevator must only rise on one of two conditions: if the player explicitly instructs the elevator to rise or if the player stands on the elevator when it is lowered. The *condition* of those transitions should not be based on time or percentage, as it is now with *Exit Time*. Rather, the *condition* should be based on states in the

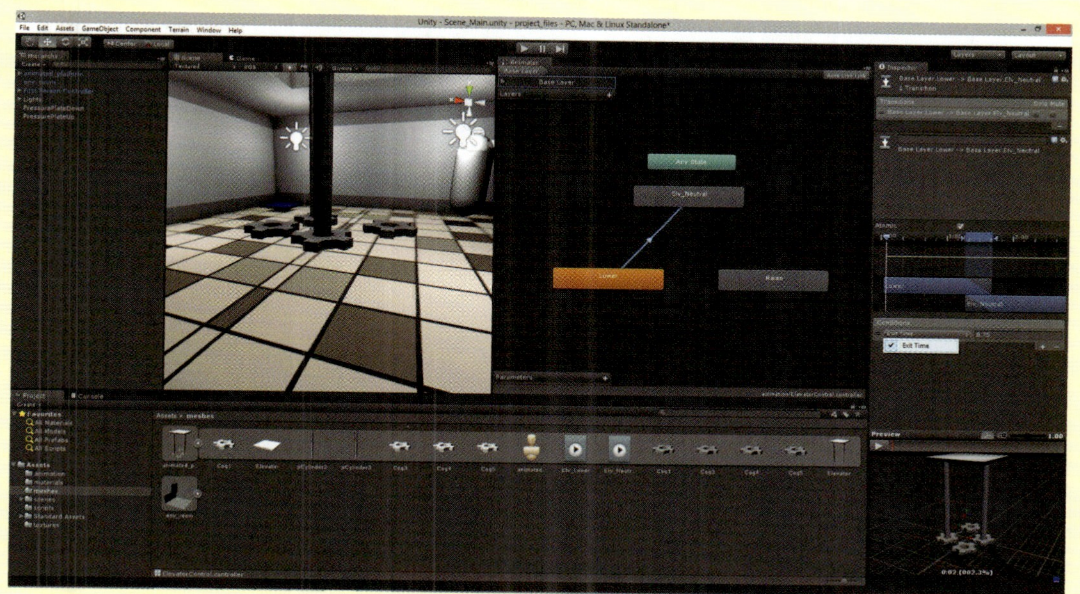

Figure 11.16 Exploring conditions to control the playback of transitions

scene that the player controls and affects. We need to control and play the transitions based on what the player actually *does*. If you click on the *Exit Time* condition from the Object Inspector, however, there are no other options to choose. It's now time to address this to get the control we need. See Figure 11.16.

11.6 Changing States – Exploring Parameters

The Animator graph features three separate states: the Raise state for playing an 'elevator rising' animation, the Lower state for an 'elevator lowering' animation, and a neutral state for when the elevator is neither rising nor lowering. Having these states defined in the graph is not enough, however, to make them play – as we've seen. This is because further instruction must be provided to Unity for controlling when one state transitions to another and under what conditions. The *Exit Time* condition is provided by default to change from state X to state Y when playback of state X has reached a specified threshold defined in percentage terms. But this condition is inadequate for our needs because our elevator should change states based not on fixed times but on specific actions of the player, such as calling the elevator through a button press. This could occur at potentially any time during gameplay, depending on the actions of the player. To get the additional control we need through the Conditions facility, we must be able to communicate with Mecanim from script. From script, we want the ability to start a transition from one state to another and find out which state is currently active. This section demonstrates how to do this, showing how we can gain almost complete control of animation playback, and the Mecanim system generally, through scripting.

1. Clear all transitions created in the previous section, leaving a graph with three states and no transitions connecting them. Then return to the project panel and create a new C# Script file named *ElevatorControl.cs*. Assign this script as a component to the *animated_platform* object in the scene and then open the script file in *MonoDevelop*, or your editor of choice (if you're using a different editor). Then add the following code to the file.

```
Code 11.1 The Elevator Control, Skeleton Class
//————————————————————
using UnityEngine;
using System.Collections;
//————————————————————
public class ElevatorControl : MonoBehaviour
{
	//————————————————————
	//List of elevator actions
	public enum ElevatorActions {neutral = 0, lower = 1, raise = 2};
	//Reference to Animator Component
	private Animator Anim = null;
	//————————————————————
	// Use this for initialization
	void Start ()
	{
		//Get Anim Component
		Anim = GetComponent<Animator>();
	}
```

```
        //————————————————————
        // Update is called once per frame
        void Update ()
        {
        }
}
```

NOTE: The class above is a work in progress: it'll be refined as we progress through the chapter. It begins, however, by defining three elevator positional states in an enumeration: *Lower*, *Raise* and *Neutral*. Using these values we can control the *AnimationStates*. The script also retrieves a reference to the *Animator* component attached to the GameObject, in the *Start* function. This is because the Animator will be used to control and interact with the animation graph. We'll use this object later.

2. The *ElevatorActions* enumeration defined in script outlines three animation states for the elevator. These values will have a relationship with the Mecanim and our animation graph. To begin establishing a link between our code and Mecanim, we can use *parameters*. To create a parameter, return to the graph view in the *Animator* window. From the bottom-left corner of the screen, in the *Parameters* list, click the + icon to create a new *parameter*. Select *Int* from the drop-down list and name the parameter *ElevatorAction*. *Parameters* act like global variables, which can be accessed both by the animation graph and its animation states, as well as from script through the Animator class. They offer a common memory space between Mecanim and script; a way to share, set, and evaluate data. A graph can have potentially many parameters for many purposes, but here we'll use just one for purposes of controlling animation transitions. See Figure 11.17.
3. The *ElevatorAction* parameter is of an integer data type; meaning it can be any whole number, either positive or negative. Here, this value will correspond to the *ElevatorActions* enumeration defined in script. When *ElevatorAction* is set to 0 (or *ElevatorActions.Neutral*), the elevator object should be in a neutral state, 1 in a lowered state and 2 in a raised state. On this basis, we can configure the states and transitions of our animation in the graph. Select the *Neutral* state and draw a transition link to the *Lowered* state. Change the Conditions variable from *Exit Time* to *ElevatorAction*, making the condition dependent on the value of this parameter. Set the value field to *Equals 1*. This means the transition from neutral to lowered will be activated when the parameter *ElevatorAction* changes

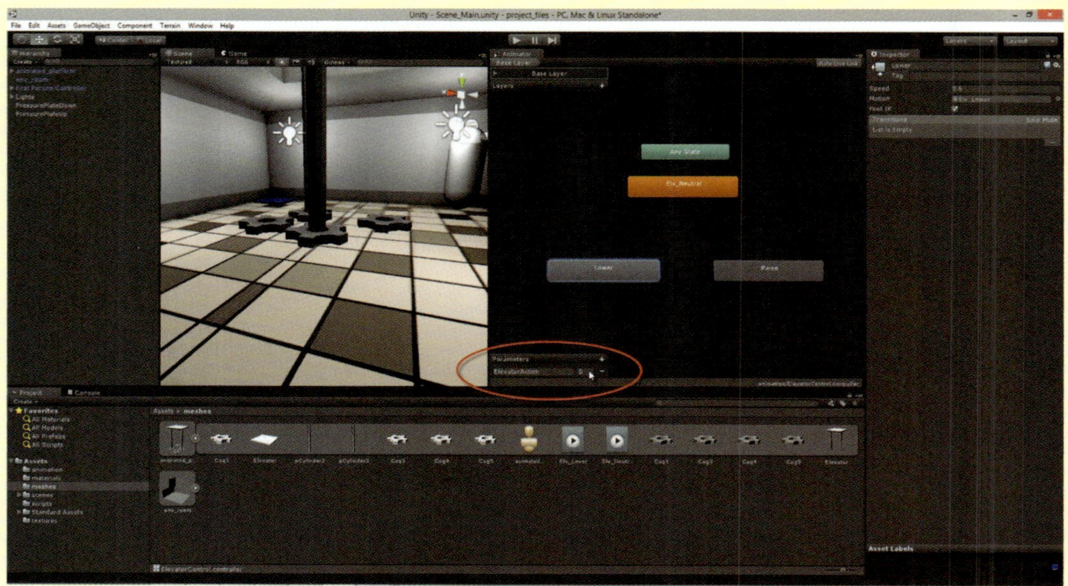

Figure 11.17 Creating a parameter. Parameters can be set and read from both script and Mecanim. They act as a bridge for moving data between the two spaces

from 0 to 1. Then use the mouse to shrink the timeline range for the transition, dragging the timeline sliders, making the start and end range equal to create an instant transition: an instant change from a neutral state to a lowered state. See Figure 11.18. This configuration, when played, will *still* not cause the elevator to lower from its default neutral state. This is because more work must be done; but we're on the right track.

Figure 11.18 Creating a transition from *Neutral* to *Lower* using parameters as conditions

4. Now let's set up a similar transition connection between the neutral and raised states in the graph, mirroring the connection between neutral and lowered created in the previous step. The condition for this connection will be based on *ElevatorAction* as before; but here its value should be *2* and not *1*, because the enum *ElevatorActions.raise* is 2. In addition to this, set up further transition connections between each of the lower and raise states, allowing the elevator to change states not just while it's in neutral mode but while it's lowering or rising too. This allows the player to call the elevator while it is rising, or vice versa, using the pressure plates on the floor as switches. See Figure 11.19 for the graph.
5. It's important to remember that individual transitions are one-way. This means the graph configuration in Figure 11.19 allows the elevator to change *from* neutral *to* any raised or lowered state and also to change between any moving states, but never to *change back* to neutral after

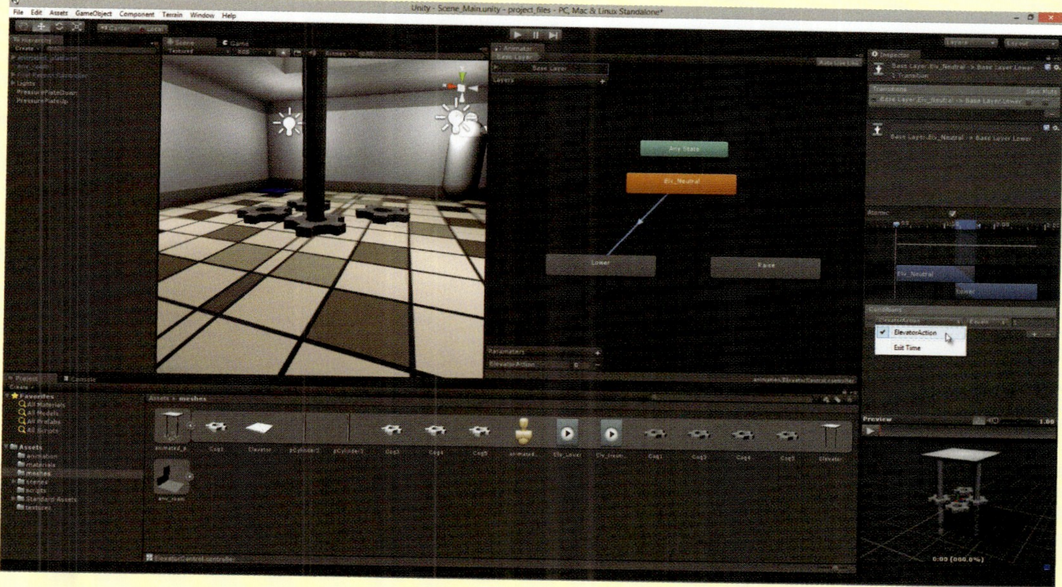

Figure 11.19 Setting up two-way transitions between lowered and raised states

raising or lowering is completed. When the elevator completes its rising, we need it change back to the neutral state. So add a backward transition leading from *Raise* to *Neutral*. But this connection will not be based on *ElevatorAction*. This is because the elevator should reset to neutral when the raise is completed, *not* when the player stands on a pressure plate. Consequently, set the condition to *Exit Time* and change the value to *1.0*. Narrow the timeline range for the transition, if necessary, to the end of the *Raise* state to switch instantly from *Raise* to Neutral. See Figure 11.20. Check the preview window to get an idea of how the transition will look. The graph is now completed.
6. The Animator graph is now configured *in theory* for controlling the elevator. But right now, nothing ever causes the graph to move away from its loop-able default state of neutral. The pressure plates on the floor are not 'linked up' to our code and to the graph. We'll address this issue in stages. First, we'll return to code and create functionality that'll set the *ElevatorAction* Parameter to appropriate values. To do this, return to the *ElevatorControl* script. Edit the code as below. Comments on the code follow in the note.

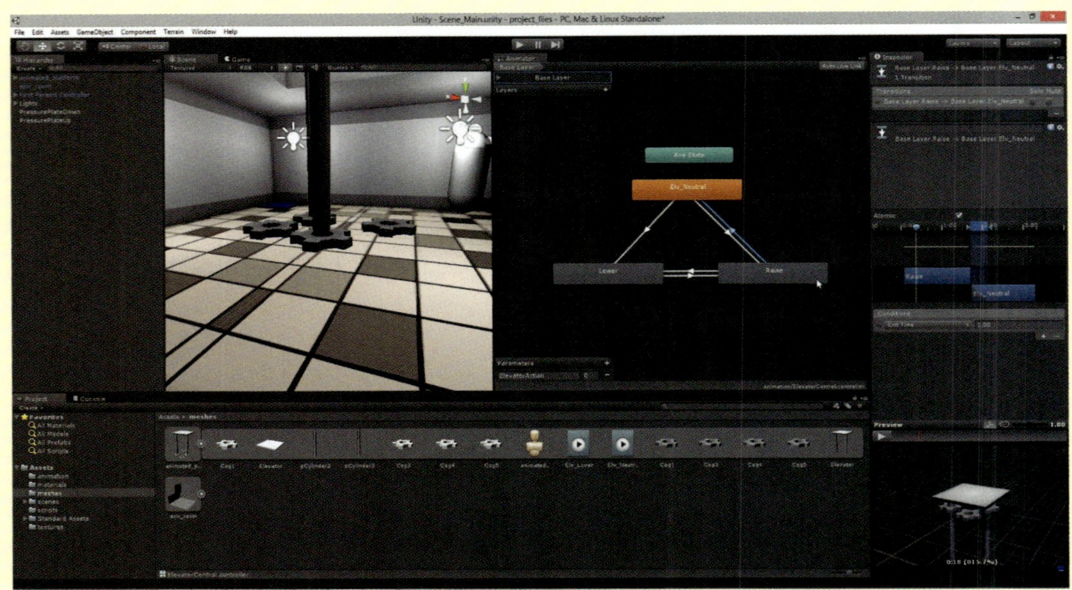

Figure 11.20 Returning from *Raise* to *Neutral*

Code 11.2 *Setting the Elevator Action*

```
using UnityEngine;
using System.Collections;
//————————————————-
public class ElevatorControl : MonoBehaviour
{
//————————————————-
//List of elevator actions
public enum ElevatorActions {neutral = 0, lower = 1, raise = 2};

//Reference to Animator Component
private Animator Anim = null;

```

```
//Get states
static int NeutralState = Animator.StringToHash("Base Layer.
Neutral");

//Should lower?
bool lowerElv = false;

//Should raise?
bool raiseElv = false;

//-------------------------------------
// Use this for initialization
void Start ()
{
//Get Anim Component
Anim = GetComponent<Animator>();
}
//-------------------------------------
// Update is called once per frame
void Update ()
{
//Get Current Animation State
AnimatorStateInfo Info = Anim.GetCurrentAnimatorStateInfo(0);

//If in neutral state or raise/lower completed
```

```
if(Info.nameHash != NeutralState && Info.normalizedTime < 1.0f)
    return;

//Get Elevator Action
int CurAction = Anim.GetInteger("ElevatorAction");

//If in raised state, then switch to neutral
if(CurAction == (int)ElevatorActions.raise)
    Anim.SetInteger("ElevatorAction", (int) ElevatorActions.
    neutral);

//Lower elevator
if(lowerElv)
    Anim.SetInteger("ElevatorAction", (int) ElevatorActions.
    lower);

if(raiseElv && Info.nameHash != NeutralState)
    Anim.SetInteger("ElevatorAction", (int) ElevatorActions.
    raise);

//Reset raise lower
lowerElv = raiseElv = false;
}
//———————————————-
//Set Lower Elevator
```

```
59    public void Lower()
60    {
61          lowerElv = true;
62    }
63    //------------------------------------
64    //Set Raise Elevator
65    public void Raise()
66    {
67          raiseElv = true;
68    }
69    //------------------------------------
70    }
```

NOTE: This code is *almost* ready to run and bring our elevator to life, but there's still a missing link – namely the pressure plate code – and we'll address that soon. Nevertheless, it features some significant features for coding with Mecanim. These are as follows, arranged by code line number:

Line 14

Uses the Animator class to retrieve a hash reference (Unique ID) to the neutral state in the animation graph. This ID is used later in code (lines 37 and 51) to determine whether the graph is in a neutral state, or not. Lines 37 and 51 both occur inside the *Update* function, called once per frame.

Line 34

Uses the Animator class to retrieve State playback information for the specified layer: the default layer has an ID of 0. The *GetCurrentAnimatorStateInfo* method returns a data structure of type *AnimatorStateInfo*. From this structure, the *normalizedTime* variable indicates how much of the active state has played in terms of animation percentage: 1.0 means the animation has played exactly once, 2.0 twice, and 3.0 three times. Decimal values such as 3.5 mean the animation has played three times and is currently halfway towards making a fourth loop. This value is used later to determine whether playback of an animation has completed (>1.0).

Line 41
This line is critical to our workflow. The function *GetInteger* of the *Animator* class is used to search the animation graph for a parameter of a specified name (*ElevatorAction*) and to return its value. This function offers us *read access* to parameters.

Lines 45, 49 and 52
These lines use the *SetInteger* function of the Animator class. These offer us write access to parameters in the graph. Note that setting parameters causes the graph to respond immediately. Calling *SetInteger* will immediately and automatically initiate the appropriate transitions in the graph if the value matches any conditions.

11.7 Finalising the Elevator

The animation graph has been configured with three states, which are connected through transitions. Further, the elevator has been fully coded and engineered to work with the animation graph through the Animator class. It does this by using the *ElevatorAction* parameter to send and receive 'messages' to and from the graph to control which transition should be activated. Though the code is correct as is, the pressure plates on the floor of the scene are intended to 'kick the code into action': these are the places where the player must stand to raise or lower the elevator. Right now, the pressure plates are simply lifeless game objects. They should be coded and customised to work with the elevator code and bring the elevator into motion. The following steps achieve this.

1. For each pressure plate object in the scene, increase its height (Y size) of its collider volume to around 16 units and enable the *IsTrigger* field. This increases the Collider volume to intersect with the player as they walk onto the plate, and the *IsTrigger* field allows the player to walk through and into the collider (to stand on the pressure plate), as opposed to being blocked and obstructed by the volume. See Figure 11.21.
2. The aim here is to code each pressure plate so that, when the player stands on it, it calls one of the *Raise* or *Lower* functions in the *ElevatorControl* class, according to the pressure plate (see lines 59 and 65 of Code Sample 11.2). These functions bring the animation to life. We *could* code each pressure plate separately to achieve this. But instead we can generalise the behaviour we need into a single class that can be applied to both pressure plates, tweaking only a few settings. So, let's create a new script file called *TriggerSender*. Add the following code.

Code 11.3 *Adding Pressure Plate Behaviour*

```
using UnityEngine;

using System.Collections;

//———————————————————-

public class TriggerSender : MonoBehaviour
```

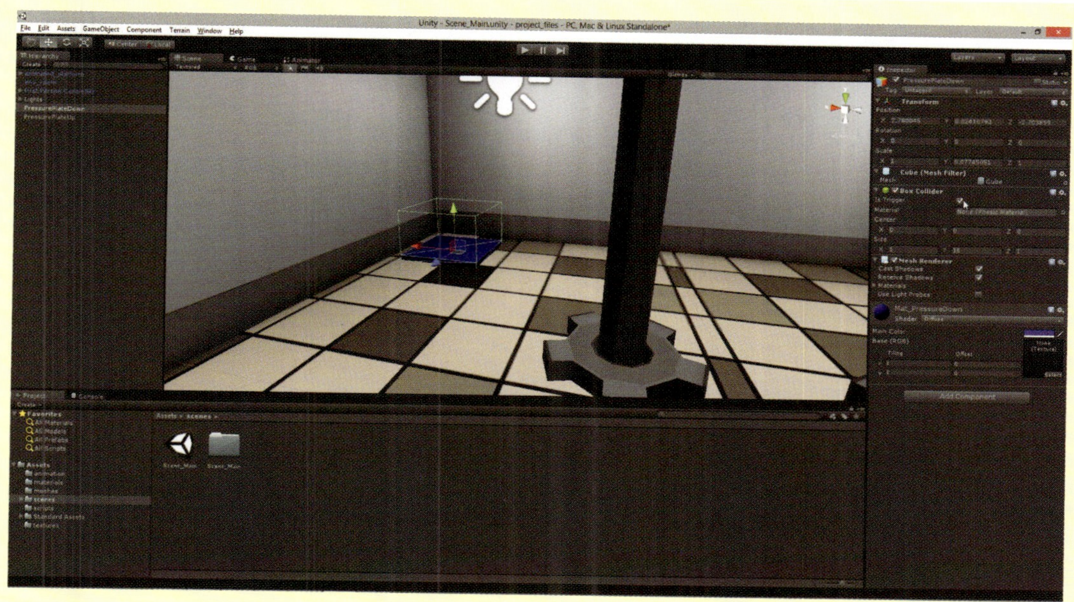

Figure 11.21 Resizing the pressure plate Collider volume

```
{
	//-----------------------------------------
	//Target Object
	public GameObject Target = null;
	//Message to Send Target on Trigger
	public string Message = "";
	//-----------------------------------------
	void OnTriggerEnter(Collider other)
	{
		//Send Message
		Target.SendMessage(Message);
	}
	//-----------------------------------------
}
```

NOTE: The *TriggerSender* class essentially *sends* a message (any message we choose) to any specified *GameObject* whenever the player collides with or enters the Trigger volume attached to the parent GameObject. By coding the class in this abstract and general way, we can assign it to both pressure plates, having each plate send a different message to the Elevator object on each collision.

3. Assign the *TriggerSender* script to each pressure plate in the scene. For both pressure plates, specify the elevator object (the object with the *ElevatorControl* script) as the *Target* object. That is, as the object to receive the message when a player collision occurs. For the *Elevator-Down* pressure plate, set the *Message* to *Lower*. For the Elevator-Up pressure plate, set the *Message* to *Up*. These will call the *Lower* and *Raise* methods of the *ElevatorControl* class respectively. See Figure 11.22. If you want, go ahead and insert an additional, empty game object as a child of the elevator, and attach to it a Collider component, making it a Trigger volume. Then assign it a *TriggerSender* component with the message *Raise*. This will allow the elevator to rise when the player stands on it too.

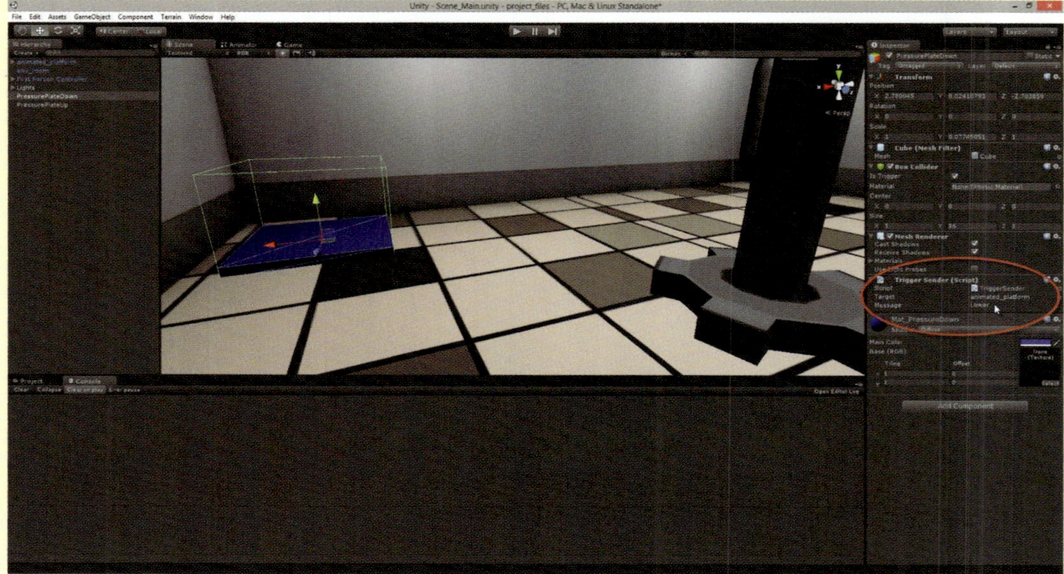

Figure 11.22 Configuring the pressure plates to initiate transitions

4. Now give the project a test run to see the results of Mecanim in action. Step on the elevator-lower pressure plate to lower the elevator to ground level, and then on the elevator-raise pressure plate to raise the elevator back to its default position in the ceiling. Then lower the elevator again and stand on it to travel upwards to the roof alcove area. Congratulations! You have successfully configured the graph

to customise the behaviour of the elevator. Notice that Mecanim is not only an animation tool but also a visual scripting tool: it allows us to customise the animated behaviour of scene objects. See Figure 11.23.

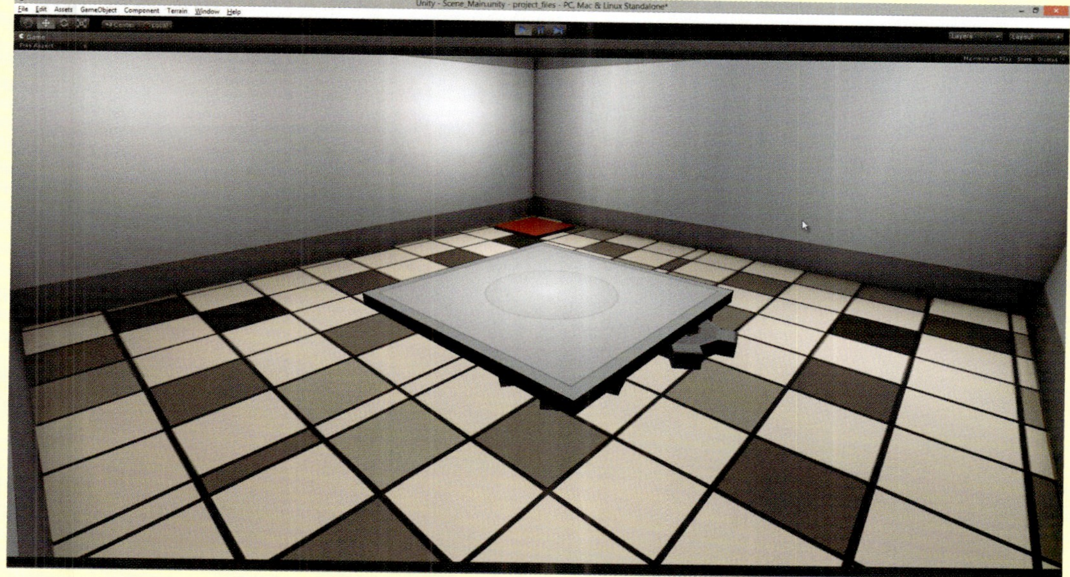

Figure 11.23 Using Mecanim and scripting to control an elevator

11.8 Finishing Touches

The elevator project so far works only with animation data baked into the mesh file. This data allows the elevator platform to rise and lower on demand. However, it's easy to see many different ways in which the project could be improved: specifically, ways in which the *animation itself* could be improved. For example, the elevator mesh at the ground level features four cogs, two of which have cylindrical supports or pillars rising up from their centre supporting the elevator platform above. However, the other two cogs have nothing at their centre even though they spin and turn as the elevator moves, and this makes them seem 'out of place' in the animation overall. It'd be more interesting if we created some additional cylindrical meshes to insert at their centre, to act as pistons, rhythmically raised and lowered as the elevator travelled up and down. This would enhance the general *mechanistic feel* of the elevator object, giving it an extra level of realism. So now the question arises as to how we can add these details and link them in with the existing motion of the elevator without resorting to lengthy scripts or re-baking the animation entirely. The answer can be found in the Mecanim feature of *curves*, which is a pro-only feature. Users of the free version can safely skip to the conclusion of this chapter. The following steps demonstrate how to work with curves.

1. Create two new cylinder objects for the pistons in the scene, using the native Unity primitives. To do this, select *GameObject > Create Other > Cylinder* from the application menu. Use the scale (*R*) tool to resize the cylinders, both in height and radius, down into the empty cogs to create an appropriate piston for each cog. The scale or measurements do not need to be exact: if it looks right, then it is right! Take a look at Figure 11.24 for a guide. Each piston can be a different size and even at a different Y position within the cog.

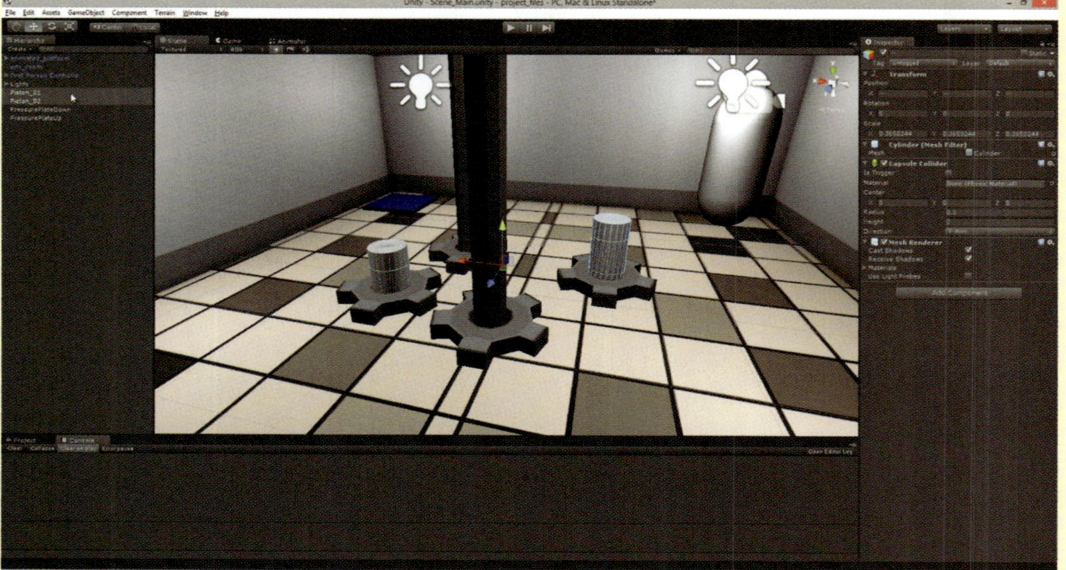

Figure 11.24 Creating piston objects and positioning them at the cog centres

2. The aim here is to animate the Y position of each cog, raising and lowering each cog, up and down, as the elevator moves, to emphasise its mechanical properties as it moves between states. We do not, however, want to animate the Y position at any time and in any way: the cogs should *only* move when the elevator platform moves, and they should raise and lower in a *predictable* and *controllable* way. The *curves* feature of Mecanim will allow us to interactively draw a line chart, plotting animation time against value (Y value) to control the position of the pistons. To get started, let's create a new parameter in the Animation graph. This parameter will define the piston's Y position in the scene. It is created as a parameter rather than a standard variable to allow both script and Mecanim to read and write to the value. So jump over to the Animator window and add a new *Float* parameter named *MachineUpDown*. See Figure 11.25.
3. Now define the Y position curves for the pistons in the *Lower* animation clip. Remember: the *Raise* animation simply plays the *Lower* animation in reverse. Both *Raise* and *Lower* are based on the same animation clip. Select the *animated_platform* mesh in the Project panel, and select the *Lower* animation clip from the *Clips* list in the Object Inspector. Un-twirl or unwind the Curves option, and click the + button to insert a new curve, ready for shaping. See Figure 11.26.
4. Let's shape this curve. Click the curve thumbnail in the Object Inspector to open the Curve editor. For information on how to use the Curve editor, consult Section 6.5 of Chapter 6 on particle systems. Think of the line graph as charting the Y position, the rising and falling, of the piston objects. The horizontal (X) axis represents *Normalized* time for the animation, ranging continuously from 0 (animation start) to 1

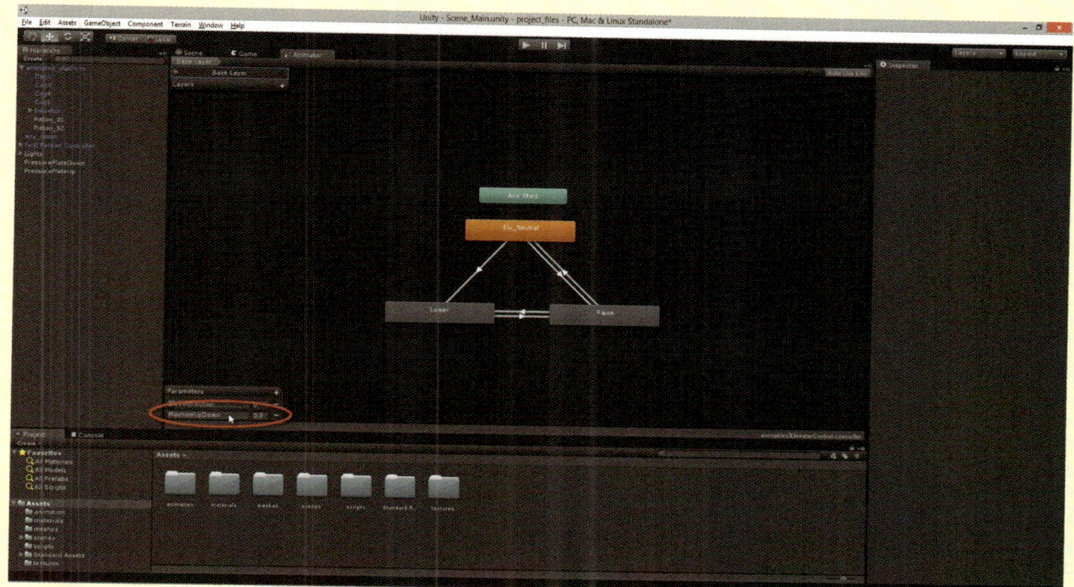

Figure 11.25 Creating a floating point parameter in the Animation graph to control the Y position of the pistons over time during an animation

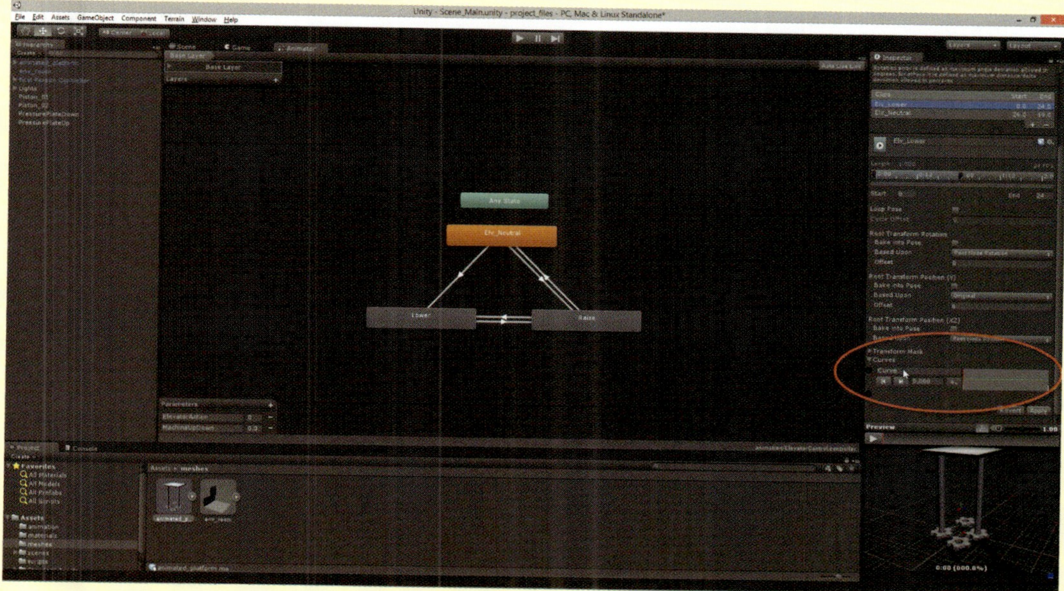

Figure 11.26 Creating an animation curve for the *Lower* animation clip

(animation end). The vertical (Y) axis represents *Value*, again ranging from 0 to 1, and it is a *generic* field, meaning whatever we want it to mean: in this case, it means *Y Position*. So the graph charts *Time* to *Y Position*. Using this graph, Mecanim *interpolates* the Y position of the pistons for each and every frame of animation, based on the line we draw. To get started, click any one of the graph presets at the bottom of the Graph editor and zoom out to see the entire graph, from 0–1 on each axis. See Figure 11.27.

5. Insert extra key frames into the graph by right-clicking the mouse and choosing *Add Key* from the context menu, and begin to shape the line into a chaotic wave, as shown in Figure 11.28. This varies the level of the pistons. Once completed, name the graph *MachineUpDown*, matching the name of the parameter *MachineUpDown*. This ensures the value for *MachineUpDown* is read from the graph at every Time *t*. *Apply* the settings.
6. By configuring the graph and the parameter *MachineUpDown* in this way we can be sure that *MachineUpDown* will always express the vertical value of the graph (0–1). Since the line varies during playback of the *Lower* animation clip, the value of *MachineUpDown* will vary too. Using these normalised values of 0–1 we can adjust the height of the pistons in script. To start, open the *ElevatorControl* script and add the following three public variables to the class.

Code 11.4 *Controlling the Pistons*

```
//Array of machine elements for interpolating Y

public GameObject[] Elements;

//Min Y Pos of Cylinder

public float MinYPos = 0.0f;

//Max Y Pos of Cylinder

public float MaxYPos = 0.0f;
```

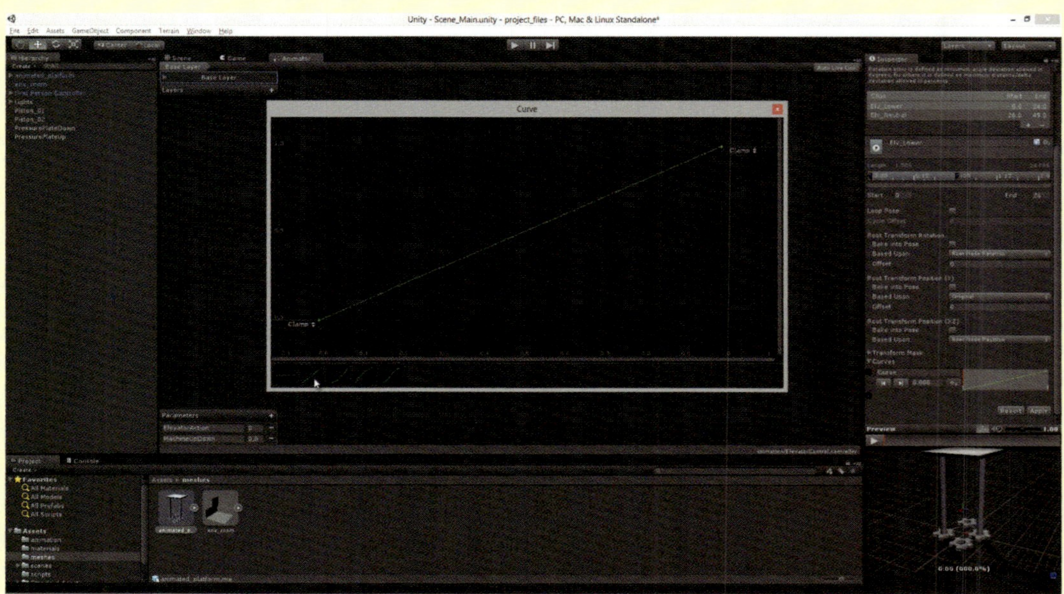

Figure 11.27 Beginning a line graph for *Time* to *Y Position*

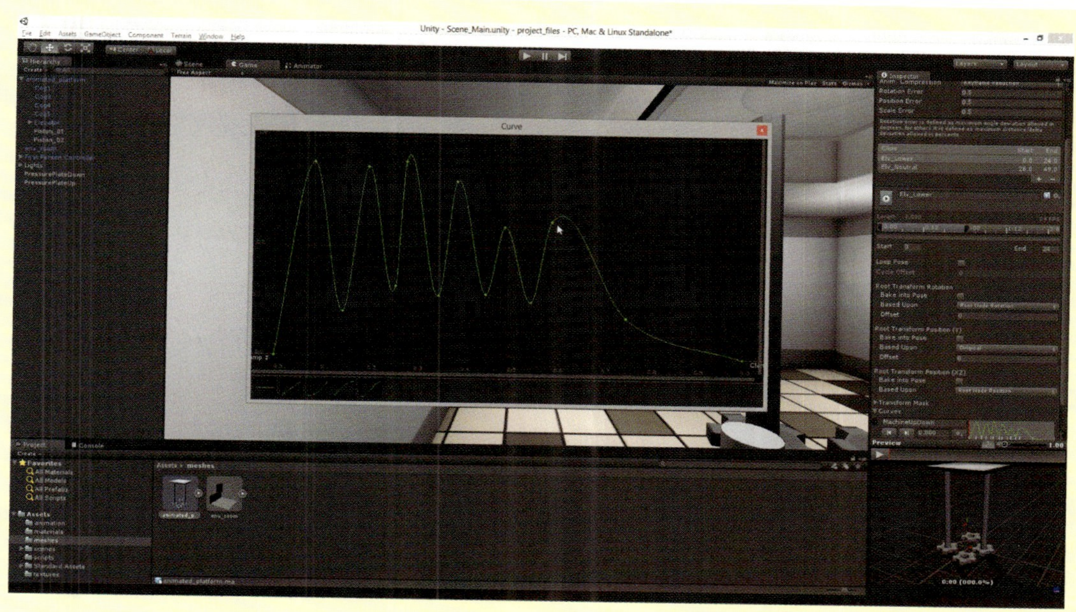

Figure 11.28 Completing the piston graph

NOTE: The three newly added properties will appear in the Object Inspector when the elevator object is selected. Using them, we can configure the pistons for animation. The Elements array is an array of *GameObjects* – a list of all objects to animate using the curve. This will include our two piston objects in the scene, although you could add more. The *MinYPos* and *MaxYPos* values represent the minimum and maximum values for the Y position that Mecanim should interpolate using the normalised 0 to 1 values from the graph. For MinYPos I have specified *-0.06018591* and for MaxYPos *0.5071337*. You can choose different values. To find out what works best, use the transform gizmo to move the pistons to various height positions, finding a suitable position for the destination values, then copy and paste the Y position value into either the *MinYPos* or the *MaxYPos* field and undo the piston back to its original.

7. Then add the following code to the top of the *Update* function in *ElevatorControl*.

Code 11.5 *Editing Element Height*

```
//Get cylinder Y pos

float YPos = Mathf.Lerp(MinYPos, MaxYPos, Anim.
GetFloat("MachineUpDown"));
```

```
//Assign heights to all elements

foreach(GameObject Obj in Elements)

{

Obj.transform.position = new Vector3(Obj.transform.position.x, YPos,
Obj.transform.position.z);

}
```

NOTE: This code is where the piston-animating magic happens. First, the code generates an interpolated YPos value between the minimum and maximum heights. It does this by reading the value from the *MachineUpDown* parameter, controlled in turn by the custom curve of the animation clip. Then finally it cycles through all GameObjects in the Elements array and updates their Y position.

8. Let's animate those pistons now! Select the animated platform object in the scene and ensure the *MinYPos*, *MaxYPos* and *Elements* array have been specified. For the Elements array, use the Object Inspector to create two element slots, and drag and drop each piston object from the hierarchy list into each slot. See Figure 11.29.

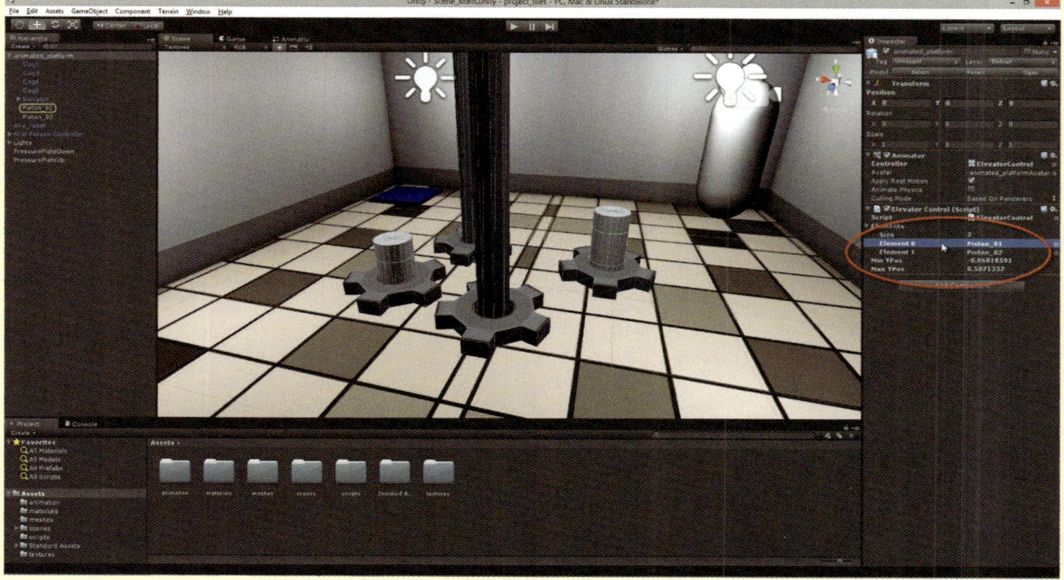

Figure 11.29 Configuring the pistons for animation

9. So finally, at long last, we can complete this scene! Take it for a test run to see the results of your hard work: see the elevator in action as before, but notice the animation of the pistons as the elevator moves up and down, their rising and falling based on the custom animation curve. Overall, this example demonstrates the awesome potential of curves for customising and tweaking animations directly from the Unity editor.

11.9 Conclusion

This chapter charted the development of a basic scene featuring an elevator that can be raised and lowered on demand using the Mecanim animation system. Despite its appearance of simplicity, it led us to flex a wide range of our *Unity-know-how* muscles. It required us to import and configure assets, plan and construct scenes, create materials, edit texture settings, use a component-based workflow, configure lighting and lightmapping, script objects, use debugging tools, Curve editors and the Animator window, and a lot more besides. Overall, this example demonstrates the awesome potential of Mecanim. However, the chapter only touches the surface of Mecanim and what it can do. There are a wide range of specialised extra features for importing and configuring animated character models: bipedal characters such as the player character, enemies, and more. Such details were not covered in this introductory title, but you've nevertheless seen enough of the Mecanim basics to explore further on your own. The final chapter considers a range of miscellaneous tips and tricks to make your Unity development experience a smoother one.

CHAPTER 12

Tips and Tricks

This final chapter takes a dramatically different form from all previous chapters of the book in how it approaches our exploration of Unity. It is neither project-based, like most chapters, nor theoretical, like some chapters. Instead, it adopts a simple question-and-answer (Q&A) format. Specifically, it raises a set of questions I find commonly asked by people new to Unity; people who have read and learned about the basics but who still have a few miscellaneous queries, the answers to which are strangely not well documented or easily found. In this chapter I pose these questions on behalf of curious students and then set about answering each of them as clearly and concisely as possible to make them practically relevant to your work. In providing an answer I am not claiming it as the *only* or even the *best* answer, but just as one *possible* answer among many. 'Better' or 'best' are relative judgements, meaning they depend on person, project and circumstance. The questions are not listed in any particular order but fired off arbitrarily, as though this were a Q&A session at the end of a class. When reading through the answers I encourage you to try out any suggestions in Unity and then think of possible alternatives. Thinking of alternatives is good practice, even if your thinking ends up providing you with nothing that is feasible. At best, the practice can offer you a more suitable alternative, and at worst it will confirm for you in that the original solution is – for the time being at least – the most suitable. So let's get started.

12.1 Scenes and Scene Changing

Q. Each scene represents a complete level in Unity. But games are typically composed of many different levels, not just one. How can I script or configure my games to handle scene changes? That is, how can I change scenes during gameplay, unloading the current scene and loading a new scene?

A. This is an important question and the answer to which is likely to raise even further questions. Changing scenes in Unity involves two main steps. These are described as follows.

1. First, add all valid scenes in your project to the *Scenes* list in the *Build Settings* Dialog. To do this, select *File > Build Settings* from the application menu, or press the *Ctrl + Shift + B* keyboard shortcut. Then drag and drop all scenes from the Project panel into the *Scene* list of the *Build Settings* dialog. On doing this, each scene will receive a *Unique ID* or number, printed on the right-hand side of the list. These IDs are significant and can be referenced in script. Ensure that your first or starting scene has an ID of 0. Scenes can be dragged and dropped and rearranged in the list to change their ID. See Figure 12.1.

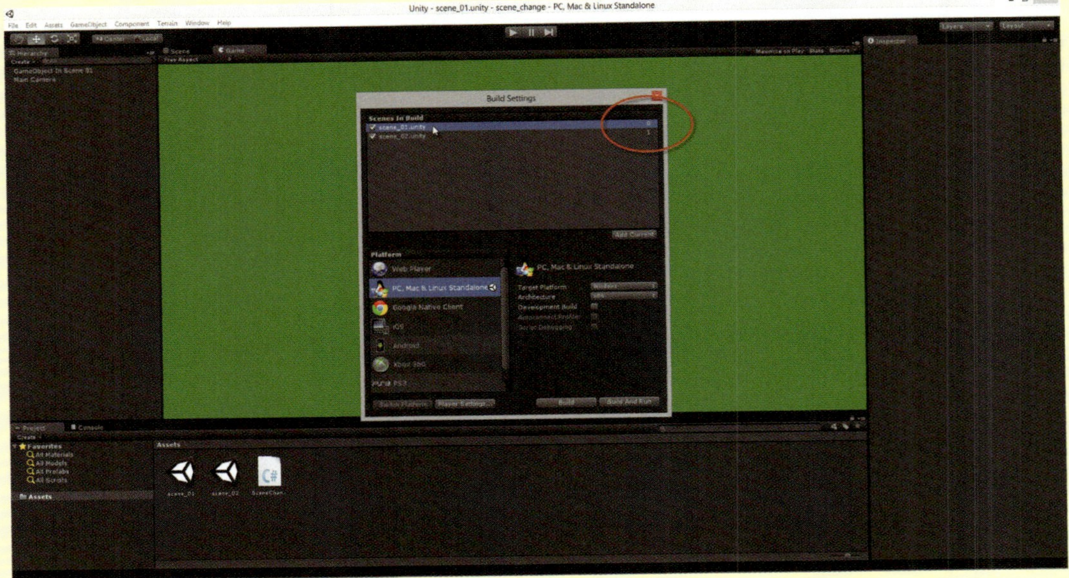

Figure 12.1 Adding scenes to the *Scenes* list in the *Build Settings* dialog

2. Once all viable scenes are added to the Build Settings dialog, you can switch between scenes dynamically in script at any time during gameplay with a call to the *Application.LoadLevel* function, which requires only the ID to the destination scene. The following code in code listing 12.1 changes between two scenes, with the IDs of 0 and 1, based on keyboard presses.

Code 12.1 *Changing the Scenes at Run-time*

```
// Update is called once per frame
void Update ()
{
        //If press A then change to Scene 01
```

```
        if(Input.GetKeyDown(KeyCode.A))
        {
                Application.LoadLevel(0);
        }

        //If press B then change to Scene 02
        if(Input.GetKeyDown(KeyCode.B))
        {
                Application.LoadLevel(1);
        }
}
```

NOTE: A scene-changing sample project can be found in the project files associated with this chapter. Look in the folder *Chapter12\Project_Files\Scene_Change*.

12.2 Persistent Data

Q. OK. So I can now change my scenes, from Scene X to Scene Y. But there's a problem. Scene-changing kills all my data! It completely destroys one scene and its data, and then loads a new scene with its default data and settings. No information from the previous scene is retained in the change. If the player collects power-ups and items in Scene X, then this information is lost when changing to Scene Y because nothing of Scene X survives the loading process. How can I keep game-critical data between scene loadings?

A. In Unity, all game-related data is encoded in the form of GameObjects and components and these are both *scene specific* structures. There is, strictly speaking, no system of global functionality or scriptable variables existing outside of scenes. However, Unity does allow us in script to mark or tag specific game objects to survive scene destruction and carry-over as game objects into the new scenes we load. Using this mechanism, therefore, it is possible to retain all game-critical data between scene loads.

For a GameObject to survive level loads, call the *DontDestroyOnLoad* function. In Code 12.2 it is being called inside the *Start* function of an object. Any object passed to this function will survive all subsequent scene changes.

```
Code 12.2 Setting the Elevator Action

// Use this for initialization

void Start ()

{

       DontDestroyOnLoad (transform.gameObject);

}
```

NOTE: A scene-changing sample, with persistent data, can be found in the project files associated with this chapter. Look in the folder *Chapter12\Project_Files\Persistent_Data*.

12.3 Persistent Data and Singletons

Q. Wait! Not so fast! What you recommend is only part of what I really meant. Sure, the *DontDestroyOnLoad* function will allow any GameObject (Object X) to survive across level loads. But if I load back the starting scene that originally featured Object X, after having switched from several other scenes, I end up with duplications of Object X in the scene. Each time I reload that original scene, I get an extra instance of Object X, and those instances survive through scenes changes because each instance calls *DontDestroyOnLoad*. This could get out of hand if the player returned to the starting scene numerous times. What I really meant was: how can I create player-specific data that survives across levels *and* remains the one and only valid instance?

A. This question might be restated as: how can I create persistent singletons? A Singleton class is one that can be instantiated once and only once – or rather: a singleton is a class for which there can be no more than one instance at any one time. The following class shown in Code 12.3 is configured to achieve this – that is, to remain the only instance.

```
Code 12.3 A Singleton Class

using UnityEngine;

using System.Collections;


public class KeepMeObject : MonoBehaviour

{
```

```
	public static KeepMeObject Instance;

	void Awake()
	{
		if(Instance)
			Destroy (gameObject);
		else
		{
			DontDestroyOnLoad(gameObject);
			Instance = this;
		}
	}
}
```

NOTE: A scene-changing sample, with persistent data and singleton behaviour, can be found in the project files associated with this chapter. Look in the folder *Chapter12\Project_Files\Singletons*.

12.4 Real-time Image Loading

Q. I'm trying to display banner ads, custom images or user-created images in my game. The problem is that Unity requires all images and texture assets to be added to the project in the Project panel at *design time*. When a project is built and shipped, it features all assets *pre-compiled* into its data files. I want to show real-time, dynamic and auto-updated content in the game. I want to show images on-the-fly at run-time, loading them into the game from sources external to the project. How can I do this?

A. There are many ways to pursue loading and streaming external content, and the professional version of Unity offers even more ways than the free version. Here I shall stick with the relatively simple case of loading only images into the project in real-time from a location on the local hard drive or via the web. The sample in Code 12.4 demonstrates how to cycle through an image set. The full project can be found in the companion files at *Chapter12\Project_Files\Dynamic_Images*.

Code 12.4 *Loading Images at Run-time*

```
using UnityEngine;
using System.Collections;
using System.Collections.Generic;
using System.IO;
using System.Linq;
using System;

public class ImageCycle : MonoBehaviour
{

public Texture2D LogoTexture = null;
public Rect LogoTextureDimensions;

// Use this for initialization
void Start () {StartCoroutine(ShowImages());}

void OnGUI()
{
    if(LogoTexture)
        GUI.DrawTexture(LogoTextureDimensions, LogoTexture);
}
IEnumerator ShowImages()
{
    //Get image files
    var set = new HashSet<string> { ".jpg", ".png" };
    string[] Files = Directory.GetFiles(Path.GetFullPath("."), "*.*",
```

```
SearchOption.TopDirectoryOnly)
    .Where(f => set.Contains(
    new FileInfo(f).Extension,
    StringComparer.OrdinalIgnoreCase)).ToArray();

    foreach(string FileName in Files)
    {
        //Create complete path
        string FullPath = "file://" + FileName;
        FullPath = FullPath.Replace('\\', '/');

        WWW URL = new WWW(FullPath);

        //Wait for load
        yield return URL;

        //Load texture
        LogoTexture = URL.texture;

        //Set texture dimensions
        LogoTextureDimensions = new Rect();
        LogoTextureDimensions.x = Screen.width/2 - (LogoTexture.
        width/2);
        LogoTextureDimensions.y = Screen.height/2 - (LogoTexture.
        height/2);
        LogoTextureDimensions.width = LogoTexture.width;
        LogoTextureDimensions.height = LogoTexture.height;
```

```
        //Show logo duration
        yield return new WaitForSeconds(2);
    }
    StartCoroutine(ShowImages());
}
}
```

12.5 Working with Movies

Q. What about cut-scenes in games? Between levels I want to show movies to the player that convey narrative and help merge the levels into a cohesive whole or story. These movies are pre-rendered into standard movie file formats. I want to play these as an animated texture in my game. How can I do this?

A. Playing pre-rendered movies in games has always been a troublesome issue, generally for performance reasons. This is because movies are typically very large files and compressed through different codecs, compression and unscrambling systems. These systems are also immersed in patenting and legal issues that can make their use problematic. Furthermore, the movie playback specifics vary greatly between platforms such as desktop and mobile devices, and some mobile systems support only a limited range of formats and only full-screen playback. The result is that even within Unity the performance you can expect from movie files varies from platform to platform. My recommendation generally is to avoid using pre-rendered movies in your games wherever possible, particularly if suitable alternatives are available. There are cases, however, where movie playback is essential. In these cases I recommend importing the movie file in the patent-free, open-source OGG Theora Format (.ogg or .ogv). These movie files can be dragged and dropped into Unity just like other assets. See code sample 12.4 for movie playback code.

```
Code 12.5 Playing Movies
using UnityEngine;
using System.Collections;

public class MoviePlay : MonoBehaviour
{
    //Reference to movie to play
    public MovieTexture Movie = null;
```

```
        // Use this for initialization
        void Start ()
        {
            //Get Mesh Renderer Component
            MeshRenderer MeshR = GetComponent<MeshRenderer>();

            //Assign movie texture
            MeshR.material.mainTexture = Movie;

            audio.clip = Movie.audioClip;
            audio.panLevel = 0;
            Movie.Play();
            audio.Play();
        }
}
```

NOTE: A movie playback example can be found in the folder *Chapter12\Project_Files\Movies*.

12.6 Dynamic Lists

Q. Throughout this book we've seen examples of code in which you have to keep lists of objects in an array or cycle through child objects or lists of things. In the previous chapter on Mecanim, for example, we had to keep an array of objects declared as *GameObject[] Elements*. This array could be built and defined in the Object Inspector. In all these cases, however, the size of the array was known in advance – we knew how many objects to store, the array was a fixed size. Yet sometimes we'll want to keep lists of things but not know in advance how many array elements we'll need: we want a dynamic array that grows and shrinks to accommodate our needs. How can this be achieved in Unity?

A. This question allows me to demonstrate an important and beautiful quality of Unity. Specifically, Unity has almost complete access to the .NET library for all platforms. This means your code can use almost any of the classes and features that are part of the .NET framework, including lists and arrays. If you are already familiar with .NET, then you'll feel at home coding in Unity. So what about dynamic lists? The .Net framework offers many kinds of dynamic lists, but I'll stick here with the standard list-type known as a *Double-Linked List*. Before showing a code sample, I want to make a recommendation: use the native, fixed array in Unity wherever possible. Only resort to a dynamic array when it is essential. Dynamic arrays are computationally more expensive than fixed-size arrays. The following code sample 12.5 allows you to *Add* an array item by pressing *A* on the keyboard, *Remove* an item with *R*, and *Print* the complete list to the console with *P*.

Code 12.6 *Dynamic Lists*

```
using UnityEngine;

using System.Collections;

using System.Collections.Generic;

public class Arrays : MonoBehaviour
{
	public List<string> Items;

	void Start ()
	{
		//Create empty list
		Items = new List<string>();
	}


	// Update is called once per frame
	void Update ()
	{
		//Add new item to list
```

```
        if(Input.GetKeyDown(KeyCode.A))
                Items.Add("Item " + Items.Count);

        //Remove last item from list
        if(Input.GetKeyDown(KeyCode.R))
                Items.RemoveAt(Items.Count-1);

        if(Input.GetKeyDown(KeyCode.P))
        {
                //Print items in list
                foreach(string Item in Items)
                        print(Item);
        }
    }
}
```

NOTE: A project for creating dynamic arrays can be found in *Chapter12\Project_Files\Arrays*.

Afterword

Congratulations on reaching the end of this book. I hope it has proved useful to you in large measure. At this point you may be thirsty for more knowledge, you may be ready to start making your masterpiece game, or you may have many more questions. Inevitably with a book entitled 'Unity 4 Fundamentals', correct content is to a degree open to interpretation because there is no agreement about exactly what the fundamentals of Unity are. Different people have different views about which topics are the most critical and in what order topics should be addressed. What I've presented here represents my view on the fundamentals. It could not reasonably represent anything else. The view I hold is that the fundamentals are the core or foundation of knowledge necessary for acting not only as a starting point for making games and further learning but also as a solid roadmap which you can independently use to decide on the direction of your future learning. This book is not – and nor is it intended to be – a book that teaches everything there is to know about Unity. No book, tutorial or college course can do that. For this reason there are still lots more things to learn and I would be very happy to know that this book has inspired you to progress further. Its aim has been to equip you with some of the most important and critical features associated with the Unity engine. That core has included:

- The Unity interface
- The transformation tools
- Scene and game modes
- The Project panel and Object Inspector
- Projects, scenes, assets, game objects and components
- Prefabs and packages
- Scripts in C#, JavaScript and Boo
- Terrain tools
- Scene design and the Modular Building Method
- Particle systems
- GUIs
- Lighting and lightmapping
- Audio and music
- Asset importing and configuration
- Debugging and building
- Post-production
- Animation and Mecanim
- Navigation and pathfinding

Many will find, however, that expanding their Unity knowledge involves not so much the learning of tools and features that have not been discussed here but learning how to use familiar tools/features in creative new ways. For those seeking further knowledge I recommend the following books and video courses:

- [Book] *Holistic Game Development with Unity: An All-in-One Guide to Implementing Game Mechanics, Art, Design and Programming*, by Penny de Byl
- [Book] *Creating Games with Unity and Maya: How to Develop Fun and Marketable 3D Games*, by Adam Watkins
- [Video] *3DMotive.com, Unity Tips and Tricks*, by Alan Thorn
- [Video] *3DMotive.com, Making 2D Games in Unity*, by Alan Thorn

Best wishes,
Alan Thorn, 2013
London.

Index

Note: page numbers in *italic* indicate figures.

C

G

I

J

K

L

M

P

Q

R

S

U

V

W

Y

Z